Environmental Regulation
in China

Environmental Regulation in China

Institutions, Enforcement, and Compliance

Xiaoying Ma & Leonard Ortolano

ROWMAN & LITTLEFIELD PUBLISHERS, INC.
Lanham • Boulder • New York • Oxford

ROWMAN & LITTLEFIELD PUBLISHERS, INC.

Published in the United States of America
by Rownman & Littlefield Publishers, Inc.
4720 Boston Way, Lanham, Maryland 20706
http://www.rowmanlittlefield.com

12 Hid's Copse Road
Cumnor Hill, Oxford OX2 9JJ, England

British Library Cataloguing in Publication Information Available

Library of Congress Cataloging-in-Publication Data

Ma, Xiaoying, 1958-
    Environmental regulation in China : institutions, enforcement, and compliance /
Xiaoying Ma & Leonard Ortolano
        p. cm.
    Includes bibliographical references and index.
    ISBN 0-8476-9398-8 (cloth : alk. paper)—ISBN 0-8476-9399-6 (pbk. : alk. paper)
    1. Environmental policy—China. 2. Water—Pollution—China. 3. Environmental
protection—Government policy—China. 4. Factory and trade waste—Environmental
aspects—China. 5. Environmental law—China. I. Ortolano, Leonard. II. Title.

GE190.C6 M3 2000
363.7′056′0951—dc21   99-086906

Printed in the United States of America

♾™ The paper used in this publication meets the minimum requirements of American
National Standard for Information Sciences—Permanence of Paper for Printed Library
Materials, ANSI/NISO Z39.48-1992.

*To the memory of Walter O. Spofford Jr.,
who inspired us in our studies of
environmental protection
in China*

Contents

List of Figures   ix

List of Tables   xi

List of Acronyms   xiii

Preface   xv

Acknowledgments   xvii

Location of the Six Cities Included in Our Study   xix

1   Environmental Costs of China's Economic Growth   1

2   Programs Regulating Industrial Pollution   13

3   Administrative Structures and Post-1978 Economic Reforms   33

4   Organizations Influencing Industrial Pollution Control   55

5   Informal Rules of Behavior Affecting Compliance   77

6   Program Design and Compliance   97

7   Enforcing Environmental Regulations   115

8   Effects of Profit, Cost, and Ownership Form on Enterprises' Response to Regulations   133

9   Comparing China and the United States   153

Appendices

A   Study Design: Objectives, Methods, and Definitions of Compliance   173

B   Classes of Water Use in China   185

C National Effluent Standards   187

D Effluent Standards Applicable to Different Classes of Water Use   189

Bibliography   191

Index   201

About the Authors   209

Figures

1.1 Ambient Concentrations of Air Pollutants in Selected Cities, 1995   5

3.1 Layers of Government Administration   34

3.2 Beijing Municipality Counties and Districts   35

3.3 Illustrative Line and Area Relationships in Beijing   37

3.4 Partial Structure of China's Administrative System   39

3.5 Exchanges between Enterprises and Local Governments   50

4.1 Organizational Structure for Environmental Protection in China   56

4.2 Jinan Municipal People's Government in the Mid-1990s   57

4.3 Organizations Reporting to Jinan EPB   61

Tables

1.1 China's Priority Environmental Problems   2

1.2 Industrial Wastewater Releases in China   3

1.3 Release of Air Pollutants by Industry   4

1.4 Production and Release of Solid Waste by Industry   6

1.5 Institutional Framework for Environmental Protection   9

2.1 Examples of Special Environmental Laws   17

2.2 Illustrative Environmental Regulations   17

2.3 Examples of International Agreements Ratified by China   18

2.4 Illustrative Surface Water Quality Standards   19

3.1 Contributions of Various Types of Enterprises to Industrial Output   41

3.2 Implementation of *Regulations on Transformation*   46

6.1 COD Concentrations in Permits for Eight Enterprises   102

6.2 COD Mass Flowrates in Permits for Eight Enterprises   104

7.1 Authorized EPB Enforcement Actions   116

7.2 Enforcement Actions Taken by EPBs (1992–93)   118

7.3 Frequency and Severity of Enforcement Actions   119

7.4 Fee-System Revenue in Municipality A   124

7.5 Fee-System Revenue in Municipality B   124

8.1 COD Releases and Fees at A1 Paper Mill   134

8.2   Compliance Rates: Profitable vs. Unprofitable Enterprises (1992)   140

8.3   A2 Chemical Fiber Plant's Cost Analysis   141

8.4   Compliance with Water Pollution Control Regulations (1992):
      TVEs vs. SOEs   144

8.5   Attributes of Enterprises Surveyed in Changzhou and Shunde   145

8.6   Government Assistance Needed by Enterprises to Comply with
      Regulations   147

8.7   Wastewater Treatment at Surveyed Enterprises in Changzhou
      and Shunde   147

A.1   Cities Participating in Initial Permit System Implementation   176

A.2   Cities Included in Our Research   177

A.3   Characteristics of Case Study Enterprises   178

A.4   Characteristics of Surveyed Enterprises   179

A.5   Sources of Data for the Six Cities   180

A.6   Compliance with Environmental Requirements in Surveyed Cities
      (1992)   182

B.1   Classes of Water Use in China   185

C.1   Comprehensive Wastewater Discharge Standards for Type I Pollutants   187

C.2   Comprehensive Wastewater Discharge Standards for Type II Pollutants   188

D.1   Effluent Standards Applicable to Different Classes of Water Use   189

List of Acronyms

BAT   best available technology
BCT   best conventional technology
CCP   Chinese Communist Party
COD   chemical oxygen demand
DPS   discharge permit system
EBCEY   Editorial Board of China Environmental Yearbook
EIA   environmental impact assessment
EIF   environmental impact form
EIS   environmental impact statement
EPB   environmental protection bureau
EPD   Environmental Protection Division
EPNRC   Environmental Protection and Natural Resources Conservation
         Committee
GDP   gross domestic product
NEPA   National Environmental Protection Agency
NGO   nongovernmental organization
NPC   National People's Congress
NPDES   National Pollutant Discharge Elimination System
PRC   People's Republic of China
QNCR   Quarterly Noncompliance Report
SDPC   State Development and Planning Commission
SEPA   State Environmental Protection Administration
SETC   State Economic and Trade Commission
SOE   state-owned enterprise
SPC   State Planning Commission
SS   suspended solids
TVEs   township and village enterprises
US EPA   United States Environmental Protection Agency
WWF   World Wide Fund for Nature

Preface

The remarkable economic development caused by China's market reforms has been accompanied by significant environmental destruction. In addition to having direct impacts within China, pollution linked to China's development contributes to several international environmental problems, including global climate change, acid rain, and the depletion of ozone in the stratosphere.

Contrary to popular opinion in the West, the Chinese government has not been insensitive to relationships between the country's rapid economic growth and its increasingly serious environmental problems. Following the introduction of the *PRC Environmental Protection Law for Trial Implementation in 1979,* China created a vast net-work of environmental protection agencies at the national, provincial, municipal, and county levels of government. Since then, China has promulgated dozens of environmental laws and created eight major pollution control programs.

Even with its sophisticated administrative structure and regulatory programs to curb pollution, China's environmental quality has continued to degrade. This raises fundamental questions: Are waste dischargers satisfying China's many pollution control requirements? And what factors influence how carefully enterprises satisfy environmental rules?

We examine these questions by investigating how Chinese enterprises comply with three water pollution control programs: the national system of wastewater discharge standards, the pollution discharge fee program, and the discharge permit system. Data for our analysis come from the following sources: interviews at environmental protection bureaus and enterprises in Anyang, Beijing, Changzhou, Chongqing, Jinan, and Shunde; a survey of managers at seventy-six enterprises in three of the cities; and in-depth studies of twelve factories in four of the cities. Our inquiry also relies on the growing literature on compliance with Chinese environmental regulations.

In addition to analyzing compliance statistics, we explore systematically the reasons that regulated parties in China do (or do not) satisfy environmental requirements. The framework for our study includes four elements: (1) *formal rules* embodied in the design of an environmental program; (2) *organizations* including regulated parties, environmental agencies, and other organizations that affect how environmental policies are implemented; (3) *informal rules* that influence interactions among participants in the regulatory process; and (4) *enforcement* actions taken by environmental agencies to monitor and encourage compliance with their rules. Our analysis pays particular attention to the customs and informal codes of behavior that govern relationships between enterprises and regulators and to the post-1978 economic and administrative reforms that are moving China toward a market economy. We put our results in perspective by comparing institutions for industrial pollution control in China with those in the United States.

This book is accessible to readers who are not China specialists. It will be of interest to a number of diffferent groups: environmental professionals and social scientists concerned with tradeoffs between economic development and environmental protection; students in courses dealing with modern China, as well as courses concerned with environmental policy implementation; and companies who want to do business in China.

Acknowledgments

We are pleased to acknowledge our debt to the many individuals who supported us during the process of data gathering and manuscript preparation. Two China scholars played a pivotal role in helping us sort out China's political and economic institutions: Michel Oksenberg of Stanford University and Scott Rozelle of the University of California at Davis. The following individuals commented on portions of the manuscript in its various forms, and we offer thanks to each of them: Earthea Bubanje-Nance, Katherine Kao Cushing, Keith Florig, Amanda Gilbert, Jacques Landy, Gilbert Masters, Sarah Middleton, Stephanie Bradley Oshita, Nina Rosenbladt, Jiang Ru, Tyson Smith, Read Vanderbilt, Kimberley Warren, Mara Warwick, Teng-Chung Wu, and Jimin Zhao.

We are grateful to many Chinese individuals and organizations for their assistance. Xia Qing of the Chinese Research Academy of Environmental Sciences played a key role in connecting us to regulatory officials in several cities, and Wang Ji of the State Environmental Protection Agency provided us with much valuable information. In addition, Yun Ping of Beijing Normal University assisted with data collection in four cities. We would also like to thank the many enterprise managers who participated in our interviews and surveys. We owe a particular debt to personnel at the State Environmental Protection Agency and at the environmental protection bureaus in Anyang, Beijing, Changzhou, Chongqing, Jinan, and Shunde. In preparing our final chapter, which compares environmental programs in the United States and China, we received help from Suzanne Clarke and from personnel at the U.S. Environmental Protection Agency offices in Philadelphia, San Francisco, and Washington, D.C., and at offices of state environmental agencies in California and Virginia.

The UPS Foundation and the Morrison Institute for Population and Resource Studies at Stanford University provided extensive support at many stages of our work. We are particularly grateful to Marcus Feldman, director of the Morrison Institute, for the assistance he provided. Xiaoying Ma's affiliation with projects the World Bank conducted in China offered us an opportunity to extend the range of our empirical work, and we are grateful for that. Nick Anderson and Lee Travers of the World Bank helped us create that opportunity.

Our deepest thanks go to Duc Wong for orchestrating all aspects of manuscript preparation. We are grateful for her extraordinary administrative ability and her unfailing patience and good humor. Thanks also to Brendan Wong for helping to prepare the bibliography, Andrea Kron for creating our maps, and Tina Katopodes for reviewing the manuscript in its final form. We are also grateful to Susan McEachern of Rowman & Littlefield Publishers for excellent editorial advice. The opinions expressed by Xiaoying Ma are her own; they do not reflect positions taken by her employer, the Asian Development Bank.

Location of the Six Cities Included in Our Study

- - - - Provincial boundary

1

Environmental Costs of China's Economic Growth

The Chinese government has introduced numerous reforms to transform its centrally planned economy into a "socialist market economy with Chinese characteristics."[1] These changes, which began in 1978, have produced spectacular economic growth and lifted millions out of poverty.[2] But this soaring economic expansion has taken an extraordinary toll on the environment. Increased pollution, deforestation, and soil erosion are only a few of the environmental problems tied to post-1978 economic growth in the People's Republic of China (PRC). Although monetary estimates of environmental damage are notoriously imprecise, the following statistics give some sense of China's loss: during the mid-1990s, the annual economic cost of air and water pollution was estimated as being between 24 and 54 billion U.S. dollars, approximately 3.5 and 7.7 percent, respectively, of China's gross domestic product (World Bank, 1997: 23).

Rapid development is not the only cause of China's environmental difficulties. Increases in China's population—which was expected to rise by at least 125 million during the 1990s—are also taking their toll.[3] The Canadian geographer Vaclav Smil offered a perspective on the effects of this population growth by calculating the grain required to provide for 125 million additional people at 1990 levels of per capita consumption in China. Smil estimated that China would have to produce an additional forty-five million tons of grain each year, which amounts to the entire grain output of Canada for 1990 (Smil, 1993: 193).

China's *urban* population grew by more than 160 million between 1980 and 1995 (World Bank, 1997: 5), and this has added to the nation's environmental problems. Air and water pollution are particularly bad in many of China's metropolitan areas. As increasing numbers of people leave farms to find jobs in cities, more people are exposed to unsafe water and polluted air.

The rise in industrialization, population, and urbanization has been accompanied by cutbacks in land under cultivation. The creation of new housing and industrial facilities and an expanded transportation network have combined to cause

1

notable decreases in farmland. Between 1959 and 1990, China lost at least 35 million hectares (Mha) of arable land, which amounted to about one-quarter of China's total farmland in 1990.[4]

CHINA'S PRIORITY ENVIRONMENTAL PROBLEMS

China's *Environmental Action Plan for 1991–2000* highlights environmental issues that national officials consider particularly significant. The Plan, which was prepared jointly by the National Environmental Protection Agency (NEPA) and the State Planning Commission (SPC),[5] focuses on the seven priority problems listed in Table 1.1. Three of the seven problems involve pollution: water and air pollution and hazardous waste. An additional three issues are linked to natural resources: water shortages, soil erosion, and loss of forests and grasslands. The final priority problem, loss of species and habitat, centers on the overall integrity of China's ecosystems.

Environmental Pollution

Many of China's rivers, lakes, and estuaries are badly fouled. For some rivers, such as the Huai and Hai, more than 50 percent of the river basin's surface waters are in the lowest category of Chinese waters, Class V.[6] These waters are so contaminated they can be employed only for industrial cooling and a few other purposes.

Water pollution from cities and industries is much easier to document than contamination from agricultural areas, but what records exist suggest that massive water pollution has resulted from use of synthetic fertilizers and pesticides on farms. Although synthetic fertilizers were not commonly employed in China before 1960, their usage has skyrocketed since then. The following figures for nitrogen fertilizer (largely urea and ammonium bicarbonate) illustrate the trend: three million tons were used in 1970 compared to more than twenty-one million tons in 1996 (Smil, 1993: 168; and Ash and Edmonds, 1998: 869). Water and

Table 1.1   China's Priority Environmental Problems[a]

- Water pollution, especially contamination by organic waste.
- Urban air pollution, as measured by particulates and sulfur dioxide.
- Hazardous and toxic solid waste in urban areas.
- Water shortages, particularly in northern China.
- Soil erosion.
- Loss of forests and grasslands.
- Loss of species and habitats, especially wetlands.

[a]Based on NEPA and SPC (1994: 206–211).

soil contamination occurs because large fractions of fertilizer and pesticide applications are carried away in flows leaving irrigated fields.

Damage tied to water pollution has been extensive. Many hectares of farmland have been taken out of production because of fouling by agrochemicals and by heavily contaminated wastewaters used to irrigate crops. In addition, pesticides, synthetic fertilizers, and waste discharges have defiled surface waters and aquifers used for drinking water and other purposes.[7] Much of the damage caused by water pollution is linked to human health. Other categories of loss include costs to industry (for example, increased water treatment costs) and drops in fish catches (Edmonds, 1994a: 145; and Vermeer, 1995: 26).

China's efforts to enhance water quality have centered on cutting industrial pollution. Municipalities, which accounted for about 45 percent of wastewater releases in 1997, have not made much progress in curbing water pollution.[8] As of the mid-1990s, about 93 percent of municipal wastewater was released without treatment (World Bank, 1997: 12). In contrast, enterprises have been treating a higher fraction of their wastewater from one year to the next. However, as Table 1.2 shows, advances in treatment have not always led to improvements sufficient to meet standards. For example, even though industrial wastewater receiving treatment jumped more than 21 percent between 1991 and 1997, wastewater meeting applicable discharge standards increased by less than 12 percent. Figures in Table 1.2 do not include wastewater from rural industrial enterprises, which were responsible for over one-third of the total value of industrial output in 1994 (Jefferson and Singh, 1997: 181).

Air pollution in China has also proven to be costly, particularly in terms of effects on human health. Studies sponsored by the World Bank tie higher sulfur

Table 1.2   Industrial Wastewater Releases in China[a]

Year	Total Discharge of Industrial Wastewater (billion tons)	Industrial Wastewater Receiving Treatment (% of total)	Industrial Wastewater Meeting Discharge Standards (% of total)
1991	23.6	63.5	50.1
1992	23.4	68.6	52.9
1993	21.9	72.0	54.9
1994	21.6	75.0	55.5
1995	22.2	76.8	55.5
1996	20.6	81.6	59.1
1997	18.8	84.7	61.8

[a]Statistics are from EBCEY (Editorial Board of China Environmental Yearbook) (1997: 149), NEPA (1997), and SEPA (State Environmental Protection Administration) (1998). This table excludes wastewater from township and village enterprises (TVEs). Beginning in 1997, national discharge statistics were reported for TVEs. For that year, TVEs released 3.8 billion tons of wastewater (SEPA, 1998).

dioxide and total suspended particulates in large Chinese cities to increased pul-
monary disorders, such as bronchitis.[9] Outdoor air pollution has been linked to
about 178,000 premature deaths in China each year.[10]

Ambient concentrations of total suspended particulates and sulfur dioxide in
some Chinese cities far exceed World Health Organization standards (see Figure 1.1). Moreover, as shown in Table 1.3, industrial emissions of sulfur dioxide
have not changed much over the past several years. Acid rain is also harmful,
particularly in cities like Chongqing, where high-sulfur coal is burned and the
natural pH of the soil is low. Damage from acid rain is illustrated by the massive destruction of pine forests in Wan County (Sichuan Province). Studies from
the mid-1980s reported that 15,000 hectares of trees in Wan County forests died
as a result of acid rain, and another 38,000 hectares of trees were dying (Smil,
1993: 120).

Air pollution problems are exacerbated by China's reliance on low-efficiency
coal stoves and outdated industrial technologies that yield high pollution loads
per unit of fuel burned. Moreover, low, government-set prices for fuel and energy reduce incentives to improve efficiency.

Solid and liquid hazardous waste releases by China's enterprises are also on
the rise. Most of this waste is not effectively regulated, and it is polluting soils
and contaminating groundwater aquifers and rivers. Although it is difficult to
distinguish between releases of hazardous and non-hazardous solid waste, the
figures in Table 1.4 provide insights into the magnitude of the hazardous waste
disposal problem.[11] While the amount of solid waste released annually by industry
has dropped recently, waste continues to pile up at dump sites. Many of these
sites are unlined and thus unable to keep contaminants from spreading to the surrounding environment, particularly to nearby aquifers. Several factors contribute to difficulties in controlling contamination from dumps and landfills; infor-

Table 1.3   Release of Air Pollutants by Industry[a]

Year	*Discharge Levels (10,000 tons)*		
	Soot	*Dust*	*Sulfur Dioxide*
1991	845	579	1,165
1992	870	576	1,324
1993	880	617	1,292
1994	807	583	1,341
1995	845	630	1,396
1996	758	562	1,397
1997	685	548	1,363

[a]Statistics are from EBCEY (1997: 149), NEPA (1997), and SEPA
(1998). Tabulated statistics do not include releases by TVEs. In 1997,
TVEs discharged the following amounts, in units of 10,000 tons: soot,
880; dust, 957; and sulfur dioxide, 489 (SEPA, 1998).

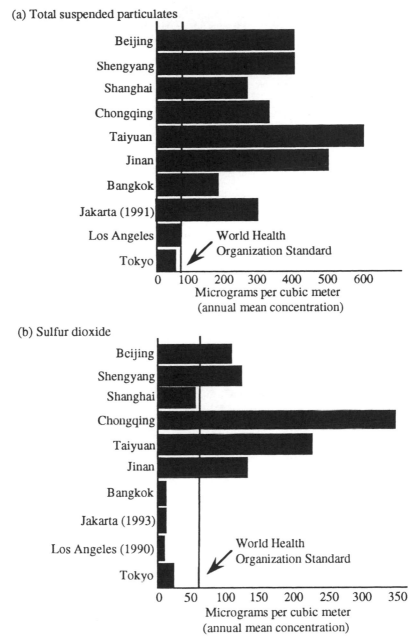

Figure 1.1   Ambient Concentrations of Air Pollutants in Selected Cities, 1995. Adapted from World Bank (1997: 6).

Table 1.4   Production and Release of Solid Waste by Industry[a]

	Industrial Solid Waste Generation and Disposal (million tons)		
Year	*Amount Generated*	*Amount Released*	*Amount Accumulating in Piles at Dump Sites*
1991	588	33.8	5,963
1992	619	25.9	5,916
1993	617	21.5	5,966
1994	617	19.3	6,463
1995	645	22.3	6,641
1996	659	16.9	6,490
1997	657	15.5	6,583

[a]Statistics are from EBCEY (1997: 149), NEPA (1997), and SEPA (1998). Tabulated statistics do not include releases by TVEs. In 1997, TVEs generated 401 million tons of solid waste and released about 169 million tons (SEPA, 1998). Natural Resources and Ecosystem Integrity.

mation on the location and condition of solid waste disposal facilities is scarce; many factories store solid waste on site, where they often escape control by environmental authorities; and, the expert knowledge needed to measure and control hazardous waste is limited (Vermeer: 1998: 981).

Natural Resources and Ecosystems Integrity

One of the natural resource issues in Table 1.1—water shortages–is tied directly to pollution. When contaminants are released to waterways, particularly to rivers in urban areas, water that was once suitable for drinking and other purposes is no longer available. Water shortages have led to extensive overpumping of groundwater aquifers, with consequent drops in groundwater levels and increases in pumping costs. Groundwater depletion has also created land subsidence problems.

Areas north of the Huai River suffer from particularly acute water shortages. This zone includes 64 percent of China's cultivated land, but it contains only 19 percent of the nation's water resources (NEPA and SPC, 1994: 208–209). Beijing's recent experiences illustrate the effects of water scarcity.[12] As a result of growth in water supply needs during the 1980s, Beijing faced a demand for sixteen billion tons of water in 1990; however, the city's waterworks could deliver no more than 700 million tons. Government officials responded by diverting to Beijing water that normally supplies Tianjin. As compensation, Tianjin received water from a new, long-distance diversion from the Yellow River. As a further response to recent droughts, water users pumped excessively from groundwater aquifers, causing drops greater than two meters during particularly dry years and leading to ground subsidence over more than 1,000 square kilometers. This pattern—inadequate surface water supply, overuse of groundwater resources, and long-distance transfers of water—is typical of what occurs in many parts of northern China during droughts.

China has also experienced increasingly serious soil erosion problems. In 1950, about 12 percent of China's land suffered from erosion, but by 1990 that figure had jumped to 16.7 percent (Edmonds, 1994b: 162). Erosion in the late 1990s adversely affected more than one-third of the nation's land and ranked among China's most pressing environmental problems.[13] Increased soil erosion results from deforestation, mining, and construction of new development projects. Agricultural activities also cause significant erosion, particularly when farmers cultivate crops on steep slopes or fail to implement erosion-control measures. Erosion is exacerbated when farmers bring pasture lands under cultivation and shift their grazing activities to dryland areas.

Soil erosion is problematic because the loss of topsoil reduces the ability of croplands to produce food. In addition, eroded material settles in reservoirs making them less effective for storing water and controlling floods. To lessen erosion, the government has tried to restrict farming on steep slopes, and to convert farm lands on slopes greater than twenty-five degrees to forests and other uses. In addition, many small dams have been constructed to collect sediment, and terrace farming is often practiced on steep slopes. The government has also tried to hold the line against deforestation.

Relative to world average forest coverage, which is above 30 percent, China's coverage—approximately 14 percent in 1996—is quite low (Edmonds, 1994b: 158; and NEPA, 1996: 4). Drops in coverage persist because farmers are clearing forests to grow crops for an expanding population, rural residents are continuing to use wood for cooking and heating, more timber is being logged, and regulations banning farming on steep slopes are often ignored.

China's government is concerned about reductions in forests—and grasslands as well—because these areas provide important natural services. When forests and grasslands are destroyed, lands have less capacity to absorb rainwater, and thus groundwater recharge declines and downstream flooding increases. The newly cleared lands are also more susceptible to erosion, and they are less suitable as habitats for species they once supported.

Although China has conducted afforestation programs for over four decades, many of those programs have failed. Smil (1993: 59) reports that while afforestation projects have taken place on 130 million hectares, "new plantings have survived on no more than 30–38 Mha, a success rate of below 30 percent." Notwithstanding the low success rate, new plantings have helped slow the rate of forest loss.

Deforestation, the conversion of grasslands to agriculture, and the increased pace of economic development have all threatened the integrity of China's ecosystems. Land areas suitable as habitats for many native species are declining. For example, a government report indicates that birds are almost extinct in many areas because farmers have overused pesticides and synthetic fertilizers (NEPA and SPC, 1994: 210).

The government's concern over the loss of species and habitats is pragmatic. For example, wetlands, forests, and other natural areas play key roles in maintaining important ecological functions, and high species diversity is essential for developing Chinese medicine and agriculture. China has tried to preserve critical habitats by introducing a system of nature reserves, but the system has functioned poorly. At the end of 1997, the total land area devoted to nature reserves amounted to about seventy-seven Mha, 7.4 percent of China's total area, but the reserves have not been well managed and destructive activities have continued (SEPA, 1998; and Harkness, 1998).

DIVERGENCE BETWEEN POLLUTION CONTROL GOALS AND ACTUAL ENVIRONMENTAL QUALITY

Serious attempts to abate pollution in China began in the late 1970s. The government promulgated in 1979 a "trial implementation" of China's basic environmental law, the *PRC Environmental Protection Law*. A decade later, that law was amended and its trial status was removed. Since 1979, the central government has established over one hundred environmental laws and regulations, and it has created eight major pollution control programs. To implement these programs, China has established a national environmental agency staffed by a few hundred people and more than two thousand local environmental protection bureaus (EPBs) that employ over sixty thousand people (Jahiel, 1998: 772; and Lotspeich and Chen, 1997: 52). Between 1988 and 1998, the national agency was called the National Environmental Protection Agency; in 1998, it was elevated in status and renamed the State Environmental Protection Administration (SEPA).

China's environmental programs and agencies provide a foundation for curtailing further degradation, but they do not ensure that environmental quality will be enhanced. A key step involves *compliance*: the full attainment of environmental requirements by organizations whose actions harm the environment. A significant gap currently exists between the goals embodied in China's environmental laws and regulations and actual levels of environmental quality, and this gap appears to be widening. In mid-1996, Xie Zhenhua, the head of NEPA, emphasized that the nation's efforts to abate pollution had slowed, but not stopped, the deterioration of environment quality.[14]

Why has China's environment continued to degrade even though the country has a sophisticated set of regulatory programs? And what role does noncompliance with regulations play in answering this question? These issues can only be probed by selecting particular regulatory programs as objects of study. Our analysis focuses on industrial wastewater control programs because they are among the oldest and most sophisticated environmental protection efforts in China.[15] In addition, programs to cut industrial wastewater have a relatively high effectiveness. Moreover, water pollution is one of the country's most pressing environmental problems. In the late 1990s, nearly 80 percent of China's urban rivers failed to meet stream quality standards for Class III water use, more than half of China's groundwater was contaminated, and the zone of coastal pollution was expanding.[16] The main pollutants found in water bodies included volatile phenols, ammonia, and contaminants that depleted dissolved oxygen in natural waters (SEPA, 1998).

INSTITUTIONAL FRAMEWORK FOR ENVIRONMENTAL PROTECTION

Our analysis of industrial wastewater management programs considers each of the following elements of China's institutional framework for environmental protection: organizations, formal rules contained in laws and regulations, informal rules reflected in unwritten codes of acceptable behavior, and mechanisms for enforcing formal rules (see Table 1.5).[17] Below we introduce each element of this institutional framework, beginning with *organizations*. Details on each element are given in later chapters.

China's State Environmental Protection Administration plays the key role in designing pollution control policies and programs, but its role in day-to-day implementation of environmental regulations is limited. SEPA, which has a staff of a few hundred people, implements rules only for projects undertaken by national-level agencies, or activities that are otherwise of national significance (for example, projects involving nuclear energy). In all other cases, environmental protection bureaus implement industrial pollution control rules. EPBs are elements of local government, where *local* refers to any level of government below the national level; for example, the Guangdong Provincial People's Government is a local government.

The regulated parties included in our study fall into two categories: state-owned enterprises (SOEs), and township and village enterprises (TVEs). In the early 1990s, when we conducted our field research, these two enterprise types accounted for about 75 percent of China's industrial activity as measured by total value of industrial output (Jefferson and Rawski, 1994: 48). Other categories consisted of urban collectives, small private enterprises, and foreign-owned firms.

An analysis of how and why Chinese companies satisfy environmental requirements cannot restrict itself to enterprises because state-owned enterprises are

Table 1.5   Institutional Framework for Environmental Protection

- **Organizations**—SEPA, EPBs, other units of government, enterprises, citizens, nongovernmental organizations, and the media.
- **Formal rules**—Environmental laws and regulations.
- **Informal rules**—Customs and unwritten codes of behavior.
- **Enforcement**—Monitoring rule compliance, and assisting or penalizing regulated parties that fail to comply.

supervised by industrial bureaus, and the majority of TVEs are owned by township governments or village committees. These governmental units affect how enterprises respond to environmental rules.

Many government agencies influence how industrial pollution control requirements are implemented. For example, a city's EPB, which is a unit of city government reporting to the mayor, works closely with many other city agencies, such as the planning commission and the economic commission. In addition, people's congresses, the media, non-governmental organizations (NGOs), and individual citizens sometimes play key roles as advocates of environmental protection.

Interactions among organizations that participate in environmental protection are guided by both formal and informal rules. *Formal rules* are the pollution control requirements detailed in laws and regulations. An example of a formal rule is the regulation stipulating that wastewater releases from many new enterprises in Beijing must have less than 100 milligrams per liter (mg/l) of chemical oxygen demand (COD), an indicator used to measure the amount of oxidizable organic material within wastewater.[18] *Informal rules* are derived from customs and unwritten codes of conduct, and they affect how environmental laws are implemented. For example, behavioral norms governing professional relationships influence how EPB personnel interact with environmental managers at regulated enterprises.

Enforcement is part of the institutional framework for environmental protection because enterprise managers make decisions based on their perceptions of what will happen if they violate rules. Information gathering plays a major role in enforcement. Enterprises need to know whether rule violations will be policed and punished. Environmental agencies, in turn, must obtain information on rule compliance. In China, as in the United States and other countries, enterprises are often required to monitor their waste releases (a process called "self-monitoring"), and to report results to environmental agencies ("self-reporting"). SEPA and EPBs conduct periodic facility inspections to gauge the reliability of self-reported data.

In enforcing rules, SEPA and EPBs incur the cost of detecting and measuring rule violations, and of reacting to violations by offering assistance or imposing sanctions. Assistance may consist of technical advice or grants to help build wastewater treatment plants. Sanctions commonly take the form of fines.

PLAN OF THE BOOK

In the next chapter, we introduce China's principal industrial pollution control programs. The four chapters that follow concern elements of the institutional framework for environmental protection (see Table 1.5). First, the main organizations affected by pollution control rules are described: enterprises, units of government, non-governmental organizations, citizens, and the media. Next, the two types of rules affecting the behavior of organizations influenced by regulations are considered: informal rules of appropriate behavior, and formal rules that define the pollution control programs included in our study. A chapter on enforcement completes our analysis of elements of the institutional framework.

The penultimate chapter identifies linkages between compliance outcomes and characteristics of enterprises, such as levels of profitability and forms of ownership. The final chapter summarizes our main findings in the context of a comparative analysis of environmental protection in China and the United States.

Appendix A describes our research approach and details how we selected the six cities included in our field investigation: Anyang, Beijing, Changzhou, Chongqing, Jinan, and Shunde (see map positioned before the beginning of Chapter 1). Appendix A also indicates how we chose our twelve case study enterprises, and how we conducted our survey of seventy-six enterprises in Anyang, Changzhou, and Shunde.

NOTES

1. Reform of the Chinese economy toward "market socialism" was initiated at the Third Plenary Session of the Eleventh Central Party Congress in late 1978.

2. With an overall rate of economic growth that averaged more than 9 percent per year in real terms from 1978 to 1993, China was the "fastest growing major industrial economy in the world over that period" (Lieberthal, 1995: 258).

3. China's population rose from 1.13 billion at the beginning of 1990 to 1.22 billion at the end of 1996 (SSB, 1996). Banister (1998: 1010) estimates that with "hardly any further decline in fertility, the population of the PRC will be about 1.26 billion in the year 2000." This would amount to an increase of 130 million over the 1990 population.

4. These estimates are from Smil (1993: 57), who also reported that China's total arable land area for 1990 was between 100 and 140 Mha. This range is large owing to difficulties in obtaining accurate statistics. One hectare equals 2.47 acres.

5. In 1998, NEPA was elevated in status and renamed the State Environmental Protection Administration (SEPA). In addition, SPC was re-named the State Development and Planning Commission (SDPC).

6. For more on pollution of these two rivers, see National Environmental Modeling Center (1999).

7. For example, a study of groundwater in forty-seven cities showed that forty-three of them were "dependent on groundwater containing toxic contaminants at levels exceeding state water quality standards" (Boxer, 1992: 299).

8. Of the 41.6 billion tons of wastewater discharged in 1997, about 18.9 billion tons came from municipalities, and the rest came from industries (SEPA, 1998).

9. Three cities were included in these studies: Beijing, Shenyang, and Chongqing (World Bank, 1997: 18). For more on adverse health effects from air pollution in China, see Banister (1998: 989–993).

10. This estimate from the World Bank (1997: 19) reflects the number of premature deaths that could be avoided annually if China met its class II air quality standards. The World Bank also estimated that 111,000 premature deaths each year were caused by indoor air pollution, particularly in rural areas, where coal and biomass are often burned for cooking and heating.

11. NEPA has estimated that 50 million tons of hazardous waste are generated each year in China (World Bank, 1994: 19). However, Vermeer (1998: 981) indicates that national data collection related to solid waste is "uneven and figures are sometimes contradictory and hard to interpret."

12. Remaining facts in this paragraph are from Smil (1993: 42–43).

13. This assertion is based on an article entitled "Soil Erosion Danger Remains" in *China Daily*, July 6, 1998.

14. This point was made by Xie Zhenhua in a speech at the Fourth National Environmental Protection Conference held in July 1996.

15. During the early 1990s, China devoted nearly 50 percent of its pollution abatement expenditures to water pollution control (Edmonds, 1994b: 167).

16. These facts are from Xie (1996) and SEPA (1998). Class III waters include sources of municipal drinking water supply with treatment required, areas for conserving common aquatic species, and areas for swimming.

17. Our conceptualization of "institutional framework" relies heavily on Douglass North and other contributors to the "new institutional economics." North (1990: 3) defines *institutions* as constraints that people devise to guide their interactions or, more colloquially, the "rules of the game in a society." We avoid using the word "institution" because it has many different meanings. For an account of competing definitions of institutions, see Scott (1995).

18. The 100 mg/l threshold for COD is illustrative; numerical limits vary depending upon the classification of the receiving water body.

2

Programs Regulating Industrial Pollution

China has a broad array of laws and programs to deal with its most pressing environmental problems. Before concentrating on industrial wastewater regulations, we introduce the legislative process and China's environmental management system.

CREATING ENVIRONMENTAL LAWS AND POLICIES IN CHINA

The principal actors in China's policy-making processes are the National People's Congress (NPC), the State Council, and the Chinese Communist Party (CCP or the Party). The NPC is the nation's top legislative body, the State Council is the leading administrative unit, and the CCP has a profound influence on both.

The NPC, the State Council, and the Party

While the impetus for many environmental policies comes from the State Environmental Protection Agency, those policies are generally legitimized by being incorporated into statutes or legally binding administrative regulations. Two types of environmental statutes exist: a "basic law" passed by the NPC and special laws, which are generally enacted by the NPC's Standing Committee. Legally binding regulations are issued by the State Council or, with the Council's approval, one or more of its ministries or commissions.

The National People's Congress has about 3,000 deputies from the provinces, in addition to deputies from the armed forces. Typically, the NPC meets for plenary sessions about once a year. Between these sessions, the Congress's work is conducted by its Standing Committee, which contains over 130 members (Charlton, 1997: 85). Although the National People's Congress has the appear-

13

ance of a traditional legislature, its activities are heavily influenced by the State Council and the CCP.

In an effort to improve the efficiency of the law-making process, the NPC created in 1993 special committees with supervisory authority for particular areas of law. One of these committees, the Environmental Protection and Natural Resources Conservation (EPNRC) Committee, has played an increasingly influential role in providing regulatory proposals to the NPC's Standing Committee.[1] During the past several years, the EPNRC Committee has been instrumental in creating or amending several environmental statutes, and it has an ambitious Environmental Legislative Plan for the 1998–2003 period. In creating legislative proposals, the Committee negotiates extensively with ministries and national-level commissions because the support of these bodies is essential for the passage and effective implementation of environmental laws.

The State Council, a collective decision-making group headed by the premier, includes leaders of ministries and national commissions. Since the founding of the PRC in 1949, the Council's size has fluctuated in response to administrative changes, such as the creation of new ministries and the elimination of old ones.[2] Key decisions are often made by the State Council's Standing Committee, which includes the premier, a few vice premiers, the secretary general, and several state councilors.

In principle, the State Council implements the laws and policies of the National People's Congress. In practice, however, the State Council drafts proposed laws and refers them to the NPC and its Standing Committee. The State Council plays this influential legislative role because it sits at the top of a vast bureaucracy that includes virtually all ministries, commissions, and other administrative agencies, and thus it has considerable access to expertise and resources.

The Chinese Communist Party influences law-making by controlling appointments to key legislative and administrative posts. The Party maintains lists of candidates acceptable for membership on the NPC's Standing Committee,[3] and it controls appointments to top positions in ministries and commissions, which is equivalent to determining who can be on the State Council. In addition, because of Party discipline exerted by NPC members, the Congress would not promulgate a law opposed by the CCP leadership (Tanner, 1994). The Party has deeply penetrated the apparatus of the state, and thus there is no advantage in distinguishing the Party from the state in our analysis of environmental policy.[4]

Promulgating Environmental Laws and Issuing Administrative Regulations

Although many Westerners envision law-making in China as a closed, top-down procedure controlled tightly by a unified CCP leadership, legislation can be influenced by national agencies and local elites. One informed analysis of recent legal reforms describes a fragmented scenario:

the Chinese law-making system should be seen as a "multi-arena" process, with draft laws passing through three major policy-making arenas: the CCP central apparatus; the State Council . . . ; and the National People's Congress system. Law-making processes and power relationships among these arenas are not clearly defined—either formally or informally—and continue to evolve. (Tanner, 1994: 57)

Because China's environmental laws are general and often intentionally ambiguous, they allow the State Council, national agencies, and local governments to add details that influence implementation. Typically, after the NPC's Standing Committee passes an environmental law, the State Council issues administrative edicts that provide particulars needed for implementation. Under Article 89 of China's Constitution, the State Council is empowered to "adopt administrative measures, enact administrative rules and regulations, and issue decisions and orders in accordance with the Constitution and statutes."[5] Administrative regulations, which may be put forth by the State Council or (with the Council's approval) one or more of its agencies, have the force of law. Enactment follows a formal procedure, and regulations are announced by being published in the *State Council Gazette* or issued by the relevant department(s).

In addition to promulgating administrative regulations, national departments can further clarify a law using "measures," "notifications," and a variety of other documents.[6] For example, three years after China's pollution discharge fee system was given a statutory foundation in 1979, the State Council enacted "provisional measures" describing how fees were to be calculated. When fees changed in 1991, the new rates were announced in a "notice" jointly issued by the National Environmental Protection Agency, the National Price Bureau, and the Ministry of Finance.

Most day-to-day implementation of a national environmental law occurs at the local level. Typically, local people's congresses and the executive branch of local governments respond to national edicts by producing their own versions of national regulations, notices, and so forth. For example, soon after the State Council issued its provisional measures for calculating pollution discharge fees, the Guangdong Provincial People's Government issued its own "measures" describing fee calculation procedures to be used throughout the province. Laws and regulations issued by sub-national people's congresses and executive branches of people's governments must be consistent with national legal enactments.

NATIONAL ENVIRONMENTAL LAWS

China's Constitution provides the underlying basis for all of the nation's environmental laws and regulations. Articles 9 and 26 call upon the state to protect the environment (including forests and rare animals and plants); eliminate pollution and public hazards; encourage afforestation; and "ensure the rational use of natural resources."[7] Below we elaborate on the hierarchy of environmental laws and regulations that are built upon this constitutional foundation: a basic law provides an overall framework for national environmental programs; special laws cover topics such as air pollution, solid waste, and so forth; and regulations and other administrative edicts contain specific instructions for implementing laws.

China's Basic Environmental Law

The Chinese government, along with many others, became increasingly concerned with the adverse effects of economic development during the 1970s. Based on several years of experience with different environmental management approaches, the NPC's Standing Committee promulgated in 1979 a tentative version of China's basic environmental law, the *PRC Environmental Protection Law for Trial Implementation*. This statute established national and local environmental protection bureaus, required polluters to comply with waste discharge standards, and directed enterprises to assess environmental impacts of proposed projects and ensure that new projects satisfied applicable environmental standards.

The trial implementation status of the basic environmental law was removed in 1989 when the NPC's Standing Committee promulgated the *PRC Environmental Protection Law*. This statute gave the regulatory programs developed in the 1970s and 1980s a solid legislative base and expanded the locus of responsibility for environmental protection. Before 1989, many Chinese authorities believed that only NEPA and environmental protection bureaus were responsible for preventing environmental destruction. With passage of the 1989 law, governments at the national, provincial, city, and county levels were given explicit environmental protection responsibilities.

China's basic environmental law contains the following four guiding principles:

- *Coordination of environmental protection and economic development.* National environmental protection plans must be integrated into national economic development plans; in addition, the state should adopt economic and technical measures that are environmentally beneficial (Article 4).
- *Pollution prevention.* While measures to abate existing waste discharges are being undertaken, future releases should be prevented, mainly by using enhanced environmental management at new pollution sources (Articles 13, 15, and 26).
- *Polluter responsibility.* Waste dischargers should bear the costs of cleaning up environmental problems they cause; thus polluters should pay discharge fees on waste releases that exceed discharge standards, and they should invest in waste treatment facilities (Articles 24, 27, 28, 29, and 31).
- *Strengthening environmental management.* Because reducing pollution by investing in new waste treatment facilities is expensive, the first line of attack is to cut waste releases by improving management procedures (Articles 9 through 15).

Specialized Environmental Laws, Regulations, and Programs

In addition to the basic environmental law, China has more than twenty special environmental statutes. As illustrated in Table 2.1, each special environmental law is directed at a particular issue. Table entries relate to some of the seven priority environmental problems identified in the *Environmental Action Plan of China: 1991–2000* (see Table 1.1).

The State Council, NEPA (and later SEPA), and other state agencies have issued numerous administrative edicts to implement environmental policies stipulated in the basic and special environmental laws. Examples of administrative regulations related to China's priority environmental problems are given in Table 2.2.

Many of the priority environmental problems are subjects of national plans and programs. Consider, for example, the "Three Norths Shelter Belt Development Program," which was initiated in 1978 in a four million square kilometer area that includes numerous provinces in northern China. The program aims to protect and enhance lands by planting trees and grasses and by preventing development on sand dunes and hillsides. As of 1996, the Three Norths Program had created over 18.5 million hectares of new forests (EBCEY, 1997: 54–75).

Table 2.1   Examples of Special Environmental Laws

Environmental Pollution
  • PRC Solid Waste Pollution Prevention and Control Law, 1995
  • PRC Air Pollution Prevention and Control Law, 1987 (revised, 1995)
  • PRC Water Pollution Prevention and Control Law 1984, (revised, 1996)

Natural Resources and Ecosystem Integrity
  • PRC Forest Law, 1984
  • PRC Grasslands Law, 1986
  • PRC Wildlife Protection Law, 1988
  • PRC Land Administration Law, 1986 (revised, 1988)
  • PRC Water and Soil Conservation Law, 1991

Table 2.2   Illustrative Environmental Regulations

Environmental Pollution
  • Collection of Pollution Discharge Fees, 1982
  • Provisional Regulations on Huai River Basin Water Pollution Prevention and Control, 1995

Natural Resources and Ecosystem Integrity
  • Water and Soil Conservation Law Implementation Regulations, 1993
  • PRC National Park Regulations, 1994
  • Natural Flora Protection Regulations, 1996

Table 2.3   Examples of International Agreements Ratified by China[a]

- Basel Convention on Control of Transboundary Movements of Hazardous Wastes, 1991
- Montreal Protocol on Substances that Deplete the Ozone Layer, 1991
- Framework Convention on Climate Change, 1992
- Convention on Biodiversity, 1992
- Convention on Combating Desertification, 1994

[a]Years shown indicate when China signed the agreements (EBCEY, 1998: 153–155 and 159).

Several of China's environmental programs are tied to international agreements. Table 2.3 lists some of the many international conventions and protocols China has ratified. Actions designed to meet China's obligations under international agreements are illustrated in the *Country Program for the Phaseout of Ozone Depleting Substances under the Montreal Protocol* approved by the State Council in 1993. This program details activities intended to eliminate the production and consumption of chlorofluorocarbons and halons in China by 2010.

NATIONAL WATER QUALITY STANDARDS

We now extend our general introduction to China's environmental laws and regulations, by considering specific programs related to our main subject of study: the regulation of industrial wastewater. We begin by discussing national standards that govern wastewater releases from enterprises.

Articles 9 and 10 of the 1989 *PRC Environmental Protection Law* authorized NEPA to establish two types of national standards: ambient environmental quality standards and waste discharge standards. *Ambient standards* are illustrated by restrictions on the minimum allowable concentration of dissolved oxygen in a stream. *Discharge standards* are exemplified by a limit on the maximum permissible concentration of mercury in a factory's wastewater release (also called *effluent*). Local governments may create ambient and discharge standards for pollutants not specified in national standards, and they may also establish more restrictive limiting values for pollutants included in national discharge standards.

NEPA and environmental protection bureaus began developing standards for ambient environmental quality and for pollutant discharges during the late 1970s. By the 1990s, eleven ambient environmental quality standards had been issued, and fifty standards had been developed for vehicular emissions and industrial effluents and emissions. In addition, over two hundred standards had been created to deal with special problems (for example, radioactive waste) and methods of sampling and analysis (CEYCC, 1993).

Ambient Water Quality Standards

China's ambient water quality standards are keyed to five categories used to classify water bodies. The classification scheme is based on types of water uses to be protected and water quality goals. Waters designated as Class I have the highest quality, whereas Class V waters have the poorest quality and can be used only for industrial cooling water and other limited purposes (see Appendix B).

Thirty water quality indicators are used to define China's ambient standards. For a water body of a given class, numerical limits are set for each of the thirty parameters. Linkages between surface water quality indicators and classification levels are illustrated in Table 2.4, which shows the limits for COD, soluble iron, and total cadmium for each class of water use. Table entries represent *concentration*; that is, the mass of pollutant per unit volume of water in units of milligrams per liter (mg/l).

Wastewater Discharge Standards

China's national effluent standards are concentration-based limits on the quality of wastewater releases.[8] In this context, "concentration" generally refers to the mass of a pollutant per unit volume of *wastewater*. At the time of our field research in the early 1990s, enterprises were bound by discharge standards that NEPA had promulgated in 1988, and those are the ones described here.[9] China's 1988 effluent standards specified the maximum allowable concentrations of twenty-nine pollutants, and these limits applied to all industrial sectors. Regulated water pollutants are divided into two types: Type I—heavy metals and other toxic substances; and Type II—conventional water pollution indicators, such as total suspended solids, COD, and pH. The 1988 national effluent standards are given in Appendix C.

Although only one set of effluent standards exists for Type I pollutants, three sets have been established for Type II pollutants, and they are linked to the five categories used to classify water bodies. Relationships between levels of effluent standards and classes of water bodies are detailed in Appendix D. Limits for Type II pollutants also depend on whether a pollution source is new or existing. New sources are regulated more tightly than existing ones.

China's effluent standards constrain concentrations, but they do *not* limit the total mass of pollutants in a discharge. The distinction between limits on mass and concentration is illustrated by considering chemical oxygen demand. The test for COD determines the amount of oxygen (in milligrams of oxygen per liter of wastewater) required to transform complex organic substances into chemically

Table 2.4 Illustrative Surface Water Quality Standards[a]

Indicator	Class of Water Use				
	I	*II*	*III*	*IV*	*V*
COD (mg/l)	15[b]	15	15	20	25
Soluble iron (mg/l)	0.3	0.3	0.5	0.5	1.0
Total cadmium (mg/l)	0.001	0.005	0.005	0.005	0.01

[a]From *Environmental Quality Standards for Surface Water*, GB 3838–88, promulgated by NEPA on April 15, 1988.

[b]Table entries are upper limits. For example, COD should be no greater than 15 mg/l in a Class I water body.

stable end products, such as carbon dioxide and water. In typical wastewater, much of the organic material is oxidized by microorganisms that break down biodegradable compounds. The remaining, non-biogradable organics can only be transformed if a strong oxidizing agent is present. The test to measure COD does not differentiate between biodegradable and non-biodegradable organic matter.

An example of a discharge standard is the 500 mg/l upper limit for COD entering a water body designated as Class V. A factory discharging wastewater with 500 mg/l of COD into a Class V water body would satisfy this standard regardless of the total quantity of waste it released each day. A factory discharging 10 liters of wastewater with 500 mg/l of COD meets the standard, as does a factory releasing 10,000 liters of wastewater with 500 mg/l of COD. Using engineering terminology, China's effluent standards do not constrain the *mass flowrate* of pollutants; that is, the mass of pollutants released per unit time expressed in units such as kilograms per day (kg/day). Mass flowrate of a wastewater is calculated as the product of pollutant concentration and *volume flowrate*, the total volume of wastewater released per unit time, in units such as liters per day.

Because China's effluent standards only constrain concentrations, they can be satisfied by diluting wastewater with uncontaminated water. Consider, for example, a factory releasing an effluent with a COD of 1,000 mg/l into a Class V river. Suppose the facility was near an inexpensive source of water in which the COD concentration was virtually nil. This factory could meet the 500 mg/l limit by simply mixing its wastewater with an equal volume of clean water. The dilution effect would cut the 1,000 mg/l of COD in half, but the total quantity of COD released to the river would remain unchanged.

National Environmental Programs to Attain Standards

China has established several national environmental programs to achieve its effluent standards. For example, the discharge fee program, and requirements to control pollution within a fixed time period are each directed at assuring that enterprises satisfy wastewater discharge requirements. Environmental monitoring stations (usually run by affiliates of EPBs) are responsible for checking up on polluters' activities, and EPBs are authorized to penalize enterprises that fail to meet effluent standards.

China has eight national programs to control urban and industrial pollution and thereby satisfy applicable standards:

- Environmental impact assessment
- Three synchronizations
- Pollution discharge fee system
- Pollution control within deadlines
- Discharge permit system
- Environmental responsibility system
- Assessment of urban environmental quality
- Centralized control of pollution

The first three of these programs were created in the late 1970s, and the last five were introduced in the 1980s to manage problems the three earlier programs could not handle. Because our research examines compliance with two of the eight programs (pollution discharge fees and the discharge permit system), only these two are described in detail.[10] We comment briefly on each of the other six programs to provide an overall perspective on how industrial pollution is regulated.[11] In this chapter we describe environmental protection rules as they appear in laws and regulations. Later chapters clarify differences between what the rules say and what actually happens in practice.

POLLUTION DISCHARGE FEE SYSTEM

Under the discharge fee system, enterprises must pay fees for releases on air-borne and water-borne pollutants that violate standards on emissions and effluents, respectively. Typically, fees are based on the pollution indicator that exceeds the discharge standard (expressed in concentration units, such as mg/l) by the greatest amount. In the case of wastewater, for example, the degree of noncompliance with the standard is used to calculate a *unit* fee, in *yuan* per ton of wastewater released. The *total* fee (in *yuan* per day) is the product of the unit fee and the wastewater discharge rate (in tons per day).[12]

Over-Standard Fees and the Four Small Pieces

In addition to paying fees for pollutants exceeding standards (referred to as *over-standard fees*), enterprises violating requirements may have to pay four other kinds of penalty charges, referred to as the *four small pieces*: (1) a 5 percent per year increase in the over-standard fee, beginning the third year the fee is assessed and continuing until the enterprise meets discharge standards; (2) a double charge for enterprises built after 1979 that violate discharge standards, close down existing treatment facilities without prior approval of the local EPB, *or* fail to comply with administrative orders requiring pollution control by a fixed date; (3) a late fee of 0.1 percent per day for failure to pay over-standard fees; and (4) a fine to compensate for economic losses or adverse human health effects caused by waste releases.

Although the fee program was included in the 1979 *PRC Environment Protection Law*, methods to calculate fees were not set until 1982 when the State Council issued *Provisional Measures for Collecting Pollution Discharge Fees* (State Council, 1982, referred to herein as *Provisional Measures*). These computation procedures ignored inflation. However, unit fees were revised in 1991 to account for inflation that had occurred since 1982.[13]

According to the *Provisional Measures*, up to 80 percent of the over-standard fees collected by an EPB is to be placed in a local *pollution levy fund* and made available as grants and low-interest loans to subsidize environmental management projects at factories that have paid fees. Enterprises may borrow (or be granted) up to 80 percent of the fees they paid.[14] The EPB retains *all* of the four small pieces plus a portion of the over-standard fees (typically about 20 percent). These funds, referred to as *self-construction fees*, can be used for environmental monitoring, research, training, and awards.[15]

If an enterprise satisfies discharge standards, it does not pay over-standard fees, but it may have to pay a volume-based wastewater discharge fee. This requirement was established in 1993 when the State Planning Commission and the Ministry of Finance jointly issued *A Notice on Collection of Wastewater Discharge Fees*. The volume-based fee is calculated by multiplying the discharge flowrate (tons/day) by 0.05 *yuan*/ton. An enterprise is *not* required to pay both an over-standard fee and a volume-based wastewater discharge fee (SPC and MF, 1993).

Five-Step Implementation Procedure

The discharge fee system is generally implemented in five steps corresponding to compliance monitoring and the determination, collection, allocation, and use of fees. For illustrative purposes, we describe how the fee system is implemented in a typical municipality.[16] In the compliance monitoring step, staff of the environmental monitoring station, an affiliate of the municipal EPB, collects wastewater samples at enterprises, analyzes the samples, and submits results to the environmental inspection station, another affiliate of the municipal EPB.[17] The inspection station then determines the total charge.[18]

In the fee collection step, the environmental inspection station notifies the enterprise of the discharge fee it must pay. Assuming the enterprise agrees to the amount, it has twenty days to ask its bank to transfer the required sum to an account in a local bank designated by the EPB. (For example, the EPB may have an account used exclusively for discharge fees at the municipal industrial and commercial bank.) If the enterprise believes the fee was not computed properly, it has fifteen days to ask the provincial EPB to review the fee calculations;[19] alternatively, the enterprise can appeal by filing a lawsuit at a local court within three months. If the enterprise neither pays the fees nor initiates an appeal, the municipal EPB can issue a notice for obtaining payment from the enterprise's bank without the enterprise's permission. If necessary, the EPB can ask the local court to enforce the rules related to fee collection. The EPB can also impose a penalty charge of 0.1 percent per day of late payment; this charge is one of the four small pieces. Once required fees and late charges are collected, the EPB transfers them to the municipal finance bureau.

In the next step, fee allocation, the municipal EPB develops a plan for distributing up to 80 percent of the over-standard fees to enterprises as grants or loans. (Each factory that paid fees may submit an application for a grant or loan to cover the cost of a proposed pollution abatement project.) The EPB also prepares a budget for the use of self-construction fees: the portion of over-standard fees retained by the EPB plus the four small pieces. The finance bureau then examines the EPB's plans for disbursing funds to enterprises and using the self-construction fees. After completing its review, the finance bureau issues a document detailing approved uses of the pollution levy fund and notifies the bank holding the discharge fees to allocate the funds to the EPB's accounts for the pollution levy fund and self-construction fees. According to the rules, discharge fees are ear-marked for industrial pollution control and for self-construction; the finance bureau has no authority to divert fees to other purposes.

The final step of the process requires both the EPB and the bank holding the fees to jointly administer the use of grants and loans by enterprises. The EPB's task is to review both the design and construction of all industrial pollution control projects supported by money from the pollution levy fund. (An enterprise can be partially exempted from repaying its loan if the EPB approves its project, and if the enterprise can prove it will have trouble making loan payments.) The bank's job is to disburse funds, receive loan payments, and help the EPB recover funds from enterprises that either default on their loans or do not build the projects described in their loan (or grant) applications.

Possible Changes in the Discharge Fee Program

During the late 1990s, changes in the use of revenues from the discharge fee program were being considered, and they could significantly affect the ability of EPBs to carry out their work. One change, which was initiated on a limited basis in the late 1990s, involves replacing pollution levy funds with new revolving funds offering loans at near market rates to enterprises to help improve their environmental performance.[20] As of 1998, about twenty EPBs at provincial and municipal levels had created "environmental protection funds" or "special foundations" with an aggregate capital accumulation of over three billion *yuan*. The future of these new investment funds was highly uncertain because of the central government's proposal to take control of pollution discharge fees away from EPBs.

In 1998, Premier Zhu Rongji and others urged a fundamental change in which the numerous special fees levied by government agencies at all levels would be brought under the control of the Ministry of Finance and the local finance commissions under that ministry.[21] Many types of fees would be involved, including pollution discharge fees. Collectively, these fees constituted a substantial fraction of the nation's fiscal revenues. Those supporting the change argued that consolidating all fees under the Ministry of Finance would reduce corruption and cut the size of the bureaucracy.

If the proposed shift was to occur, the ability of EPBs to use revenues from discharge fees would be reduced significantly. Instead of maintaining primary control over the use of fees it collected, an EPB would have to apply to the local finance bureau with a proposal detailing how the requested funds would be used. Because they derive a significant part of their total budget from discharge fees, many EPBs strongly opposed the change.

DISCHARGE PERMIT SYSTEM

In the late 1980s, some NEPA staff believed that water quality was continuing to deteriorate because existing environmental programs were based on discharge standards that constrained only concentrations of pollutants. The staff felt that water quality degradation would be reduced by establishing a discharge permit system (DPS) to limit both the concentration *and* the mass flowrate of pollutants an enterprise could discharge.

NEPA explained the rationale for the DPS as follows:

> Although pollution sources in some cities have achieved national or local effluent standards, the increase in total quantity [or volume flowrate] of wastewater has led to an increase in the total . . . [mass] of pollutants discharged and a deterioration of water quality. To change this situation, [the existing] management system based on concentration control must be gradually modified, and a system of mass-based pollution control must be carried out. (NEPA, 1988b)

Under the DPS, environmental protection bureaus issue permits that limit both the quantities and concentrations of pollutants in an enterprise's wastewater. EPBs also enforce permit conditions. In 1987, NEPA selected seventeen cities and one river basin to participate in a trial implementation of the DPS.[22] By the end of 1991, a trial version of the DPS had been implemented at about 3,600 enterprises in 106 cities. In March 1994, NEPA announced the end of the trial and the extension of the DPS throughout China. By the end of 1997, more than 50,000 discharge permits had been issued. As of 1999, the extension of the permit system was still underway.

DPS rules issued by NEPA in 1988 require EPBs and enterprises implementing the permit system to employ the following steps. Enterprises must register with EPBs and apply for permits. EPBs then allocate allowable pollution loads to enterprises, issue discharge permits, and enforce permit conditions.[23] Unlike the discharge fee system and some other environmental programs in China, the DPS has not been affirmed by legislation.[24] It is based on administrative edicts.

OTHER PROGRAMS REGULATING INDUSTRIAL WASTE

Discharge fees and permits are only two of the eight national schemes for regulating industrial waste. This section introduces the other six programs.

Environmental Impact Assessments and the Three Synchronizations

Requirements for environmental impact assessments and the three synchronizations policy are integral parts of the process of constructing industrial projects, and they each have a foundation in the 1989 *PRC Environmental Protection Law*.

Article 13 requires that a proponent of a construction project assess the project's environmental impacts, and Article 26 requires *three synchronizations*: the design, construction, and operation of a new industrial enterprise (or an existing factory that is expanding or changing its production processes) must be synchronized with the design, construction, and operation of appropriate waste treatment facilities.[25]

The procedure for managing a construction project in China includes the following steps: registration of the proposed project with appropriate authorities; feasibility study (which includes the project's conceptual design); detailed design; construction; and inspection and approval of the completed facility. An environmental impact assessment is supposed to be performed at the time of the feasibility study. Assessment results, including plans for pollution abatement, are generally specified in an *environmental impact statement* (EIS). Those plans provide a basis for the first of the three synchronizations: design of pollution control facilities and the main elements of the proposed project occur at the same time. The remaining synchronizations are conducted in the last two steps of the project development cycle: enterprises must build waste management facilities at the same time as the main project, and environmental agencies are required to inspect and approve pollution control works at the same time as other agencies inspect and approve the main project.

In 1986, the State Council, the State Planning Commission, and the State Economic Commission jointly issued *Management Guidelines on Environmental Protection for Construction Projects* (State Council, SPC, and SEC, 1986). This document (referred to herein as the *Management Guidelines*) instructs project proponents on how environmental impact assessments and the three synchronizations fit into the project development cycle. For most projects, EPBs are responsible for reviewing EISs and supervising implementation of the three synchronizations.[26] However, SEPA assumes these responsibilities for a project that is very large, involves nuclear devices, or crosses provincial boundaries.

If the local environmental protection bureau fails to approve an EIS for a project, the *Management Guidelines* require the following: the local planning department is not supposed to approve the feasibility study; the land management department should refuse to authorize use of land previously designated for the project; and the local bank is to deny any loans. The *Management Guidelines* also instruct officials on what to do if requirements of the three synchronizations are violated. Before a construction project begins, the local EPB must examine and approve the design of any required environmental management facilities. If the EPB withholds its approval, licenses for the construction and operation of the project must be denied. Moreover, the department responsible for supplying construction materials and equipment is not supposed to provide them. If construction begins without the local EPB's approval, an order to stop construction can be issued, in which case the project proponent would have to go through additional formalities to satisfy the three synchronizations policy. If project operations begin without approval from the local EPB, the owner of the project is legally responsible for the consequences.

In many instances, the sanctions noted above have not been applied. Notwithstanding the many departures from the rules, several studies have shown that EISs have been effective in reducing adverse effects of many industrial projects.[27] Those studies also show that EISs have not generally influenced industrial siting decisions because siting is generally approved by local leaders *before* environmental impact studies are undertaken. The three synchronizations policy has played an important role in stimulating investment in waste treatment facilities at industrial enterprises, especially at new factories. However, as we explain in Chapter 4, simplified permitting procedures established during the early 1990s to encourage industrial growth have made it easier for companies to circumvent rules calling for EISs and the three synchronizations. Moreover, these rules have been evaded by many township and village enterprises.

Pollution Control Within Deadlines

Under the 1989 *PRC Environmental Protection Law*, governments can require polluting enterprises to control their waste releases by specific dates, a policy called "pollution control within deadlines." Clean-up deadlines for enterprises can only be imposed by national or local people's governments, but local governments sometimes give EPBs the authority to set deadlines. Enterprises that do not abate pollution on time risk being fined or shut down.

Local governments do not frequently issue orders for enterprises to cut pollution by a fixed date, but a single order might apply to dozens of enterprises. Once an enterprise is ordered to abate pollution by a particular date, enterprise managers feel enormous pressure to comply.

An example of pollution control within deadlines is the Shandong Provincial People's Government issuance (in 1995) of a *Notice of Factory Closings, Limitations on Production and Pollutant Discharges, and Pollution Control Within Deadlines at Several Industrial Enterprises in the Four River Basins*. This notice included cleanup orders for 127 enterprises, primarily pulp and paper factories, distilleries, breweries, and chemical plants. Some of these factories were required to meet effluent standards by the end of 1995, others by the end of 1996, and still others by the end of 1997.

Centralized Pollution Control and the Environmental Responsibility System

Until the 1980s, China's pollution reduction efforts focused on treatment by individual enterprises. This strategy can be inefficient because, in general, the larger the treatment plant, the lower the cost per unit of waste treated. Recognizing the possible economic advantages of building large treatment plants, the State Council and NEPA issued documents requiring governments at all levels to promote centralized control of wastes within their jurisdictions. However, centralized control has not yet developed into a significant environmental program.

The 1979 *PRC Environmental Protection Law for Trial Implementation* gave NEPA and EPBs responsibility for environmental quality, but those agencies had little influence on economic development decisions affecting the environment. Late in the 1980s, NEPA proposed an "environmental responsibility system," in which provincial governors, city mayors, and county magistrates would be responsible for overall environmental quality in their jurisdictions. The 1989 *PRC Environmental Protection Law* reinforced NEPA's concept by making governments at county levels and above responsible for protecting and improving environmental quality within their jurisdictions.

Instead of issuing detailed guidelines for implementing the environmental responsibility system, NEPA encouraged local innovation. Some municipalities responded by creating formal contracts between mayors and directors of industrial bureaus, or between mayors and heads of urban districts and rural counties. These contracts spelled out mutually agreed upon environmental goals and cleanup targets. In other cities, the environmental responsibility system has been implemented using informal contracts between EPBs and managers of enterprises. Although the environmental responsibility system has been influential in many parts of China, it did not have much effect on enterprises included in our research.[28]

Assessment of Urban Environmental Quality

In 1988, the State Council's Environmental Protection Commission issued a "decision" instructing NEPA to conduct annual assessments of environmental quality in thirty-two major Chinese cities (SCEPC, 1988). The cities are ranked annually according to a numerical evaluation system created by NEPA, and the results are widely published.

Twenty-one indices have been developed to measure and evaluate the level of urban environmental protection in a city. Indices are grouped into three subject areas: (i) *urban environmental quality*, as indicated by parameters such as concentration of total suspended particulates and fraction of drinking water supplies meeting potable water standards; (ii) *control of urban pollution*, gauged, for example, by percentage of soot emissions that meet applicable discharge standards; and (iii) *availability of urban infrastructure*, measured, for instance, by fraction of an area served by district heating.

In addition to assessments of thirty-two cities, which are now carried out by SEPA, provincial EPBs conduct annual appraisals of environmental quality for other large cities. Assessments of urban environmental quality are influential primarily because of the publicity—both positive and negative—that they generate.

STRATEGIES FOR CONTROLLING POLLUTION IN THE LATE 1990s

During the 1990s, China's environmental policy began to shift. In a speech at the Second National Conference on the Control and Prevention of Industrial Pollution in 1993, Xie Zhenhua, NEPA's Administrator, outlined the following components of an emerging new strategy for industrial pollution control:

- Move from concentration-based standards to a system combining both concentration-based and mass-based standards.
- Rely less on waste treatment at individual enterprises and more on a combination of centralized treatment facilities and treatment plants at individual enterprises.
- Employ cleaner production methods to prevent pollution, instead of generating waste and then treating it. (CEYCC, 1994)

Amendments to the Water Pollution Control Law

The three approaches highlighted in the speech by Zie Zhenhua are embodied in the amended *Water Pollution Prevention and Control Act* enacted in 1996. Article 16 of the Act addresses one of the three elements by authorizing national and provincial agencies to employ mass-based pollution control systems for water bodies that would not meet ambient standards even if all discharges met concentration-based effluent standards. This new scheme is to supplement, not replace, existing effluent standards. Article 16 also requires use of a "check and ratification system," which (apart from its name) is similar to the discharge permit system.[29]

A second part of the approach advocated by Xie Zhenhua is addressed by Article 19, which directs governments at all levels to integrate plans for water source protection and water pollution abatement into their urban infrastructure plans. Governments are also instructed to include centralized waste treatment facilities in urban infrastructure plans.

Article 22 addresses the remaining element of the new strategy by calling on enterprises to adopt *cleaner production technologies*; that is, production methods with a high efficiency of raw material use and low quantities of pollutants per unit of output. Article 22 also stresses management procedures as a tool for pollution prevention. For example, enterprises can often decrease waste loads by improving their chemical handling and storage procedures. This focus on cleaner production and pollution prevention represents a significant shift from China's traditional reliance on waste treatment as an environmental protection strategy.

China's new emphasis on cleaner production extends well beyond the 1996 revisions to the Water Pollution Prevention and Control Act. For example, the State Economic and Trade Commission and SEPA have been working with the National People's Congress to prepare a draft cleaner production law for 2002. In addition, SEPA has implemented a "Ten, One Hundred, One Thousand, Ten

Thousand" plan. According to this plan, which was initiated in 1995, cleaner production will be promoted in ten heavily polluting industrial sectors in one hundred cities throughout China. The goal is to implement cleaner production in one thousand enterprises and to train ten thousand people in cleaner production concepts and methods. In implementing its cleaner production goals, China will face challenges in gaining access to up-to-date production technologies and organizing the human and financial resources needed to put those technologies to use.[30]

Environmental Protection at TVEs

During the 1990s, the environmental problems created by township and village enterprises attracted the attention of China's top leaders. As detailed in later chapters, many governments at the village, township, and county level derive substantial revenues from TVEs, and thus they often have weak incentives to enforce environmental regulations. Indeed, many township governments and village committees own TVEs, and thus they often have vested interests in shielding these enterprises from environmental requirements. In addition, many TVEs have modest financial resources and limited technical capability, and this can limit their ability to satisfy regulations. Moreover, because many TVEs are widely scattered in rural locations, environmental regulators frequently have trouble monitoring their activities. Finally, environmental management at TVEs is regulated by two different agencies: SEPA and the Ministry of Agriculture.

Environmental problems caused by TVEs came into the national spotlight in 1994 when pollution caused by TVEs (along with state-owned enterprises and municipalities) caused massive water quality degradation in the Huai River basin. Pollution incidents in July 1994 led to dramatic losses: more than 11 million kilograms of fish were killed, fish farms were destroyed, factories were forced to close, and several thousand people became ill with severe gastrointestinal problems (Jahiel, 1998: 781).

Small TVEs, particularly paper mills, were among the major targets of efforts to clean up the Huai River. In responding to the 1994 problems caused by TVEs in the basin, the State Council issued (in 1995) *Provisional Regulations on Huai River Basin Water Pollution Prevention and Control*. This edict required the governments of Anhui, Henan, Jiangsu, and Shandong provinces to close all pulp and paper mills (in the basin) producing less than 5,000 tons/year. As of the June 30, 1996 closure deadline, 1,094 pulp and paper mills had been shut (CEYCC, 1997: 109). However, these closure statistics cannot be taken at face value because some factories that closed may have been scheduled to be shut anyway as a result of China's economic restructuring. In addition, some profit-making TVEs included in the shut-down order may have resumed business under different names in nearby locations.

Attention on pollution problems caused by TVEs was maintained in the *State Council Decisions Concerning Certain Environmental Protection Issues* (State Council, 1996). One portion of these decisions singled out for closure fifteen categories of small enterprises (the "fifteen smalls"). Examples of the fifteen smalls are pulp and paper mills with annual production capacities of less than 5,000 tons and tanneries with annual production of less than 30,000 equivalent cow hides. In 1997, NEPA, the Ministry of Agriculture, and two other national agencies jointly issued *Regulations Concerning Environmental Protection at Township and Village Enterprises* (NEPA et al, 1997), which ordered the closure of all TVEs included among the fifteen smalls. The regulations also prohibited the formation of new factories of these types.

The 1997 *Regulations Concerning Environmental Protection at Township and Village Enterprises* also included a separate set of requirements for all TVEs— not just the fifteen smalls—contained in the "three rivers and three lakes": Huai River, Hai River, Liao River, Tai Lake, Chao Lake, and Dinanchi Lake. Each of these water bodies has suffered from extraordinarily heavy pollution and been the subject of national attention since the mid-1990s.

Ninth Five Year Plan for Environmental Protection

In 1996, the National People's Congress approved China's *Ninth Five Year Plan for Social and Economic Development*, which included environmental goals to be met through the beginning of the next century. Several months later, the State Council issued the *Ninth Five Year Plan for Environmental Protection and Long Term Targets for the Year 2010* (referred to herein as the Plan). Two implementation strategy documents were attached to the Plan: one described a national program to control total waste discharges and a second detailed China's "Trans-Century Green Project." The latter includes over 800 water pollution abatement projects.

The notion behind controlling total waste releases—referred to in the Plan as the "Total Amount Control of the Main Pollutants Discharged During the Ninth Five Year Plan Period"—is to limit both the mass as well as the concentration of waste discharges. The Plan calls for mass-based controls on twelve pollutant indicators, including, for example, COD, cyanide, and mercury. Aggregate limits are set for future years. For instance, the Plan requires cutting the 1995 COD discharge of 22.33 billion tons down to 22.20 billion tons by the year 2000.

Implementing the Plan will involve challenges for provincial and municipal officials, who have expressed concerns about the adequacy of their environmental protection budgets and staff allotments and their problems in enforcing environmental requirements at TVEs (Vermeer, 1998). These challenges will be explored in later chapters, as we elaborate on the implementation of industrial pollution control programs that will be used to meet the Plan's objectives.

NOTES

1. The EPNRC Committee received its current name in April 1994; when it was formed in April 1993, it was called the Environmental Protection Committee. Qu Geping, the first director of NEPA, was appointed to lead this NPC committee.

2. For details on temporal fluctuations in the composition of the State Council, see Zheng (1997: 79–80 and 200–202). A major administrative downsizing occurred in March 1998, when eleven of China's forty ministry-level entities were slated for elimination.

3. Use of lists to control appointments to key posts is part of the *nomenklatura* system, a term borrowed from the former Soviet Union. The CCP maintains "lists of leading positions over which party units exercise the power of appointment and dismissal, lists of reserve candidates for those positions, and rules governing the actual processes of appointments and dismissals" (Lieberthal, 1995: 209).

4. See Zheng (1997) for an analysis that distinguishes between the CCP and the Chinese government.

5. This translation of Article 89 is based on Corne (1997: 62), and facts in the following two sentences are from Corne (1997: 67).

6. Examples of administrative acts commonly used in implementing environmental programs include regulations (*faqui*); decrees (*guizhang*); orders (*mingling*); provisional measures (*zhanxing banfa*); measures (*banfa*); decisions (*jueding*); resolutions (*jueyi*); directives (*zhishi*); and notifications (*tongzhi*) and administrative circulars (*tongbao*). See Zhang and Ferris (1997) for more on this subject.

7. These constitutional provisions are summarized by Palmer (1998: 791). The 1978 Constitution included modest commitments to environmental protection, but those commitments were expanded considerably by the above noted articles in the 1982 Constitution.

8. Effluent standards were first specified in the *Industrial "Three Wastes" Discharge Standards* issued in 1973 (SPC et al., 1973). The standards were revised in 1988 (NEPA, 1988a), and again in 1996 (NEPA, 1996).

9. In October 1996, NEPA issued new effluent standards that differ somewhat from the ones applicable during the time of our field studies. The 1996 standards, which are not uniformly more stringent than the 1988 standards they replaced, are being introduced in phases. For details on the 1996 standards, see NEPA (1996).

10. Appendix A explains why we focused on the discharge fee and permit programs.

11. For details on all eight programs, see Sinkule and Ortolano (1995) and Wang and Bloomquist (1992).

12. A *yuan* is a unit of Chinese currency. In 1994, one U.S. dollar was equivalent to about 8.5 *yuan*. Although the Chinese discharge fee program has been promoted as a system based on economists' theories of efficient resource allocation, it is more accurately viewed as a non-compliance penalty scheme (Krupnick, 1991).

13. The new fees for industrial wastewater are contained in NEPA, SPB, and MF (1991). As of the mid-1990s, discharge fees for industrial waste gas and solid waste had not been revised since they were first issued in 1982.

14. Regardless of the size of the loan or grant, an enterprise is required to come up with matching funds from its own coffers, other sources, or both.

15. A city EPB may be required to give a fraction of the over-standard fees to the provincial EPB.

16. Steps at the municipal level are similar to those used at other levels of government.

17. The average frequency of compliance monitoring at heavily polluting enterprises in the six cities we studied ranged from two to four times per year. Monitoring was less frequent at small- and medium-sized enterprises.

18. Fee calculations are based on formulas in NEPA, SPB, and MF (1991).

19. Fee computations would be reviewed by the provincial EPB responsible for supervising the municipal EPB.

20. This paragraph is based on Jahiel (1998: 776) and Bohm et al (1998: 35).

21. This account of the proposed change is based on an anonymous news report in *China Environmental Review*, II, 2 (December 1998-January 1999) and a conversation on April 12, 1998, with Qu Geping, head of the NPC's Environmental Protection and National Resources Conservation Committee.

22. In China, a new program is frequently implemented on a trial basis at several "experimental points," such as a few enterprises or cities. Details about implementation procedures emerge as local agencies develop specific responses to the program. After evaluating a program's trial implementation, the central government may decide to expand the program to the whole country, change the implementation process, or discontinue the program.

23. The 1988 rules are in NEPA (1988c and 1988d). More detailed rules were issued a year later (NEPA, 1989).

24. Only registration with EPBs is required by a statute: the 1989 *PRC Environmental Protection Law*.

25. We translated the program name, *san tongshi zhengce*, as three synchronizations policy. The name has also been translated as "three simultaneouses" or "three at-the-same-time."

26. A short "environmental impact form" (EIF) can be used for small construction projects that have minor environmental impacts; for simplicity, we omit reference to EIFs. Results of an EIS generally detail the pollution abatement facilities to be designed, built, and operated when implementing the three synchronizations policy. The *Management Guidelines* were revised by the State Council in 1998, but the environmental impact statement process described herein is still required.

27. See, for example, Spofford et al (1996a) and Sinkule and Ortolano (1995).

28. For insights into the effects the environmental responsibility system has had in some Chinese cities, see Jahiel (1998: 777).

29. According to NEPA staff we interviewed, several ministries objected to the proposal by NEPA that the Act refer to (and thereby legitimize) the discharge permit system. As a compromise, the language "check and ratification system" (*heding zhidu*) was used.

30. For information on China's progress in implementing cleaner production, see Ortolano, Cushing, and Warren (1999).

3

Administrative Structures and Post-1978 Economic Reforms

At the time of our field research in the early 1990s, the majority of Chinese enterprises were owned and closely-supervised by government bodies. Ownership patterns have changed rapidly throughout the 1990s, and Chinese enterprises are increasingly being encouraged to function like privately-owned companies in the West. This chapter analyzes the administrative structure in which enterprises operate because that structure affects how enterprises respond to environmental rules. Our analysis also considers how the diminished role of government in the activities of enterprises has made it more difficult—in the short term—for environmental agencies to perform some aspects of their work.

CHINA'S ADMINISTRATIVE SYSTEM

Levels within the Administrative Hierarchy

China's government is organized as a hierarchy. Three distinct entities operate one level down from the national level, also called "the Center": provinces; autonomous regions; and centrally administered municipalities (i.e., Beijing, Chongqing, Shanghai, and Tianjin). Each of these three types of entities is at the provincial-level of government (see Figure 3.1).

We use Beijing to illustrate the structure of government below the provincial-level. As shown in Figure 3.2, Beijing includes numerous districts and counties. Each urban district is divided into sub-districts. Within Beijing's counties and non-urban districts, there are many townships and villages.[1]

The Beijing example illustrates political jurisdictions for a municipality that reports directly to the Center, but the example does not fully characterize prefectural-level cities; that is, cities that report to governments of provinces and autonomous regions.[2] Prefectural-level cities (or "municipalities") can include three types of entities that are one level down in the hierarchy: counties, districts,

33

Figure 3.1   Layers of Government Administration

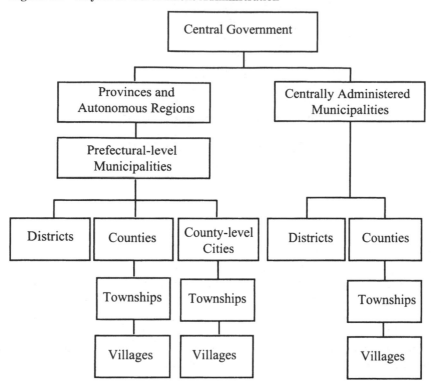

and county-level cities. Each of these entities is at the "county level" of government. Townships are one level below the county level, and villages are a level down from townships (see Figure 3.1). All governments below the Center are referred to as "local."

Governments at the township level and above are "official" in the following sense: they receive budgetary support from the Center and their employees are government staff. In contrast, the governing body in a village is called a "village committee"; it consists of a leader, a deputy leader, an accountant, and so forth.

Administrative Rank of Government Units

Each government unit above the village level has an administrative (or bureaucratic) rank, which is an important reflection of power and status. The highest ranking units under the State Council are the comprehensive commissions, such as the State Development and Planning Commission (SDPC) and the State Economic and Trade Commission (SETC); these units have responsibilities that cut across economic sectors and geographic regions. A ministry has the same administrative rank (*buji*) as a provincial-level government. Other examples of rank (in

Figure 3.2   Beijing Municipality Counties and Districts

BEIJING MUNICIPALITY

4 Urban Districts:	4 Suburban Districts:	3 Countryside Districts:	7 Counties:
Chongwen	Fengtai	Fangshan	Changping
Dongcheng	Chaoyang	Mentougou	Daxing
Xicheng	Haidian	Tongzhou	Huairou
Xuanwu	Shinjingshan		Miyun
			Pinggu
			Shunyi
			Yanqing

descending order) are vice-ministry (*fubuji*) and bureau (*juji*) within a ministry; the latter also corresponds to the rank of a department within a provincial government.

State-owned enterprises (SOEs) are affiliated with industrial bureaus, and those enterprises also have a place in the hierarchy defined by rank. An SOE supervised by a state industrial bureau within the State Economic and Trade Commission will generally outrank one reporting to an industrial bureau within a provincial-level government, and so on down the line for SOEs affiliated with industrial bureaus at lower levels of government. The rank of an SOE signals the political and social status of its managers and workers, and SOEs with high ranks often offer relatively good wages and fringe benefits. An enterprise's rank also influences its interactions with other government organs. For example, rank has been linked to an enterprise's ability to bargain with government officials over tax reductions and subsidies (O'Brien, 1992).

Rank has special significance for an environmental agency because governmental units holding the same rank cannot issue binding orders to each other. Kenneth Lieberthal, an expert on China's political system, argues that as a consequence of this rule, governmental units have "a tremendous need to build a consensus in order to operate effectively in China." As a result, "negotiations aimed at consensus building are a core feature" of China's government system (Lieberthal, 1997: 3). The State Environmental Protection Administration has a high rank (i.e., ministry), but it is under continual pressure to build a broad consensus in support of its regulations. When SEPA is able to gain a consensus, it can have its proposed regulations issued by the State Council, and those regulations would be binding on governmental units at or below the ministerial level.

Line and Area Relationships

At the township level and above, government organs are interconnected in two distinct ways: by function and by geographical area. A local agency's connection with its functionally-related agency at the Center (or with a functionally-related agency below it) is described as a line (*tiao-tiao*) relationship, whereas the unit's linkage with other government organs within the same jurisdiction is called an area (*kuai-kuai*) relationship. Bureaucratic control is exercised by function using line relationships and within geographic regions using area relationships.

Each work unit (*danwei*) within the administrative system reports to both an upper-level department in the same functional area and the government of a geographic area. For instance, Beijing EPB reports to its upper-level functional department, the State Environmental Protection Administration, and it also supervises the work of EPBs within Beijing's districts and counties (see Figure 3.3). These are both line relationships. At the same time, Beijing EPB is part of the Beijing Municipal People's Government (by area), and thus it is under the jurisdiction of the Mayor's Office in Beijing. As another example, the Beijing Chemical Industry Bureau is part of the Beijing Municipal People's Government; it also reports to the State Bureau of the Chemical Industry, and it supervises the chemical industry bureaus that are units of the county and district governments within Beijing.[3] In Figure 3.3, the vertical lines from the central government down to

Figure 3.3   Illustrative Line and Area Relationships In Beijing

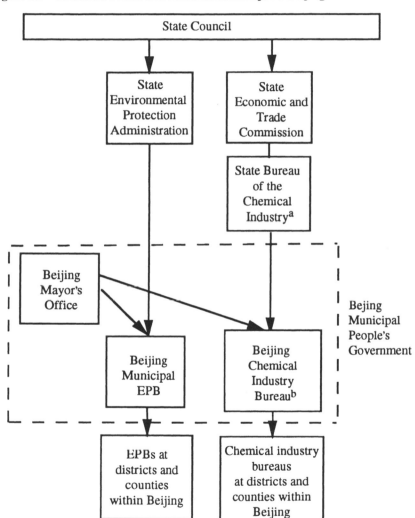

[a]Before March 1998, this bureau was the Ministry of the Chemical Industry.
[b]For part of the 1990s, this bureau was called the Beijing General Company of the Chemical Industry, but (despite its name) it still functioned as an administrative unit.

county-level governments depict bureaucratic control by function (*tiao-tiao*), and slanted lines within the dashed box show area relationships (*kuai-kuai*).

As a result of a government restructuring in March 1998, the State Bureau of the Chemical Industry ranks below the State Environmental Protection Administration. (Formerly, this state bureau was the Ministry of the Chemical Industry.) The State Bureau of the Chemical Industry and analogous state bureaus for other industrial sectors report to the State Economic and Trade Commission. The latter, like SEPA, has a direct link to the State Council.

Lines and areas are sometimes described as a multi-layer, multi-regional organizational system (Qian and Xu, 1993). The Center controls about thirty provincial-level regions (areas) and a few dozen functional ministries (lines). The hierarchical structure of each region at each level mirrors the central government's structure. For example, a typical prefectural-level municipality contains several districts and counties. The municipal government supervises its own agencies through area relationships, and it directs heads of districts and magistrates of counties using line relationships.

Figure 3.4 represents illustrative line and area relationships in contexts involving cities, such as Jinan, that report to a provincial government. The figure is analogous to Figure 3.3, but it shows more levels of government: national, provincial, municipal, and county. Boxes created by dashed lines represent people's governments; those boxes contain only a few of the many agencies that make up a typical local government. Townships are omitted from Figure 3.4 because the structure of a township government is less complete than that of higher level governments; moreover, county-level governments are the lowest ones responsible for implementing many of China's environmental laws. For simplicity, Figure 3.4 also omits county-level cities, autonomous regions, and municipalities reporting to the central government.

The vertical lines below SEPA in Figure 3.4 represent a typical set of *tiao-tiao* relationships: an agency supervises counterpart units at lower levels of government. However, the vertical lines below the State Economic and Trade Commission are not typical because the commission supervises a wide variety of units: economic commissions, as well as different types of industrial bureaus.

Relationships between governments and enterprises below the county level are different from those between industrial bureaus and SOEs. What are commonly referred to as "state-owned enterprises" exist at the county level and above, and they were a part of the original planned economy. Collectively-owned enterprises at the township and village level are also government owned, but they are owned by township governments and village committees, and they were not part of the centrally planned economy (Oi, 1998: 96)

The lines framework facilitates a nationwide coordination of effort within an industrial sector, but it is poorly suited for coordinating economic activities *across* functions. Within the lines framework, each government department develops its own plans separately, and then sends orders to units it supervises at the next lower

Figure 3.4 Partial Structure of China's Administrative System

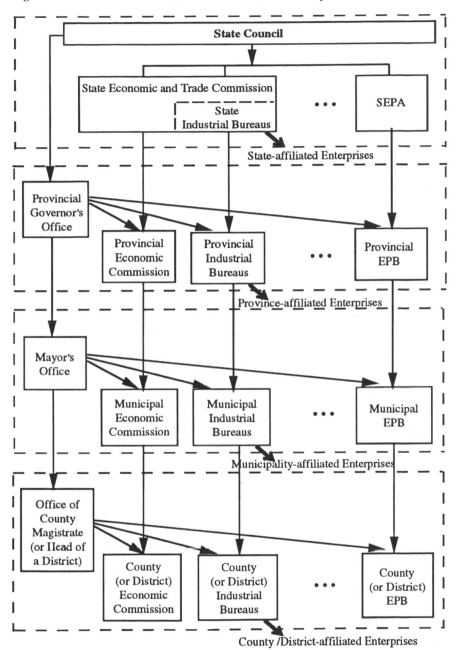

hierarchical level. Under the planned economy (and even under the quasi-market system in place in the 1990s), effective communication and cooperation among government units belonging to different functional lines occurred infrequently. When cooperation did occur, it usually resulted from a mandate by a higher-level department.

China began decentralizing its economic system in the early 1980s. Since then, the Center's role in resource allocation has decreased relative to that of local governments. Although the Center still makes broad policy decisions, local governments have more authority over and responsibility for industrial activities within their jurisdictions. A major result of economic reforms since 1978 is that area controls now have priority over line, or functional, controls (Lieberthal, 1997: 4).

FORMS OF ENTERPRISE OWNERSHIP

An enterprise can be state-owned, collectively-owned, or privately-owned. Theoretically, the means of production of a state-owned enterprise belong to everyone in the PRC, assets of a collectively-owned enterprise belong to the people within the collective organization, and the capital of a privately-owned enterprise belongs to private parties.

In 1980, before the initial economic reforms had much influence, about 76 percent of the total value of industrial output was produced by SOEs (i.e., the "state sector"), and nearly all the rest was produced by collectives, primarily collectively-owned enterprises in urban areas (see Table 3.1). Thus, even before the first economic reforms took hold, many production decisions were made outside the context of economic plans developed by the Center.

The post-1978 reforms fostered the creation of many new TVEs and joint-ventures. Collectively-owned township and village enterprises are owned by township governments and village committees, respectively. Thus, even though they are not in the state sector, many TVEs are government-owned. Another form of ownership, the joint-venture, commonly refers to a Chinese enterprise owned by two or more entities, one of which may be foreign. The joint-venture classification is further subdivided as follows: state-owned joint-venture, collectively-owned joint venture, and privately-owned joint venture.

The economic reforms introduced competition in China's markets and shifted the relative importance of different types of enterprises. As shown in Table 3.1, after 1980 there was a notable drop in contributions to total output from SOEs and a corresponding rise in contributions from private companies and collectively-owned TVEs. Starting in the mid-1990s, China began transforming many SOEs into corporations owned by shareholders. At the same time, a significant fraction of the total value of industrial output began coming from the private sector, including privately-owned TVEs.

Table 3.1   **Contributions of Various Types of Enterprises to Industrial Output**[a]

	Shares of Output (%)			
	1980	1992	1994	1996
State-Owned Enterprises	76.0	48.4	34.1	28.5
Collectives				
Urban	13.7	11.8	7.6	8.2
Township-Village[b]	9.9	26.2	33.4	31.1
Small Private[c]	0	6.8	11.5	15.5
Other[d]	0.5	7.2	13.6	16.6
	100	100	100	100
Total Value of Industrial Output (billion *yuan*)	515	3,707	7,691	9,959

[a]Based on Jefferson and Rawksi (1994: 48) and Jefferson and Singh (1997: 181). Percentages may not add to 100 due to rounding off.

[b]The terms "township enterprise" and "village enterprise" were not used in 1980. What are now called "townships" and "villages" were called "communes" and "brigades," respectively (Naughton, 1995: 148).

[c]"Small Private" refers to enterprises with less than eight workers.

[d]"Other" includes private firms with more than eight workers, joint ventures, and foreign-owned firms.

Our field research was conducted in the early 1990s, when state-owned enterprises and collectively-owned TVEs dominated the Chinese economy. For this reason, we limited our study of compliance with environmental regulations to enterprises in those two categories. Because we did not examine privately-owned enterprises, "TVE" is used hereafter as a shorthand for "collectively-owned TVE."

INFLUENCE OF POST-1978 REFORMS ON STATE-OWNED ENTERPRISES

Below we highlight aspects of China's economic reforms bearing on environmental protection efforts. In addition to providing a perspective on the changing incentives faced by SOEs and local governments, we show how the increased autonomy granted to firms in the state sector has, in some instances, decreased the ability of EPBs to regulate them. Reforms in China are a vast work in progress, and our treatment of the subject is necessarily selective.

Limited SOE Autonomy Before 1979

In 1978, just prior to China's initial economic reforms, SOEs had weak control over key decisions affecting production and profits. Planners at the Center developed annual production targets for selected products in different industrial sectors, and industrial ministries allocated these targets (via *tiao-tiao* relationships) to individual SOEs. Industrial ministries and bureaus linked the central government to SOEs by allocating production targets, auditing performance, supplying key inputs, and so forth.

State-owned enterprises submitted their profits to the state and operated with budgets allocated by their supervisory industrial bureaus and ministries. A typical SOE also interacted with several other government departments that sought either to extract revenues or to offer funding for expansions and renovations. The most significant of these other local institutions were finance and taxation bureaus, banks, planning and economic commissions, and the office of the local government leader, such as the mayor. In addition, the Chinese Communist Party played a dominant role in decision-making, particularly decisions related to personnel. The *nomenklatura* system—in which the CCP controlled the appointment, promotion, and dismissal of personnel—was used widely by Party committees within factories (Naughton, 1995: 107).

In addition to producing economic goods, a typical SOE delivered social services to its workers and their families. At the time of the initial economic reforms, an SOE's internal structure included an "administrative and service system" concerned with the following: personnel, labor and capital, education, security, health, general affairs, family planning, food, and housing (Jiang and Guan, 1991: 108). SOEs took responsibility for almost every aspect of their workers' lives, including retirement pensions and even workers' funeral arrangements.

First Phase of Reforms: 1979–1983

During the first phase of reforms, the period from 1979 to 1983, the central government showed little interest in creating a market economy (Rawski, 1995: 1151). Rather, it aimed to improve economic performance by modifying incentives faced by SOEs.

Enhanced Control of Profits by Enterprises

A key aspect of the early reform agenda involved giving enterprises incentives to enhance their economic performance by letting them keep part of their profits. Under a "profit-retention system" introduced in 1979, the portion of total profit to be turned over to the state was negotiated between an enterprise and its supervisory industrial bureau or ministry and formalized in a contract. Once the contract target was met, the enterprise retained profits from additional output.[4] Because profit-retention rates were negotiated periodically on a factory-by-factory basis, state budgetary revenues fluctuated. Moreover, the profit-sharing scheme did not diminish the government's ability to interfere in business (Wang, 1994: 85).

In 1983, as a partial response to deficiencies of the profit-retention system, the central government replaced it with a "tax-for-profit" scheme for state-owned enterprises (Chai, 1997: 73). Instead of submitting a negotiated fraction of their profits to the state, all large and medium-sized SOEs, except for unprofitable ones, were required to pay a standardized amount: a tax of 55 percent on all profits.[5] This new scheme was expected to reduce bargaining between government departments and enterprises and to stabilize the revenue enterprises contributed to the state's coffers. Notwithstanding these expectations, the tax system had problems. For example, the amount of after-tax profit was generally low and provided little incentive for enterprises to increase productivity (Yang, 1989). In addition, because loan payments were tax-deductible, enterprises had incentives to borrow money and invest in projects that were not economically efficient (Du, 1992).

Fiscal Decentralization

The introduction of the tax-for-profit system was part of a broader decentralization program in which local governments received both enhanced opportunities to obtain revenues and increased responsibilities for implementing national mandates. Some local revenues were classified as "within budget," and they included money collected from income taxes as well as a number of industrial and commercial taxes. The amount retained locally depended upon the tax source; a local government received no revenues from SOEs supervised by industrial ministries, but it could keep significant fractions of taxes from SOEs supervised by local industrial bureaus. In contrast, local governments retained 100 percent of revenues classified as "extra budgetary." These included property taxes, other local taxes, and numerous "non-tax revenues," such as fees and surcharges that local governments could collect from SOEs supervised by local industrial bureaus (Oi, 1999: 39).

The program of fiscal decentralization that began in the early 1980s gave local governments strong incentives to protect established SOEs and to invest in new economic growth. The more vibrant the local economy, the more opportunities for local governments to extract within-budget and extrabudgetary revenues from enterprises and thereby carry out the new duties they inherited under decentralization, such as responsibilities to implement increasingly higher national standards for health and education (Wong, 1991: 705). Increased revenues for local governments also meant higher bonuses for government officers and enhanced political stature for local officials (Oi, 1999: 47–50).

The push for development that accompanied fiscal decentralization had implications for environmental protection. As detailed in the following chapter, environmental protection bureaus received budget and staff allocations from leaders of local governments. Under the circumstances, EPBs had to be sensitive to how their enforcement of environmental requirements affected enterprises, particularly SOEs supervised by local industrial bureaus and favored by local leaders.

Second Phase of Reforms: 1984–1991

During the second phase of reforms, from 1984 to 1991, the focus shifted from how to divide SOE profits to how to free SOEs from government. Two particular changes—a program replacing grants with loans, and a revival of contracts detailing profit-retention rates—merit attention because they affected SOEs' abilities to raise capital for environmental projects.

Grant-to-Loan Program

During the early 1980s, many SOEs relied on non-repayable government grants to fund new facilities and renovate existing factories. Government planning departments selected the projects, finance departments arranged for funding, and state banks granted money and supervised its use. Since SOEs did not have to repay the funds, they had little incentive to minimize the cost of new projects, and thus many projects were uneconomically large and poorly managed. To prevent such misallocations of funds, a trial program to replace grants with loans was started in 1981 and extended to the entire country in 1985. Since then, SOEs have depended increasingly on bank loans and retained earnings to finance investments. For example, state-owned enterprises obtained 54 percent of their investment funds from government budgets in 1980, but only 27 percent in 1989 (Dong, 1991).

As a part of the grant-to-loan program, EPBs generally stopped giving enterprises grants from pollution levy funds, and this cut enterprises' motivation to build waste treatment plants. However, this disincentive was offset somewhat since the loans from pollution levy funds had low interest rates, and EPBs sometimes forgave the principal on loans and only required repayment of interest.

Contract Responsibility System

The use of contracts as a mechanism for profit-sharing, which had been introduced and then abandoned during the first phase of reform, was reinstated during the second phase. By 1988, a contracting approach referred to as the "contract responsibility system," replaced the previously installed tax-for-profit scheme at over 80 percent of the SOEs (Yeh, 1993: 21). The new system aimed to transform SOEs from subsidiaries of the state into independent businesses capable of making their own decisions and taking responsibility for profits and losses. Contracts negotiated in the late 1980s permitted enterprises to retain a much larger share of realized profit than before. In addition to specifying the base amount of profit to be retained, contracts also included targets for technology renovation, and limits on the rate at which enterprises could increase wages when contract targets were met (Koo, Li, and Peng, 1993).

Bargaining between enterprises and their supervisory industrial bureaus (or ministries) over specific targets had been a universal phenomenon prior to economic reform and, as of the early 1990s, it was as pervasive as ever. In fact, bargaining had become even more complex because it extended beyond details of the plan to encompass a complicated mixture of plans, exchanges, and redistributions (Naughton, 1992). Also, since retained profits often covered only a fraction of an enterprise's investment costs, SOEs had to rely even more heavily on bank loans to implement projects, and frequently had to negotiate tax breaks with local governments in order to repay their loans.[6] As SOEs increased their reliance on loans and retained earnings to fund new activities, environmental projects had to compete for capital against factory renovation and expansion projects.

Increase in Number of Money-Losing SOEs

Contracts negotiated in the late 1980s permitted state-owned enterprises to retain a much larger share of profits compared to the first phase of the reform. Despite the change, the fraction of industrial SOEs incurring net losses increased. For example, the percentage of industrial SOEs losing money rose from 13 percent in 1986 to 44 percent in 1995 (Jefferson and Singh, 1997: 187).

Some analysts blamed the contract responsibility system for the poor economic health of many state-owned enterprises.[7] For example, because contract periods were usually less than five years, managers tended to focus on the short-term by deferring maintenance and investing only in projects delivering quick payoffs (Yeh, 1993: 21). Moreover, the contracted amount was generally based on actual profits before the contract system's introduction. When an enterprise increased its profits, a supplementary tax was imposed, which was equivalent to taxing profitable enterprises more heavily than those running poorly (Walder, 1992: 318–322).

Other explanations for the poor performance of SOEs center on "soft budget constraints," a term introduced by Hungarian economist Janos Kornai to explain chronic shortages and enterprise bargaining in socialist Hungary (Kornai, 1980). An enterprise with a soft budget constraint does not risk bankruptcy if it exceeds its budget allocation in a given year, and thus its managers are not forced to face the full consequences of a failure to earn profits. Still another explanation of the weak financial performance of SOEs relates to their obligations to provide worker housing, education, health care, and other social services. Because SOEs had to shoulder these burdens, they had difficulty competing with TVEs, most of which were unencumbered by social service obligations.

Money-losing SOEs pose problems for environmental agencies. EPBs tend to avoid requiring these enterprises to satisfy environmental requirements because the money to pay for environmental facilities would generally have to come from the state. Moreover, local government leaders would be unlikely to support an EPB that imposed demands on a money-losing SOE supporting large numbers of workers or retirees.

Third Phase of Reforms: Post-1991 Period

The lack of profitability in a notable fraction of SOEs in the early 1990s encouraged the State Council to promulgate *Regulations on Transformation of Management Mechanisms at State-Owned Industrial Enterprises* (referred to herein as *Regulations on Transformation*). This document, issued in 1992, granted fourteen "autonomous rights" to managers of state-owned enterprises, including, for example, the right to make decisions concerning product prices, material purchases, and capital investments (State Council, 1992).

Enterprise Autonomy and Tax Rates

The autonomous rights in the *Regulations on Transformation* have been exercised at different levels. Survey results summarized in Table 3.2 indicate that many enterprises have fully employed the autonomous rights related to production decisions, sales, and purchasing. In contrast, however, only 21 percent of the surveyed enterprises have used their right to refuse unauthorized requests by governments for funds to cover the cost of public projects.

An unintended side effect accompanied the *Regulations on Transformation*: EPBs lost some of their ability to regulate SOEs. As detailed in the next chapter, many EPBs had negotiated agreements whereby other local agencies, such as planning and economic commissions, took no actions on proposed industrial

Table 3.2   Implementation of *Regulations on Transformation*[a]

Autonomous Rights	% of 156 Enterprises Indicating Full Implementation
Production decisions (e.g., product type and output)	96
Product pricing	73
Sales (e.g., choice of product purchasers)	97
Purchasing (e.g., choice of input providers)	94
Import and export rights	39
Investment financing	47
Use of retained earnings	78
Disposition of assets	37
Ability to form joint ventures or conduct mergers and acquisitions	40
Hiring of workers	58
Management of personnel	55
Determination of wages and bonuses	65
Organizational restructuring	78
Right to refuse unauthorized government requests for funds	21

[a]Results of a survey of 156 SOEs conducted by the World Bank (1996: 22).

projects until EPBs had given their stamps of approval. These arrangements gave EPBs excellent access to information on new industrial projects and ensured that their opinions would be considered. After the *Regulations on Transformation* were implemented in 1992, enterprises could accomplish much more without having to obtain approvals from planning and economic commissions, particularly if they did not need government loans. When enterprises proceeded on their own, EPBs lost access to the information and power they enjoyed as a result of the above-noted interagency agreements.

In 1994, China modified its tax system to eliminate a perceived bias against some SOEs. Before the change, large- and medium-sized SOEs paid 55 percent of their profits as an "income tax," but small-sized SOEs laid out only between 7 and 55 percent of profits, and TVEs paid between 10 and 55 percent (Oi, 1992 and Wang, 1994: 85–86). Under the tax system introduced in 1994, all enterprises were subjected to a 33 percent tax on profits.

Reforms Under Jiang Zemin

The reforms were further advanced in 1997 at the Fifteenth National Congress of the Chinese Communist Party. At that meeting, China's President Jiang Zemin laid out the CCP's blueprint for establishing a modern enterprise system with "'clearly established ownership,' well defined power and responsibility, [and] separation of enterprises from administration."[8] Under the proposed scheme, large- and medium-sized SOEs would be converted into corporations in which the state would have partial equity rights and limited responsibility for debts incurred. The corporations would have complete control of their profits and full responsibility for their losses.

Although limited experimentation with converting SOEs into corporations had been carried out in Shanghai and other cities since the mid-1990s, the 1997 CCP National Congress signaled the Party's endorsement of ownership systems based on shareholding. While specific targets for SOE conversions were not detailed at the Congress, one China scholar suggested that the following changes were in the offing:[9]

- One thousand of China's largest SOEs in strategic industrial sectors would be merged to form corporate conglomerates with dominant state ownership but autonomous management.
- The remaining large- and medium-sized SOEs would become "mixed" firms with the state holding some (but necessarily a majority) of the shares.
- More than 85,000 small-sized SOEs would eventually become "joint stock cooperatives" with staff members holding equity shares.

Many details associated with this proposed SOE conversion remain to be worked out, including problems caused by the anticipated down-sizing of some SOEs and closure of others.

Increased efforts to extricate the state from the operation of firms and to use markets instead of plans to allocate resources were accompanied by changes in the role of state and local industrial bureaus. As of the late 1990s, many industrial ministries had been downsized and downgraded to state industrial bureaus under SETC, and a number of industrial ministries had been eliminated or merged. In some cases, the status of former ministries had changed more than once over several years. For example, the Ministry of Light Industry had been changed to a sectoral association in 1992 and was transformed in 1998 to a bureau under SETC. As examples in later chapters demonstrate, reductions in the number of environmental engineering staff within industrial bureaus has had short-term adverse effects on the ability of EPBs to conduct their work.

THE NON-STATE SECTOR IN RURAL AREAS

Growth of TVEs

China's economic reforms have had particularly notable effects on collectively-owned enterprises in rural areas. Before the reforms, most rural enterprises were cooperatives owned by communes and brigades. With the elimination of communes and brigades in the late-1970s, these collectives fell under the ownership of township governments and village committees, respectively. Although TVEs are free from constraints tied to the Center's economic plans, they are subject to control by the township governments and village committees that own them.

TVEs proliferated during the 1980s. Jean Oi, a political scientist who has studied rural enterprises extensively, has argued that the dramatic growth of TVEs is tied to actions of the "local corporate state" consisting of village, township, and county governments.

> Somewhat akin to a large multi-level corporation, the county can be seen as being at the top of a corporate hierarchy as the corporate headquarters, the townships as the regional headquarters, and the villages as companies within the larger corporation. (Oi, 1995: 1138)

As previously noted, economic reforms instituted in the early 1980s gave local governments strong incentives to protect and expand local industry. In the context of the local corporate state, government officials became economic actors as well as government administrators. Rapid economic growth enhanced local income and employment, increased bonuses of government officials, and made it possible for township governments and village committees to augment their budgets using a variety of within-budget taxes and extrabudgetary revenues. The spectacular rise in output from TVEs is reflected in Table 3.1.[10]

How TVEs Differ from SOEs

TVEs differ from state-owned enterprises in several important ways. Township and village enterprises have more flexibility in recruiting and hiring employees and establishing worker compensation rates. Also, because TVEs operate outside the context of production targets and other requirements established by the central government, they have greater autonomy. Moreover, TVEs have fewer responsibilities for providing social services.

Although TVEs have more flexibility than SOEs in making decisions, they have greater responsibility for shouldering results of poor investments. Also, because they operate outside of China's central plans, TVEs cannot rely on subsidized rates for energy, raw materials, and bank loans. Unlike SOEs, township and village enterprises cannot operate for long when their revenues fail to cover costs. Bankruptcy is a reality they must face because their owners—township governments and village committees—lack the resources to sustain unprofitable enterprises for very long (Chai, 1997: 173). Thus, compared to state-owned enterprises, TVEs are more accustomed to the normal concerns of free market entrepreneurs: labor productivity, production process optimization, incentive schemes, marketing, and so forth. However, efforts to reform SOEs in the 1980s blurred differences in the entrepreneurial orientation of managers of SOEs and TVEs.[11] By the late 1980s, SOEs had become increasingly profit oriented in many respects (Chai, 1997: 191).

TVEs and SOEs also differ in terms of their sources of capital. TVEs rely heavily on their own earnings and on bank loans and profits from community enterprises pooled by township or village industrial corporations, whereas SOEs can seek government grants to supplement retained earnings and bank loans.[12]

Compared to SOEs, most township and village enterprises have weaker technological and management capabilities. Although TVEs have often been started by rural residents with little formal education and no prior business experience, leaders of many TVEs have learned modern business practices on the job (Wong and Yang, 1995: 27). However, they have been less successful in picking up engineering and technical skills. The majority of China's engineers and technicians are employed by SOEs and research institutes attached to industrial bureaus (Wong and Yang, 1995: 32). TVEs have employed the following strategies to obtain needed technological skills:[13]

- Hiring an engineer or technician from an SOE either permanently or as a part-time consultant.
- Contracting with one of China's many technology firms or agencies, which commonly provide services under contract to TVEs.
- Engaging engineers and technicians who take second jobs at TVEs on a fee-for-service basis.
- Forming a joint venture with an organization that can transfer needed technology and technical know-how.

- "Reverse engineering" by purchasing equipment and then working backwards to learn how to reproduce it.

TVEs and SOEs also differ in terms of relative numbers. Although China had only about 100,000 industrial SOEs in the early 1990s, it had over a million collectively-owned, industrial TVEs. Because they are abundant and widely disbursed, TVEs pose special challenges for environmental agencies. Many EPBs cannot even maintain accurate inventories of where TVEs are located, not to mention what wastes they are releasing.

EXCHANGES BETWEEN ENTERPRISES AND LOCAL AGENCIES

Both SOEs and TVEs have close connections with local governments. As illustrated in Figure 3.5, local agencies extract funds from SOEs and TVEs by means of taxes, ad hoc fees, and unauthorized requests for funds (*tanpai.*).

Except for villages, local governments keep some of the taxes paid by enterprises under their jurisdictions. Tax revenues have been shared in different ways:

> Some places use an overall ratio, such as 70:30, where the locality keeps 70 percent [of tax revenues collected] and 30 percent is sent to the next higher level. In other cases the locality pays a set quota to the next higher level, but once the quota is met, the locality retains all or at least the bulk of the remaining tax revenues. (Oi, 1992: 103)

These tax-sharing arrangements give governments above the village level incentives to support the growth of SOEs and TVEs.

Figure 3.5   Exchanges Between Enterprises and Local Governments

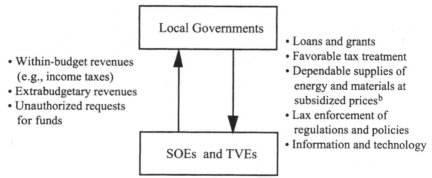

---

[a] Based on Huang (1990: 453).

[b] TVEs operate outside of China's plans and cannot rely on subsidized prices.

Village committees have access to after-tax earnings of the enterprises they own. Thus, in addition to imposing taxes (which are sent to the appropriate township government), village committees can make claims on earnings of collectively-owned village enterprises using a variety of mechanisms: a contracted share of enterprise profits; management fees; contributions for various purposes (e.g., old age pensions, buildings, and cultural and education programs); and "voluntary contributions" (sometimes requested as donations). For example, one village collected about 70 percent of enterprise profits as either taxes sent to the township or fees retained by the village (Oi, 1992: 112).

Township governments supplement their share of tax revenues (i.e., "within-budget revenues") by extracting extrabudgetary revenues from township enterprises. For example, it is common for a local economic commission to take profits from rich enterprises when it needs extra funds for the following:

> to pay off debts incurred by one of [its] enterprises, or to expand production in one of its enterprises. One township economic commission took over 3 million *yuan* for these purposes between 1986 and 1988. (Oi, 1992: 111–112)

At the *county* level and above, funds are extracted from SOEs (not TVEs). State-owned enterprises may be asked to pay taxes and ad hoc fees to be used at the discretion of the fee-collecting government organ. This is illustrated by an industrial bureau in Hejin County (Shanxi Province) that levied ad hoc fees amounting to 1.7 million *yuan* on its sixteen subordinate enterprises between 1984 and 1986 (Huang, 1990: 45). The bureau used the funds to renovate staff housing, build a staff hospital, and offer bonuses to its workers.

Notwithstanding complaints from enterprise officials, governments at all levels often make unauthorized requests for funds from profitable enterprises. The *Regulations on Transformation* give enterprises the right to refuse unauthorized government requests for funds, but the practice still continues (see Table 3.2).

The flows of funds in Figure 3.5 are not all in one direction. Enterprises can receive several types of funding from local governments. Support for TVEs can take the form of start-up capital or government infusions of money to undertake facility expansions. For SOEs, governments might provide grants to enlarge factories or to cover losses during unprofitable years. Frequently, local finance and taxation bureaus can arrange low interest loans and favorable tax treatment, respectively. Local agencies are also able to expedite licenses and permits for enterprises, and they play a key role in procuring energy and other production-process inputs. Moreover, many local governments have been aggressive about providing enterprises within their jurisdictions "with an array of essential services and information about new products, technology, and markets for finished goods" (Oi, 1999: 123).

As the previous discussion demonstrates, local governments at all levels have strong incentives to support industrial development. By creating new enterprises and supporting existing ones, local governments create sources of revenue for themselves, employment opportunities for local workers, and prestige and bonuses for local officials. As one China scholar has observed,

> increased revenue flows [from economic development] have vastly expanded the funds that local officials can use for local construction and other government expenditures—and these, not unimportantly, include office buildings, automobiles, fax machines, long-distance and international telephone lines, and expanded housing for government officials. (Walder, 1998: 23)

Under the circumstances, it is not surprising that local officials and agencies are often characterized as economic actors playing multiple roles: mobilizing investment funds, targeting promising firms and sectors for growth, conducting market research, and brokering deals between enterprises.

In subsequent chapters, we explore how the ties between governments and enterprises compromise the ability of SEPA and environmental protection bureaus to regulate enterprises. The potential for compromise is included in Figure 3.5 as "lax enforcement of regulations and policies." We begin our exploration of this subject in Chapter 4, which details the structure and function of organizations influencing compliance with environmental rules.

NOTES

1. "When the non-agricultural population in a 'township' or *xiang* has increased to exceed a certain level, it can be renamed 'town' or *zhen* upon the approval of the provincial government" (Wong and Yang, 1997: 20). For simplicity, we use only the term "township," and we do not distinguish between towns and townships.

2. Although prefectural governments are no longer common in all parts of China, the term prefectural-level city is still widely used. For our purposes, the key characteristic of a prefectural-level city is that it reports to a province or an autonomous region.

3. During the mid-1990s, many industrial bureaus were renamed as "general companies," but some of them reverted to their earlier names after the 1998 creation of state industrial bureaus under the State Economic and Trade Commission. Moreover, many general companies functioned as administrative organs. For simplicity, we will refer to both general companies and industrial bureaus as "industrial bureaus." According to Zhang and Ferris (1997: 10229), the long-term effect of transforming industrial bureaus to general companies "may be the withdrawal of administrative powers from general companies."

4. By the end of 1979, profit retention had been adopted by 6,600 mostly large SOEs that accounted for 60 percent of the state-sector's output (Naughton, 1995: 100).

5. Definitions for large-, medium-, and small-sized SOEs vary by industrial sector. Depending on the sector, these terms are defined in terms of number of workers, total value of output, or total value of assets. The 55 percent tax rate was applied only to profitable, large- and medium-sized SOEs. The rate was lower for many other enterprises.

6. For more on financial relationships between enterprises and local governments, see Walder (1992), Wong (1993), and Oi (1999).

7. For a summary of the problems faced by SOEs, see Naughton (1995: 284–287).

8. This phrase is from Jiang Zemin's keynote address at the 1997 CCP Congress as quoted by Baum (1998).

9. Observations below are based on a report by Baum (1998) on events at the Fifteenth National Congress of the CCP.

10. As Table 3.1 indicates, the relative importance of collectively-owned TVEs began to fall in the mid-1990s. Oi (1999: Chapter 3) details the changes in physical and economic conditions that caused many township governments and village committees to shift their attention to privately owned TVEs during the 1990s.

11. In China, free markets are not the norm, even for TVEs. Many township governments and village committees engage in "local protectionism" by, for example, purchasing all their building materials from firms they own (Wong and Yang, 1995: 26–27).

12. However, TVEs are often able to obtain bank credits and local grants from the township governments or village committees that own them (Chai, 1997: 190).

13. This list is based on Wong and Yang (1995: 34–37).

4

Organizations Influencing Industrial Pollution Control

It is impossible for an environmental agency to conduct its work in isolation. Relationships between regulatory bodies, other agencies, and citizens invariably affect how environmental policy is executed. In examining those relationships below, we demonstrate how actions by disparate governmental units and citizens can influence enterprises' responses to environmental rules.

ADMINISTRATIVE SYSTEM FOR ENVIRONMENTAL PROTECTION

As shown in Figure 4.1, government organizations involved in environmental protection are organized hierarchically along three lines: (a) environmental protection committees of people's congresses,[1] (b) SEPA and environmental protection bureaus, and (c) environmental protection commissions of people's governments. Although all organizations in the figure are involved in pollution control, they have different responsibilities. Environmental committees under people's congresses propose environmental laws, SEPA formulates environmental policies and programs, EPBs implement local and national regulations, and environmental commissions of people's governments coordinate agency responses to pressing environmental problems.

We use Jinan to illustrate how people's congresses and elements of a local people's government influence pollution abatement.[2] Jinan, the capital of Shandong Province, is an industrialized city with more than five million people. The governmental structure within Jinan is typical of many Chinese cities. Examples from other municipalities are introduced to further explain interactions among agencies involved in controlling pollution.

Figure 4.2, which shows the structure of the Jinan Municipal People's Government, delineates relationships between the local people's congress, the mayor's office, and various agencies and enterprises. Jinan contains several county-level

55

Figure 4.1 Organizational Structure for Environmental Protection in China

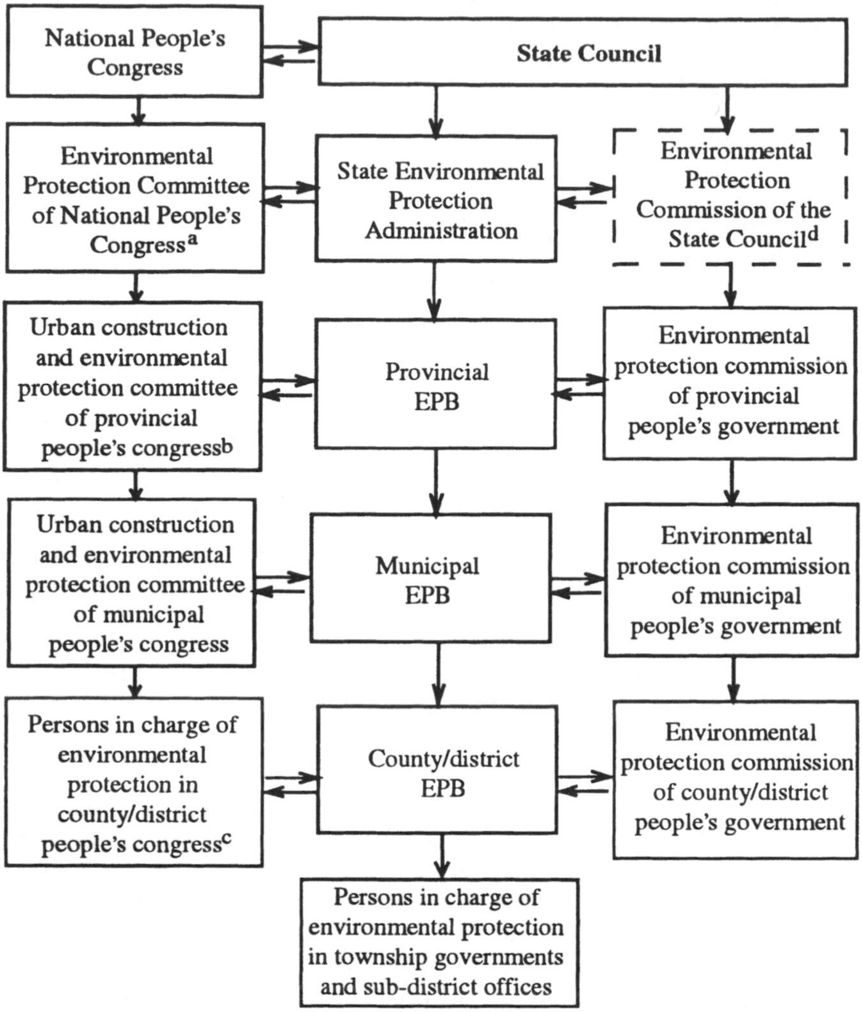

```
┌─────────────────────┐       ┌─────────────────────────────────────┐
│ National People's   │◄─────►│           State Council              │
│ Congress            │       │                                      │
└─────────────────────┘       └─────────────────────────────────────┘
         │                              │                      │
         ▼                              ▼                      ▼
┌─────────────────────┐  ┌──────────────────┐  ┌─────────────────────────┐
│ Environmental       │  │ State            │  │ Environmental           │
│ Protection Committee│◄►│ Environmental    │◄┤ Protection              │
│ of National People's│  │ Protection       │  │ Commission of the       │
│ Congressᵃ           │  │ Administration   │  │ State Councilᵈ          │
└─────────────────────┘  └──────────────────┘  └─────────────────────────┘
```

(diagram boxes)

- National People's Congress
- State Council
- Environmental Protection Committee of National People's Congress[a]
- State Environmental Protection Administration
- Environmental Protection Commission of the State Council[d]
- Urban construction and environmental protection committee of provincial people's congress[b]
- Provincial EPB
- Environmental protection commission of provincial people's government
- Urban construction and environmental protection committee of municipal people's congress
- Municipal EPB
- Environmental protection commission of municipal people's government
- Persons in charge of environmental protection in county/district people's congress[c]
- County/district EPB
- Environmental protection commission of county/district people's government
- Persons in charge of environmental protection in township governments and sub-district offices

[a] The full title of this organization is the Environmental Protection and Natural Resources Conservation Committee of the National People's Congress; it was formed in 1993.

[b] "Province" is used here to mean provinces, autonomous regions, and centrally-administered municipalities.

[c] For simplicity, no reference is made to county-level cities or counties reporting directly to provincial governments.

[d] In 1998, the Environmental Protection Commission of the State Council was eliminated in an effort to streamline the government's administrative structure. The committee had been established in 1984.

Figure 4.2   Jinan Municipal People's Government in the Mid-1990s[a]

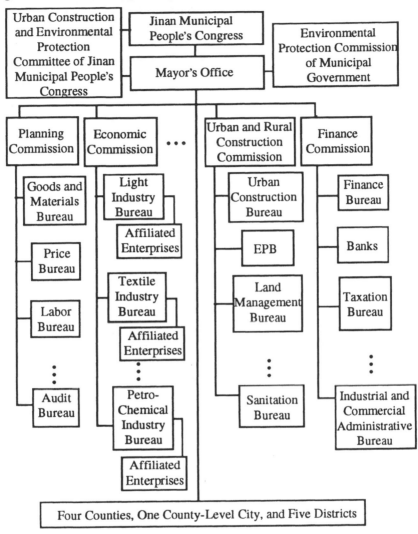

[a] Adapted from Spofford et al. (1996a: 2-38). The figure provides only a partial representation of the many units within a municipal government.

administrative areas: districts, counties, and a county-level city. Each county and county-level city contains numerous townships and villages. The structure for each county-level and district government mirrors the municipal government's administrative form.

Having introduced the administrative structure of a typical municipality, we now examine governmental bodies participating in the regulatory process. Our analysis is directed by two questions:

- What roles are played by government organs that affect industrial waste management?
- How have China's economic reforms influenced pollution abatement?

We begin by considering local lawmakers.

LOCAL PEOPLE'S CONGRESSES

Lawmaking by local people's congresses has become stronger since reforms began in the late 1970s. In addition to creating environmental statutes, many congresses also maintain offices where citizens can register complaints about environmental problems. Local people's congresses also supervise and inspect the work of EPBs (Interview No. 101895).[3]

Many people's congresses have established urban construction and environmental protection committees to assist with their environmental work (see Figure 4.1). Members of the committee in Jinan include the *former* directors of several local agencies, including Jinan EPB. Several full-time staff members carry out the committee's daily work, which includes approving local environmental regulations, inspecting environmental protection work carried out by local agencies, and keeping those agencies informed of environmental problems raised by citizens.

Jinan EPB has close ties with Jinan People's Congress and its Urban Construction and Environmental Protection Committee. Because the congress lacks technical specialists capable of drafting environmental rules, it relies on Jinan EPB to do so. Before finalizing a regulation proposed by the EPB, Jinan People's Congress generally solicits views of agencies having an interest in the proposed requirement. The EPB then revises its draft regulation based on comments offered by reviewing agencies.

The existence of close working relationships between an EPB and a local people's congress is not unique to Jinan. For example, the director of Chongqing EPB stressed the importance of being backed by the local congress:

> If we get supported by the [Chongqing] People's Congress, we are represented at the top level. In recent years, we have tried to convince staff of the people's congress of the importance of environmental protection, and we have established a good relationship with them. (Interview No. 70894)

EPBs in Beijing, Anyang, and Shunde also work closely with their congresses to gain support for regulatory proposals and programs.[4]

Local people's congresses provide an important channel for citizen participation in the formulation of environmental policy. For example, starting in the late 1980s, people's congresses of both Jinan Municipality and Shandong Province received many complaints about water pollution from farmers, fishermen, and residents along the Xiaoqing River which flows through Jinan. As a result, the municipal and provincial legislatures introduced numerous proposals to cut pollution in the river.

Provincial and municipal people's congresses also supervise EPB enforcement of environmental requirements. Congressional staffs routinely visit municipal EPBs to receive briefings, ask questions, and uncover environmental problems. In addition, congressional staffs periodically join EPB personnel in inspecting rivers and making spot checks of polluters. Some provincial and municipal people's congresses develop joint plans for conducting annual inspections of environmental conditions.

The role of legislatures in enforcement is exemplified by the case of a paper mill with about 600 employees in Chongqing County, which is a part of Jinan. The county government closed the mill temporarily in 1995 when the people's congresses of Jinan Municipality and Shandong Province determined that the mill's untreated effluent was causing a black belt of pollution in the Yellow River. Both congresses required Jinan EPB and Chongqing County People's Government to take action, which included the threat of closing the mill permanently if it did not meet effluent standards (Interview No. 102495).

ENVIRONMENTAL PROTECTION COMMISSIONS OF PEOPLE'S GOVERNMENTS

Environmental protection commissions of municipal people's governments typically consist of high level officials—including agency directors or deputy directors—with responsibilities for coordinating interactions between EPBs and other government organs. For example, the Environmental Protection Commission of the Jinan Municipal People's Government is headed by a deputy mayor, and it includes directors or deputy directors of the Planning Commission, the Economic Commission, the Finance Bureau, and various industrial bureaus. The Jinan government's environmental protection commission meets on an ad hoc basis to coordinate agency activities related to pollution abatement, and to settle disputes, such as differences of opinion between Jinan EPB and industrial bureaus on whether proposed industrial projects should be approved. The commission also coordinates how Jinan's agencies respond to "environmental accidents," such as an unexpected release of toxic waste into a river.

In some cities, for instance Guangzhou, the mayor heads the environmental protection commission. The Office of the Environmental Protection Commission in Guangzhou is the city's "highest policy making body" for the environment (Chan, Cheung and Lo, 1993: 66). The commission provides a forum in which all Guangzhou municipal agencies involved in environmental protection (including agencies concerned with economic development) have an opportunity "to exchange information and feedback, to obtain financial and personnel support, and to negotiate."[5] Environmental protection commissions in Nanjing and Zhengzhou serve the same purposes.

As of mid-1998, the future of environmental protection commissions was uncertain (Jahiel, 1998: 760). As part of the national government's reorganization during March 1998, the State Council's Environmental Protection Commission was abolished, and its coordination responsibilities were transferred to SEPA. This change at the national level might eventually affect environmental protection commissions at local levels.

ENVIRONMENTAL PROTECTION BUREAUS

Environmental protection bureaus at municipal levels and below implement environmental regulations and deal with enterprises on a daily basis. We use Jinan to illustrate common features of EPBs and their affiliates. Jinan includes one county-level city, four rural counties, and five urban districts. Each county has several townships, and each district is divided into subdistricts. The environmental protection system in Jinan, as in other municipalities, includes three levels: (1) the municipal EPB; (2) county-level EPBs (i.e., EPBs at the county-level city, the counties, and the districts); and (3) officials in charge of environmental protection in sub-district offices and township governments (see Figure 4.1). Environmental protection organizations at each level implement national and local environmental programs. In townships and villages without environmental protection staffs, county-level EPBs implement environmental rules.

In Jinan and dozens of other cities, the municipal EPB reports to the urban and rural construction commission, which in turn reports to the mayor's office[6] (see Figure 4.2). Jinan EPB has supervisory authority over the county-level EPBs, and it also has several affiliated work units. Three of these are shown in Figure 4.3: Jinan Environmental Monitoring Center, which measures ambient environmental conditions and factory discharges; Jinan Environmental Inspection Unit, which collects pollution discharge fees and enforces regulations; and Jinan Environmental Protection Investment Company, which manages the pollution levy fund.

Jinan EPB sits at the top level of the environmental protection system in Figure 4.3. County-level EPBs report to Jinan EPB, and environmental protection staff in sub-districts and townships report to the EPBs in districts and counties, respectively. Each EPB represents and reports to its next higher level EPB, and each higher level EPB assists those under it in executing environmental programs.

Monitoring and enforcement tasks are divided between municipal and county-level EPBs based on the type of monitoring to be conducted and the affiliation

Figure 4.3   Organizations Reporting to Jinan EPB

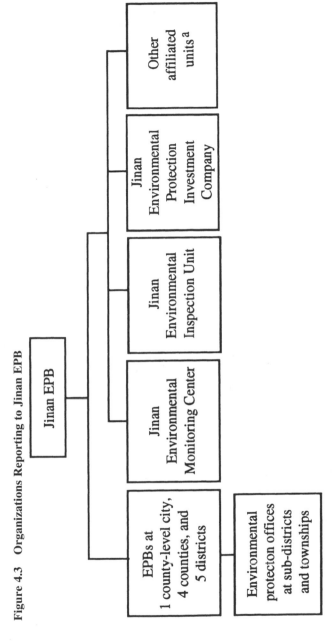

[a]Other units include: Jinan Environmental Protection Research Institute, Jinan Environmental Protection Technology Development Center, and Jinan "Environment News" Agency.

relationship of regulated enterprises. In general, a municipal EPB monitors *ambient* environmental quality and conducts monitoring and enforcement at enterprises affiliated with municipal and higher level governments. EPBs in districts, counties, and county-level cities typically monitor waste discharges and enforce regulations at enterprises affiliated with governments at the county level and below.[7]

EPBs within Jinan receive funds from pollution discharge fees and their local people's governments.[8] Revenues from discharge fees have been important for EPBs in Jinan and many other cities. For example, discharge fees provided 87 and 95 percent of the 1994 operating expenditures of Jinan municipal EPB and its county-level EPBs, respectively.[9]

One aspect of China's administrative reform since the late 1980s has been intense central government pressure on agencies to support themselves. For many EPBs, the local government provides funds to cover salaries of workers classified as "administrative" and included in the EPB's official staff allotment. Additional staff must be paid from other sources, and discharge fees are often the most important of these (Jahiel, 1997: 98–99). Many EPB affiliates generate substantial revenue by conducting environmental impact assessments on proposed development projects. This has led to potential conflicts of interest, since EPB staff often wind up evaluating impact assessment documents prepared by their colleagues in EPB affiliates (Tang et al., 1997: 871–872).

Because a municipal EPB is a unit of municipal government, the mayor plays the key role in appointing the EPB director. In Jinan and other cities, the mayor nominates the director of the municipal EPB, and the municipal people's congress approves the nomination and makes the appointment. Similarly, the district EPB director is nominated by the head of the district and appointed by the district people's congress. An analogous procedure is used in counties and county-level cities. Mayors also affect decisions regarding staff size for EPBs. For example, the mayor's office in Jinan proposes the number of regular staff for Jinan EPB and submits it to the municipal people's congress for approval.

As part of a 1992 reform, Jinan Municipal People's Government changed the classification of all county EPBs from *administrative* units, which are fully funded by government allocations, to *service* units, which obtain some of their funds as fees paid for services. This change was notable because the 1989 *PRC Environmental Protection Law* grants authority to enforce environmental regulations to administrative units, not service units. When the county EPBs were converted to service units their standing as organizations capable of enforcing environmental rules became ambiguous.

The diminution of authority for county-level EPBs has not been restricted to Jinan. According to Jahiel (1997: 93), administrative reforms in 1994 caused a number of counties to eliminate their EPBs or downgrade their status. This drop in status was compounded by staffing problems. At the Fourth National Environmental Conference held in Beijing in 1996, a number of officials complained about the lack of adequate environmental staff at the county and township levels of government. The decrease in status and lack of staff added to the difficulties county-level EPBs had in managing pollution from TVEs (Vermeer, 1998: 962).

MAYORS' OFFICES

As the highest administrative officer within a municipality, the mayor is responsible for executing national and provincial mandates, as well as laws and policies of the municipal people's congress. Personnel within the mayor's office wield considerable power because of their close working relationships with the mayor. Typically, the mayor's office makes key decisions on large investment projects involving industrial development and environmental protection.[10] It also settles disputes between the municipal EPB and enterprises supervised by a municipality's industrial bureaus. In general, only major disputes are sent to the mayor's office for resolution.

The mayor's office typically tries to balance its obligations for both economic development and environmental protection.[11] As in other cities, the mayor's office in Jinan often favors industrial growth over pollution abatement when economic and environmental goals conflict. This is not surprising, because China's post-1978 decentralization policies gave local officials strong financial incentives to expand their economies. As a consequence of decentralization, much municipal government revenue comes from enterprises in the form of income taxes, industrial and commercial taxes, and extrabudgetary fees. Moreover, increased local industrial growth also means more jobs for local unemployed workers and more prestige for local officials.

Enforcement of national environmental laws is supposed to be obligatory, but laws are often vague and a mayor's office can influence how an EPB interprets requirements. Mayor's offices in many cities commonly employ two strategies to influence enforcement of environmental rules: asking an EPB to "give the green light" to an enterprise's new project, even though the enterprise failed to satisfy regulations; and requesting that an EPB drop enforcement actions at factories violating requirements.

Instances in which a mayor's office interfered with an EPB's work are common. A typical case involves a mayor's office that asked an EPB to return fines that an enterprise paid to the EPB. The fines were imposed because the enterprise had installed a new boiler without satisfying the three synchronizations policy. The mayor's office argued that the enterprise had financial problems, and the EPB's fines made the enterprise's position even worse. The EPB returned the fines to the enterprise (Interview No. 100995).

In another city, government leaders offset an EPB fine for an enterprise by giving the enterprise a tax break proportioned to the size of the fine. These actions served two purposes at once: the EPB satisfied its obligation to enforce environmental rules, and government leaders met their responsibility to safeguard local jobs and income (Lieberthal, 1997: 6).

Although a mayor can exert significant power over a city EPB, that power can be checked by provincial officials if the negative effects of a mayor's actions attract the provincial EPB's attention. This is exemplified by a case in which the mayor of a city in Hunan Province wanted the city EPB to approve a port project, even though the EPB opposed it.[12] The EPB's environmental impact studies had demonstrated that pollution linked to operations at the proposed port would contaminate the city's drinking water supply. Although the city EPB felt it couldn't deny the mayor's request, it did not want to be held responsible for environmental damage caused by the port. The city EPB sought help from the provincial EPB, which also became convinced of the port's potential to cause serious environmental problems. In the end, the provincial EPB together with the city EPB convinced the mayor not to proceed with the proposed port.

The provincial EPB's intervention to counterbalance the mayor's pressure on the city EPB was not an isolated event. In Hunan Province at least, the provincial EPB will confront a mayor as long as a city EPB presents solid evidence that the mayor's proposed action would cause significant environmental damage. In routine circumstances, however, Hunan EPB does not participate in municipal-level decisions.

Although some mayors have interfered with the work of municipal EPBs, others have used their influence to solve environmental problems. During the past several years, for example, the mayor's office in Jinan played a key role in having two centralized plants built to treat domestic and industrial wastewater. Our main point is that mayors have enormous incentives to promote local economic development and are thus likely to interfere with municipal EPBs when the economic stakes are high.

PLANNING COMMISSIONS AND ECONOMIC COMMISSIONS

Unlike municipal agencies that are responsible for particular functions, planning commissions and economic commissions are "comprehensive decision-making departments" (according to China's official language). For example, Jinan Planning Commission prepares Jinan's five-year economic and social development plans, and coordinates activities of other departments to fit into those plans (Interview No. 101795a). The Jinan Economic Commission carries out the following work: adjusting the proportion of enterprises in different sectors to meet local needs, approving industrial renovation projects, promoting technological innovation, and helping the mayor's office conduct "macro-economic management" (Interview No. 101795b).

In contrast to planning commissions, which focus on long-term issues, economic commissions coordinate production to eliminate bottlenecks in the execution of annual plans. Another difference is that planning commissions arrange funding for large, basic construction projects, whereas economic commissions approve renovation projects, which are usually smaller and more numerous.[13]

Planning commissions at the county level and above are responsible for revising EPBs' environmental protection plans and integrating them into local economic and social development plans (SPC and NEPA, 1994). Despite these integration efforts, environmental and economic components of development plans are often inconsistent. This occurs, in part, because agencies often fail to communicate with each other during plan preparation. For example, in one of the cities we studied, the EPB consistently lacked funds to meet its pollution control goals because of poor coordination between the EPB and departments in charge of allocating funds. In that city, plans created by industrial bureaus, the economic commission, and the EPB were often inconsistent.[14]

Coordination of city-wide plans has often been problematic, but interagency cooperation on individual projects was effective in many cities, at least until 1992. In Jinan, for example, the planning commission would inform the EPB of proposed construction projects, and the commission would not act on those projects until it had heard from the EPB. The economic commission employed a similar procedure for proposed factory renovation projects.

This interagency coordination was impeded by the State Council's 1992 *Regulations on Transformation of Management Mechanisms at State-Owned Industrial Enterprises*, which allowed enterprises to undertake projects without obtaining approvals from planning or economic commissions if the enterprises had sufficient funds to undertake their projects. However, even when enterprises had their own funds, the *Regulations on Transformation* required that proposed projects be registered at planning or economic commissions *before* the start of construction.

The problem for EPBs in Jinan and other cities was that many enterprises registered their projects *when* they began construction. Indeed, some enterprises only registered *after* construction had started. Moreover, because the planning and economic commissions in Jinan were no longer required to approve industrial projects that did not involve municipal funds, these commissions were often unable to give Jinan EPB timely information about new projects. In addition, Jinan EPB could no longer count on having the planning and economic commissions withhold project approvals based on EPB recommendations. Since 1992, there have been instances where Jinan EPB only learned of new projects *after* they were built.

INDUSTRIAL BUREAUS AND THEIR ENVIRONMENTAL PROTECTION DIVISIONS

Many industrial bureaus play significant roles in day-to-day industrial pollution abatement. A number of industrial bureaus have environmental protection divisions (EPDs) that assist enterprises associated with their bureaus with technical aspects of pollution control. EPDs also help settle disputes and improve communications between enterprises and EPBs.

In all six cities included in our research, especially the more industrialized cities, EPDs have reduced the information-gathering requirements of EPBs. Compared to environmental protection bureaus, EPDs generally have more contact with their affiliated enterprises and know more about their pollution problems. Moreover, in comparison to EPB staff, the educational backgrounds of EPD personnel are often more closely related to the technologies employed in factories affiliated with their bureaus.

Circumstances in Beijing illustrate the significance of EPDs in pollution control. Between 1990 and 1992, Beijing had more than 1,600 large and middle-sized enterprises, but only four members of Beijing EPB administered the discharge permit system. The EPB found it easier to issue permits by working through EPDs. Under Beijing's discharge permit scheme, Beijing EPB calculated a total allowable pollution load and allocated portions of that load to various industrial bureaus. EPDs of the bureaus then divided their assigned loads among affiliated enterprises participating in the trial implementation of the permit system.

Environmental protection divisions of industrial bureaus often help enterprises determine how to meet environmental rules. Managers of many enterprises believe EPDs know more about their factories than EPBs, and that EPD staff can be trusted to make good recommendations for pollution abatement. In addition, enterprise managers commonly believe it is more effective to bargain with an EPB through an EPD than to negotiate directly. Moreover, enterprises often seek help from EPDs in applying for loans or grants to finance environmental projects.

The role of EPDs in pollution abatement has diminished since the early 1990s, when industrial bureaus in many cities were required to trim their size, disband completely, or transform themselves into "general companies" or trade associations. When industrial bureaus made cutbacks, EPDs were often either scaled back or eliminated. When the bureaus were converted to companies, relationships between former bureaus and their affiliated enterprises became similar to linkages between parent companies and their subsidiaries.

An example of how relationships have changed is given by the Beijing Chemical Industrial Bureau, which in 1991 was transformed into the General Company of the Beijing Chemical Industry. The latter was classified as an enterprise unit and was expected to operate without government budget allocations. The director of the EPD at the company, whose staff was cut from five to three, described the new relationship with the Beijing EPB as follows:

[Before 1991,] Beijing EPB relied on us a lot for activities such as [treatment plant] inspections and coordination between the EPB and enterprises. As a result of the change, it will be impossible for us to do much to help Beijing EPB. (Interview No. 30293)

As of the late 1990s, the nomenclature and status of industrial bureaus were in transition. Under a reorganization of the central government that took place in 1998, many industrial ministries were reduced in size and became state industrial bureaus within the State Economic and Trade Commission. In addition, some general companies that had continued to carry out administrative duties were renamed as industrial bureaus. Moreover, units serving similar purposes were called general companies in some municipalities and industrial bureaus in others. For simplicity, we use the term "industrial bureau" to include both general companies and industrial bureaus.

Some analysts believe that EPBs' long-term abilities to enforce environmental regulations will be enhanced as China shifts to a market economy in which government and enterprises are clearly separated (Ross and Silk, 1987). In the short run, however, changes within industrial bureaus have caused problems for EPBs, since they cannot depend on EPDs to either provide environmental engineering services or settle EPB disputes with enterprises.

FINANCE BUREAUS AND LOCAL BANKS

Municipal finance bureaus manage city revenues and expenditures and play important roles in the pollution discharge fee system. In Jinan, for example, discharge fees collected by EPBs within the city go into two funds: a *pollution levy fund*, which provides grants and loans for pollution abatement; and a *self-construction fund*, which supports operations of EPBs within Jinan. In Jinan and many other cities, the finance bureau must approve the municipal EPB's annual plans for use of each of the two funds.

Regulations require that pollution levy funds support waste management at enterprises, but finance bureaus sometimes divert these funds to other purposes. This occurred, for example, in Chongqing between 1982 and 1993. During that period, Chongqing Finance Bureau diverted 23 percent of pollution discharge fees collected (57.4 million *yuan*) to activities unrelated to environmental protection.[15]

Although EPBs have complained about finance bureau diversions of pollution levy funds to purposes unrelated to pollution abatement, regulations contain no provisions to punish finance bureaus for siphoning off funds. Some finance bureaus argue that it would be more economically efficient to make all discharge fees collected by EPBs a part of the budgets of local governments. Notwithstanding this argument, the diversion of earmarked funds by finance bureaus violates the law.

Local banks also play key roles in administering discharge fees. In Jinan, for example, once the finance bureau approves the EPBs plans for use of the pollution levy fund, it requests that Jinan Industrial and Commercial Bank allocate funds to a pollution levy fund account administered by Jinan EPB. The bank plays no role in determining how enterprises use the money or whether they can repay loans from the fund. The bank simply allocates money once the EPB and the finance bureau decide to make a loan or grant, and later the bank helps the EPB obtain loan payments.

A loan or grant from a pollution levy fund usually covers only a small part of an enterprise's cost for a waste treatment facility, and enterprises often look to commercial banks for additional money. Obtaining a bank loan can be problematic. For instance, enterprises in Jinan had trouble getting bank loans for pollution reduction projects in the early 1990s because bad investments by some enterprises had created a capital shortage. According to a World Bank study,

> Twenty-two percent of the 12.4 billion *yuan* in loans outstanding [from commercial banks in Jinan] are overdue, and their repayment is uncertain. This has made the banks especially cautious and hesitant to provide new loans to industrial enterprises in Jinan. (Spofford et al., 1996a: 5–40)

INDUSTRIAL AND COMMERCIAL ADMINISTRATIVE BUREAUS

Industrial and commercial administrative bureaus play a role in pollution control by requiring enterprises to obtain approvals from EPBs as a condition for obtaining business licenses. This requirement, which was created in response to the 1986 *Management Guidelines on Environmental Protection for Construction Projects*, allowed EPBs to affect proposed industrial development projects (State Council, SPC, and SEC, 1986). It is analogous to previously discussed requirements in which planning and economic commissions withheld their approvals of proposed development projects until EPBs signed off on them. As in the case of planning and economic commissions, cooperative interactions between EPBs and industrial and commercial administrative bureaus were hampered by the 1992 *Regulations on the Transformation of Management at State-Owned Industrial Enterprises*.

Circumstances in Jinan illustrate how interactions between some industrial and commercial administrative bureaus and EPBs changed in 1992. Before that year, Jinan Industrial and Commercial Administrative Bureau would not issue a business license without getting Jinan EPB's consent. After 1992, the Bureau issued numerous business licenses to enterprises, particularly small ones, that lacked the EPB's stamp. The Bureau felt justified in proceeding this way because Jinan Municipal People's Government had called for streamlined administrative procedures that would promote economic development. An official at the Bureau rationalized the organization's position as follows:

> Each year we issue about two to three thousand business licenses. Before we issue a license to an industrial enterprise we are supposed to get approvals from at least four units [i.e. the public health bureau, the fire brigade, the bureau of power supply, and the EPB]. It is difficult for us to deal with such a huge workload in this period of rapid economic growth. We issued licenses to some small factories [without the EPB's stamp] when the factories told us they did not have pollution problems. (Interview No. 102095)

Once the new procedure was put in place, Jinan EPB could no longer rely on the Bureau for information about proposed projects.

The ability of enterprises to obtain business licenses from an industrial and commercial administrative bureau without an EPB stamp is not limited to Jinan. For example, in 1992 Chongqing Municipal People's Government eliminated the need for enterprises in several industrial sectors to obtain Chongqing EPB's approval for new projects. As in Jinan, this action was intended to streamline administrative procedures and thereby promote economic development. Using the new procedures, many enterprises received licenses to operate projects without EPB approval, and some of those projects caused significant pollution. Chongqing EPB responded to this situation in 1994 by urging the municipal government to reestablish the requirement for an EPB stamp of approval in managing new industrial projects (Interview No. 71394).

URBAN CONSTRUCTION BUREAUS

Compared with interactions between EPBs and the local agencies described above, relationships between EPBs and urban construction bureaus have been unique and often contentious. Disputes have arisen because EPBs are legally required to enforce discharge standards on releases from municipal wastewater treatment works, which are built and operated by urban construction bureaus. Tensions between EPBs and construction bureaus are exacerbated by the administrative structure of city governments. Municipal urban construction bureaus have *tiao-tiao* (i.e., vertical) reporting relationships with urban and rural construction commissions. Although municipal EPBs have *tiao-tiao* linkages with provincial EPBs, a number of them are under urban and rural construction commissions in the hierarchy of local government (see Figure 4.2). This positioning is a consequence of history: before 1984, what is now the State Environmental Protection Administration was the Environmental Protection Bureau within the Ministry of Urban and Rural Construction and Environmental Protection.

Because the majority of municipal treatment works in China are new, most EPBs have not yet monitored flows from municipal plants, nor have they tried to collect discharge fees from urban construction bureaus that operate plants violating effluent standards. Thus many EPBs have not faced the inevitable conflicts that will arise when they try to extract fees from another unit within the same government.

However, sharp tensions between EPBs and urban construction bureaus already exist over who should collect fees from enterprises that release waste violating effluent standards and flowing to municipal treatment plants. Before these plants were built, EPBs collected the fees. After the treatment plants were up and running, urban construction bureaus were supposed to collect the fees, but many EPBs have been reluctant to give the fees up. Urban construction bureaus believe it is unfair for EPBs to collect the fees, since construction bureaus must run the municipal treatment plants that handle the factories' wastes. Construction bureaus feel it would be more equitable and consistent with discharge fee regulations if they collected the fees from factories and used the money to operate municipal treatment facilities.

Disagreements between municipal EPBs and urban construction bureaus have impeded environmental protection efforts. Even though China has relatively few municipal treatment works, many run below capacity because construction bureaus claim they lack operating funds. Construction bureaus feel they could operate municipal plants at full capacity if they collected fees from factories contributing waste to those plants. In contrast, EPBs argue that construction bureaus should not receive any fee-based revenues because municipal plants are not being operated at capacity. This impasse has existed for only a few years, since most municipal treatment works in China were built recently. Conflicts between EPBs and construction bureaus are of concern to the State Environmental Protection Administration. As of 1999, the issue was unresolved.

CITIZENS, THE MEDIA, AND NGOs

Having analyzed the roles of government organizations, we now consider how individual citizens, nongovernmental organizations (NGOs), and the media participate in environmental protection. Contrary to popular belief in the West, Chinese citizens have opportunities to influence compliance with environmental regulations, and the growing importance of the media and environmental NGOs have extended those opportunities.

Channels for Citizen Complaints

China has a tradition of allowing people to make complaints to government authorities that dates back more than two thousand years, and the Chinese Community Party embraced that tradition after assuming power in 1949 (Shi, 1997: 60). In contemporary China, citizens can express dissatisfaction at "offices of letters and visits" at various levels of government. For example, Beijing Municipal People's Government has a Department of Letters and Visits to accommodate citizen concerns. To reduce the risk of retaliation, many people send unsigned letters of complaint. In many provinces, anonymous notes account for between 25 and 50 percent of all citizen complaint letters (Shi, 1997: 63).

In addition to relying on governments' offices of letters and visits, citizens can direct their concerns about environmental matters to one or more of the following:

- Environmental protection bureaus—Many EPBs have the equivalent of a "complaint division" to hear the public's concerns.
- Mayor's offices—Many cities have a vice mayor whose responsibilities in-

clude environmental protection, and the staff of this vice mayor accepts citizen complaints.

- Local people's congresses—Citizens frequently bring environmental complaints to their elected representatives on people's congresses and to staffs of urban construction and environmental protection committees of people's congresses.

Many cities have established hotlines for residents to call and talk about environmental problems. For example, Dalian City (Liaoning Province) installed a 24-hour telephone hotline to receive citizen complaints about the environment. The city also has a radio talk show that gives people an opportunity to discuss their environmental concerns.[16]

Citizen queries regarding the environment generally center on obvious pollution, such as excessive noise from factories, sooty plumes from smokestacks, and wastewater releases causing fish kills. Less evident problems, such as discharges of colorless, odorless, toxic substances, often escape the public's attention.[17] Frequently, citizens first complain to the factory causing the problem and turn to government authorities or the media only if the factory is unresponsive.

The extent of the public's use of government channels to express dissatisfaction is illustrated by data regarding complaints to EPBs. From 1991 through 1993, citizens sent over 55,000 complaint letters annually and made about 80,000 complaints in person each year. Approximately 90 percent of these complaints concerned air and water pollution and noise. There were as many as 20 to 30 complaints per 100,000 inhabitants in prosperous eastern provinces and centrally administered cities, and as few as 3 to 4 complaints per 100,000 inhabitants in China's least economically developed areas—the western hinterlands. In most provinces, EPBs responded to over 80 percent of the issues raised by citizens.[18]

EPBs also receive anonymous telephone calls tipping them off to factories violating environmental rules. Judging from the technical details given in some of these calls, workers appeared to be using EPB complaint lines to expose health and safety problems at their own factories.[19]

Letters, visits, and telephone calls to EPBs represent the most common means for registering environmental complaints, but citizens also have rights to sue companies that pollute and EPBs that fail to carry out national laws.[20] Although citizens do not use their rights to bring suit frequently, the number of citizen-based environmental court actions is rising. In one instance, citizens sued a county EPB for failing to enforce an environmental law (Harkness, 1998: 933). In addition, multiple parties have used the 1991 *PRC Civil Procedure Law* to bring class-action suits, and some of those suits have been against local authorities who failed to implement national laws. Other class-action suits have involved citizens' attempts to obtain compensation for damages from air and water pollution and excessive noise (Note, 1998: 1530).

In contrast to the situation in many Western democracies, Chinese citizens have no systematic means for expressing dissatisfaction about proposed projects that would impact them. Existing channels only allow citizens to complain *after* negative effects of development projects become apparent.

Another contrast with the West concerns the types of actions that citizens feel free to criticize. In Western democracies, many people feel comfortable pointing out faults in national environmental policies. In contrast, Chinese citizens are normally quite hesitant to criticize the central government openly.[21] Recently, however, the Center has encouraged citizens to expose enterprises that violate environmental rules and to pressure local governments to enforce environmental requirements strictly. For example, the 1996 *State Council Decision Concerning Certain Environmental Protection Issues* calls for establishing a mechanism to "encourage the public to participate in the work of environmental protection and to report and expose various actions that violate environmental laws and regulations" (State Council, 1996: Section 10). Thus, while individual citizens are still reluctant to criticize national environmental policies, they have become more comfortable in exposing polluters and criticizing how local governments enforce environmental policies.

NGOs and the Media

Although NGOs and the media in China play important roles in protecting the environment, they do not have the autonomy of NGOs and media outlets in Western democracies.[22] All Chinese NGOs must be registered with and approved by the government, and many are established to meet government agency objectives. In addition, the principal media outlets in China are sponsored by the Chinese Communist Party and serve as government spokespersons. Under these circumstances, neither NGOs nor the media are free to criticize the government's environmental policies and programs. While media accounts may be accurate, they often reflect the biases of their sponsoring governmental bodies.

NGOs and the media have limited ability to obtain information that may reflect poorly on the government's environmental protection efforts. This is reflected in practices of the Environmental Publicity and Education Center, which produces (among other things) reports and videotapes detailing China's significant environmental problems. Many of these materials are distributed only to high-level government officials. Citizens, NGOs, and the media cannot access these videotapes and reports (Interview No. 120898).

Notwithstanding the limited access to information and other restrictions faced by NGOs, they have done much to protect the environment during the past few years, mainly by raising public awareness of environmental problems, carrying out campaigns to change behavior (e.g., by encouraging recycling), and conducting studies of environmental issues aimed at influencing national leaders.[23] Consider, for example, the work of *Friends of Nature*, a "Western-style" NGO established in 1993 under the Academy of Culture.[24] The organization has over 400 members, many of whom are journalists and teachers. Much of Friends of Nature's work involves enhancing the environmental awareness of citizens. The organization's surveys of newspaper accounts of environmental subjects in 1995 (and later years) stimulated increased coverage of environmental topics in Chinese newspapers. In addition, the newsletter published by Friends of Nature has provided material that many of its media-based members have used in their own news stories. Other activities sponsored by Friends of Nature include tree plantings, birdwatching events, and Green Forums on Earth Day. Although the organization does not lobby the government on environmentally sensitive topics, it has waged media-based campaigns to address particular issues, such as environmental destruction in the upper-most portions of the Yangtze River basin (Wandi, 1996).

Another NGO, the *Global Village Environmental Culture Institute*, was registered in the mid-1990s under the Chinese Commercial Agency. This NGO has focused on two main activities: producing environmental documentaries for regular airing on Chinese Central Television, and promoting materials recycling and reuse by households. Among other things, the NGO has made citizens aware of numerous opportunities for incorporating environmentally-friendly behavior into their daily lives.

Some Chinese NGOs conduct research that explores new approaches to environmental planning and decision making. This organizational type is illustrated by the *Beijing Environment and Development Institute*, established in 1995 with the support of the People's University Institute of Environmental Economics. This NGO's efforts to influence environmental policy are illustrated by its re-evaluation of development plans in Heilongjiang's Three River's Plain region, where key issues center on conflicts between agricultural activities and wetlands preservation.

International environmental NGOs have become increasingly active in China, and their work has heightened the environmental awareness of government officials. For example, in 1994, the *World Wide Fund for Nature* (WWF) joined with China's Ministry of Forestry to produce a major audit of China's nature reserve system. The Ministry of Forestry/WWF team pointed out serious gaps in the system and made numerous recommendations for government action (Harkness, 1998: 922–923).

In addition to the types of formal NGOs mentioned above, a number of student-organized environmental organizations have recently surfaced on college campuses.[25] For example, as of 1997, at least twenty such groups existed in Beijing and more than ten campus groups had been established in other parts of the country. Some campus groups had as many as 400 members. In March 1996, an unofficial organization, Green Student Forum, was created to network among the various campus groups. The Green Student Forum publishes a newsletter, and it has organized "Green Camps" for projects such as opposing deforestation by loggers in Tibet.

Chinese newspapers and television have been active in promoting NGO activities. More generally, the media plays an important role in raising public awareness of environmental issues and publicizing violations of environmental regulations. In addition to being covered in China's regular newspapers, environmental issues are also featured in special newspapers put out by environmental agencies. For example, *China Environmental News*, published by an affiliate of SEPA, is circulated to about half a million readers and focuses exclusively on environmental subjects.

The news media and environmental NGOs sometimes work in tandem. For example, as part of its effort to block the clearcutting of virgin forests in Denqin County (Yunnan Province), Friends of Nature launched a major publicity campaign using television and the press. In one particularly dramatic effort, a television station showed panic stricken golden monkeys terrified by the roar of machinery used for construction activities within the forest. This caused a nationwide response that contributed to the central government's decision to force Denqin County to halt the logging (Wandi, 1996).

During the early 1990s, when our field research was conducted, few environmental NGOs existed, and the media confined itself to "lecturing the public on the need to protect the environment, but failed to inform people on how or what they should do" (Bo, 1998: 89). Citizen complaints were influential, but citizens only had an opportunity to react to existing problems. The 1996 *State Council Decision Concerning Certain Environmental Protection Issues* signaled a turning point by strongly encouraging both the media and citizens to expose illegal actions that caused environmental damage. By the late 1990s, the media and environmental NGOs had become increasingly influential. NGOs prodded the media to provide increased coverage of environmental affairs, and to publicize NGO activities and thereby gain public support for causes advanced by NGOs. In addition, the media began advocating environmental protection on its own initiative.

NOTES

1. The national-level unit is called the Environmental Protection and Natural Resources Conservation Committee of the National People's Congress. Analogous units under local people's congresses are also in charge of urban and rural construction. They are usually called urban and rural construction and environmental protection committees.

2 Some material concerning Jinan in this chapter is based on Spofford et al. (1996a: Chapter 2); it was prepared by Xiaoying Ma with the assistance of Walter Spofford, Jr.

3. Information in this paragraph is based, in part, on one of our interviews. Because most interviewees spoke on the condition of anonymity, we cite all interviews using only a code number representing the interview date, in this case, 10–18–95. For more on people's congresses, see Tanner (1995).

4. This assertion is based on our interviews with EPB staffs in Beijing, Anyang, and Shunde.

5. The quote is from Chan, Wong, Cheung, and Lo (1995: 336); their article is also the basis for the assertion in this paragraph about Nanjing and Zhengzhou.

6. As of the end of 1992, 66 of 315 municipal environmental protection organs were under urban construction departments. However, the majority (176) were independent "first-tier" organizations within their local governments (Jahiel, 1998: 772).

7. Although some townships and villages have their own environmental protection organizations, the number of staff engaged at these levels constitutes less than 2 percent of the total number of EPB staff (SEPA, 1998).

8. As noted in Chapter 2, EPBs can use all of the four small pieces and up to 20 percent of over-standard fees for environmental monitoring, research, training, and awards.

9. Fees are collected by EPBs at both the municipal and county levels and then distributed to three levels: the provincial EPB, the municipal EPB, and the EPBs in county-level governments. For details on how fees are distributed, see Ma (1997: 90).

10 For more on the functions of a mayor's office, see Walder (1992: 317–318).

11. Under the 1989 *PRC Environmental Protection Law*, people's governments at all levels are responsible for environmental protection within their jurisdictions.

12. This case and observations in the next paragraph are based on June 1998 interviews with Shasha Hu, who had just completed a study in Hunan Province investigating how environmental impact assessments were being conducted. Ms. Hu's work was part of her undergraduate research project at Stanford University.

13. For more on differences between planning and economic commissions, see Walder (1992).

14. Examples of coordination problems noted in this paragraph were given by EPB staff in one of the six cities included in our field research.

15. These figures are from interviews we conducted with Chongqing EPB staff.

16. Information about phone hotlines and Dalian's radio show is from reports of the Working Group on Environment in U.S.-China Relations, November 1996-July 1997, as summarized in the first issue of the *China Environment Series* published in 1997 by the Woodrow Wilson Center, Washington, D.C. (pp. 55 and 57).

17. For an analysis of how citizen complaints might divert EPB resources away from low visibility, high-risk problems, see Dasgupta and Wheeler (1996).

18. Facts in this paragraph are from Dasgupta and Wheeler (1996: 18–20).

19. This point was made by our colleague, Kimberley Warren, based on her interviews with EPB staff in Qingdao City in the mid-1990s.

20. As indicated by Zhang and Ferris (1997), Chinese citizens can initiate environmentally-based court actions using a variety of statutes, including the *PRC Administrative Litigation Law* and the *PRC Environmental Protection Law*.

21. Vocal public opposition to the Three Gorges Dam in the late 1980s and 1990s represents a notable exception.

22. This discussion of NGOs and the media relies heavily on Knup (1997), Bo (1998), and personal correspondence with Read Vanderbilt. For details on the rigorous registration process that must be followed to become an official NGO in China, see Palmer (1998: 795–796).

23. We do not discuss so-called "government-organized NGOs" which Chinese agencies sometimes create to enter agreements with or raise funds from foreign NGOs. An example is the *China Environmental Protection Foundation*, established in 1993 under NEPA. This organization's "own literature states its first general principle is 'to facilitate the donation of funds and goods in order to help develop environmental protection undertakings in China'" (Knup, 1997: 11).

24. See Dunn (1997) and Wandi (1996) for additional information about Friends of Nature.

25. Information in this paragraph is from Jahiel (1998: 786).

5

Informal Rules of Behavior
Affecting Compliance

The institutional framework for environmental protection in China includes both formal rules, as exemplified by effluent standards, and informal rules embodied in the social norms and unwritten codes of conduct that influence interactions among people in China. In this chapter, we introduce several informal rules and demonstrate how they can either promote or impede compliance with effluent standards and other formal rules. We emphasize informal rules related to authority, social connections, and the Chinese concept of face, because these rules play strong roles in environmental policy implementation.[1]

RESPECT FOR AUTHORITY

Since the time of Confucius (551–479 B.C.), a person's position within a hierarchy has helped define appropriate behavior in China. Although the influence of Confucian teachings has varied over the centuries, the Confucian tradition is still important in China. In this tradition, correct behavior is defined in terms of reciprocal exchanges between individuals in different positions, such as ruler and subject, father and son, husband and wife, elder brother and younger brother, and friend and friend. Confucius used these particular role combinations to explore a wide range of human interactions.

According to Confucian teachings, social order and harmony are maintained when individuals behave in ways consistent with their roles. Consider, for example, the connection between a father and a son. A son is expected to demonstrate unwavering loyalty to his father and to care for him as he grows old. A father, in turn, *reciprocates* the reverential behavior of his son by treating him as he (the father) would have liked to be treated if he were the son. Thus, for example, the father would nurture a young son and remain forever loyal to him.

For Confucians, a person's position in a hierarchical system determines how one should behave toward the person. A ruler is at the top level of the hierarchy, and thus subjects owe the ruler respect and loyalty. As in the linkages between father and sons, the relationship between ruler and subjects involves reciprocity. Confucian teachings make it clear that a ruler gains a right to the loyalty of his subjects by acting benevolently towards them. The wealth and authority of rulers will not be questioned, provided they act to improve the welfare of their subjects.[2]

The Confucian tradition has long been reflected in the hierarchical nature of Chinese political systems: a small number of individuals at the top levels of national and local political hierarchies have governed large numbers of people. Despite the egalitarian ideals of Chinese leaders in the period following establishment of the People's Republic of China in 1949, position within a political hierarchy continues to symbolize and legitimate power.

CHANGES IN STATUS FOR CHINA'S TOP ENVIRONMENTAL AGENCY

Hierarchical position is important for organizations as well as individuals, and this is well illustrated by the history of SEPA, China's leading environmental agency. The first version of China's top environmental agency was the Environmental Protection Office, a unit with a staff of twenty set up in 1974 under the State Council. The Environmental Protection Office had no authority over lower levels of government and it concentrated on planning. However, the office could exert an indirect influence on other governmental organizations by working through its supervisory organ, the State Council's Leading Group for Environmental Protection.

In 1982, three years after promulgation of the *PRC Environmental Protection Law for Trial Implementation*, the State Council set up the Ministry of Urban and Rural Construction and Environmental Protection (referred to herein as the Ministry of Construction), and it made China's top environmental agency a bureau within this ministry. Qu Geping, who had been China's representative to The United Nations Environment Programme since 1976, was selected to head the new Environmental Protection Bureau. While creation of this unit was a significant event, the Bureau "resembled an appendage rather than an integral component of the new ministry, with most of its offices located in a separate compound" (Ross, 1988: 141). The ability of the Environmental Protection Bureau to influence activities of other agencies was limited: as a unit within the Ministry of Construction it could only issue orders to lower-level units within that ministry. Moreover, the State Council abolished its Leading Group on Environmental Protection when it created the Ministry of Construction. This was a loss, because the Leading Group had been able to coordinate the environmental protection activities of various ministries.

Elevated Status for Environmental Protection in 1984

In 1984, the State Council took several steps to enhance the status of the Environmental Protection Bureau: the unit was renamed the National Environmental Protection Bureau; its staff size was doubled (from 60 to 120 persons); and it became responsible to both the Ministry of Construction and the State Council's Environmental Protection Commission. The Commission had been created earlier in 1984 to coordinate environmental efforts of ministries and to resolve controversial elements of proposed environmental laws. With a membership that included thirty-one ministries and commissions and several representatives of large enterprises and the media, the Commission could play an active role in policy making. The expanded and newly named National Environmental Protection Bureau provided staff support to the State Council's Environmental Protection Commission and drafted environmental policy documents for the Commission's consideration.

Although the National Environmental Protection Bureau reported to the Ministry of Construction, it also reported to the State Council's Environmental Protection Commission, which meant it could issue regulations binding all ministries by having its proposed regulations issued by the Commission. The 1984 change also allowed the Bureau to carry out its environmental protection activities more effectively.[3]

The creation of the State Council's Environmental Protection Commission and the elevation in status of the former Environmental Protection Bureau had impacts at lower levels of government. Many provincial, city, and county governments established environmental protection commissions in "accord with the spirit of the State Council's decisions" (Qu Geping, as quoted by Jahiel, 1994: 110). In addition, many local governments strengthened the authority and capability of their environmental protection bureaus.

Creation of NEPA in 1988

The status of China's top environmental agency was raised again in 1988 when the National Environmental Protection Bureau was brought out from under the Ministry of Construction and renamed the National Environmental Protection Agency. In making this change, the State Council increased the organization's authority, more than doubled its staff size (from 120 to 321 people), and signaled that the State Council attached importance to environmental protection. Like main line ministries, NEPA had direct links to the State Council.

The 1988 changes are also notable for how they affected the administrative rank of China's national environmental protection unit. In China, all government organizations have administrative ranks, and staff members within those organizations also have ranks. When NEPA was created, it was given the rank of a vice-ministry, which meant it could issue binding orders to government units with ranks below the vice-ministerial level. As important as this change was, it still left the nation's key environmental protection agency with less prestige and status than a full ministry.

Creation of SEPA at Full Ministerial Rank

As part of a major restructuring of the central government in 1998, NEPA was transformed into the State Environmental Protection Administration, a government organization with full ministerial rank. The restructuring also involved dismantling the Ministry of Forestry and consolidating some of its staff and functions within SEPA. By granting SEPA ministerial rank when many ministries were being dismantled, China's leaders once more signaled their interest in addressing the nation's environmental problems. In an effort to clarify lines of authority and cut non-essential government units, the 1998 reorganization also dismantled the State Council's Environmental Protection Commission. The elimination of the Commission left no doubt that SEPA was the nation's leading environmental protection organization.[4]

SEPA's increased status within the government bureaucracy led to subtle, but nonetheless notable, changes in the deference given to the opinion's of SEPA's administrator, Xie Zhenhua, in meetings of the State Council. When he was head of NEPA, Xie Zhenhua's views were sometimes discounted by ministers because they held a higher rank. With Xie Zhenhua's elevation to full ministerial rank, his opinions were given greater weight. Significantly, SEPA's status was further augmented because the former Minister of Geology and Mineral Resources had been made a vice administrator of SEPA during the 1998 governmental restructuring. In addition, vice ministers of two other organizations that had been eliminated—the Ministry of Forestry and the Ministry of the Chemical Industry—were made vice administrators of SEPA. As an agency that included an administrator holding the rank of minister, a former minister, and two former vice-ministers, SEPA's status was enhanced. Notwithstanding this increase in stature, SEPA remained far less powerful than some key national organizations, such as the State Development and Planning Commission and the State Economic and Trade Commission.

STATUS OF EPBs CAN ADVERSELY AFFECT POLLUTION REDUCTION EFFORTS

The importance of status is illustrated by difficulties that SEPA has had in trying to resolve disputes between urban construction bureaus and EPBs (see Chapter 4). Even though many municipal EPBs and urban construction bureaus now have the same administrative rank, that was not the case in the past. Between 1982 and 1984, the unit that eventually became SEPA was a mere bureau within the Ministry of Urban and Rural Construction and Environmental Protection, the precursor to the Ministry of Construction. Similarly, most municipal EPBs were units within municipal bureaus of urban and rural construction and environmental protection, the precursors to municipal urban and rural construction commissions. Many officials at municipal construction bureaus do not treat their counterparts at EPBs equally because EPBs were once parts of their organizations. This negative view of EPBs has made it more difficult for SEPA to resolve differences between municipal EPBs and construction bureaus.

Administrative Rank Influences Policy Implementation

Another instance in which status issues adversely affected an environmental agency's work involves one of our case studies, A1 Power Plant in Anyang. Under the trial implementation of the discharge permit system, Anyang EPB proposed a new method of calculating discharge fees based on the total mass of pollutants released. In 1989, Anyang Municipal People's Government approved the proposal when it promulgated the *Methodology for DPS Management in Anyang (Trial)* (referred to herein as *the Methodology*).[5]

Initially, A1 Power Plant refused to pay fees calculated using the new method. Plant managers claimed that the government of Anyang had no authority to regulate A1 Power Plant because the plant was affiliated with Henan Province Electric Power Department, a part of Henan Provincial People's Government. Unlike other enterprises in Anyang, which typically had a lower administrative rank than Anyang EPB, the power plant had the same rank as the EPB, and thus it was not formally obliged to obey the EPB's orders.

In July 1990, Anyang EPB responded to A1 Power Plant's challenge by requesting that Henan Provincial People's Government approve *the Methodology*. The provincial government granted its approval several months later. Since then, A1 Power Plant has not questioned the legitimacy of *the Methodology*. As a result of pressure from Anyang EPB and mediation efforts of Henan EPB and Henan Province Electric Power Department, A1 Power Plant eventually paid the discharge fees it owed.

Other cases in which administrative rank affected environmental policy implementation have occurred in Guangzhou, the capital of Guangdong Province and one of the pace setters in China's expanding economy (Chan, Cheung, and Lo, 1993: 79). In one instance, staff of Guangzhou Environmental Protection Office was not allowed to monitor wastewater releases from Guangzhou Paper Manufacturing Company because the administrative rank of the environmental protection office's director was lower than the rank of the company's director. In another case, environmental agency staff in Guangzhou were blocked from inspecting the Retired Air Force Personnel Recreation Club because many club members had a higher party seniority than that of the party general in Guangzhou. As this case illustrates, hierarchical position is also delineated by status in the Chinese Communist Party.

Leaders Sometimes Encourage Rule Violations

Hierarchical position also played a role in an EPB's approval of a 1992 proposal for a large manufacturing facility in Chongqing, a case that demonstrates the power of local leaders to make decisions that override environmental requirements.[6] According to regulations governing environmental impact assessment (EIA), Chongqing EPB was required to approve an EIA for the proposed factory before it could be constructed. In this instance, the economic importance of the manufacturing facility caused the mayor's office to demand and receive the EPB's stamp of approval of the project's EIA, even though an EIA had not been conducted. A year later, when Chongqing EPB tried to inspect the manufacturing facility during construction, factory managers refused to allow the inspection. Once more, the mayor's office intervened. In this case, it instructed Chongqing EPB not to inspect the factory.

In principle, the EPB director could have challenged the demands of the mayor's office. However, doing so would have been risky since the EPB sits below the mayor in the local political hierarchy. An EPB director that attempts to challenge a mayor that violates the law runs the risk of being fired for violating unwritten rules about the ability of top officials to violate environmental laws with impunity. The Chongqing case is not unique.[7]

GUANXI: SOCIAL CONNECTIONS

The Chinese word *guanxi* is frequently translated as "social connections," but it is more than just a crude form of favoritism.[8] A more complex, less pejorative conceptualization of *guanxi* clarifies why more than simple partiality is involved. *Guanxi*, which has long been an element of Chinese life, is based on a blend of exchanges and mutual affection that "create feelings of responsibility and obligation on the one hand and indebtedness on the other" (Pye, 1981: 139). While *guanxi* is often nurtured over long periods, in the initial instance it is often based upon "a shared particularism—a common place of origin, a shared teacher, grandfathers who were friends, and the like"[9] (Pye, 1981: 142).

In one of its simplest forms, *guanxi* is maintained by trading favors over long periods. These exchanges are often viewed as creating a resource that can be used to get things done. The following interpretation of the interchanges that strengthen *guanxi* is instructive:

> Many Westerners never quite learn the reciprocal nature of *guanxi* even when they consider themselves ace players in the Chinese game of *guanxi*. It's never enough to say "thank you, my friend, that's very kind of you to have done all this for me"; you must consciously realize you are in debt . . . and remember you may have to pay it back one way or another or you risk losing this *guanxi* of yours who could be very important in your future business. It's not necessarily a one-for-one mechani-

cal tally—it's seldom that way, as a matter of fact—but it should be reciprocal on the whole. (Ju, 1996: 51)

Guanxi Can Assist in Enhancing Environmental Protection

How does *guanxi* relate to environmental regulation? A common illustration concerns ties that develop between EPB staff and environmental specialists at regulated enterprises. In some countries, the fact that regulators develop enduring and mutually supportive ties with regulated parties would be frowned upon. In China, the practice is routine.[10] Enterprise personnel develop *guanxi* with EPB staff because they hope to gain favorable treatment, whereas many EPB staff feel that *guanxi* makes it easier for them to gain information about the environmental performance of enterprises. EPBs do not consider it a conflict of interest to develop *guanxi* with enterprises they regulate because EPBs view SOEs as units linked to industrial bureaus and township and village enterprises as units directly controlled by township governments and village committees, respectively. Indeed, for many EPB staff, "conflict of interest" is not a meaningful concept (Sinkule and Ortolano, 1995: 177).

Relationships that develop between EPB staff and environmental protection workers at regulated enterprises facilitate productive exchanges of ideas and information. This *guanxi* often reflects mutual concern. For example, a factory director might feel grateful for an EPB's suggestion on how to recycle waste to cut pollution, and an EPB might feel sympathy for an enterprise that tried to meet environmental requirements but failed because it had an unprofitable year. Although *guanxi* between environmental regulators and enterprise personnel does not eliminate all conflicts, it generally reduces both the frequency and severity of serious disagreements.

An example from Abigail Jahiel's study of environmental protection in Wuhan, a city in Hubei Province, illustrates the significance of *guanxi* in controlling pollution. Before 1990, Wuhan EPB could only comment on a proposed project after enterprise officials and city government leaders had agreed on a site and a conceptual design for the project. Wuhan EPB staff felt they could be more effective in preventing pollution if they could appraise a proposed project *before* decisions were made by key units within the Wuhan Municipal People's Government: the Planning Commission, the Economic Commission, and the Commission for Foreign Trade. In 1990, Wuhan EPB approached these commissions and asked to be consulted about new projects before the commissions approved them. Each of the three commissions consented.

Why did the commissions accept Wuhan EPB's proposition? Jahiel (1994: 319) points to the *guanxi* that had developed as a consequence of "long-time interaction" between the head of Wuhan EPB's Pollution Prevention Division and key staff in each of the three commissions. As a result of these exchanges, the EPB division head "had developed rapport (or, as the Chinese would say, *guanxi*) with each of these individuals." In an interview with Jahiel, the division head explained that he could easily get the commissions to accept the EPB's prior consultation scheme because he had been in his job "for a long time and [was] very familiar with the people" in the three commissions.

Using *Guanxi* to Avoid Compliance

While *guanxi* can enhance environmental protection, it can also have the opposite effect. Studies of how investors from Taiwan and Hong Kong have operated in China demonstrate ways in which *guanxi* has been used to short-circuit regulations. Based on numerous interviews with foreign business executives, one analyst found that investors often employed "the 'Chinese Way' of getting things done" to circumvent laws (Pearson, 1997: 108). Typically, this involved *guanxi* between the entrepreneurs and local officials.

An example of how *guanxi* has been used to sidestep regulations involves a Hong Kong business manager who ran a factory producing computer parts in Guangdong Province. The manager felt that *guanxi* enabled him to operate his factory with minimal interference from local authorities. His *guanxi* was nurtured by two factors: he was born in a nearby village, and he paid a "monthly fee" to local officials (Weidenbaum and Hughes, 1996: 148).

In the course of developing *guanxi* with private entrepreneurs, government officials often use their *guanxi* networks to help secure required project approvals. In return for this form of support for entrepreneurs, government officials can enrich themselves in numerous ways, including the following:

> through "management fees," . . . or through "voluntary donations" and authorized and unauthorized fees and taxes levied on private businesses. They may take "power shares" in private enterprises in return for protection and favors. Cadres also rely on private businesses to be channels for re-selling at higher market prices goods bought at low state-set prices. . . . Indeed, local cadres sometimes have become the embodiment of the private-official linkage by running private enterprises themselves (with spouses or family members as "fronts"), using their political connections to advantage. (Pearson, 1997: 112–113)

Gains to local officials are often in forms other than cash; for example, officials may obtain valuable gifts, invitations to prestigious events and banquets, and all-expense-paid trips abroad. (Interview No. 60499).

While use of *guanxi* opens the door to bribery and corruption, it is possible to exchange favors and gifts without violating anti-corruption laws. A perspective on the subtleties involved in distinguishing between *guanxi* and bribery is provided by a Chinese businessman who had spent time outside of China:

> China wants reforms. But business professionals also reach private understandings with officials. It is illegal to take a cash bonus if you are an official. But in the U.S.

if you give money to your congressman's favorite charity, the congressman will like it—and he then has an interest in what you're doing. There are always ways to befriend an individual, and the law on this [in China] is not clear. If you think hard enough about it there is always something you can do to meet the interests of an official. (Pearson, 1997: 114)

Clearly, a fine line exists between the widespread practice of using social connections for personal gain and the exchange of gifts and favors that constitutes bribery.

Although some analysts have argued that a "climate of corruption and insider dealing is pervasive" in many parts of China, the situation appears to be changing.[11] The central government's efforts to establish a functioning legal system and its campaigns to weed out corruption have made it more perilous to use *guanxi* to subvert regulations and thereby gain financially. A 1995 survey conducted in Shanghai indicates that many Chinese business managers consider it normal practice to use *guanxi*, in the sense of "connections," to conduct business (Guthrie, 1998). However, a number of the 155 survey participants expressed reservations about the use of relationships cultivated by exchanging gifts and favors to get things done (for example, to obtain a government permit or to secure scarce raw materials). While some interviewees felt this use of *guanxi* was on the decline, many indicated that it remained significant, particularly below the municipal level of China's administrative hierarchy.

SAVING AND LOSING FACE

The Chinese concept of "face" has approximate counterparts in Western countries, but (compared to China) face has less influence on the implementation of environmental regulations in the West. The Chinese interpretation of face, which is complex and multifaceted, plays an important role in defining an individual's standing within a group or community.

The Concept of Face In China

Face has two aspects for the Chinese: moral authority and accomplishments. As indicated by the excerpt below, face can be characterized as a form of social currency.

Loss of face, and particularly of moral authority, is deeply threatening, and through long processes of socialization Chinese people are taught to build and protect it. Because of its salience as social currency, it is a matter for open discussion, comment and comparison, and an important part of the system of status ascription. (Redding, 1996: 320)

An examination of the numerous ways in which face is gained and lost within China is well beyond the scope of this book. Some indication of how face is exchanged is given by the following informal rules from a recent book intended to assist foreigners living in China.

- A direct rebuttal of one person's statement or claim, especially in front of others, can cause loss of face [for the person rebutted].
- Putting someone on the spot is almost always taken as a loss of face for the party involved [i.e., the person on the spot].
- Failure to follow traditional custom, especially as regards a display [e.g., giving an appropriate wedding gift] . . . is often directly seen as a loss of face.
- Anything which might lead to a very good or positive impression, especially as regards a display of power, connections, generosity, etc. is generally viewed as getting face. (Hartzell, 1988: 321, 323, and 326)

Gaining face is related to enhancing dignity and honor, and losing face is akin to being embarrassed or shamed, but relationships between these English words and the Chinese concept of face are imprecise.[12]

In China, much significance is attached to the integrity of social networks, such as those existing in work units, and face-saving behaviors play an important role in maintaining this integrity. Causing a member of one's network to lose face can be very disruptive. Maintaining harmony in relationships is important to the Chinese, and they sometimes go to great lengths to avoid causing others to lose face. Because environmental agency personnel often have social relationships with managers of enterprises they regulate, interactions between environmental regulators and enterprise managers can involve behaviors intended to prevent losses of face.

Causing Loss of Face Can Impede Environmental Protection

Face-saving behavior in the context of EPB-enterprise interactions is illustrated by a case in which fishermen complained to an EPB about fish kills in a stream being polluted by a weaving and dyeing factory in Shenzhen City (Guangdong Province).[13] When Shenzhen EPB staff went to the factory to investigate, factory managers said one of their pipes had ruptured and the mishap had caused a release of untreated wastewater. However, while at the factory, EPB personnel noticed a permanently installed pipe that discharged untreated wastewater directly to the river. Using this pipe allowed the factory to bypass its wastewater treatment plant, thereby saving on costs of operating the plant.

When questioned about the extraordinary practice of releasing wastewater without sending it through the factory's treatment plant, managers claimed "they were unaware of this discharge and that it had resulted from a blocked pipe to the wastewater treatment works" (Sinkule and Ortolano, 1995: 109). Even though Shenzhen EPB personnel were completely unpersuaded by this explanation, they did not challenge the factory managers' story. If the managers had been put on the spot by a direct challenge, the risk of causing them to lose face would have been high. Eventually, Shenzhen EPB forced the factory to improve its environmental performance significantly, but it did so without challenging the unconvincing story about the blockage in the pipe to the treatment plant.

Another illustration of the way face-saving behavior can influence the implementation of environmental regulations is given by an American journalist with lengthy experience in China:

> many citizens do not want to get involved in reporting illegal factories or taking a strong stand in . . . forcing them to cease operations, even when noise, health, sanitation, and other environmental laws are being broken. This is because they do not want the businessmen or employees to lose face. They often feel that if they cause trouble then they themselves lose face as well. . . . [T]he Chinese idea of conducting oneself in a proper manner is much more concerned with saving face for all those involved in a dispute than in determining each party's legal position. (Hartzell, 1988: 344)

Winning Environmental Awards Enhances Face

Environmental awards can foster pollution abatement because winning them enhances face. This is demonstrated by Kimberley Warren's analysis of pollution prevention at "Red Star," an SOE in Qingdao City (Shandong Province) that manufactures equipment parts for the military.[14] At Red Star, materials recycling and other pollution prevention measures were more sophisticated than at any of the other eight factories in Warren's analysis. Two factors explained Red Star's high motivation to prevent pollution: (1) the prospect of increasing profits, and (2) the desire to win the "Armed Forces Clean Factory Award." Each year Qingdao EPB works with the Navy and Army departments in Qingdao to host an environmental competition between military facilities. The Clean Factory Award has become a prestigious designation, one strongly coveted by many of Qingdao's military units. Despite intense competition, Red Star has won the award for several consecutive years. Managers at Red Star felt that winning the award was a great honor and they did not want to lose it.

The significance of environmental prizes in stimulating factory cleanup extends well beyond the case of Red Star in Qingdao. In our survey of seventy-six enterprises in Anyang, Changzhou, and Shunde, we found that environmental managers at more than half those enterprises felt that government awards for compliance with environmental regulations would be an effective technique for encouraging enterprises to meet environmental goals. The prospect of winning an environmental prize and thereby increasing face for company staff is an important motivation for many factory leaders.

Face-Saving Behavior and Information Flows

When unpleasant information must be reported, the Chinese commonly use round-about ways of speaking to allow all affected parties to save face. This practice affects flows of information between EPBs and SEPA. In reports to SEPA regarding the effectiveness of its policies, EPB staff may leave out negative opinions to avoid causing SEPA staff to lose face.

We learned of this practice of omitting criticism from reports in a meeting we organized with ten EPB staff in one of our case study cities. The meeting was held to discuss problems in implementing the discharge permit system. During the meeting, it became evident that many of the staff's problems with the permit system were omitted from the EPB's reports to NEPA (the predecessor to SEPA) summarizing the EPB's experience with permits. As one EPB official put it,

> NEPA staff who were responsible for designing the discharge permit system may not know the practice here [i.e., in our city]; they should come to see the real world. (Interview No. 52893)

When one of us asked why the EPB staff did not include their problems with the permit system's design in their reports to NEPA, those present at the meeting laughed, and one EPB official responded by saying, "You are Chinese, so you should know why." His meaning was unmistakable: the EPB withheld criticism of the permit system to avoid causing the system's designers to lose face.

While SEPA staff may be deprived of accurate information about their policies in formal EPB reports, they may learn of EPB difficulties with policies indirectly, via more traditional Chinese approaches to offering criticism. In some settings—particularly private conversations after a meeting or at an informal dinner—EPB staff may offer accurate criticism of SEPA policies. Even in these contexts, circumlocutions would generally be employed. By being indirect, EPB staff can offer criticism without causing anyone to lose face.

Linkages between Face and *Guanxi*

Face is linked to *guanxi* in the following sense: when a person makes a positive, face-enhancing gesture in relation to another, the *guanxi* between the individuals can be strengthened.[15] The example below demonstrates how an EPB's innovative solution to a problem encountered by enterprises simultaneously increased the EPB's face and improved the bureau's *guanxi* with the enterprises.

A suburban district EPB in Changzhou learned that three enterprises were operating wastewater treatment plants without adding chemicals needed to treat their waste. Because the EPB often conducted inspections without analyzing wastewater samples, factories could operate plants without adding chemicals for months before the practice would be detected.[16] Soon after identifying this problem, the EPB learned of its cause: a market shortage existed for two chemicals the factories needed for waste treatment (aluminum chloride and ferrous sulfate), and the price of these chemicals had increased sharply. Moreover, factories had trouble locating the chemicals, and often the chemicals they could purchase were of poor quality.

Instead of punishing the enterprises for discharging untreated wastewater, the EPB solved the underlying problem: the absence of high-quality, reasonably-priced, and easily-obtainable treatment chemicals. The EPB located a dependable chemical supplier and made bulk purchases of high-quality aluminum chloride and ferrous sulfate. After making the purchases, the EPB sold the chemicals to eleven enterprises that needed them. Because the EPB purchased in bulk, it obtained a low price, which it passed on to the enterprises. In addition, the EPB negotiated a deal in which the supplier agreed to deliver the chemicals directly to each of the enterprises.[17] Soon after the purchasing program went into effect, the quality of effluents improved at the eleven factories.

The suburban district EPB in Changzhou gained face because of its accomplishment in arranging to supply enterprises with chemicals. The vice director of one of the factories praised the EPB's work: "This program has reduced our efforts to purchase chemicals. We feel the EPB is helpful, and we want to do a better job in controlling pollution. We should have more programs like this one" (Interview No. 120893a).

In addition to gaining face, the EPB also strengthened its *guanxi* with the enterprises. EPB staff we interviewed felt the chemical purchasing program improved their relationships with participating factories. They also felt that managers at most of the eleven factories would be more cooperative in exchanging information and reducing pollution (Interview No. 122093). The chemical purchasing program yielded an additional benefit. By keeping track of the amount of chemicals purchased, the EPB could easily identify enterprises operating treatment plants without adding chemicals (Interview No. 120893b).

RESOLVING DISPUTES AND INTERPRETING LAWS

We continue our analysis of informal rules by examining, more systematically, how respect for authority, *guanxi*, and face affect procedures for settling conflicts.

Mediation and Conciliation Instead of Adjudication

In China, parties in dispute prefer to resolve their differences using informal negotiations in which compromises are made by opposing sides in the interest of reaching a consensus[18] Third parties often facilitate conflict resolution by means of *mediation* and *conciliation*. These two approaches differ:

> mediation implies a more active role on the part of the intermediary in terms of proposing compromise solutions to the parties for their voluntary acceptance.

> Conciliation by contrast implies an effort by the intermediary to reduce friction be-
> tween the parties to the dispute so they themselves can reach an amicable solution,
> without the intermediary proposing the solution. In China, the process clearly tends
> toward the mediation side of the continuum. (Ross, 1989: 30)

Legal institutions have become increasingly significant in China, but mediation
and conciliation continue to be important, particularly in the context of environmental policy implementation.

Following Lester Ross (1989: 15–18), an expert on Chinese environmental law
and policy, we offer three explanations for the reliance on intermediaries to settle
disputes outside of the judicial system. First, the Confucian tradition emphasizes
moral values and moral instruction (not fear of legal sanctions) as a basis for
guiding behavior and maintaining social order.[19] Second, the Chinese Communist Party has long viewed the legal system as a means to implement state policy,
not as a basis for articulating and guaranteeing the rights of citizens.[20] Under the
circumstances, ordinary citizens had little reason to look to the courts for help
in safeguarding their rights.[21] Third, and finally, the Chinese legal system is un-
derdeveloped. Few statutes existed before 1979, and because little legal education took place in the 1960s and 1970s, well trained judges have been in short
supply. Legal specialists point to the following additional inadequacies: judicial
ignorance of the law, corruption within the judicial system, pressures on judges
from local government and CCP officials, and the inability of courts to enforce
their own judgments (Clarke, 1991: 257–268).

Beginning in the 1980s, there has been increased use of the courts to resolve
disputes, particularly economic disputes. Notwithstanding the rising importance
of the legal system, most conflicts related to environmental protection are settled
without going to court.[22] There are several reasons for this: most EPBs do not
have legally trained staff, vaguely drafted statutes often make it difficult to allocate responsibility and liability, legal procedures are not well developed, and
substantial resources can be required to prepare cases for trial. Moreover, EPB
staff and enterprise managers know that going to court will place severe strains
on their future relationships. They often consider it more appropriate to resolve
disputes in the traditional way, with each side making concessions in order to
reach a workable compromise.

Deciding Factors: Affection, Reason, Law, and CCP Policy

Even when courts are used, the letter of the law is typically just one of several
factors considered in enforcing environmental rules. Recent research on how
Chinese judges resolve contract disagreements illuminates how factors other than
the law affect judicial decisions. In one study, economic court judges in Shanghai and Tianjin were asked what they considered in deciding contract disputes.[23]
Some judges responded by citing the following adage: "*Heqing, Heli, Hefa* which

translates as 'according to people's feelings or affection, according to propriety or reason, according to law'" (Cheng and Rosett, 1991: 224). Most economic court judges interviewed in the study felt that a rigid insistence on the precise terms of a contract was not the best enforcement approach. Instead, the letter of the law "must be softened by deference to the relationship of the party and the moral demands of accommodation" (Cheng and Rosett, 1991: 225).

A similar investigation of judicial decision making concluded that Chinese laws and regulations served largely as "decisional guides." The study found that courts decided cases by relying on CCP policy, the views of the local government, and "a court's individual sense of justice and fairness in contractual dealings" (Chang, 1989: 138).

The tendency of judges to balance the letter of the law with other factors is consistent with the approach often followed by EPBs in enforcing regulations. Factors such as *guanxi* between EPB staff and enterprise managers, interventions by local officials, and an enterprise's profitability often lead to outcomes that depart substantially from those specified in environmental regulations.

The enforcement of wastewater discharge standards at pharmaceutical factories in Shenyang City (Liaoning Province) illustrates how contextual factors affect the interpretation of rules. In Shenyang, the regulatory limit on chemical oxygen demand in wastewater from pharmaceutical factories is typically 150 mg/l, but most local pharmaceutical companies routinely discharge more than three times that much. Katherine Kao Cushing interviewed several officials at Shenyang EPB to clarify why violations of the 150 mg/l COD standard at pharmaceutical plants were routinely ignored. EPB staff felt it would be unreasonable to require enterprises to incur the high cost of renovating their production and treatment facilities in order to meet the 150 mg/l limit. A remark by one of Cushing's interviewees clarifies this point:

> The economic and technical conditions of the industry are very difficult. They use all kinds of treatment equipment . . . but the [COD concentration in the] effluent is still very high. . . . So you can see that their situation is very difficult . . . this is a headache for me because there is no way they can meet the [150 mg/l COD waste-water discharge] standards. You want them to meet the standards, but it is impossible for them. (Shenyang EPB officials as quoted by Cushing, 1998: 150)

Shenyang EPB considered factors unrelated to the law—waste treatment efforts already being made and the cost burden that would be imposed by additional treatment—in allowing pharmaceutical factories to violate discharge standards.

Ambiguity Allows Flexibility in Interpreting Laws

The vagueness of many Chinese environmental statutes offers judges and environmental regulators flexibility. At the national level, a law typically includes only broad policy statements. Key terms are often left undefined and precise targets are generally not specified. Ambiguities in Chinese environmental statutes are illustrated by the following statement, which appears in several national laws: "If regulations are violated, an environmental protection bureau should impose sanctions based on the seriousness of the violation."[24] This provision includes no details regarding types of violations, and it makes no reference to minimum or maximum values for penalties. An EPB can use its own judgment to decide on the timing and severity of sanctions.

A rationale for keeping national laws ambiguous was offered by the director of the NPC's Judicial Committee in 1985. The director argued that excessively specific laws would "tie our hands and feet in the face of the rapidly changing situation" (Wang Hanbin as quoted by Gao, 1989: 113). When statutes are vague they also allow local decision makers to account for particular circumstances during implementation. China occupies an enormous land area and its cities and counties vary in terms of topography, climate, natural resources, and levels of economic development. Each area has its own features and problems.

The vagueness of national edicts allows local governments to interpret them in ways that are as consistent as possible with local objectives. The Chinese even have a common saying, "national policies, local countermeasures," to describe the practice of exploiting the ambiguity of national laws and regulations to figure out ways around them.[25] The ability to interpret vague laws and regulations in different ways is also what allows individuals with extensive *guanxi* networks to influence greatly how regulations are implemented.

As detailed in Chapter 2, lower levels of government are expected to issue their own regulations to implement national environmental statues. After analyzing several cases of moving from a national law to local regulations, one student of Chinese law characterized the end result as follows:

> law is treated as only a flexible guideline that sets the parameters within which administrative discretionary lawmaking authority can be practiced. Administrative organs are thus free to reinterpret laws as they see fit, either to reflect department [or agency] policy or to reflect the conditions of local reality. (Corne, 1997: 145)

Ambiguity Can Impede Court Enforceability

The ambiguity of China's environmental legislation allows local officials to exercise discretion during implementation, but it also hampers the court enforcement of environmental rules. Problems caused by statutory ambiguity are illustrated by Changzhou EPB's attempt to sue a local chemical company for failing to pay discharge fees of 1.37 million *yuan* for 1992 and 1993.[26] Because of unclear language in laws and regulations establishing the discharge fee system, the EPB could not determine whether grounds for its lawsuit rested on the enterprise's failure to pay the four small pieces or its failure to pay over-standard fees.

Changzhou EPB faced a second problem. According to the Changzhou court that would hear the EPB's case, an inconsistency seemed to exist between national regulations defining the fee system and rules Changzhou EPB developed to implement the national regulations. Because of clouded phrasing in applicable rules and the possible inconsistency between national and local regulations, the Changzhou Court advised the EPB to avoid making a hasty decision on whether to sue the chemical plant.

In the six cities included in our research, EPBs rarely used courts to enforce environmental requirements. This outcome is only partially explained by ambiguities in environmental rules. Many EPBs lack staff members with legal training.[27] In addition, informal rules of appropriate behavior—such as concepts related to respect for authority, *guanxi*, and face—caused many EPBs to favor conciliation over lawsuits.

NOTES

1. For details on the many informal rules of behavior that operate in modern China, see Pye (1981), Lockett (1988), and Ju (1996).

2. The following excerpt characterizes the Confucian view on appropriate relationships between ruler and subjects: "There has never been a situation in which a ruler liked to express good will (*en*) and the people did not like to reciprocate (*li*). There has never been a situation in which people liked to reciprocate and the public business was not carried out fully. And there has never been a situation in which there was objection to the wealth of such a state being in the ruler's warehouses." [Bahm (1969: 152) translating the teachings of Confucius as recorded in *Great Wisdom*]

3. See Jahiel (1994: 109–110) for details on how the new status of China's top environmental agency influenced the conduct and scope of its work.

4. For more on the transformation of NEPA to SEPA, see *China Environmental Review*, 1998, 1(4): 4–5. In 1998, SEPA had approximately 200 members, about two-thirds the number of staff at NEPA before the latter was transformed. This cut was part of the Center's effort to downsize the entire government bureaucracy.

5. For details on *the Methodology*, see Anyang EPB (1989).

6. This case, which involves a diesel engine facility owned by the Qingling Automobile Company, is based on an unpublished report (in Chinese) of the Chongqing Working Group of the China Environment and Development International Cooperation Committee: "A Report of Chongqing's Industrial Pollution Control Strategy and Policy Research" (p. 20). The project cost approximately 595 million *yuan* (about 120 million U.S. dollars using the applicable exchange rate). At that time, Chongqing was within Sichuan Province. It has since been elevated to a municipality that reports directly to the central government.

7. The term "mayor's project" is often used to refer to a project that a mayor follows closely and supports for economic or political reasons. In one province in South Central China, government insiders used the term "leading cadre's project" to refer to a proposed development project in which a mayor asks the local EPB to approve the project without

conducting the required environmental impact assessment. Sometimes, compromise deals are struck whereby the EPB approves the project with the understanding that an EIA will be completed during construction (Interview 60398).

8. The meaning of *guanxi* depends on the context. In many circumstances, *guanxi* is translated as "relationship." For example, to say that the Chongqing mayor has *lingdao-beilingdao guanxi* with the director of the Chongqing Finance Bureau means that these two government officials have a leader-subordinate relationship within the administrative structure of the Chongqing government: the finance bureau director reports to the mayor.

9. A distinction is often made between *guanxi* among family members and "social *guanxi*"; only the latter is considered here.

10. Chapter 7 describes informal visits and other ways that EPBs develop cooperative relationships with regulated enterprises.

11. The quote is from Weidenbaum and Hughes (1996: 144), who provide a summary of problems related to corruption in China. Details on corruption in Guangdong Province, a hot-bed of entrepreneurial activity, are given by Vogel (1989: 409–413).

12. For a comparative analysis of Chinese and American concepts of face, see Hu and Grove (1991: 115–120).

13. This case is from Sinkule and Ortolano (1995: 94 and 109).

14. "Red Star" is a pseudonym; the Red Star case is detailed by Warren (1996: 210–214).

15. The opposite is also possible: causing someone to lose face diminishes *guanxi*.

16. EPB inspectors frequently conducted "walk through inspections" when treatment plants appeared to be operating normally.

17. The factories paid the transportation fees.

18. Shirk (1993: Chapter 5) documents the key role of concensus in the Chinese government bureaucracy.

19. In the Confucian tradition, there is "hostility toward the very concept of law: laws make people cunning, they foster amorality and cynicism, ruthlessness and a perverse spirit of strife and contention" (Leys, 1997: 176). For accounts of the Confucian view of law, see Ch'ü (1961: 226–241) and Cohen (1966: 1208).

20. Between the 1950s and the 1980s, the prevailing policy was that "whenever there was a conflict between law and Party policy, policy took precedence" (Lo, 1995: 46).

21. Citizens rely heavily on People's Mediation Committees to resolve a wide range of conflicts including, for example, disputes related to marriage, inheritance, and house sites. According to Clarke (1991: 294), mediation in China "has come more and more to resemble adjudication. This is both because of the coercive features of mediation and because of the weakness of adjudicatory institutions such as courts."

22. For an overview of aspects of Chinese legal procedures (including criminal law provisions) that pertain to environmental issues, see Zhang and Ferris (1997). See Lubman (1999) for a survey of ongoing legal reforms in China.

23. The study was by Cheng and Rosett (1991: 144); they interviewed numerous participants in contract law in Shanghai and Tianjin in the mid-1980s.

24. For other examples of ambiguity in Chinese laws, see Corne (1997).

25. National policies, local countermeasures is a translation of *shang you zheng ce xi you dui ce*.

26. This attempted court action involves one of our case studies, the C1 Chemical Plant (see Appendix A).

27. EPBs in three of the six cities we studied did not have a single staff member holding a law degree in 1995. Among the six cities, Beijing had the greatest number of EPB lawyers: two out of 113 EPB staff members held law degrees in 1995.

6

Program Design and Compliance

How do the formal rules that constitute the design of a regulatory program affect compliance? We explore this question by analyzing the discharge permit system, a controversial program that has received much less attention than either effluent standards or discharge fees.[1]

China's discharge permit program has been much less effective at reducing pollution than regulators and enterprises expected it to be. Of the seventy-six enterprises we surveyed in the early 1990s, only 9 percent reported that DPS had influenced them significantly in abating pollution, reusing materials, or paying discharge fees.[2] In addition, EPB staff in each of the six cities in our study felt the permit system was far less effective at reducing pollution than the discharge fee program, the three synchronizations policy, or the use of cleanup deadlines. Some EPB staff characterized the discharge permit system as "a mere formality," and as a program that "gives us no power to control pollution."

Although many of the people we interviewed during the early 1990s believed the permit system had not had much effect, opinions differed as to why the program was unsuccessful. Environmental regulators offered three distinct explanations for the program's ineffectiveness. First, enterprises failed to satisfy DPS requirements because the program was established by administrative rules instead of a statute. Second, enterprises did not satisfy permit conditions because EPBs did not enforce the program's rules.[3] Third, rules that defined the permit system were crafted in ways that made the program unworkable.

Which, if any, of these explanations of the permit system's ineffectiveness is valid? The explanation related to the lack of a statutory foundation is unpersuasive. We investigated whether the non-statutory basis of DPS was problematic at 243 enterprises participating in the DPS trial implementation in Anyang, Beijing, Changzhou, and Shunde. None of those enterprises was much affected by the permit system's being based on administrative regulations instead of law. The explanation related to poor enforcement of DPS rules is also unconvincing: 69 percent of the seventy-six enterprises in our survey met their permit requirements, a compliance percentage that is high for China.[4] Our analysis demonstrates that the permit system's ineffectiveness during the early 1990s resulted from problems with the program's rules.

OVERVIEW OF THE DISCHARGE PERMIT SYSTEM

Rationale for Creating the Program

During the late 1980s, NEPA felt a discharge permit system that would limit both concentration and mass flowrate could overcome the following two shortcomings in China's national wastewater discharge standards.[5] First, in some cities national effluent standards had been satisfied, but stream quality continued to drop because no constraints on mass flowrate existed. Second, in other cities watercourses had unused "assimilative capacity;" that is, watercourses could accept additional wastewater discharges without violating ambient water quality standards. NEPA staff who designed DPS felt it was "wasteful" to force enterprises to meet national effluent standards in circumstances where watercourses had the capacity to assimilate additional discharges without violating ambient standards.[6]

To eliminate these two shortcomings, NEPA staff designing the DPS decided not to require the allowable wastewater concentrations in permits to be the same as the national effluent standards. NEPA staff expected that allowable concentrations in permits would be *more* stringent than national effluent standards in areas where ambient water quality continued to deteriorate even though effluent standards were being met. The staff also expected that allowable concentrations in permits would be *less* stringent than effluent standards in areas where the assimilative capacity of receiving waters was not being fully utilized. Assimilative capacity could be put in quantitative terms using water quality models.

Steps in Program Implementation

In 1988, NEPA issued guidance requiring EPBs in cities selected for the DPS trial implementation to issue permits to all large, heavily-polluting enterprises (NEPA, 1988b and 1988c). A permit was to stipulate limits on both mass flowrate *and* concentration of pollutants in an enterprise's effluent.

NEPA prescribed the following four-step DPS implementation procedure:

- *Registration and application.* Each enterprise in the DPS trial implementation registers with the local EPB and completes a permit application that includes the amount and type of pollutants discharged.
- *Allocation of total loads.* Each EPB in the program first determines the total allowable pollution load that can enter local waters; it then distributes this load by stipulating the mass flowrate of pollutants that each enterprise can release.

- *Issuance of permits.* EPBs issue each enterprise a permit, which is good for either two or five years. The former type, called a "temporary permit," is for enterprises incapable of meeting the discharge limits in their permits.
- *Monitoring and enforcement.* Enterprises monitor their waste loads and concentrations and report results to local EPBs. Environmental protection bureaus enforce permit conditions by issuing warnings, imposing fines, and revoking permits.

NEPA allowed EPBs to use their own discretion in establishing requirements for nearly all steps in the implementation process. The one exception is the registration process: the 1989 *PRC Environmental Protection Law* requires all enterprises to register with EPBs.

Inconsistency Between DPS and the Fee Program

When the permit program was introduced, it was inconsistent with the long-standing discharge fee system. Although discharge fees are calculated using concentrations in effluent standards, the permit system is based on both mass flowrates *and* concentrations of contaminants in discharges. Moreover, allowable concentrations in permits can be different from limits in effluent standards. When the restrictions differ, two questions arise. First, which of the two concentration limits should enterprises be required to meet? Second, should the existing, concentration-based fee program be replaced by a new fee system based on allowable concentrations and mass flowrates in permits?

The lack of consistency between pollution limits in discharge permits and effluent standards frustrated many EPB staffs. They felt it would be difficult to implement the permit program without changing the existing fee system, but they also felt powerless to change the fee program because both the effluent standards and the method for calculating fees were specified by law.[7]

NEPA staff who designed the permit system recognized that inconsistencies between the permit and fee programs might obstruct implementation of DPS. Guidance issued by NEPA in 1988 highlighted the problem but left it to EPBs to find their own solutions:

> During DPS implementation, [EPBs] should have the courage to face the challenge of inconsistency between DPS and existing [environmental] policies. Creative experiments are allowed as long as the environmental goals can be achieved at the least-cost. (NEPA, 1988c: 21)

We describe some of the "creative experiments" EPBs have undertaken in the final section of this chapter. As of the summer of 1999, NEPA had not issued new DPS guidelines to eliminate inconsistencies between the permit and fee programs. However, changes to eliminate the inconsistencies were expected to be made during implementation of the *National Plan for Total Amount Control of the Main Pollutants Discharged during the Ninth Five-Year Plan Period* (see Chapter 2).

DETERMINATION OF PERMIT CONDITIONS

In general, discharge permit systems require environmental regulators to tackle a difficult question: How can limits on enterprises' mass flowrates and concentrations of pollutants be set such that ambient water quality goals are attained? We contend that the formal rules defining DPS allowed EPBs to sidestep the question, and to negotiate outcomes with enterprises that allowed many permit holders to meet permit conditions without reducing pollution. Our analysis demonstrates that the following two expectations of NEPA staff who designed DPS were not met: the staff assumed that (1) concentration limits in permits would be more rigorous than national effluent standards in areas where water quality continued to deteriorate even though effluent standards were being satisfied, and (2) concentration limits in permits would only be less stringent than national effluent standards in areas where watercourses could assimilate additional waste without violating ambient water quality standards. We show that permit conditions were often so lax they had little effect in reducing pollution in the six cities we studied. We also demonstrate that modeling guidance NEPA issued to help EPBs determine allowable waste discharges was so complex that many EPBs ignored it.

Lack of Stringency in Permit Conditions

EPBs have generally used either a goal-based or a capacity-based approach to establish permit conditions (Zhu et al., 1991). Using a capacity-based scheme, an EPB must first use water quality models to determine the receiving water's *assimilative capacity*; the latter consists of the total pollution load a water body can receive without falling below ambient water quality standards. Once the total load that just meets ambient standards is calculated, that load is divided among enterprises. As we demonstrate later in this section, this capacity-based approach was too complex for many EPBs. Indeed, only Shanghai and a few other municipalities used it.

Most cities adopted the goal-based approach, and they often used the following modest goal: maintain wastewater releases at existing levels while allowing industries to expand. To implement the goal-based approach, EPBs often set permit conditions based on the actual concentrations and flowrates released by enterprises as specified in their initial permit applications.

Permit conditions were frequently based on case-by-case negotiations between EPBs and enterprises. Since most enterprises in the cities we studied did not meet national effluent standards when DPS was initiated, allowable pollutant concentrations in permits were often less rigorous than concentration limits in effluent standards.[8] This meant enterprises could satisfy permit conditions even when they violated effluent standards. For enterprises that had satisfied effluent standards before DPS was adopted, permit concentrations were at least as strict as the effluent standards. The approach described above was followed in five of the six cities we studied. The exception was Chongqing, which used permits to force enterprises to meet effluent standards.

Next, consider how allowable *mass flowrates* were specified in permits. EPBs in the six cities often determined an enterprise's total allowable pollutant load by multiplying the allowable concentration specified in a permit by the volume flowrate of wastewater reported by the enterprise. In other words, mass flowrate was computed as

$$\text{concentration} \times \text{volume flowrate,}$$

where: mass flowrate = mass of pollutant/time,
concentration = mass of pollutant/volume of wastewater, and
volume flowrate = volume of wastewater/time.

Permits often included relatively lenient concentration limits because EPBs felt that many enterprises lacked the ability to meet effluent standards. The following explanation was typical of what we heard from our interviewees at EPBs:

> Many enterprises were not even meeting the existing [concentration-based national effluent] standards; it was unrealistic for us [refers to the EPB] to require enterprises to meet a more stringent mass-based standard. (Interview No. 121093)

In addition, EPBs often felt that the goal of "increasing industrial production without increasing pollution levels" was more realistic than trying to cut the total pollution load, given the rapid economic growth taking place in the early 1990s. Moreover, many EPBs felt they could tighten up permit conditions gradually as permits came up for renewal.

Low Influence of the DPS on Pollution Reduction Decisions

Our case studies provide additional insights into how EPBs set permit limits. Table 6.1 contains allowable concentrations of chemical oxygen demand (COD) in the permits of eight case study enterprises that failed to meet effluent standards when their permits were issued. We focus on COD because environmental officials in China use it as the key indicator of water pollution consisting of organic matter. As shown in the table, the maximum allowable COD concentration in a permit can be much higher than 200 mg/l, the highest COD limit specified (for enterprises) in the national effluent standards.

For five of the eight enterprises, COD concentrations in permit applications decreased over time. For instance, when B1 Brewery applied for its permit in

Table 6.1   COD Concentrations in Permits for Eight Enterprises[a]

City	Enterprise	Year(s) of of Permit Validity	COD Concentration in Permit Application[b] (mg/l)	Allowable COD Concentration in Permit (mg/l)
Anyang	A2 Chemical	1989–90	2,945	980
	Fiber Plant	1991–92	1,895	950
	A3 Paper Mill	1989–90	7,718	3,147
		1991–92	2,852	2,852
Beijing	B1 Brewery	1990–91	3,700	3,700
		1992	1,331	1,331
		1993	500	500
	B2 Eastern	1989–91	310	310
	Chemical Works	1992–95	331	331
Changzhou	C1 Chemical	1989–90	650	650
	Plant	1991–92	780	780
	C2 Chemical	1989	1,500	1,500
	Works	1990–92	950	950
	C3 Printing and	1989	1,052	1,052
	Dyeing Plant	1990	240	240
		1991–92	500	500
Shunde	S3 Dyeing	1990	280	210
	Company	1991–92	360	250

[a]Of the twelve case study enterprises included in our research, COD limits in discharge permits for the eight enterprises above were less stringent than national effluent standards. Three of the four other enterprises had already met effluent standards, and data was not available for the fourth.

[b]This represents the maximum COD specified in an enterprise's permit application for the initial year of a permit's validity.

1993, it listed a maximum COD of 500 mg/l, which was much lower than the target the brewery applied for in both 1990 (3,700 mg/l) and 1992 (1,331 mg/l). When we asked the brewery's managers why they decided to reduce their COD, they told us the cuts were called for by the three synchronizations policy. As explained in Chapter 2, an enterprise expanding production capacity must synchronize the design, construction, and operation of its expansion with the design, construction, and operation of its waste treatment facilities.

In 1990, B1 Brewery decided to augment its annual beer production capacity from 50,000 tons to 110,000 tons. To meet three synchronizations' requirements, the brewery began building a wastewater treatment plant containing a biochemical oxidation unit. The plant started operating in 1992. A year later, the treatment plant was able to attain an effluent COD of 500 mg/l, and this is why the brewery listed a COD of 500 mg/l in its 1993 permit application. When asked whether the discharge permit program had affected their decision to abate pollution, managers at the brewery responded as follows:

> The [Beijing] EPB almost always approved what we applied for [in terms of] the allowable pollution discharge in the permit. . . . They [refers to the EPB] still monitor concentration, but they rarely monitor wastewater flow. There has not been any punishment for violations of DPS. . . . The permit seems just like a "certificate of merit" to be hung on the wall. (Interview No. 51393)

In short, the permit system had no effect on the brewery's decision to decrease its COD concentration.

Several of our other case studies were analogous to B1 Brewery in the following sense: enterprises cut pollution primarily in response to the three synchronizations policy, but not the permit system. Of the eight enterprises in Table 6.1, five applied for successive permits in which the COD concentration decreased over time. Of these, three (B1 Brewery, C1 Chemical Plant, and C3 Printing and Dyeing Plant) released less waste because of the three synchronizations program. One of the five (A3 Paper Mill) lowered pollution for reasons unrelated to pollution abatement efforts: the mill discharged less waste only because it slashed its total output. Only one enterprise—A2 Chemical Fiber Plant—lowered pollution because of the discharge permit program, and in this case the influence of the DPS was only partial.

The pollution cutback at A2 Chemical Fiber Plant resulted from the combined influence of DPS *and* the discharge fee program. In response to problems caused by inconsistencies in concentrations used in the fee and permit systems, Anyang EPB revised completely its basis for calculating fees in 1989. As a result, A2 Chemical Fiber Plant faced a 35 percent rise in discharge fees for 1990 (an annual increase of about 100,000 *yuan*), and this was a key incentive for the plant to decrease pollution.

As Table 6.1 suggests, EPBs in Beijing and Changzhou generally set allowable COD concentrations in permits based on concentrations listed by enterprises in their permit applications. The same holds for these EPBs' decisions on permitted COD loads (that is, mass flow-rates). Table 6.2 compares COD loads in permit applications with those in permits for the same eight enterprises in Table 6.1. In all but one instance (B1 Brewery in 1989–91), the allowable COD loads of factories in Beijing and Chongzhou were identical to the allowable loads the enterprises asked for.[9] According to EPB staff we interviewed in Beijing and Chongzhou, those EPBs typically approved the concentrations and mass flowrates enterprises requested in permit applications.

EPBs in Anyang and Shunde set COD limits in permits below what applicants applied for. The quantity the Anyang and Shunde EPBs subtracted from the COD in a permit application depended upon the applicant's profitability and the nature of its production technology. EPBs and enterprises negotiated the targets in permits.

Table 6.2   COD Mass Flowrates in Permits for Eight Enterprises

City	Enterprise	Year(s) of of Permit Validity	COD LOAD in Permit Application (ton/yr)	Allowable COD Load in Permit (ton/yr)
Anyang	A2 Chemical Fiber	1989–90	4,297	4,178
	Plant	1991–92	3,630	3,630
	A3 Paper Mill	1989–90	3,981	3,981
		1991–92	2,671	2,671
Beijing	B1 Brewery	1989–91	1,490	1,350
		1992	1,578	1,578
		1993	1,020	1,020
	B2 Eastern	1989–91	627	627
	Chemical Works	1992–95	1,029	1,029
Changzhou	C1 Chemical Plant	1989–90	880	880
		1991–92	798	798
	C2 Chemical	1989	1,269	1,269
	Works	1990–92	1,170	1,170
	C3 Printing and	1989	1,760	1,760
	Dyeing Plant	1990	896	896
		1991–92	1,038	1,038
Shunde	S3 Dyeing	1990	210	130
	Company	1991–92	231	157
		1993	616	216

Difficulty of Using Models to Allocate Waste Loads

NEPA's modeling guidance on how to distribute total allowable pollutant discharges among enterprises was not used by any of the six cities in our study. According to the *Several Suggestions for Trial Implementation of DPS* issued in 1988, the allocation of total load was to be carried out using mathematical optimization procedures (NEPA, 1988c). NEPA issued a follow-up *Technical Manual for Controlling the Total Amount of Pollution Discharges* (referred to here as the *Technical Manual*) to help EPBs carry out two key tasks:

(1) determine the total allowable pollutant discharge into a water body, and
(2) allocate that total among enterprises.

The *Technical Manual* includes a three-step procedure to determine the total allowable pollutant load. First, a river is divided into several sections; for each section, ambient water quality goals are based on water uses to be protected (e.g., drinking water and irrigation). Second, mathematical models are used to calculate the total allowable load into a river section; this load is the maximum mass flowrate of pollutant satisfying ambient water quality goals specified in the first step.[10] Third, mathematical optimization procedures are employed to calculate how the total allowable load should be distributed among dischargers in each of the river sections to minimize pollution abatement costs while still meeting ambient water quality goals. Step 2 represents a quantification of assimilative capacity, and step 3 consists of allocating portions of that capacity to individual dischargers.

Limitations of the Modeling Approach

In the early stages of DPS implementation, NEPA staff visited EPBs in Anyang and Shunde to run water quality and optimization models for those EPBs. However, neither of the bureaus used the modeling results to issue permits. An EPB staff member in charge of issuing permits explained why:

> It is not realistic for us to use those [water quality and optimization] models for issuing permits. Those mathematical models are too theoretical. We need to consider many practical factors to make decisions about permits. (Interview No. 51894)

Another EPB staff member pointed to the excessive complexity of models in the *Technical Manual*. He felt that his bureau could "determine clean-up objectives and allocate pollution loads [to enterprises] in a much simpler way" (Interview No. 120393).

During a meeting we organized at one EPB office to discuss the permit system, an EPB official offered the following explanation for why models were not used to allocate total allowable loads among enterprises:

> NEPA staff came here to guide us in running the mathematical models, but many alternative pollution control plans [used in] operating the models were determined theoretically by NEPA and EPB staff, not by the enterprises themselves. Thus the outputs of those models are not workable. Moreover, our own [EPB] staff does not exactly understand those models. (Interview No. 52893)

A provincial EPB official at the meeting added the following point:

> We don't have good models. Even if we can develop some good models, it is doubtful that we can obtain all the data we need to run those models. . . . There is still a long way to go to establish appropriate models and use those models in implementing DPS. (Interview No. 72595)

In summary, EPBs offered three reasons for why they did not use models in the *Technical Manual* to allocate pollution loads. First, they distrusted the models; even if appropriate models could be provided, EPBs often lacked data to run the models. Second, few EPBs had staff trained in using mathematical models. Third, optimization models themselves are too narrowly focused; EPBs consider other factors, such as an enterprise's financial status, in determining allowable waste loads.

Waste Load Allocation Difficulties Faced by Jinan

An extreme case demonstrating difficulties in allocating waste loads is given by Jinan, a city in Shandong Province that discontinued its trial implementation of the DPS. In 1990, Jinan EPB issued its first round of permits to the thirty enterprises initially selected for the DPS trial implementation. In 1993, the EPB issued permits to another twelve enterprises. Unlike the other five EPBs included in our study, Jinan EPB did not reissue any permits, nor did it require the original thirty enterprises receiving permits to apply for new ones. Moreover, Jinan EPB did not penalize enterprises for violating permit conditions. As of 1995, the permit system in Jinan had "ceased to exist except in name" (Interview No. 73195).

The failure of the DPS in Jinan was tied directly to difficulties in calculating total allowable waste loads. Unlike other cities participating in the trial implementation, Jinan and Zibo (another city in the upper Xiaoqing River basin) could not distribute allowable loads to enterprises until they received a total load allocation from Shangdong Province EPB. The provincial EPB was responsible for determining the total allowable load for the upper Xiaoqing River basin and for dividing that load between the two cities. EPBs in Jinan and Zibo then divided their load allocations among enterprises in their cities.

Jinan discontinued its implementation of DPS mainly because Shangdong EPB did not give it a total discharge allocation after the first-round permits expired (Interview No. 73195a). In explaining the difficulties in coming up with total loads for Jinan and Zibo, an official from Shangdong EPB cited the need to "use several scientific methods to calculate and allocate allowable loads; this involved considerable administrative work" (Interview No. 73195b). Although the failure to continue the permit system in Jinan is an extreme out-come, it demonstrates how regulatory schemes requiring burdensome calculation procedures can overwhelm EPBs.

INCONSISTENCIES BETWEEN DPS AND THE FEE PROGRAM

We conclude our analysis of formal DPS rules by examining how EPBs and enterprises responded to inconsistencies between the fee and permit systems. Fees are based on concentration-based effluent standards, whereas permits limit both mass flowrates and concentrations. An inconsistency problem arises when concentration limits in permits are different from those in effluent standards. Below we examine how five of the six cities included in our study responded to this inconsistency problem.[11] Our analysis demonstrates the discretion local governments have in responding to national environmental rules.

Beijing Enterprises Object to a Dual System

Beijing EPB dealt with the inconsistency problem by retaining its original discharge fee system and creating a new enforcement program to deal with permit violations. Enterprises not participating in the DPS trial implementation were unaffected by the new enforcement scheme; they paid fees only if they violated effluent standards. The following "dual system" of enforcement applied to enterprises participating in the DPS trial. Enterprises violating effluent standards but satisfying permit limits paid only discharge *fees*, whereas those violating permit conditions while meeting effluent standards paid only *fines*. However, enterprises violating both effluent standards and permit conditions paid *both* fees and fines. EPBs in Jinan, Changzhou, and Shunde created similar dual systems.

In 1989, Beijing EPB prepared a *Trial Methodology of the DPS Management in Beijing* (referred to here as *the Methodology*), which authorizes the EPB to respond to permit violations by issuing warnings or, in serious cases, imposing fines. However, as of 1994, Beijing EPB had not imposed any such fines because the Beijing Municipal People's Government had not approved *the Methodology*, and thus no legal basis existed for imposing fines (Interview No. 72791). An EPB official explained why the government had not approved *the Methodology*:

> The procedure of [legal document] approval is very complicated, and the Beijing Municipal Administration Commission has quotas each year for the number of regulations or legal documents to be approved. Ours [refers to *the Methodology*] has to be in line in order of importance from the point of view of the Commission. [The Beijing government will not issue a legal document that has not been approved by the Commission.] However, we did not push that hard because we felt there are some problems with the permit system we have not yet solved, mainly the inconsistency between the permit system and the discharge fee system. . . . Some enterprises argued that they should not be charged for both pollution discharge fees and DPS fines. We are worried that this might cause us problems in implementing the permit system. (Interview No. 72791)

Our interviews with enterprise managers in Beijing clarified the EPB's concerns about the difficulty of imposing both fees for failing to meet effluent standards and fines for violating permit conditions. One manager summarized the problem as follows:

> You [refers to the EPB] can charge me [refers to the enterprise] with either pollution discharge fees or fines for DPS [violations]. You should not charge me twice. . . . We have been meeting the permit conditions, but we are still required to pay discharge fees. We do not understand the role of the permit system. Why do we need it? (Interview No. 20693)

This manager and others we interviewed questioned the necessity of having two distinct systems of enforcement, one based on discharge fees and another based on permits.

Jinan's Problems with the Dual System

As in Beijing, the EPB in Jinan set up a dual system involving fees for violations of effluent standards and fines for permit infractions. If infringements of permit conditions were serious, the EPB could revoke permits. The EPB's implementation approach is detailed in the *Methodology of the DPS Management in Jinan* (JMPG, 1990), an EPB document that Jinan Municipal People's Government approved in 1990.

As previously noted, Jinan EPB stopped issuing new permits in 1995 because it had not received a total allowable waste load allocation from Shangdong Province EPB. However, even when the permit system was being implemented during the early 1990s, Jinan EPB had difficulties with it, primarily because of excessive monitoring and administrative work. A Jinan EPB staff member highlighted the problems:

> We intended to use fines to enforce DPS, but we found it difficult [to employ fines]. This [refers to the imposition of fines in response to permit violations] involves a tremendous monitoring task, since we must measure both concentrations and wastewater flows to compute the total quantity of pollutants being discharged. The lack of instruments to measure wastewater flow is also a big problem. Without monitoring data, we do not have evidence needed to fine enterprises. (Interview No. 73195)

Another Jinan EPB staff member complained about the considerable "administrative burden" involved to "impose both fees based on effluent standards and fines based on permit conditions" (Interview No. 73195).

Jinan was not the only city troubled by the lack of instruments for measuring wastewater flowrates. EPB staff in each of the other five cities included in our study commented frequently on difficulties caused by a lack of reliable flow monitoring devices. This equipment is in short supply because, prior to DPS, both EPBs and enterprises only measured pollutant concentrations. Few enterprises had flow meters when DPS was introduced. As part of the DPS trial implementation, EPBs in many cities required selected enterprises to install meters to monitor wastewater releases. Although about twenty types of flow meters had been developed and used in the DPS trial implementation, approximately two thirds of them were dropped because of problems with installation or repairs. As of the late-1990s, high quality, reliable instruments for measuring wastewater flows were not available for purchase in many places.[12]

Changzhou's Controversial New Fee Calculation Method

Changzhou EPB also adopted a dual system of fines and fees to deal with inconsistencies between the permit and fee systems. Unlike Beijing and Jinan, where fines for permit infractions existed only in principle (as of 1994), Changzhou EPB exercised its authority to fine enterprises. The EPB was also successful in reissuing permits. How did Changzhou EPB manage to handle the monitoring and enforcement difficulties that plagued EPBs in Beijing and Jinan?

To reduce the monitoring and administrative burdens of its dual system of enforcement, Changzhou EPB developed an innovative fee assessment procedure. Instead of calculating fees based on monitoring data, the EPB computed over-standard discharge fees based on allowable pollutant concentrations in enterprises' permits. Using this scheme, Changzhou EPB could compute discharge fees without measuring concentrations of contaminants.

Under the new fee calculation procedure, monitoring served primarily to discover permit infractions. If monitoring indicated permit conditions were met, an enterprise paid no fine. However, the enterprise was required to pay a discharge fee if allowable concentrations in its permit violated effluent standards. The concentration limits in permits were often the values enterprises listed as actual concentrations in their permit applications.

If monitoring data revealed a permit violation, an enterprise faced a penalty with two parts: (1) double the over-standard fee if monitoring data showed the enterprise violated allowable *concentrations* in its permit; and (2) a once-a-year fine for exceeding the allowable *quantity* of pollutant discharge (in tons per year) specified in the permit.[13] This innovative approach to calculating fees and fines allowed Changzhou EPB to cut back on monitoring needed to enforce both DPS and the fee program.

Changzhou EPB also hoped its new approach to calculating fees and fines would discourage enterprises from misrepresenting amounts of pollutants listed in permit applications. The EPB assumed that enterprises would not *overstate* concentrations in their applications because this would force them to pay greater over-standard fees than necessary. Enterprises also had a disincentive to *under-state* concentrations in permit applications. If an enterprise understated its concentrations, it ran the risk of being fined if EPB monitoring revealed a permit infraction.

Despite the expectations of Changzhou EPB, many enterprises overstated their pollution releases when they applied for permits. One enterprise manager clarified the incentive to overstate concentrations:

> We applied for [a permit by listing a load that was] more than we actually discharged. This gave us leeway for future development. Maybe someday we will need to increase our production capacity. Most likely the EPB will not allow us to discharge more pollutant [loads] when we increase our production capacity. However, we can have extra room to discharge more [pollutant loads in the future] if we apply for more than we can use now. Even if we currently have to pay more pollution discharge fees, we think it is worth it. (Interview No. 121393)

This tendency for enterprises to overstate their actual loads was problematic because the total amount of pollution was not being controlled. For example, suppose an enterprise actually released 200 tons of COD annually, but it overstated its COD load by claiming in its permit application to discharge 250 tons per year. In a typical situation, Changzhou EPB would have approved the permit application. In this instance, the enterprise could have made future increases in its annual COD discharge by 50 tons without violating permit conditions.

Some enterprises opposed Changzhou EPB's scheme for calculating discharge fees because it did not use monitoring data to determine discharge fees. For example, one factory manager we interviewed argued as follows:

> Under the new method, we sometimes pay more than we should pay, since no matter how much we actually discharge, the EPB charges us based only on information [specified] in the permit. . . . We should pay if monitoring data show that we do not meet the [effluent] standards. Monitoring is the EPB's job. It [refers to the new method for calculating fees] is unreasonable. (Interview No. 121393)

Changzhou EPB recognized shortcomings of its procedures, but it felt the simplicity of the fee calculation method was needed to reduce the work of monitoring and enforcing the permit system. A Changzhou EPB staff member justified the EPB's position:

> DPS is only one of our jobs. [Because] our monitoring work load was already very heavy before DPS was applied, we had to find some way to implement all environmental programs without increasing our monitoring and administrative work load too much. (Interview No. 121093)

Shunde's Dual System Appears Unfair to Enterprises

Shunde is still another city that adopted a dual system to deal with inconsistencies between the permit and fee systems. An important difference between the system in Shunde and those of other cities we studied concerns the EPB's authority to sanction enterprises violating permit conditions by imposing both a fine (up to 10,000 *yuan*) and a fee equal to three times the over-standard fee.[14]

Unlike Changzhou, where fines were imposed only once a year, Shunde EPB imposed fines once a quarter. In Shunde, the size of a fine was usually negotiated between the EPB and an enterprise. Shunde EPB used its own data to assess discharge fees. However, to decrease its monitoring burden, the EPB relied on enterprises' self-monitoring data to assess fines for permit infractions.

The fairness of Shunde EPB's fines were often challenged by enterprises selected for the DPS trial implementation. They questioned the validity of fines by arguing that enterprises not included in the DPS trial faced no similar penalties. Shunde EPB's director offered a perspective on the subject:

> It is impossible for us to issue discharge permits to the majority of enterprises and then monitor them. Given the tremendous monitoring and administrative work load to implement the discharge permit system, the unfairness issue has to be left unresolved. (Interview No. 52494)

Enterprise managers in the other five cities we studied also complained about the lack of equity in imposing permit requirements on only a subset of enterprises.

Anyang's Mass-Based Discharge Fee Scheme

Anyang EPB responded to incompatibilities in the permit and fee programs by replacing its existing concentration-based discharge fee program with a mass-based scheme. Under the new scheme, enterprises paid fees based on the mass of pollutant discharged (in kilograms) instead of concentration. The new fee system was used only at enterprises participating in the DPS trial.

In 1989, Anyang Municipal People's Government issued a notice that formally approved both Anyang EPB's mass-based fee system and its *Method of Computing Pollution Discharge Fees Based on the Total Amount of Pollutant Discharges* (referred to herein as *the Method*).[15] To ensure a smooth change from the old concentration-based fee system to the new, mass-based fee system, Anyang EPB employed the following constraint: the *increase* in total fees collected under the new scheme could be no more than 30 percent of the total fees collected under the old system (Interview No. 51893). Anyang EPB's new system introduced a fundamental change. Before 1989, enterprises only paid fees if their discharges violated concentration-based effluent standards, and fees were imposed only on the pollutant exceeding the standard by the greatest amount. Using *the Method*, fees were assessed not only on pollutants *violating* permit restrictions but also on pollutants *satisfying* those restrictions.[16] Moreover, instead of charging enterprises for only one pollutant, the new method for calculating fees applied to three pollutants: COD, suspended solids, and oil.

The mass-based fee scheme created by Anyang EPB solved the problem of inconsistency between DPS and the existing fee program. However, some environmental regulators at NEPA and elsewhere felt that Anyang's fee scheme undermined the national effluent standards (Interview No. 121093 and Interview No. 12193). These regulators argued as follows: discharge fees in Anyang are paid only for releases violating permit conditions on *total allowable loads*, not concentrations. Moreover, enterprises that meet permit conditions often do not satisfy effluent standards. Because fees are no longer imposed on violations of effluent standards, enterprises have less incentive to attain them.

FINDINGS RELATED TO DPS DESIGN

Flaws in the design of the permit system were responsible for the system's poor performance during the trial implementation. A root cause of deficiencies in the system was the absence of a rule forcing concentration limits in permits to be at least as stringent as the national effluent standards. Without such a rule, EPBs and enterprises were free to negotiate concentration limits that were equal to levels enterprises were releasing at the time DPS was introduced. Consequently, many firms violated effluent standards though at the same time they satisfied concentration targets in their permits. If, as frequently occurred, limits in an enterprise's initial permit were based on actual wastewater (volume) flowrates and concentrations, the enterprise would satisfy those limits without curbing pollution.

In setting initial permit conditions equal to an enterprise's releases, EPBs were not caving in entirely to industry pressures. Some EPBs took a long-term view and negotiated tighter permit restrictions as permits came up for renewal. However, the best occasions for tightening occurred when enterprises renovated or enlarged their facilities. These were opportune moments because EPBs could invoke the three synchronizations policy to demand new treatment facilities.

Another program design difficulty relates to differences between resources available to EPBs and those required to implement the permit system. For example, many EPBs were unable to use the sophisticated water quality models and mathematical optimization procedures that NEPA offered as the suggested approach to determining allowable discharges from enterprises. In addition to requiring staff with experience in mathematical modeling, the suggested approach required data that was unavailable to many EPBs. Another data problem occurred because EPBs and enterprises often lacked instruments needed to measure wastewater flowrates.

Finally, the use of mass-based requirements in permits was incompatible with the fee system, which relied on concentration-based effluent standards. Although EPBs responded to this inconsistency creatively—in many cases by developing dual systems of enforcement— their responses often led to new problems and caused enterprises to complain that DPS was neither fair nor rational.

We do not mean to suggest that controls on mass flowrates embodied in the permit program are a bad idea. The contrary is true. Restrictions on total pollutant releases are necessary if ambient water quality goals are to be attained. However, as our analysis shows, a mass-based pollution control program can yield disappointing results if it includes modeling procedures that EPBs are unable to implement and yields outcomes that are inconsistent with rules of other environmental programs.

Permit system design problems are certainly not unique to China. Designers of permit programs in all countries face difficulties in forecasting how regulators, enterprises, and others will respond to the rules they create. China's reliance on trial implementations of the DPS and related programs provides opportunities for improving program rules based on implementation outcomes.

NOTES

1. See Jahiel (1994 and 1997) and Sinkule and Ortolano (1995) for analyses of China's discharge standards and fees. Other studies of links between program design and

compliance have been conducted by Sabatier and Mazmanian (1983), Bartel and Thomas (1985), and DiMento (1986).

2. An additional 28 percent of the survey respondents said the DPS had *no* substantive influence on their decisions. The remaining 63 percent of the seventy-six enterprises reported that the permit system had minor or moderate effects. Enterprises took the following actions in response to DPS: writing informative slogans and messages regarding DPS on blackboards in a factory; sending an environmental manager to participate in an EPB's training workshop; explaining the permit system to top-level managers; and installing meters to measure wastewater flowrates.

3. Those advancing the poor enforcement argument point to the EPBs' lack of equipment to monitor wastewater flowrates and the rare use of permit revocations to sanction enterprises violating permit conditions.

4. By comparison, only 36 percent of the seventy-six enterprises we surveyed satisfied effluent standards.

5. Motivations for creating DPS noted in this paragraph are given in NEPA (1988d, and 1993: 14) and Zhu et al. (1991: 4); they were also mentioned in our interviews with NEPA staff who designed the permit system.

6. Another perceived shortcoming of the national effluent standards related to the ability of enterprises to satisfy concentration-based limits by diluting discharges with water instead of reducing waste releases. Dilution only makes sense for enterprises with access to inexpensive water sources. Managers of some enterprises included in our study told us they often diluted waste just before EPB staff came to conduct inspections.

7. Observations in this paragraph are based on our interviews with EPB staffs in six cities. For a general discussion of problems caused by inconsistencies in fee and permit programs, see Bernstein (1993: 11).

8. Our assertion that most enterprises in the six cities violated effluent standards is based on our survey results (see Appendix A); data for Jinan and Chongqing given by Spofford et al. (1996a and 1996b); and NEPA-compiled data reported by enterprises in Beijing (NEPA, 1987 and CEYCC, 1995). These data show compliance rates ranging from 35 percent for Anyang in 1992 to nearly 70 percent for Beijing in 1994. Most of the data show compliance rates between 35 and 45 percent for the 1992–1994 period.

9. When asked to clarify why Beijing EPB permitted enterprises to release the COD loads and concentrations in their permit applications, a staff member simply indicated that the EPB had done careful monitoring to verify that actual COD data in permits "reflects the real discharge conditions at these enterprises." The inference was that it would have been unreasonable to use DPS to force enterprises to cut pollution further. As explained in this chapter's final section, Changzhou's rationale for permitting enterprises to release COD at levels they requested is linked to changes in the Changzhou EPB's method of calculating discharge fees.

10. The *Technical Manual* includes numerous models, including a one-dimensional model for predicting biochemical oxygen demand and dissolved oxygen, and a stochastic water quality model, the "probability dilution model," contained in a manual issued by US EPA (1984).

11. The sixth city, Chongqing, is not considered because we could not obtain information on how Chongqing EPB treated the inconsistency problem.

12. Problems tied to the lack of reliable monitoring instruments are documented by NEPA (1993).

13. The enterprise *may* also have to pay an over-standard discharge fee if concentrations in its permit violate effluent standards.

14. Based on our interviews, Shunde EPB seldom used its authority to impose triple over-standard fees on enterprises violating permit conditions.

15. For details on the notice, see AMPG (1989).

16. Fees are based on load (i.e., mass flowrate) restrictions in permits. If an enterprise satisfies permit conditions it pays a single fee. However, if an enterprise violates permit conditions by exceeding its allowable load, the enterprise pays *two* fees: one for the portion of its total load that is consistent with permit conditions and a second for the remainder of its total load.

7

Enforcing Environmental Regulations

We complete our study of the institutional framework for environmental protection by examining EPBs' actions to enforce regulations. In the six cities we studied, EPBs exercised much discretion in deciding whether and how to enforce environmental rules. We demonstrate this by comparing enforcement actions EPBs were authorized to take with measures they actually employed.

AUTHORIZED ENFORCEMENT ACTIONS

Table 7.1 characterizes the severity of enforcement actions EPBs can take in response to violations of rules for discharge standards, permits and fees. Enforcement options include issuing warnings, imposing fees and fines, revoking permits, and gaining court assistance to collect fees.[1] These measures differ in harshness: warnings are less severe than fees and fines, whereas court actions and permit revocations have the highest degree of severity.

Suppose an enterprise violates *effluent standards*. In this case, an EPB can issue warnings and impose over-standard fees, and it can hike those fees by 5 percent per year starting in the third year fees are assessed. For factories built after 1979, EPBs can charge double the over-standard fees. Compared to other enforcement options, these fees and fines involve a similar level of penalty: we classify them as being of medium severity. Notwithstanding this equal classification of fees and fines, enterprises experience fees as somewhat less onerous than fines because fees count as a production cost that can be subtracted from profits, thereby reducing an enterprise's tax burden. In contrast, fines must be paid from after-tax profits.

If an enterprise violates its *discharge permit requirements*, an EPB can issue warnings, impose fines, or revoke permits. Two types of violations can be distinguished: improper actions during permit registration (for example, providing false information) and releasing pollutants in excess of allowable limits.

115

Table 7.1 Authorized EPB Enforcement Actions

Program	Type of Enforcement Action	Severity Level of Action
Effluent Standards	• Issue warnings when standards are violated	Low
	• Collect over-standard fees	Medium
	• Increase over-standard fees by 5% per year, beginning the third year a fee is assessed (one of the four small pieces)	Medium
	• Impose double the over-standard fee at enterprises built after 1979 that violate effluent standards (one of the small four pieces)	Medium
Discharge Permits	• Issue warnings for refusing to register or cheating during registration	Low
	• Impose fines for refusing to register or cheating during registration	Medium
	• Issue warnings for violating permit conditions	Low
	• Impose fines for violating permit conditions	Medium
	• Revoke permits for serious violations of permit conditions	High
Discharge Fees	• Issue warnings when fees are not paid on time	Low
	• Impose a penalty of 0.1% per day on over-standard fees paid late (one of the four small pieces)	Medium
	• Initiate a court action if an enterprise refuses to pay fees, and the enterprise neither applies for reconsideration by a higher level EPB nor files a suit at a local court within three months	High

Enterprises can be fined as much as 5,000 *yuan* for refusing to register or cheating on their permit applications and up to 10,000 *yuan* for each permit infraction.[2]

Now suppose an enterprise violates provisions of the *discharge fee* program by either failing to pay fees or delaying their payment. Depending on the circumstances, an EPB can respond by issuing warnings, imposing fines for late payments, or requesting a local court to intervene in collecting fees. Fines on delayed payments are more severe than warnings. Bringing an enterprise to court is the harshest action an EPB can take against an enterprise that fails to pay fees.

ENFORCEMENT MEASURES USED IN PRACTICE

A wide gap exists between what EPBs are authorized to do and what they actually do when enterprises violate environmental rules. EPBs are highly pragmatic;

in some cases they impose heavy penalties, and in others they help enterprises resolve their noncompliance problems and impose no sanctions at all. The stringency of enforcement depends on the circumstances.

Low Inter-City Variation in Use of Enforcement Actions

Table 7.2 shows types and frequencies of enforcement measures taken by the EPBs in each of the six cities in our study. We developed a five-point scale (*almost always, frequently, sometimes, rarely, and never*) to characterize the frequency of use of each enforcement action.[3]

With few exceptions, EPBs in the six cities we studied responded to rule violations in similar ways. Table 7.2 notes exceptions for Anyang, but these concern enforcement measures that were not applicable because they were not part of Anyang's new mass-based scheme for calculating discharge fees.[4] The exceptions for Beijing and Jinan resulted because, as of 1995, Beijing did not enforce permit conditions, and Jinan stopped issuing or renewing permits.[5] The only additional frequency variations across cities concerns use of warnings. While these variations are notable, they are not significant enough to alter our finding that the six cities use particular enforcement actions with similar levels of frequency.

Reliance on Low and Medium Severity Actions

Table 7.3, which aggregates information in Table 7.2, indicates the approximate frequency with which different enforcement measures were employed. The measures in the table are grouped according to level of severity. As might be expected, low-severity actions were taken frequently. Interestingly, each of the six EPBs almost always tried to collect over-standard discharge fees, an action we classified as moderately severe. The interest of EPBs in collecting money from enterprises is also reflected in the frequent use of two types of fines: double-over standard fees and 5 percent annual increases in fees.

As shown in Table 7.3, the six EPBs *sometimes* issued warnings for irregularities in DPS registration, and they *sometimes* requested court assistance in collecting fees. However, court actions were rare, except during environmental enforcement campaigns, when EPBs increased their inspections and severely punished enterprises violating rules. The six EPBs *rarely* imposed fines for late fee payments,[6] and they *never* revoked discharge permits or imposed fines for failure to comply properly with permit application procedures. Below we use our case studies and surveys of enterprises to explain the outcomes in Table 7.3.

Assessing and Collecting Fees Based on Circumstances

Although the six EPBs frequently issued notices to collect discharge fees, amounts of fees were generally negotiated rather than calculated using formulas detailed in regulations. Moreover, the EPBs were pragmatic: the pressures they exerted

Table 7.2 Enforcement Actions Taken by EPBs (1992-93)[a]

	Anyang	Beijing	Changzhou	Chongqing	Jinan	Shunde
Effluent Standards						
• Issue warnings	*Sometimes*[b]	Frequently	Frequently	NA	NA	Frequently
• Try to collect fees	Almost always	Almost always	Almost always	Almost always	Almost always	Almost always
• Impose double over-standard fees and/or 5% annual fee increases	*Not applicable*	Frequently	Frequently	Frequently	Frequently	Frequently
Discharge Permits						
• Issue warnings for irregularities in registration	Sometimes	Sometimes	Sometimes	NA	Sometimes	*Frequently*
• Impose fines for irregularities in registration	Never	Never	Never	Never	Never	Never
• Issue warnings for permit violations	Frequently	*Sometimes*	Frequently	Frequently	*Rarely*	Frequently
• Impose fines for permit violations	*Not applicable*	*Never*	Frequently	Frequently	*Never*	Frequently
• Revoke permits	Never	Never	Never	Never	Never	Never
Discharge Fees						
• Issue warnings	Frequently	Frequently	Frequently	Frequently	Frequently	Frequently
• Impose penalties for late payments	Rarely	Rarely	Rarely	Rarely	Rarely	Rarely
• Apply for court assistance to collect fees[c]	Rarely	Rarely	Rarely	NA	Rarely	Rarely

[a]Table entries are based on interviews we conducted with EPB staff in each of the six cities included in our study. "NA" means not available. *Italics* highlight exceptions to the general patterns shown in the table; *not applicable* means the action does not apply because Anyang did not include the action when it switched to a mass-based discharge fee system.

[b]"*Sometimes*" means the EPB sometimes took the action.

[c]For the entry related to court action, "rarely" means the EPB rarely took the action if an environmental campaign was not being conducted; however, EPBs sometimes used court actions during campaigns.

Table 7.3   Frequency and Severity of Enforcement Actions[a]

Enforcement Measure	Frequency	Severity
Warnings for not paying fees on time	Frequently	Low
Warnings for violating effluent standards or permit conditions	Frequently	Low
Warnings for irregularities in DPS registration	Sometimes	Low
Over-standard fees	Almost always	Medium
Double over-standard fees	Frequently	Medium
5% annual fee increases	Frequently	Medium
Penalties for late fee payments	Rarely	Medium
Fines for irregularities in DPS registration	Never	Medium
Court assistance in collecting fees	Rarely/Sometimes[b]	High
Permit revocation	Never	High

[a]Table entries are derived from general patterns of Table 7.2.

[b]"Rarely" means that court assistance in collecting fees was rarely sought during periods in which there was no environmental enforcement campaign; however, court actions were sometimes used during campaigns.

on enterprises to pay fees on time depended heavily on particular circumstances. As the following examples demonstrate, EPBs take account of an enterprise's profitability and other particular conditions in deciding on the severity of enforcement.

Economic Status is Considered in Determining Fees

EPBs often consider an enterprise's economic status, or ability to pay, when determining discharge fees. A money-losing enterprise may be asked to pay a lower fee than the one spelled out in regulations. In contrast, EPBs follow applicable rules closely when computing fees for profit-making enterprises.

Consider two contrasting examples in Anyang. The first, A3 Paper Mill, was unprofitable in 1989 and during the early 1990s. The mill was supposed to pay hefty fees during 1990 and 1991. During negotiations with Anyang EPB, the mill's managers argued that EPB's fee assessment should be slashed because the enterprise was unprofitable and had no funds to pay fees (APM, 1989). In response to these pleas, Anyang EPB agreed to let the factory pay 37,000 *yuan* per month instead of the more than 100,000 *yuan* per month required by applicable regulations (Interview No. 102593a). A3 Paper Mill paid the 37,000 *yuan* for two months in 1990, after which it renegotiated the fee and paid only 17,000 *yuan* per month. During the renegotiations, the enterprise continued to argue that it should pay less than legally required amounts because it was losing money.

The second example involves A1 Power Plant, one of the fifty enterprises in Anyang that received a first-round discharge permit in 1989. In comparison to requirements imposed on other enterprises, permit conditions at the power plant were stringent. For example, the mill was required to restrict its effluent COD to 11 mg/l, which is much lower than the 100 mg/l COD required by national effluent standards. The manager of A1 Power Plant complained about the stringency of the plant's permit conditions:

> We never complied with requirements because limits set by the EPB in the permit were ridiculous. We made no efforts to cut pollution to the level required by the permit because it would even be impossible for the most advanced power plant to meet those conditions. . . . The fees we pay now are about ten times as much as the fees we paid before [the DPS implementation] based on the national effluent standards. (Interview No. 102293)

The manager explained why the plant had accepted the stringent permit conditions and had been willing to pay the fees:

> EPB staff told us this permit would be applied only for a short time during a trial implementation of the permit system. They said it would not last very long. However, three years have passed, and we still have to pay discharge fees based on those unreasonable requirements. . . . The fees are not that large (70,000 *yuan* per year). In addition, the fees are not paid by us but by Henan Province Electric Power Department.[7] (Interview No. 102293)

When we asked Anyang EPB staff why they issued such rigorous permit conditions for A1 Power Plant, the staff indicated that an EPB can exercise discretion when it implements the DPS. In the case of A1 Power Plant, EPB staff characterized the COD concentration in the permit as a "trial value." At the end of the DPS trial implementation, the EPB could change the limit if it proved unworkable.

In Anyang and other cities in our study, managers of profitable enterprises often used the colloquial phrase "whipping the fast oxen" to complain of unfair treatment by EPBs. In this context, the "fast oxen" are the profitable enterprises that have tried to control their pollution, and "whipping" refers to an EPB's vigorous efforts to force those enterprises to abate pollution or pay discharge fees.[8]

Factors Influencing an EPB's Enforcement Strategy

One of our case studies, C1 Chemical Plant in Changzhou, further demonstrates the pragmatic enforcement approach taken by EPBs. The plant was losing money in the early 1990s, and it failed to pay the 1.37 million *yuan* of discharge fees imposed by Changzhou EPB in 1992 and 1993. Although it knew of the difficulties in enforcing regulations at an unprofitable factory, the EPB decided to be strict and try to force the chemical plant to pay the required fees.

The magnitude of the C1 Chemical Plant's waste releases made the plant hard to ignore. The EPB ranked the factory as the number one industrial polluter in Changzhou in terms of both wastewater discharge and imposed discharge fees.

For example, in 1993, C1 Chemical Plant's fees amounted to 14.5 percent of the discharge fees collected by the EPB from the entire urban area of Changzhou. From 1991 to 1993, the factory did not meet either its effluent standards or its permit conditions. In addition, the enterprise ignored the EPB's warnings and formal notices requiring payment of fees during 1992 and 1993. The deputy director of the Changzhou EPB summarized the case against the factory:

> We must deal with the problem of the [C1] Chemical Plant seriously because of its important contribution to pollution and its [refers to the enterprise] bad attitude. . . . This case is not only about problems caused by the chemical plant. This case concerns the credibility of EPB's enforcement. That is why we are actively preparing a lawsuit. If we win, it will put us in a good position to enforce environmental regulations in the future. If we lose, we will be in trouble. (Interview No. 120393)

Factors other than an enterprise's waste load, profitability and attitude toward an EPB can also affect an EPB's enforcement strategy. As previously noted, during environmental enforcement campaigns organized by higher authorities, EPBs apply rules strictly. Because the performance of EPBs is monitored closely during these campaigns, EPBs have incentives to enforce rules vigorously. More generally, EPBs often receive enforcement signals from local leaders. For example, if a mayor wants a particular stream cleaned up, the EPB has incentives to enforce rigorously, and it knows it will be supported by the mayor and other local agencies. However, as demonstrated in Chapter 4, a mayor can also signal an EPB to back off if enforcement of environmental rules would interfere with a project favored by local leaders.

Cooperative Approaches Employed by EPBs

The pragmatism of EPBs is also reflected in the many cooperative programs they have created to encourage enterprises to meet regulations. These programs have been local inventions; they are not called for in national laws or regulations.

In one commonly used cooperative approach, EPBs invite environmental specialists from local enterprises and industrial bureaus to meetings that focus on compliance problems and possible solutions. Such meetings have been held once or more per year in at least three of the six cities included in our study.[9] According to Beijing EPB staff, these occasions provide an opportunity for "increasing understanding of each other." Changzhou EPB staff call this type of conference a "sincere discussion." These efforts to enhance cooperation are illustrated by one of Shunde EPB's quarterly meetings with staff from enterprises and industrial bureaus. At a meeting in May 1994, EPB officials reported on the main reasons for permit infractions at each of several enterprises.[10] The officials also praised enterprises with good records and encouraged problematic enterprises to learn from those who met permit conditions.

Another EPB activity that enhances cooperation involves informal factory visits to discuss pollution problems and provide assistance. This kind of visit is unrelated to formal compliance inspections. EPBs often make informal visits to factories violating requirements or encountering problems with their treatment facilities.

We used part of our survey of enterprises in Anyang, Changzhou, and Shunde to learn about the frequency of EPB factory visits. We found that EPBs made informal visits to more than two-thirds of the seventy-six surveyed enterprises about twice a year, which is about the same as the annual frequency of formal factory inspections made by EPBs in Chinese cities.[11] It is also notable that EPBs in Anyang, Changzhou, and Shunde made informal visits to some factories as often as once every two months.

In addition to meeting informally with enterprise staff, EPBs frequently run training workshops to help enterprises implement environmental rules. We found that staff at about three-quarters of the seventy-six enterprises we surveyed had participated in EPB training workshops.

Some EPBs have developed unique programs of cooperation with enterprises. The EPB effort to help factories in Changzhou obtain wastewater treatment chemicals provides an example (see Chapter 5). Another illustration comes from Jinan, where the EPB took advantage of a Jinan Municipal People's Government program encouraging the exchange of managers in agencies and industries. Under this program, an official from Jinan EPB switched positions with an environmental manager at Jinan Yuxing Chemical Plant during 1994 and 1995. Both the EPB official and the enterprise manager considered the program valuable in strengthening relationships (*guanxi*) between the EPB and the enterprise.[12]

As demonstrated by the examples above, EPBs do not pursue a rigid enforcement strategy. Both coercive and cooperative approaches are employed, depending on what EPBs think will be effective in a particular situation.

WHY EPBs FREQUENTLY IMPOSE FEES AND FINES

Table 7.3 makes it clear that the most frequently employed enforcement actions consist of warnings and the collection of fees and fines. It is easy to understand why warnings are commonly used. It takes little time and effort to issue warnings, and many EPB staff believe an enterprise should have at least one chance to correct rule violations before facing penalties. The rationale for the EPBs' frequent use of discharge fees is less obvious because administrative burdens are involved in fee collection, and, as many analysts have noted, China's fees on COD and other conventional pollutants are too low to motivate enterprises to cut pollution.[13]

Importance of Fee-Based Revenues

EPBs in the six cities we studied were highly motivated to implement the fee system because it yielded substantial revenues. EPBs could retain as much as 20 percent of over-standard fees they collected. In addition, they retained 100 percent of the four small pieces, such as the 0.1 percent per day late payment penalty and the 5 percent annual increase in over-standard fees imposed on enterprises that paid fees for more than two years. For many EPBs, the retention of a fraction of over-standard fees and all of the four small pieces is essential for their survival and growth.[14]

The importance of fee-based revenues is illustrated by circumstances in Municipalities A and B, cities that provided us with financial data on the condition of anonymity. In 1995, total operating expenditures for Municipality A's EPB amounted to nearly 1.7 million *yuan*. (This figure excludes expenditures for EPBs in the municipality's districts and counties.) The municipal government provided only 40 percent of the funds needed to cover the EPB's operating expenses. The remaining 60 percent of the EPB's budget came from the four small pieces and a fraction of over-standard fees. The portion of the operating budget received from fee-based revenues was even higher for EPBs in Municipality A's districts and counties. Those EPBs spent about 8.6 million *yuan* in 1993, but only 4 percent of this total was provided by district and county governments. The remaining 96 percent came from over-standard fees and the four small pieces.

EPBs in Municipality B also relied heavily on fee-based revenues. During 1994, an average of 90.8 percent of the total operating expenditures for Municipality B's EPB *system* came from fee-based revenues. The following figures represent percentages of operating expenditures covered by over-standard fees and the four small pieces for units within the EPB system:

- Municipal EPB – 87 percent
- Municipal environmental monitoring center—69 percent
- Municipal environmental inspection station—100 percent
- District and county EPBs—95 percent[15]

During the early 1990s, EPBs in both municipalities retained an increasing fraction of the total fees collected. In Municipality A, the fraction of total fees used by the EPB jumped from 20 percent in 1990 to 70 percent in 1994, whereas in Municipality B, the fraction rose from 41 percent in 1990 to 61 percent in 1994 (see Tables 7.4 and 7.5). These increases reflect growth in the relative importance of the four small pieces, since EPBs retain 100 percent of these funds. In both municipalities, total fee-based revenues generally increased (except for 1993 in Municipality A), but the amount used to subsidize waste treatment plants either decreased or remained about the same. Although financial data from the other four cities included in our study were not available, EPB staff in those cities confirmed that similar trends existed in the use of fees.

Table 7.4   Fee-System Revenue in Municipality A

Year	Support for Pollution Control at Enterprises		Support for EPB Operations[a]		Total Fee-System Revenue Collected[b] (1000 yuan)
	Amount (1000 yuan)	% of Total Revenue Collected	Amount (1000 yuan)	% of Total Revenue Collected	
1990	20,950	80	5,373	20	26,323
1991	14,300	73	5,341	27	19,641
1992	15,000	52	14,100	48	29,100
1993	12,000	55	9,802	45	21,802
1994	6,100	30	14,071	70	20,171

[a]Expenditures for EPB operations include support for the municipal EPB's operations, as well as operations of district and county EPBs.

[b]Total revenues include only discharge fees controlled by the municipal EPB. Fees collected by district and county EPBs are not included.

EPBs are becoming increasingly dependent on discharge fees for core support rather than for supplemental support, as was originally intended. This has had some positive effects. The EPB staff is motivated to monitor pollution sources carefully, and fee-based revenues have allowed many EPBs to grow. Stronger EPBs with increased man-power can do a more effective job in controlling pollution. However, as demonstrated below, the heavy reliance of EPBs on fee-based revenues can also impede progress in meeting the original goal of the fee system: providing enterprises with incentives to curb pollution.

Table 7.5   Fee-System Revenue in Municipality B

Year	Support for Pollution Control at Enterprises		Support for EPB Operations[a]		Total Fee-System Revenue Collected[b] (1000 yuan)
	Amount (1000 yuan)	% of Total Revenue Collected	Amount (1000 yuan)	% of Total Revenue Collected	
1990	10,904	59	7,568	41	18,472
1991	11,282	54	9,500	46	20,782
1992	13,266	52	12,349	48	25,615
1993	11,803	43	15,580	57	27,383
1994	11,509	39	18,218	61	29,727

[a]Expenditures for EPB operations include support for the municipal EPB's operations as well as operations of district and county EPBs.

[b]Total revenues include discharge fees collected by the municipal EPB *and* all lower-level EPBs in Municipality B.

Setting Permit Conditions to Maximize EPB Revenues

An example from Municipality X, another city that shall remain anonymous, illustrates the conflict EPBs face between augmenting fee-based revenues and cutting pollution. Typically, the EPB in Municipality X sets allowable pollutant concentrations in an enterprise's permit at or below values listed in the enterprise's permit application. Allowable concentrations of pollutants in the permit are taken as actual concentrations for purposes of calculating over-standard fees. Monitoring data is not used in calculating fees, but it is used to discover permit infractions. If permit conditions are violated, an enterprise faces a fine equal to double the over-standard fee.

At a meeting in late 1993, EPB staff in Municipality X argued over the limits to be set in the 1994 permit of an enterprise that violated effluent standards. Because the enterprise expected its COD to increase as a result of a planned expansion, in 1994 the enterprise applied for COD concentration and mass flowrate limits higher than those in its 1993 permit.

Before acting on the enterprise's permit application, the EPB director asked his staff to estimate fees and fines the EPB would collect under each of two scenarios: (1) increase the allowable COD in the permit to match values listed in the enterprise's 1994 application, and (2) maintain the allowable COD in the 1994 permit at the value specified in the enterprise's 1993 application. Under scenario 1, the EPB would increase the COD limit, and thus it would collect a higher over-standard fee. This follows because the (higher) COD concentration limit in the permit would be used in calculating the fee. For scenario 2, in which the EPB would keep the allowable COD at the lower (1993) permitted level, the prospect of collecting fines equal to double the over-standard fee for permit infractions would be higher. By using the 1993 COD limit, the EPB would be more likely to find that the enterprise violated its permit conditions because of its 1994 factory expansion.

The EPB director wanted the COD limit in the 1994 permit set to yield maximum income for the bureau. When some EPB staff argued that maximizing fee-based revenues should not be a criterion for setting limits in permits, the EPB director responded as follows:

> I know there is a conflict between increasing fees and decreasing pollution. But what can I do? I need money to operate the EPB. And next year the budget will be even tighter because the provincial government will require us to give it 5 percent of the fees collected. What do you want me to do? (Interview No. 122093)

In the face of the provincial government's requirement for a 5 percent share of fees and only modest funds from the municipal government, the EPB director felt justified in maximizing the EPBs income from fees.

Municipality X's interest in maximizing fee-based revenues is not unique. In Wuhan, for example, the municipal EPB has enhanced its income by setting annual quotas on fees collected by Wuhan's six district EPBs. Fee collectors in the districts receive financial rewards when quotas are met.[16] National statistics provide an additional perspective on the importance attached to fees. Between 1992 and 1995, the number of fee collectors nearly doubled, and the number of work units paying fees tripled.[17] Many EPBs have augmented the fee system's original pollution abatement goal with a revenue generation goal.[18] However, as the experience in Municipality X suggests, the two goals are not always compatible.

Monitoring to Collect Fees Rather Than Ensure Compliance

The existence of conflicting goals for the fee system also affects how EPBs monitor factory discharges, and this is demonstrated by Municipality Y. EPB staff in this city usually stopped monitoring at a factory for three to six months after they determined that effluent standards were being violated. When asked why the EPB did not increase its monitoring frequency to check on the enterprise's environmental performance, EPB staff explained that increased monitoring might reduce the bureau's revenues. If new monitoring data showed the enterprise complied with standards, the EPB could no longer collect fees.

During our interviews at factories in Municipality Y, enterprise managers frequently complained about having to pay fees even after they made changes to meet effluent standards. Enterprise managers in another city in our study indicated that they asked the EPB to monitor their effluents soon after they had improved their performance, only to be told that the EPB staff had no time. Several managers we interviewed felt it was unfair for an EPB to collect fees from enterprises for three months or longer based only on one-time monitoring of a problem that was corrected soon after it was discovered.

Can EPBs be faulted for viewing the discharge fee system primarily as a mechanism to expand their budgets? As one China specialist has noted, the EPBs' emphasis on generating income through fee collection is consistent with the stress on money-earning that characterizes contemporary China (Jahiel, 1997: 78). In addition, the Center's call for self-supporting government agencies together with local government cuts in EPB funding enhance the drive to maximize fee-based revenues.

WHY EPBs RARELY OR NEVER EMPLOY SOME TYPES OF ENFORCEMENT MEASURES

Enforcement Actions Never Conducted

EPBs in the six cities we studied almost never revoked discharge permits when enterprises violated permit conditions (see Table 7.2). When we asked why permits weren't revoked, EPB staff generally referred to the importance of maintaining harmonious relationships with enterprises. Many interviewees indicated that revoking a permit would seriously damage an EPB's relationship (*guanxi*) with an enterprise, an outcome one person described as "not being good for anyone." EPB staff we interviewed felt that, for the most part, enterprise managers were "reasonable," and that most noncompliance problems could be resolved effectively by negotiation instead of confrontation.

We also asked EPB staff why they almost never fined enterprises for irregularities in the permit application process (for example, for the submission of false information regarding pollution loads). Interviewees indicated that such fines were uncalled for because almost all enterprises complied with DPS registration and permit application procedures. Some EPBs found it difficult to detect irregularities in permit application data because it was too expensive to monitor factory effluents on a systematic bases. One EPB official elaborated on this point:

> Even if the data reported by an enterprise does not make sense, it is very difficult to claim the enterprise is cheating. Cheating sounds very bad. In addition, the data reported by the majority of enterprises make sense. (Interview No. 51993)

Accusing an enterprise of cheating on its permit application is considered risky because it could lead to a loss of face and damage an EPB's *guanxi* with an enterprise. Several EPB officials explained that accusing an enterprise of cheating implies an enterprise knowingly violated the law; thus, accusing an enterprise of cheating would be equivalent to questioning the moral integrity of enterprise managers. Cheating would be considered more serious than violating effluent standards, since the latter could be rationalized in terms of technical and economic factors.

Enforcement Actions Rarely Conducted

Tables 7.1 and 7.2 show that EPBs in the six cities rarely imposed a late payment penalty. The following is a typical EPB explanation for this outcome:

> These enterprises often told us about their difficulties in paying discharge fees on time and promised to pay later. They had a good attitude. If they promised to pay later and paid as they promised, how could we be so unreasonable as to impose fines on their late payment? (Interview No. 122093)

Some EPB staff also felt that an enterprise penalized for being late might *never* pay its over-standard fees.

Court actions represent another enforcement measure EPBs rarely use. As detailed in Chapter 5, courts are not used for several reasons, including shortcomings of the Chinese legal system and the strong preference of the Chinese to resolve conflicts by making concessions to reach a compromise. In the six cities included in our research, court actions against polluters who refused to pay discharge fees were sometimes taken during environmental campaigns, such as the three-year "Inspection of Environmental Enforcement Campaign" launched by the central government in 1993. This campaign, which was organized jointly by the NPC's Environmental Protection and Natural Resources Conservation Committee and the State Council's Environmental Protection Commission, had two main objectives:

- to use legal instruments, publicity, and the mass media to improve enforcement of environmental regulations; and
- to remedy the commonly observed problem of "law without compliance, violation without enforcement, and enforcement without seriousness." (CEYCC, 1994:105)

EPBs enforce environmental rules more strictly than usual during campaigns because their enforcement efforts are assessed by inspection teams organized by SEPA and by national and provincial people's congresses. For example, in the first year of the Inspection of Environmental Enforcement Campaign, national teams evaluated EPB actions at 166 enterprises in forty-five cities and counties in seven provinces (CEYCC, 1995: 95). EPBs view environmental enforcement campaigns as opportunities to enhance their credibility with polluters and demonstrate their accomplishments to high-level officials.

EPB ENFORCEMENT IS PRAGMATIC

EPB enforcement personnel often use discretion to determine whether they will enforce requirements strictly in a particular case. Some analysts have argued that this exercise of discretion constitutes a problem of "underenforcement and selective enforcement of environmental control."[19] However, we believe the approach used by EPBs is more aptly characterized as *pragmatic enforcement*, an approach in which the choice of enforcement action has more to do with the particular case at hand than with a rigid attachment to a single approach, such as insisting on strict compliance with environmental rules.[20]

Arguably, the institutional context of environmental protection in China leaves EPBs with little choice. They must exercise discretion in enforcement in order to use their limited resources effectively and gain local government support for their actions. EPBs have little hope of taking enforcement steps opposed by local leaders or powerful agencies.

Pragmatism is reflected in EPBs' reliance on *guanxi* with regulated enterprises. Many EPB staff believe the way to bring most enterprises into compliance is by developing mutual understanding, providing technical and financial assistance, and negotiating reasonable compliance deadlines. Of course, when emergency situations prevail, negotiation may not be appropriate. In situations where timely action has been essential, EPBs, with support of local leaders, have taken strong enforcement actions against enterprises.

Another reflection of pragmatism is EPBs' avoidance of court actions, except in the context of environmental enforcement campaigns. When campaigns were not being waged, the six EPBs we studied rarely used the courts because they wanted to avoid the cost of gathering data needed to support a legally convincing argument. In addition, many EPBs lack staff with legal training. EPBs also know that the traditional use of negotiation to settle disputes with enterprises is more likely preserve their *guanxi* with enterprises.

Still another manifestation of EPB pragmatism is the approach they have taken to implement the discharge fee system. Many EPBs collect discharge fees systematically because fees are a major source of income. EPBs view revenue generation as a key objective of the fee system because they depend on fees to support core activities. Although the original goal of the fee program was to motivate enterprises to cut pollution, many EPBs operate with a second, potentially conflicting goal: to maximize funds collected in the form of over-standard fees and the four small pieces.

In general, pragmatic enforcement appears to be common when regulated parties have widely varying characteristics (Hunter and Waterman, 1996). Case examples in this chapter show how diversity in pollution load and enterprise profitability can influence the enforcement actions taken by EPBs. We continue exploring this theme in the next chapter, which shows how the form of enterprise ownership (TVE vs. state-owned enterprise) as well as enterprise profitability and the cost of pollution abatement affect behaviors of both EPBs and enterprises.

NOTES

1. If an enterprise fails to pay fees because it believes the EPB calculated fees incorrectly, it must apply to have the fees reconsidered by a higher level EPB within fifteen days or file a complaint at a local court within three months. If the enterprises does not apply for reconsideration, and neither initiates a court action nor pays the fees within three months, the EPB can ask the local court to enforce fee system rules (State Council, 1982).

2. The fine imposed for exceeding permit limits is double the over-standard fee the enterprise pays for violating effluent standards (NEPA, 1988b). This blending of the fee and permit programs simplifies the administrative burdens faced by EPBs.

3. In conducting interviews with EPB staff in six cities, we posed the following question for each of several types of requirements: "For every 10 violations of the requirement, how many times did the EPB respond by taking a certain type of enforcement action?" If the answer was 9 or 10 times, we classified the frequency as *almost always*; if the answer was 7 or 8 times, we classified the frequency as *frequently*; and so on as indicated below:

Answer to the question posed:	Frequency level:
9 or 10 times	almost always (*zongshi*)
7 or 8 times	frequently (*jingchang*)
3 to 6 times	sometimes (*yonshi*)
1 or 2 times	rarely (*bujingchang*)
0	never (*zonglai meiyon*)

We created this procedure for defining frequency level based on discussions with Beijing EPB staff.

4. See Chapter 6 for a discussion of Anyang's mass-based fee system. In developing its new system, Anyang EPB did not include fines based on the four small pieces.

5. These facts about Beijing and Jinan were introduced in Chapter 6.

6. For example, thirty enterprises in Anyang failed to pay about one million *yuan* of fees on time in 1992, but the EPB did not impose any payment penalties. Similarly, forty-three enterprises in Changzhou delayed paying fees amounting to about five million *yuan* during 1992 and 1993. They paid late payment penalties of less than five hundred *yuan*.

7. A1 Power Plant is affiliated with Henan Province Electric Power Department. As of 1993, all production costs, including pollution discharge fees, were paid from a budget managed by that department.

8. This increased pressure on profitable enterprises is also reflected in an observation from Vermeer's study of pollution abatement at Chinese enterprises: "In Chinese practice, many legal obligations are negotiable for poor enterprises, while rich enterprises may be forced by local governments to pay more than their due" (Vermeer, 1991: 37).

9. These types of meetings were held in Beijing, Changzhou, and Shunde. We were unable to determine whether such meetings took place in Anyang, Chongqing, or Jinan.

10. Xiaoying Ma attended the May 1994 meeting as an observer.

11. The percentages of enterprises visited informally by EPBs at least twice a year in Anyang, Changzhou, and Shunde were 68 percent, 76 percent, and 69 percent, respectively. For details on this portion of our survey results, see Ma (1997: Tables 8.4 and 8.5).

12. Information about the effectiveness of the position exchange is based on interviews with Jinan EPB staff.

13. For evidence that fees on COD are too low to motivate cleanups, see Krupnick (1991); Sinkule and Ortolano (1995); and Jahiel (1997). In contrast, Warren (1996) demonstrates that fees on some heavy metals are high enough to motivate enterprises to cut releases of these materials.

14. For examples of EPBs that depend heavily on fee-based revenues, see Sinkule and Ortolano (1995).

15. Both the monitoring center and the inspection station are semi-autonomous organizations affiliated with the municipal EPB. The EPB system for Municipality B included a few other affiliated units, but information on their use of fee-based revenues was not available.

16. The Wuhan example is from Jahiel (1997: 97).

17. The number of fee collectors jumped from 10,000 in 1992 to 19,000 in 1995, whereas the number of enterprises paying fees increased from 100,000 in 1992 to 300,000 in 1995 (Jahiel, 1997: 98).

18. For additional evidence supporting the dual goals of the fee system, see, for example, Jahiel (1997); and Sinkule and Ortolano (1995).

19. The quoted phrase is from Chan, Cheung, and Lo (1993: 65).

20. Interestingly, Hunter and Waterman (1996) introduced the term "pragmatic approach" to describe how the United States Environmental Protection Agency enforced its wastewater discharge permit program.

8

Effects of Profit, Cost, and Ownership Form on Enterprises' Response to Regulations

Even though compliance with environmental rules depends heavily on particular circumstances, some patterns exist in the way EPBs and enterprises approach regulations. In this chapter we show that three characteristics of enterprises—profitability, compliance cost, and form of ownership—influence actions of both EPBs and enterprises and help explain why some enterprises have better environmental performance than others.

RULE ENFORCEMENT AT UNPROFITABLE SOEs

In the previous chapter we used two enterprises in Anyang to demonstrate that EPBs consider factories' economic status in deciding whether to enforce environmental rules strictly. Here we explore this subject further by examining how EPBs enforce regulations at unprofitable state-owned enterprises. During the time we conducted our fieldwork in the early 1990s, SOEs operated with soft-budget constraints, and unprofitable state-owned enterprises could continue operating year after year. Since the time of our fieldwork, the central government has greatly reduced its support of unprofitable firms. However, until the state completely eliminates soft-budget constraints, SOEs that are consistently unprofitable will continue to exist.

A1 Paper Mill

Anyang EPB's experience with A1 Paper Mill demonstrates that environmental regulators have few enforcement options when dealing with money-losing SOEs that have large staffs. A1 Paper Mill, which uses rice straw to produce both pulp and paper, was established in 1958. The mill is a state-owned enterprise that employed nearly 1,000 people in the early 1990s. Mill operations yielded wastewater with high concentrations of chemical oxygen demand and suspended solids (SS).[1] The main wastewater treatment facilities at A1 Paper Mill were two sets of air flotation units which reduced COD and SS in "white liquor," the discharge from paper production. However, wastewater from pulp production, referred to as "black liquor," is far more potent and it was not treated. The mill installed its air flotation units in 1986 in response to requirements of the three synchronizations policy.

In 1989, Anyang EPB issued a permit to A1 Paper Mill that allowed COD releases of 20,000 kg per day in 1989 and 1990. However, the actual COD discharged was over 34,000 kg/day in that period.

When the DPS was implemented in 1989, Anyang changed its procedures for calculating discharge fees by moving from a concentration-based method to a mass-based approach. Under the *old* fee-calculation scheme, A1 Paper Mill was required to pay 10,500 *yuan* per month during 1989. Using the fee calculation procedure implemented in 1990, fees imposed on A1 Paper Mill skyrocketed to over 100,000 *yuan* per month (see Table 8.1). However, as a result of negotiations between plant managers and Anyang EPB staff, discharge fees were reduced to values below those indicated by applicable regulations.

In 1991, Anyang EPB issued a second permit to A1 Paper Mill. While its second discharge permit was in effect, the mill cut its releases significantly and permit conditions were, for the most part, satisfied.[2] However, the waste release was lowered only because poor economic conditions forced the mill to scale back its operations.

Table 8.1   COD Releases and Fees at A1 Paper Mill[a]

| | COD Releases 1,000 kg/day | | Discharge Fees 1,000 yuan/month | | |
Year	Actual maximum	Allowable maximum	Fees based on regulations[b]	Fees based on negotiation	Fees paid
1989	34.4	20.0	10.5	NA[c]	10.5
1990	38.1	20.0	142	17	17 or 0[d]
1991	8.4	17.3	107	17	0
1992	12.8	17.3	NA	17	0

[a]Data are from annual environmental reports submitted by the factory to Anyang EPB, discharge permits issued by Anyang EPB, interviews at the factory, and Anyang EPB's monitoring records.

[b]The jump in fees between 1989 and 1990 occurred because Anyang EPB introduced a new fee system. Before 1990, enterprises had to pay fees based only on the one pollutant *exceeding* the standard by the greatest amount. Starting in 1990, fees were assessed not only on pollutants exceeding the allowable mass flowrate of pollutants (kg/day) set by permit conditions, but also on pollutants discharged in amounts *less than* allowable quantities. In addition, charges under the new fee-calculation procedure were imposed on both COD and SS, instead of only on one pollutant.

[c]NA = not available

[d]The factory paid discharge fees of 17,000 *yuan*/month during the first part of 1990, but it did not pay fees after April 1990.

Beginning in 1989, A1 Paper Mill's output became unstable because of short-ages of raw materials, and strong competition from township and village enter-prises producing paper. Once the mill started losing money in 1990, it tried to cut costs by operating its wastewater treatment facilities only several hours per day, depending on the quantity and quality of wastewater.

The mill was supposed to pay discharge fees of more than 100,000 *yuan* per month during 1990 and 1991, but it negotiated with EPB to have its fees cut to 17,000 *yuan* per month (see Table 8.1). Negotiations began in December 1989 when A1 Paper Mill submitted a report to Anyang EPB offering three reasons why the new fee calculation procedure should not be applied to the mill. First, the enterprise was losing money and had no funds to pay discharge fees. Sec-ond, monitoring data were so inaccurate that the EPB's calculated fee could rep-resent an overcharge. Third, if Anyang EPB forced A1 Paper Mill to pay the re-quired fees, the mill might have to close, resulting in extensive unemployment and related social problems (APM, 1989).

Negotiations between A1 Paper Mill and Anyang EPB yielded an agreement whereby the mill would pay 37,000 *yuan* per month instead of more than 100,000 *yuan* per month of fees as required by applicable regulations. After paying the 37,000 *yuan* for two months in early 1990, the enterprise negotiated a new deal in which it would pay only 17,000 *yuan* per month. In negotiating the agreement, the enterprise continued to argue that it should pay less because it was losing money. After a few more months, in July 1991, the mill stopped paying any dis-charge fees at all.[3]

Interactions between Anyang EPB and the factory in July 1991 illustrate how fruitless it can be to try to collect fees from a money-losing enterprise. When the EPB first gave the mill its regular monthly notice for fee collection in July 1991, the enterprise director ignored the notice. In response, EPB officials followed procedures authorizing it to transfer the required fee from the enterprise's bank account to the EPB's account at the Industrial and Commercial Bank in Anyang.[4]However, the EPB discovered that no money was left in the special ac-count A1 Paper Mill had established for paying its discharge fees. After press-ing the factory for payment on several subsequent occasions, EPB officials gave up.

The assistant director of A1 Paper Mill explained why the mill ignored the EPB's requests for payment: "We are a poor, money-losing factory. Because we have so many workers to feed, the EPB must let us survive" (Interview No. 52393). The assistant director pointed out that A1 Paper Mill paid fees as required before 1990, a period during which it was profitable. When we asked him whether he cared about the enterprise's losing face for violating regulations, the assistant director said the factory had already lost the "face of profitability." Since the enterprise even had problems paying taxes to the government, he felt there was no reason to care about the "face of environmental protection."

EPBs are authorized to enforce DPS and discharge fee regulations by imposing fines and revoking discharge permits, but Anyang EPB never took those actions against A1 Paper Mill. Anyang EPB staff argued that it was pointless to do so in a case where a factory was losing money. As one EPB official put it, "We don't want to exert effort for nothing." (Interview No. 51993)

The A1 Paper Mill case illustrates a phrase we heard many times during our field work: "dead pigs are not afraid of boiling water" (*sizhu bupa kaishui tang*). In the context of environmental policy, the "dead pigs" refer to unprofitable enterprises, and the "boiling water" refers to the sanctions that EPBs can impose.

C1 Chemical Plant

C1 Chemical Plant, another SOE employing about 1,000 people during the early 1990s, further illustrates the problems EPBs have in enforcing environmental rules at money-losing SOEs. The case is also notable because the factory built a treatment plant while it was unprofitable, and its wastewater release was *worse* after plant construction than before.

Difficulties in Enforcing Environmental Rules

C1 Chemical Plant, which had the largest industrial wastewater load in Changzhou as of 1990, had an unremarkable environmental record during the 1980s. Although the enterprise violated discharge standards between 1983 and 1990, it consistently paid required discharge fees on time. This changed in 1991 when the enterprise started operating at a loss. Although the factory failed to pay fees during 1992, it was not until mid-1993 that Changzhou EPB began to apply significant pressure. In August of that year, the EPB formally notified C1 Chemical Plant that it owed 1.37 million *yuan* of fees for its 1992–93 wastewater releases. Payment was due by September 10, 1993.

In response to the formal notification, the factory director wrote to the Changzhou EPB director promising to visit the bureau to discuss the fees personally, but the factory director never followed up. In December 1993, Changzhou EPB began contemplating use of a court action to force C1 Chemical Plant to pay its fees. Even after the plant's top managers learned of the EPB's intentions to file a lawsuit, they showed no sign of paying the fees.

Although EPB officials started preparing for their lawsuit, they hesitated to take the case to court because they could not count on support from Changzhou's government leaders. EPB officials felt that the leaders would want to avoid the social consequences of shutting down the chemical plant. Another stumbling block was that Chang-zhou EPB was short on staff. Moreover, even though EPB personnel in charge of collecting discharge fees wanted "to take enforcement action, [they felt it would be] very difficult, because of the factory's poor economic health." (Interview No. 122093)

The vice director of C1 Chemical Plant explained the enterprise's failure to pay its discharge fees:

I want to pay the fees. I don't want to violate the law, but I have no money. We did not even pay "taxes to the state and grain to the emperor" *(guo zhai huang liang)*, let alone the pollution discharge fees. (Interview No. 122193)[5]

The vice director elaborated:

In theory, EPB staff can take enforcement action, but in practice, they cannot, because we don't have money. Can they take our machines away? . . . If EPB forces us to close, it would be better. Then the workers will not ask me for their rice bowl; they will go to EPB for the rice bowl. I will see how EPB deals with it.

The vice-director's use of "rice bowl" (a shortened form of "iron rice bowl") refers to the lifetime employment expected by many workers at SOEs. Employment at an SOE was accompanied by a broad array of social services, including housing and medical care.

Installation of a Treatment System

The C1 Chemical Plant case is unusual because the enterprise completed construction of a new wastewater treatment facility in 1993, a time when the factory was operating at a loss. Why did the enterprise continue investing in a new treatment system when it claimed it lacked funds to pay discharge fees? The answer relates to both timing and funding. Changzhou municipal government first required C1 Chemical Plant to build a treatment plant in 1986 as a project under the national program of "pollution control within deadlines."[6] Treatment plant construction started in 1990, *before* the factory started operating at a loss. Moreover, the enterprise did not use any of its own funds to build the plant. Of the total construction cost of 6.2 million *yuan*, 3.4 million *yuan* came as a subsidy from Changzhou EPB's pollution levy fund, and 2.8 million *yuan* was a loan from the World Bank.

The treatment plant project was completed and approved by Changzhou EPB in 1993, but the plant performed poorly. Although a small volume of wastewater was occasionally treated to keep the treatment process bacteria alive so the facility could function, most waste-water was discharged untreated because the factory did not want to pay for treatment chemicals.

The vice-director of C1 Chemical Plant clarified why the enterprise completed treatment plant construction at a time the enterprise was steadily losing money: "EPB compelled us to build the treatment plant. All right, I built one for you [refers to Changzhou EPB], but I don't have the money to operate it" (Interview No. 122193). In building the wastewater treatment facility, the enterprise lost nothing. The money from the pollution levy fund was a (non-repayable) grant, and Changzhou Municipal People's Government, not the factory, had guaranteed repayment of the World Bank loan.[7]

Another reason C1 Chemical Plant completed construction of the treatment system was that factory managers believed costs for operating the system would be lower than fees the factory would have to pay for releasing untreated wastewater. According to calculations by the Huabei Civil Engineering Design Institute, the group that designed the treatment plant, annual discharge fees would be 1.08 million *yuan*, and annual operation and maintenance cost would be 0.92 million *yuan*. However, the operating cost estimate was low because it did not account for inflation. Discharge fees are not adjusted for inflation.[8]

The quality of C1 Chemical Plant's effluent, in terms of phenols, pH, and COD, deteriorated after the enterprise became unprofitable in 1991. Based on our interviews with the plant's environmental manager, the increased pollution after 1991 was linked to drops in employee morale once large bonuses were dropped because the factory was losing money. After the bonus structure was weakened in 1991, the quality of work fell off significantly. For example, laborers frequently spilled chemicals on the factory floor, and the spilled materials became pollutants when the floor was washed and the chemicals went down the drains. This and other "poor housekeeping" practices contributed to a boost in waste load.

C3 Printing and Dyeing Plant

Although TVEs have different relationships with local governments than state-owned enterprises, EPBs consider the profit status of TVEs when deciding on enforcement measures. This is demonstrated by EPB actions at C3 Printing and Dyeing Plant, a TVE in a rural section of Changzhou. The enterprise was established with two workshops in 1978, before China's three synchronizations policy had been implemented. In 1987 when the enterprise added a third workshop in 1987, it failed to satisfy requirements of the three synchronizations program. In response, Changzhou EPB issued a limited time treatment order requiring the factory to clean up its wastewater. The enterprise complied with the order in 1989 by investing 700,000 *yuan* in chemical air flotation units.[9] According to the EPB, in building these treatment works, the enterprise was "making up a missed lesson of the three synchronizations" (Interview No. 120893).

Later in 1989, when C3 Printing and Dyeing Plant began operating at a loss, it started treating less than 10 percent of its wastewater. As a consequence, the factory violated its permit conditions and applicable effluent standards. Although the EPB had several enforcement options available, it chose only to impose discharge fees. The fees were 125,000 *yuan* in 1990 and the enterprise paid the full amount. By treating only a small fraction of its wastewater, the factory incurred only minimal operating costs, less than 11,000 *yuan* for the year. In 1991 when the factory's profit status improved, it treated all its waste-water again, and it was able to satisfy all restrictions on its wastewater discharges. Although it was not obligated to pay discharge fees once it satisfied requirements, the plant incurred substantial costs for running its treatment facility (e.g., 342,000 *yuan* in 1991).

The director of C3 Printing and Dyeing Plant clarified the factory's motivation to pay the relatively high treatment plant operating costs and bring the factory into compliance with requirements:

> We are profitable, and we can afford the operation and maintenance costs to run the treatment facilities. Also, the EPB would not allow us to violate pollution control requirements because we are profitable and have no excuse [for violations]. (Interview No. 120893)

This case demonstrates that, while EPBs are sometimes lenient with money-losing enterprises, an EPB's views can change quickly once an enterprise starts earning profits.

The above three cases—A1 Paper Mill, C1 Chemical Plant and C3 Printing and Dyeing Plant—demonstrate that enterprises are less likely to comply with regulations when they are operating at a loss. The cases also demonstrate how EPB enforcement actions are influenced by the economic positions of enterprises. Our survey results corroborated this point.

Table 8.2 includes survey responses from seventy-six enterprises, twenty of which were classified as unprofitable in 1992. The table shows that the rate of compliance with environmental rules was significantly higher for profitable enterprises than for unprofitable ones. While 82 percent of the money-making enterprises paid discharge fees on time, only 33 percent of unprofitable enterprises did so. The rate of compliance with permit conditions was also much higher for profitable enterprises (83 percent) than for money losers (31 percent). Moreover, about 40 percent of economically healthy enterprises met effluent standards, compared with only 25 percent for enterprises operating at a loss. On average, fewer enterprises complied with effluent standards than with discharge permits because effluent standards were usually much more stringent than discharge limits in permits.

INFLUENCE OF COMPLIANCE COSTS ON ENTERPRISE DECISIONS

The decision of a Chinese enterprise to satisfy environmental regulations is affected by the enterprise's profit status and its costs of compliance.[10] Even managers at a profitable enterprise might resist meeting regulations if they felt compliance costs were unreasonable. Our case studies allowed us to investigate the kinds of cost analyses Chinese enterprise managers conduct in deciding whether to meet regulations or risk facing EPB sanctions.

Compliance Costs at A2 Chemical Fiber Plant

The case of A2 Chemical Fiber Plant in Anyang demonstrates how costs figure into compliance decisions. The plant, a middle-sized SOE established in 1966,

Table 8.2   Compliance Rates: Profitable vs. Unprofitable Enterprises (1992)[a]

	Enterprises		
	Total	*Profitable*[b]	*Unprofitable*
Effluent standards[c]			
Number of enterprises in compliance	26	21	5
Number of valid observations	73	53	20
Compliance rate	36%	40%	25%
Discharge permits			
Number of enterprises in compliance	47	41	6
Number of valid observations	68	49	19
Compliance rate	69%	83%	31%
Discharge fees			
Number of enterprises in compliance	22	19	3
Number of valid observations	32	23	9
Compliance rate	68%	82%	33%

[a]Compliance rates with effluent standards and permit conditions are calculated based on survey data in three cities (Anyang, Changzhou, and Shunde).The compliance rate for the discharge fee program is calculated based on survey data in two cities (Changzhou and Shunde); fee-system compliance data for Anyang were not available. Appendix A explains how "compliance" is defined for each of the three regulatory programs. For each regulation, the number of valid data points in the sample is lower than the total sample size because of incomplete or inconsistent answers to survey questions.

[b]Enterprises are classified as "profitable" if annual after-tax revenues exceeded costs for 1992.

[c]In each city included in our survey, local effluent standards were identical to national effluent standards.

had been profitable from 1978, when China's economic reforms were being started, until the time of our field work in the early 1990s.

Before 1989, when A2 Chemical Fiber Plant obtained its first discharge permit, the enterprise had made few investments in pollution control. Its only treatment facility was a 5,000-ton per day wastewater treatment plant built in 1981. During the 1980s, the factory increased its output, and its wastewater discharge rose to around 12,000 tons per day. Because of inadequacies in treatment plant capacity, the factory violated effluent standards by a wide margin. By the late 1980s, treatment facilities at the factory were badly out of date and were operated only about 120 days each year. A2 Chemical Fiber Plant simply paid discharge fees imposed by the EPB instead of trying to meet effluent standards.

The enterprise's incentives to satisfy environmental requirements changed in 1989 when Anyang EPB reworked its fee calculation procedure from a concentration-based approach to a mass-based approach (in response to the city's implementation of the discharge permit system). Following this change, A2 Chemical

Fiber Plant's discharge fees increased about 35 percent, from 23,000 *yuan* per month in 1989 to 31,000 *yuan* per month in 1990.[11]

When A2 Chemical Fiber Plant received its first discharge permit in 1989, its COD load violated permit conditions. At that time, the enterprise invested 950,000 *yuan* to expand its treatment facility's capacity to 12,000 tons per day and thereby attain compliance with permit limits.[12] Before deciding to meet permit requirements, managers at A2 Chemical Fiber Plant made a rough estimate of compliance costs. According to the head of the factory's environmental protection unit, their calculations showed that compliance would not be too much of a burden, even though it "would be more expensive to treat wastewater than to pay discharge fees" (Interview No. 102593b). Enterprise managers calculated compliance costs without considering either an inflation rate or an interest rate.

The economic analysis performed by factory managers involved one scenario for compliance and another for noncompliance. For the compliance scenario, the annual cost of operation and maintenance (O&M) plus discharge fees amounted to 558,000 *yuan* (see Table 8.3). Interestingly, "compliance" meant satisfying discharge permit limits, but it did not involve meeting the effluent COD standard of 150 mg/l. In the early 1990s, the factory's effluent COD was approximately six times as high as the 150 mg/l standard. Moreover, using Anyang's new fee calculation procedure, the factory was required to pay discharge fees even though it satisfied permit conditions. The compliance scenario also included a treatment plant construction cost of 950,000 *yuan*, but this cost had little impact on the factory's decisions because half of it was covered by a grant from the EPB's pollution levy fund. Although the factory paid the other half of the construction cost, that amount was comparable to the cost of running the treatment plant for a single year.

Under the noncompliance scenario, the factory incurred only minimal O&M costs, but its discharge fees were substantial (see Table 8.3). The difference between the annual costs of compliance (558,000 *yuan*) and noncompliance (432,000 *yuan*) amounted to 126,000 *yuan*.

From the factory managers' perspective, the additional 126,000 *yuan* per year to meet permit restrictions was small (about 1 percent of total production costs), and compliance carried political and social benefits. For example, by satisfying permit conditions, enterprise managers felt they could improve their position in

Table 8.3   A2 Chemical Fiber Plant's Cost Analysis[a]

Scenario	*Annual Costs(1,000 yuan/year)*		
	Operation and Maintenance	*Discharge Fees*	*Total*
Compliance with permit	438	120	558
Noncompliance with permit	60	372	432

[a]For details on how individual table entries were estimated, see Ma (1997: 228).

bargaining over future permit limits. Being in compliance also improved the factory's image. In addition, the factory director believed that compliance would yield a long-term cost advantage: "The discharge fee rate is getting higher and higher, and environmental regulations will be increasingly stringent. Therefore it is better to control pollution sooner rather than later" (Interview No. 102593c). Another indication of the factory director's sensitivity to cost is the deliberate decision not to satisfy the 150 mg/l COD effluent standard. Although factory managers felt the 150 mg/l was attainable from a technical perspective, they chose not to meet that limit because of the high cost involved.

"Saving Money in EPB" by Overpaying Fees

During our fieldwork in Changzhou in 1993, we learned that several enterprises had voluntarily paid discharge fees in excess of required amounts. Two factors contributed to this counterintuitive outcome: (1) the Changzhou EPB policy of giving enterprises grants from the pollution levy fund, and (2) the Chinese tax code. These factors gave some enterprises an opportunity to increase profits by as much as 35 percent of their annual discharge fees. Aspects of the tax code that allowed this to occur involve distinctions between realized profit (RP) and net profit (NP).

For a Chinese enterprise, annual *realized profit* is yearly profit before paying income tax, and it is calculated as:

$$RP = I - C - PT,$$

where   I   = income from product sales,
        C   = cost, and
        PT = product tax.[13]

In the absence of discharge fees, the annual *net profit* is:

$$NP = RP - IT,$$

where   IT = income tax (i.e., tax on annual realized profit).

While all enterprises pay a product tax each year, only *profitable* enterprises pay an income tax. Before changes in the tax code were made in 1994, large- and medium-sized SOEs paid an income tax equal to 55 percent of annual realized profit (i.e., 0.55 RP). For such enterprises, only 45 percent of realized profit remained as net profit.[14]

To see why a large- or medium-sized SOE in Changzhou might pay discharge fees in excess of required amounts, consider two scenarios. In the first, the enterprise pays no discharge fees and its annual net profit is simply

$$NP_1 = 0.45 \, RP,$$

where subscript "1" denotes the first scenario. In the second scenario, the enterprise pays an annual discharge fee of F *yuan*. In this instance, the net profit is affected in three ways: (1) the enterprise must subtract F from realized profit, (2) the enterprise pays less income tax because its realized profit is lower by F, and (3) the enterprise can augment its net profit by 0.8F to reflect the nontaxable grant of 80 percent of fees the enterprise was eligible to receive from Changzhou EPB's pollution levy fund.[15] In algebraic terms, the resulting net profit is

$$NP_2 = (RP - F) - 0.55(RP - F) + 0.8F,$$

where the subscript "2" denotes the second scenario. After some algebraic simplification, NP_2 can be written as:

$$NP_2 = 0.45RP + 0.35F.$$

The 0.8F grant from the pollution levy fund is for use in pollution abatement. However, if Changzhou's factory managers felt they would make investments in pollution control, they could count on eventually obtaining 80 percent of the discharge fees they paid. Comparing NP_2 with NP_1, a factory that paid F *yuan* in fees could increase its annual net profits by 0.35F.

Some enterprise managers called the process of paying excess fees "saving money in EPB" because they viewed paying fees like putting money in a bank. Eventually they would withdraw 80 percent of their fee payments and, in the meantime, they could enjoy higher profits because they paid lower taxes.

Although several SOEs in Changzhou paid more discharge fees than required in the early 1990s, they stopped doing so for two reasons. First, under the tax code China adopted in 1994, their income tax rate was cut from 55 percent to 33 percent. This change reduced the magnitude of the possible increase in net profits.[16] Second, changes in rules for using Changzhou EPB's pollution levy fund meant enterprises could not be sure they would receive 0.8F as a non-repayable grant. The 0.8F might come as a low-interest loan.

The experience of Changzhou SOEs in "saving money in EPB" shows how sensitive enterprise managers can be to subtleties in the tax code that allow them to enhance after-tax profits. The experience also demonstrates how the design of an environmental program, in this case the discharge fee system, can yield responses from enterprises that would be very difficult for the program's creators to anticipate.

FORMS OF ENTERPRISE OWNERSHIP

State-owned enterprises and TVEs differ in numerous ways, including access to capital and responsibility for providing social services. Our survey results from Changzhou and Shunde, the two cities in which we surveyed both SOEs and TVEs, allow us to examine whether the form of ownership affects the degree of compliance with environmental rules.[17]

Forms of Ownership and Degrees of Compliance

Table 8.4, which summarizes our survey results from Changzhou and Shunde, demonstrates that the rate of compliance with effluent standards is quite similar for SOEs (37 percent compliance) and TVEs (33 percent). The table also shows that rates of compliance with permit conditions are similar for SOEs (76 percent) and TVEs (71 percent). The discharge fee system is the only one of the three programs where compliance rates for SOEs and TVEs are notably different. Only 59 percent of the SOEs paid fees on time compared to 90 percent of the TVEs. Moreover, the one TVE that delayed payment paid required fees at a later date. Of the nine SOEs that did not pay fees on time, only one eventually paid. Before analyzing aspects of Table 8.4, we introduce a caveat: because both SOEs and TVEs included in our survey are heavily polluting enterprises that are regulated carefully by local EPBs, the enterprises are not representative and our results cannot be generalized. In contrast to the TVEs in our survey, many TVEs are rarely monitored by EPBs. Moreover, TVEs included in our survey are not average because the level of economic development in rural portions of Shunde and Changzhou is atypically high. Rates of TVE compliance with environmental requirements are much lower in many areas, particularly in central and western China (Zhou and Tang, 1996).

Table 8.4 Compliance with Water Pollution Control Regulations (1992): TVEs vs. SOEs[a]

	SOEs	TVEs
Sample size	35	15
Effluent standards[b]		
Number of enterprises in compliance	13	5
Number of valid observations	35	15
Compliance rate	37%	33%
Discharge permits		
Number of enterprises in compliance	25	10
Number of valid observations	33	14
Compliance rate	76%	71%
Discharge fees		
Number of enterprises in compliance	13	9
(i.e., enterprises that paid fees on time)		
Number of valid observations[c]	22	10
Compliance rate	59%	90%

[a]This table is based on our survey data for Changzhou and Shunde. See Appendix A for details on how "compliance" is defined and determined for each of the three types of regulatory programs.

[b]For each regulation, the number of valid data points in the sample is lower than the total sample size because of incomplete or inconsistent responses to survey questions.

[c]Local effluent standards in Changzhou and Shunde are identical to national effluent standards.

TVEs Were More Likely to Pay Fees Than SOEs

We begin our analysis of the influence of ownership form on compliance by addressing the following question: Why is it that 90 percent of the surveyed TVEs in Changzhou and Shunde paid fees on time compared to only 59 percent of the SOEs? One factor explaining this outcome is profitability. In comparison to TVEs in our survey, a higher fraction of SOEs were unprofitable (see Table 8.5), and, other things being equal, money-losing enterprises are less likely to pay fees on time. Another factor contributing to the comparatively higher fee payment rate for TVEs relates to differences in the social consequences of plant closures that could result from tough enforcement of environmental rules. Several attributes of the surveyed enterprises in Changzhou and Shunde suggest that shutting down an SOE would be much more disruptive than closing a TVE. Size is one such attribute. As shown in Table 8.5, 94 percent of the SOEs in our survey are large- or medium-sized, compared to only 47 percent of the TVEs. Also, the SOEs typically employed more people. The average number of employees per state-owned factory in our survey was 1056, compared to 443 for TVEs. In addition, many of the SOEs were responsible for paying retirement pensions and for providing workers with housing, health care, and other social services.[18] In contrast, most TVEs in our survey were new and had no responsibility for retired workers. Moreover, many TVE employees had previously been farmers. In the face of a TVE closure, many of those workers could return to farming. Because of differences in social effects of plant closures, EPBs in Changzhou and Shunde were less likely to enforce discharge fee rules stringently at money-losing SOEs in comparison to unprofitable TVEs.

The general argument that local governments hesitated to enforce discharge fee payment rules at money-losing SOEs is further supported by events in

Table 8.5   Attributes of Enterprises Surveyed in Changzhou and Shunde

	SOEs	*TVEs*
Sample size	35	15
Unprofitable enterprises[a]	14 (40%)	3 (20%)
Large- and medium-sized enterprises[b]	33 (94%)	7 (47%)
Small-sized enterprises	2 (6%)	8 (53%)
Old enterprises[c]	31 (89%)	4 (27%)

[a]Data outside parentheses are the number of enterprises with the corresponding attribute. Data within parentheses represent the percentage of enterprises with the corresponding attribute.

[b]Definitions for large-, medium-, and small-sized SOEs vary by industrial sector.

[c]A "new" enterprise is one established after September 13, 1979, when the *PRC Environmental Protection Law for Trial Implementation* was promulgated. This definition of an "old" enterprise was consistent with common usage within NEPA at the time of our survey.

Chongqing during 1989.19 At that time, Chong-qing Municipal People's Government announced that 82 "difficult state-owned enterprises" that were in poor economic health would be exempted from paying discharge fees (and some taxes). Following the government's announcement, several other SOEs applied to be classified as "difficult." In 1993, Chongqing Municipal People's Government exempted from pollution discharge fees all money-losing state-owned enterprises in the textile industry (CCICED, 1994; Interview No. 71394).

The relatively tough positions EPBs have taken against TVEs for violating environmental rules are also reflected by events in Shandong Province. In April 1996, Shandong Provincial People's Government issued *A Public Notice on Closing Down Small-Sized Paper Mills*. This notice required the closure and dismantling (by June 30, 1996) of all enterprises in the province that had an annual pulp production capacity of less than 5,000 tons *and* failed to meet national effluent standards (SPPG, 1996a). In April 1996, the provincial government also issued *A Decision on Strengthening Water Pollution Prevention and Control* requiring enterprises with annual pulp production capacities of less than 10,000 tons to shut down by the end of 1997 if they failed to meet effluent standards. This decision also required the closure of "small-sized chemical, tannery, printing, and dyeing plants that [were] heavily polluting and unprofitable" (SPPG, 1996b). According to Shandong EPB staff we interviewed, TVEs accounted for more than 95 percent of the enterprises forced out of business as a result of the above-noted April 1996 edicts.

TVEs and SOEs Violated Rules for Different Reasons

Rates of noncompliance with permit conditions and effluent standards were similar for TVEs and SOEs (see Table 8.4). However, our interviews at twelve case study enterprises indicate that reasons for noncompliance by TVEs and SOEs can be quite different.20 Factory managers at our nine case study SOEs explained their failure to meet environmental rules by describing their enterprises' poor economic health or the high cost of compliance. In contrast, managers at our three case study TVEs did not dwell on cost issues. Instead, they cited poor management of wastewater treatment facilities as the most important reason for noncompliance.

Our survey results from Changzhou and Shunde are consistent with the view that SOEs fail to meet environmental rules because of financial difficulties, whereas TVEs fail because of poor environmental management capabilities. Table 8.6 summarizes survey responses to the following question: "What kinds of government assistance does your factory need most to enhance your ability to comply with environmental regulations?" As shown in the table, 93 percent of the TVEs in our survey felt that lack of *environmental management training for staff* was a serious obstacle to pollution abatement, but only 40 percent of the SOEs considered this troublesome. In contrast, shortage of *capital for pollution control* (e.g., grants and loans) is viewed as a problem by 66 percent of the SOE

Table 8.6   Government Assistance Needed by Enterprises to Comply with Regulations[a]

	SOEs	*TVEs*
Sample size	35	15
Environmental management training for staff	14 (40%)	14 (93%)
Information on pollution abatement technology and management	22 (63%)	10 (66%)
Awards for compliance	24 (68%)	7 (46%)
Capital for pollution control	23 (66%)	5 (33%)
Reliable technology for pollution abatement	7 (20%)	5 (33%)
Demonstration projects for pollution abatement	3 (12%)	1 (7%)
Other	1 (3%)	0 (0%)

[a]Data outside parentheses are the number of enterprises checking the corresponding listed answer. Data within parentheses represent the percentage of enterprises considering the answer important. Response items are listed in descending order of importance for surveyed TVEs.

managers, but only by 33 percent of the TVE managers.21 Because we have already discussed how funding problems caused SOEs to violate environmental rules, we focus here on environmental management shortcomings at TVEs.

Eight of the nine case study SOEs had a special administrative unit for environmental management, while no such unit existed at any of the three case study TVEs. Our survey results for Changzhou and Shunde reinforce the view that TVEs have poor environmental management capabilities in comparison to SOEs. The average number of full-time environmental managers per surveyed enterprise was much smaller for TVEs (0.26) than SOEs (0.83). Moreover, the average number of environmental managers (including both full-time and part-time managers) having a college degree was 1.1 for SOEs, but only 0.5 for TVEs.

Entries in Table 8.7 make it clear that the lack of equipment to control pollution was not a major obstacle to pollution reduction at TVEs we surveyed. Because those TVEs were relatively new—nearly three-quarters of the fifteen TVEs were built in the 1980s and 1990s—they had been subjected to requirements of the three synchronizations policy. As a consequence, 93 percent of the TVEs had

Table 8.7   Wastewater Treatment at Surveyed Enterprises in Changzhou and Shunde

	SOEs	*TVEs*
Number of enterprises surveyed	35	15
Percent of enterprises with wastewater treatment facilities	80%	93%
Percent of industrial wastewater treated	50%	76%
Percent of treated industrial wastewater meeting effluent standards	62%	50%

wastewater treatment works (compared to only 80 percent of thesurveyed SOEs). Table 8.7 also shows that while TVEs treated a larger percentage of their waste-water than SOEs, a smaller fraction of their *treated* wastewater met effluent standards. The relative ineffectiveness of treatment suggests that treatment facilities at the TVEs were either poorly designed or, as is more likely, poorly operated.

Survey results in Table 8.6 are further reinforced by our case studies. We found that (compared to the nine SOEs) environmental managers at the three TVEs had a less complete understanding of pollution problems and treatment technology. The environmental management limitations that we observed at TVEs are consistent with findings in Kimberley Warren's empirical study of pollution prevention at Chinese electroplating factories. She concluded that limited technical knowledge and capability was the key barrier to adoption of pollution prevention measures by the TVEs she investigated. Warren characterized the technical capabilities of directors and staff at her case study TVEs as follows:

> Even when directors were eager to reduce pollution in their factories, they did not have the capacity to identify and design pollution prevention alternatives. Directors and staff in [the case study TVEs] often lacked basic knowledge about technical processes, sources of pollution during production, or the type, scale, and effects of the pollutants generated by their firms. (Warren, 1996: 345)

High turnover of environmental managers also contributes to the problems TVEs have had in managing waste. Unlike the employment system at SOEs, where workers tend to stay with their firms, environmental managers at TVEs frequently leave to take advantage of better employment opportunities. Environmental personnel who quit are often replaced by less experienced staff. As a result, many environmental managers at TVEs do not have the experience needed to effectively operate their wastewater treatment facilities.

One of our case studies—S3 Dyeing Company, a medium-sized township enterprise in Shunde—illustrates the problems TVEs have with high turnover of environmental staff. All wastewater at this factory was treated, but none of it met effluent standards in 1992 and 1993. According to managers at S3 Dyeing Company, the biochemical oxidation technology used in the treatment plant was extremely unstable, and difficulties in using this technology prevented the factory from meeting effluent standards. The enterprise's problems were compounded when the factory's one experienced environmental manager quit in 1992. At that point, no one at the factory had the background to solve the technical problems causing poor performance of the treatment system (Interview No. 51694). Our interviews at the Shunde EPB indicated that high turnover of environmental personnel at TVEs was a common problem. EPB staff in Shunde complained about how frustrating it was to train environmental managers at TVEs, only to learn that the managers quit their jobs soon after they completed their training.

The relatively weak environmental management capabilities of TVEs in our survey is also reflected in their poor monitoring capabilities. About 26 percent of the surveyed TVEs did not test their wastewater.[22] Monitoring problems were generally linked to a lack of equipment and staff needed to sample wastewater and conduct laboratory analyses to determine pollutant concentrations. Because of this limited monitoring capability, many TVE managers were unable to understand pollutant discharge patterns, such as temporal variations in effluent quality, linkages between operating conditions in production workshops, and concentrations of pollutants in wastewater releases. This lack of awareness compounded the problems TVEs had in meeting environmental rules.

Compliance with environmental regulations is clearly influenced by socioeconomic context, and thus our findings in this chapter apply only for the period of our field research—the early 1990s. Chinese enterprises have been forced to respond to many changes in their social and economic contexts throughout the 1990s. These changes affected each of the three enterprise characteristics examined in this chapter: profitability, compliance costs, and form of ownership. During the ongoing transition to a market economy, the profitability of many Chinese enterprises has been unstable, and short-term changes in policies governing taxation, prices, and inflation have affected compliance costs. In addition, transformations in forms of ownership have occurred at many enterprises. For example, many SOEs have become corporations owned by stockholders that include state agencies, corporate investors, and individuals.[23] Because enterprise characteristics that influence compliance can fluctuate from year to year, it is difficult to predict if any particular enterprise will continually satisfy environmental rules. During the transition to a market economy, enterprises may move from compliance to noncompliance, and vice versa, over short periods. The high rate of change in institutions during the transition poses challenges to environmental policy makers. They can only keep up with the rapid changes by evaluating policy implementation regularly, and by modifying environmental programs in response to results of those evaluations.

NOTES

1. Suspended solids in an untreated wastewater can lead to sludge deposits and anaerobic conditions in the water body receiving the discharge.

2. The second permit was written for the period from December 1991 to December 1992. However, conditions in the second permit remained in effect until the third permit was issued in June 1993.

3. Facts in this paragraph are based on Interview No. 102593a.

4. In Anyang, the process of collecting discharge fees includes several steps. First, the EPB issues a notice specifying the discharge fee an enterprise should pay. If it agrees with the EPB's assessment, the enterprise has twenty days from the time the notice is received to inform its bank to transfer the money to an EPB bank account used for discharge fees. If the enterprise disagrees with the EPB's assessment, it has twenty days to submit a report to the EPB describing its disagreement. If the enterprise does not pay the

fee within three months, the EPB is authorized to transfer the money from the enterprise's account to the EPB's account without the enterprise's permission.

5. "Taxes to the state and grain to the emperor" refers to the tax on profit the factory is supposed to submit to the government. We heard this Chinese phrase often when we visited enterprises that were losing money and violating environmental requirements.

6. Pollution control within deadlines is one of eight national environmental programs described in Chapter 2.

7. A Chinese enterprise cannot obtain a World Bank loan unless the local government, typically the local finance bureau, guarantees repayment.

8. Facts in this paragraph are from Interview No. 122193.

9. The enterprise used its own funds to cover 235,000 *yuan* of the capital investment for the air flotation units. The remainder was subsidized by a grant (265,000 *yuan*) and a loan (200 thousand *yuan*) from the Changzhou EPB's pollution levy fund.

10. For more on this point, see case studies in Warren (1996) and Sinkule and Ortolano (1995).

11. See Chapter 6 for details on how Anyang EPB modified its fee calculation procedures.

12. The treatment plant's capacity was raised from 5,000 to 12,000 tons per day, and average removal rates of SS and COD were raised to 75 percent and 45 percent, respectively.

13. Product tax rates range from 3 to 60 percent of the income from sales, depending on the product type; rates are set by the National Taxation Bureau. For details on taxes faced by enterprises, see Du (1992).

14. This result follows because

$$NP = RP - (0.55\ RP) = 0.45\ RP.$$

For details on income tax rates before the 1994 changes, see Oi (1992) and Wang (1994: 85–86).

15. There is an upper limit to the amount a factory can expect to receive from the levy fund: the cost of building a treatment facility to reduce the factory's pollution discharge. This limit sets a bound on the amount an enterprise would pay over and above its required discharge fees.

16. The 1994 change in the tax code imposed a uniform tax—for SOEs and TVEs—amounting to 33 percent of realized profit. Using the same reasoning employed in deriving the equation for NP_2 above, it can be shown that the potential for "saving money in EPB" dropped from 0.35F to 0.13F after the tax code was changed in 1994.

17. In Anyang, the third city in our survey, we surveyed only SOEs.

18. In several of our case study SOEs, retired workers accounted for one-third of the number of people linked to the enterprises.

19. The proposition that governments were more concerned about the viability of SOEs compared to TVEs is also supported by outcomes from a nationwide austerity program initiated in 1989. As a result of that program, about three million TVEs were forced into bankruptcy or were taken over by other TVEs. But during the same year, nearly all unprofitable SOEs avoided bankruptcy by being bailed out by the state (Qian and Xu, 1992).

20. Appendix A provides basic information about the twelve case study enterprises.

21. Changzhou and Shunde differ in terms of need for capital for pollution control technology: 61 percent of enterprises we surveyed in Changzhou expressed a need for capital, but the corresponding figure in Shunde was only 38 percent. This may reflect differences

in economic development in the two cities. In 1993, the gross domestic product per capita was 10,224 *yuan* for Shunde (GDSB, 1994), compared to 6,798 *yuan* for Changzhou (JSSB, 1994).

22. By comparison, only 6 percent of the surveyed SOEs in Changzhou and Shunde failed to monitor their wastes.

23. For details on the major types of stock companies created in China during the mid-1990s, see Ji (1998: Chapter 8).

Comparing China and the United States

We conclude our analysis of compliance with China's water pollution control requirements by comparing Chinese programs with their United States counterparts. Because the United States does not have a national pollution discharge fee program,[1] our comparative analysis is restricted to only two of the three programs we investigated in China: effluent standards and the discharge permit system.

In the United States, the counterparts to Chinese effluent standards and discharge permits are embodied in the National Pollutant Discharge Elimination System (NPDES), which Congress created in 1972.[2] Under NPDES, environmental agencies issue permits that indicate allowable concentrations and mass flowrates of pollutants in a wastewater discharger's release. These limits on concentration and flowrate, which are set on a case-by-case basis, constitute a de facto effluent standard. The United States does not employ uniform national effluent standards of the type used in China.

Our comparison of China and the United States is structured around elements of the institutional framework for environmental protection employed in previous chapters: organizations, formal and informal rules, and enforcement. For each of these elements, we first summarize findings from previous chapters regarding China. Then we introduce corresponding information about the United States and provide a comparative assessment.

ORGANIZATIONS INFLUENCING COMPLIANCE WITH POLLUTION CONTROL RULES

Chinese Organizations

In contrast with most other countries, China's national environmental agency—the State Environmental Protection Administration—plays a minor role in the day-to-day implementation of environmental rules. Although SEPA helps draft environmental laws and regulations, most national water pollution control requirements are implemented by EPBs.

An environmental protection bureau is part of a local government *and* a unit in the administrative hierarchy that has SEPA at the top. Thus an EPB has two formal reporting relationships: *kuai-kuai* relations connect an EPB with the head of its local government, and *tiao-tiao* relations link an EPB with an environmental agency one level up in the hierarchy. Local government leaders control an EPB's budget and staffing, and thus they typically have a stronger influence on routine EPB actions then the next highest environmental agency in the hierarchy.

Because of the institutional setting in which it operates, an EPB cannot be effective unless it secures the backing of local political leaders and other agencies, such as the local economic commission and industrial bureaus that supervise state-owned enterprises. For example, without the support of the mayor, a municipal EPB could not hope to enforce costly environmental rules at enterprises that provide important sources of revenues to the municipal government and jobs for local residents.

Many local agencies have assisted the EPBs in their areas, but their ability to do so was weakened as a result of the *1992 Regulations on Transformation of Management Mechanisms at State-Owned Industrial Enterprises*. For example, before 1992, all new industrial construction projects had to be examined and approved by a municipality's planning commission. In many cities, planning commission staff informed EPBs of large projects and solicited opinions of EPBs before deciding whether to approve those projects.

Flows of information from local agencies to EPBs were cut substantially after the 1992 *Regulations on Transformation* were issued. For example, in the post-1992 context, enterprises with sufficient financial resources could build new factories without obtaining approvals from planning commissions. Even though enterprises are legally bound to register proposed new projects with planning commissions, this requirement has been ignored frequently. Many enterprises have registered their projects at the time of construction and some have even delayed registration until project completion. In some instances, EPBs first learned about new projects after they had been built. As a result of changes in information flows that followed the 1992 *Regulations on Transformation*, EPBs can no longer depend on other agencies for information on proposed industrial development projects and renovations of existing factories.

Although EPBs have been less able to count on local agencies for information and support in recent years, they have enjoyed increased backing from local people's congresses and from the media and individual citizens. Many people's congresses have become advocates of environmental protection and have provided citizens with mechanisms for registering complaints about environmental problems. Moreover, the media is playing an increasingly important role in environmental affairs. The media's significance was emphasized by Qu Geping, the first head of NEPA:

Using the media to expose violators and to praise enforcers of environmental regulations was the main tool the NPC could use to get local government compliance with national environmental protection regulations. (Qu Geping as quoted by United States Embassy, Beijing, 1998)

In the past few years, China's moves toward political liberalization and a market economy have been accompanied by the emergence of environmental nongovernmental organizations. While these organizations must be sanctioned by the government and do not have the independence and enforcement authorities of environmental NGOs in the United States, they represent early signs of an environmental movement that has the potential to help EPBs carry out their work. For example, some NGOs have concentrated on raising citizen awareness of environmental problems and requirements, and an informed citizenry can provide support for EPB activities.

Enterprises are the main targets of environmental regulations in China, and the participation of local governments in enterprise supervision or ownership leads to special challenges for environmental agencies. While China has a growing private sector, most industrial enterprises are still classified as either state-owned enterprises or township and village enterprises. Most TVEs are themselves owned by either township governments or village committees.

Before recent efforts to weaken ties between firms and governments, many enterprises could satisfy environmental rules by simply adding environmental investment costs and discharge fee payments to other costs of doing business, and then requesting government funds to cover those costs. Market reforms have changed that. Now that enterprises receive less government support, they must rely more on bank loans and retained earnings to build treatment works. As a result of cuts in government funding, enterprises have greater incentives to delay meeting environmental requirements.

U.S. Organizations

In contrast to the situation in China, the national-level environmental agency in the United States—the United States Environmental Protection Agency (US EPA)—*is* responsible for implementing (or ensuring adherence with) national water pollution control laws. In most states, US EPA delegates much of the day-to-day work of implementation to state environmental protection agencies that are interested in doing the work and have the required capacity. In instances where state agencies do not implement NPDES permit requirements, regional offices of US EPA run the permit program. Ten regional offices are distributed across the country and each has responsibility for a particular group of states.

In order for a state to carry out the federal permit program, it must demonstrate that it has the necessary staff, statutory authority, monitoring capabilities, and other required resources. As of the late 1990s, US EPA had given over forty states primary responsibility for NPDES permits. In those states, permits are is-sued and enforced by state agencies, but US EPA is responsible for ensuring that NPDES is implemented properly. While states receive funding from US EPA to administer NPDES, the funding does not generally cover all operating costs. States are willing to pay the remaining costs in exchange for maintaining con-trol over how the federal permit program is run.

Organizations Influencing Day-to-Day Implementation of NPDES

Because the agencies administering NPDES are not bureaus of local government, they are not subject to the intensity of local political pressure faced by Chinese EPBs. Environmental agencies in the United States certainly face political pres-sure, but the influence of that pressure varies. Arguably, federal water pollution control programs administered by US EPA regional offices are subject to less political manipulation than are comparable state-run programs, and enormous variations exist in the mix of political forces within states. Political influence on NPDES implementation is greater at the state level because the head of each state's environmental agency is appointed by the governor, and agency budgets are typically set by state legislatures.[3]

One aspect of the NPDES permit program *is* implemented in an organizational context similar to the one faced by EPBs in China. The NPDES program requires local agencies that operate publicly-owned treatment works to issue *pretreatment* permits to firms that discharge into their sewer systems. Many operators of these treatment facilities are agencies of local governments, and those governments rely on taxes and fees from local firms as revenue sources. The NPDES pre-treatment permit program resembles the discharge permit system in China in terms of its susceptibility to local political forces. In both countries, industry can exert pres-sure on local officials in an attempt to obtain favorable treatment, and local gov-ernments depend on revenues from firms.

Interesting differences exist in the way environmental rules are applied at municipalities in the United States and China. In China, only a small fraction (about 7 percent) of municipal wastewater is treated. Moreover, because most municipal treatment plants in China are new, many EPBs have not monitored municipal discharges carefully. Consequently, enforcement of discharge limits at municipal plants has been weak or nonexistent. In contrast, discharge permit conditions have been enforced carefully at many municipal plants in the United States. In addition, US EPA and delegated state environmental agencies can in-tervene if a municipality is not properly implementing NPDES pretreatment re-quirements.

In the United States, the ability of political officials to influence individual permits is checked by the transparency of the permit process and by the watch-dog role played by citizens and NGOs. Under the U.S. Clean Water Act, citizens and NGOs can (and do) bring lawsuits against dischargers that violate NPDES permit conditions, and they can also sue US EPA for failure to enforce rigorously the Clean Water Act. In preparing for court actions, citizens and NGOs can obtain much information from environmental agencies. For example, citizens can review NPDES permits as well as the discharge monitoring reports that permit holders must routinely submit to US EPA and state environmental agencies.

The United States and China differ in term of how courts are used for environmental enforcement. In China, courts are not often used to settle environmental disputes, and agencies cannot depend on courts to enforce environmental laws. In contrast, US EPA and state agencies rely on court actions and the threat thereof as mechanisms for enforcing NPDES permit conditions.[4] As mentioned, U.S. citizens and NGOs frequently use the courts for this purpose. In addition, even regulated parties—primarily firms and municipalities—bring lawsuits to challenge provisions of regulations that US EPA develops to implement the Clean Water Act.

Another point of contrast in the way organizations influence environmental protection relates to the mass media. While television stations and newspapers in China have recently become advocates of environmental protection, the media within the United States has promoted public awareness and support for environmental programs since the 1960s. Media coverage in the United States has been significant in informing citizens about environmental problems, instructing citizens on opportunities to improve environmental quality, exposing polluters, and criticizing agencies for lax enforcement of environmental rules.

Other organizational differences concern the parties regulated by discharge permit programs. Whereas China's permit system regulates mainly enterprises, NPDES regulates municipalities and federal facilities (such as military bases) as well as companies.[5] Moreover, firms in the United States do not have the same respect for government authority as their counterparts in China. Indeed, the attitude of many U.S. businesses toward government has been "deeply adversarial" (Andrews, 1997: 84). While some U.S. corporations have taken strong pro-environmental positions, many believe environmental regulations are excessively stringent and do not produce benefits that justify the costs of compliance.

Organizations Influencing General Administration of NPDES

We conclude our analysis of organizations influencing NPDES by examining how top-level elected and appointed officials can affect the administration of the permit program. Our discussion uses US EPA as an example, but similar points could be made about state agencies that issue NPDES permits. The Office of the President can influence NPDES activities by its choice of top US EPA officials, and by its proposals for the agency's funding in the president's budget. Congress can also affect NPDES implementation because it sets US EPA's final budget. Moreover, the Senate can overturn the President's choice of top agency officials, and congressional committees can hold hearings to oversee NPDES implementation.

Combined effects of presidential and congressional influence on NPDES activities are difficult to disentangle because effects sometimes cancel each other out. In addition, US EPA can exercise its own initiative (e.g., by controlling information flows to Congress) to counteract or reinforce actions taken by the President or Congress.

A recent study by Hunter and Waterman (1996) demonstrates the difficulties in sorting out these combined effects. The analysts conducted statistical studies to examine how political hierarchy influenced US EPA's implementation of the NPDES during the Reagan administration (1980–88). Hunter and Waterman hypothesized that NPDES enforcement would fall between 1980 and 1983, since Reagan's first US EPA Administrator, Anne Gorsuch, was decidedly pro-business and took steps to dismantle the agency's enforcement program. The analysts also hypothesized that NPDES enforcement would increase during 1983–84, when Reagan replaced his first US EPA Administrator with William Ruckleshaus, who gave priority to enforcement activities.

Some relationships that Hunter and Waterman expected to see between NPDES enforcement and controls exerted by the President and Congress were supported by their statistical results. In particular, they found that increased attention by the House of Representatives to water-related issues and a high frequency of congressional hearings on environment were associated with increased facility inspections by the agency's NPDES personnel. Counterintuitively, the researchers found the opposite relationship for the Senate. Surprisingly, they also determined that NPDES enforcement did not decrease under Gorsuch, whereas it did increase (as they hypothesized) under Ruckleshaus. Overall, Hunter and Waterman (1996: 121) found that US EPA staff are accountable to the President and the Congress, but the influences of the President, the Senate, and the House of Representatives are difficult to sort out when they act at cross purposes.

The impact of the judiciary on NPDES implementation is more clear-cut: U.S. courts have affected NPDES implementation often and with great effect. Courts have ruled frequently on cases challenging effluent guidelines used in setting permit conditions, as well as cases involving complaints against polluters brought by environmental agencies, citizens, and NGOs. Many of these lawsuits have influenced the overall direction of the NPDES permit program.[6]

FORMAL RULES: PERMIT SYSTEM DESIGN

China's Discharge Permit System

The permit system that China implemented on a trial basis required environmental protection bureaus to establish, for each regulated enterprise, limits on concentrations and mass flowrates of pollutants in the enterprise's wastewater. National rules governing how permits were written did *not* require concentration limits to be as stringent as effluent standards. Because many permits had less demanding concentration restrictions than those in effluent standards, it was common to find enterprises that satisfied permit conditions while violating effluent standards.

Environmental protection bureaus were given freedom to tailor DPS requirements to meet local circumstances. Many EPBs expressed this freedom by adopting a modest goal for the permit system: maintain current levels of environmental quality in the face of increasing industrial output. This goal, which endorsed existing levels of pollution, was considered reasonable by many EPBs because of China's focus on industrial growth during the 1990s.

For EPBs that selected the above-noted DPS goal, the allowable concentration of chemical oxygen demand in an enterprise's first permit was often set equal to the actual COD the enterprise specified in its permit application. This allowable COD was then multiplied by the existing volume flowrate of wastewater to yield the allowable mass flowrate of COD. When this procedure was followed, enterprises could satisfy permit requirements without reducing pollution because allowable COD limits were equivalent to pre-permit discharge conditions.

Sometimes EPBs insisted on making allowable COD concentrations lower than values specified in permit applications, and EPBs frequently cut allowable COD concentrations and mass flowrates when permits came up for renewal. In these instances, EPBs and enterprises negotiated permit limits. Objective criteria were not used in setting permit conditions.

For most of the six EPBs in our study, relationships between wastewater discharges and ambient water quality did not play an important role in setting permit requirements. In order to make an explicit connection between wastewater releases and stream quality, EPBs would have had to construct mathematical models. The six EPBs in our study were not prepared to do this because they lacked the technical ability and data needed to run mathematical water quality models. Moreover, many EPBs questioned whether mathematical models provided an appropriate basis for setting permit limits.

NPDES in the United States

Permit writers in China have extraordinary flexibility, but writers of NPDES permits must follow a well-defined procedure. The centerpiece of the procedure is a set of US EPA regulations that details the agency's minimum expectations for constraints on wastewater releases from factories in about fifty industrial categories and municipalities. These regulations, commonly referred to as "effluent guidelines," constitute a body of administrative law.[7] In addition to being consistent with effluent guidelines, permit restrictions must protect receiving water quality.

At the time NPDES was started in 1972, permits were based on effluent guidelines specifying "best practicable control technology currently available." When the first round of permits came up for renewal after five years, permit writers had to use a more demanding set of effluent guidelines based on "best available technology economically achievable" (BAT). An exception was made for traditional measures of pollution, such as COD, suspended solids, and pH. For these "conventional pollutants," permit limits were based on "best conventional pollution control technology" (BCT).

When an environmental agency receives an NPDES permit application from a wastewater discharger, the agency's permit writers use effluent guidelines that delineate BAT and BCT to determine limits on the applicant's wastewater release. For firms having facilities not covered by effluent guidelines, permit writers must conduct ad hoc studies to determine discharge restrictions based on BAT and BCT. In such cases, permit writers use "best professional judgment," which is frequently informed by studies conducted by environmental engineering consulting firms.

Procedures for setting NPDES permit conditions based on BAT and BCT establish a minimum set of discharge limits, but those limits are not necessarily final. US EPA's regulations require permit writers to examine whether the quality of the watercourse receiving the permit applicant's discharge would violate ambient water quality standards if a release based on BAT and BCT were made. In principle, this determination is based on mathematical modeling exercises. If it turns out that ambient standards would be violated, permit conditions based on BAT and BCT need to be tightened: limits on concentrations and mass flowrates must be such that ambient water quality standards would be satisfied.

In practice, permit writers have sometimes had problems implementing procedures for ensuring that ambient water quality standards would be met. One difficulty is that, until recently, many states did not have numerical standards for some regulated pollutants, particularly toxic substances. Along the same lines, many ambient standards used descriptive criteria, such as the obligation of polluters to avoid interference with recreational uses of streams and lakes. Permit writers have had problems using such general criteria to set numerical permit limits. Finally, the complexity and expense of using mathematical models to estimate how much different polluters contribute to decreases in ambient water quality have also caused difficulties in setting permit restrictions.

In contrast to the ambiguous rules governing permit conditions in China, formal requirements used to establish permit limits in the United States restrict greatly the types of issues waste dischargers can negotiate with permit writers. Negotiations center on technical matters, such as the applicability of particular mathematical models and the professional judgment used in setting BAT and BCT limits (in cases where US EPA's effluent guidelines do not apply.)[8]

Another difference between the permit programs in the United States and China is that Chinese discharge permits often cover a much narrower range of contaminants than NPDES permits. For example, in the many permits we examined in six Chinese cities, at most four parameters were listed: COD, suspended solids, pH, and oil. In contrast, NPDES permits can require dischargers to monitor as many as thirty pollutants, and permits can also include limits for 126 toxic substances (U.S. Council on Environmental Quality, 1993: 89).

Permit systems in the United States and China also differ in the types of facilities that require permits. As noted, China's permits are mainly for enterprises, whereas U.S. permits are used to regulate municipalities and federal facilities, as well as firms. The inclusion of municipalities in the U.S. permit system is notable because in addition to wastewater releases from publicly owned treatment plants, municipal coverage involves:

- Industrial wastes flowing to municipal sewer lines.
- Surface runoff draining to municipal stormwater sewers.
- Semisolid residues, commonly termed "sludge," from municipal treatment facilities.

INFORMAL RULES

Pragmatic Administrative Approach in China

Our introduction to informal rules in Chapter 5 centered on three concepts: respect for authority, *guanxi*, and face. We now summarize how those concepts apply to China's permit system and introduce an informal rule not mentioned in our previous discussion.

Respect for authority is reflected in the way EPBs carry out their work. In the context of DPS, the need to respect authority is but one of several factors EPBs consider in setting and enforcing permit conditions. For example, if a mayor or other top official suggests that an EPB relax its efforts to enforce a rule, the EPB is likely to accede. This reflects traditional Chinese respect for authority, but, more significantly, it is also a response to the power wielded by local leaders. EPB directors are very sensitive to the control mayors and other local leaders can exert on their budget and staff allocations.

Many environmental regulators believe they can make better progress in abating pollution by maintaining good relationships (*guanxi*) with enterprises. EPB personnel often told us that most companies they worked with were trying to clean up the environment. And when enterprises failed, it was typically because they lacked resources or technical know-how, not because they did not care if they polluted the environment.

The importance of maintaining *guanxi* was reflected in the unwritten rules that guided the enforcement activities of the EPBs we studied. The following enforcement actions were used sparingly because they would damage the *guanxi* between EPBs and enterprises:

- Charging an enterprise with falsifying information on a permit application.
- Revoking a discharge permit.
- Using court actions to enforce environmental requirements.

The desire of EPBs to maintain good *guanxi* is not the only reason these strategies were not often used. For example, court actions were rarely initiated (except during enforcement campaigns) because of the high cost of preparing for trial and because many EPBs lacked legally trained staff.

Our field research did not uncover many instances where face-saving (or face-enhancing) behaviors had a direct influence on DPS implementation. However, face-saving behaviors played an indirect role because of close connections between face and *guanxi*. For example, charging an enterprise with falsifying information on a permit application would damage *guanxi* because the accused party would lose face.

Arguably, one of the most common informal rules used by EPBs is one used widely in administering the discharge fee program: if an enterprise does not discharge waste causing evident damage to humans, then its violations of effluent standards can be ignored provided the enterprise pays its discharge fees on time.[9] This rule, which amounts to equating compliance with payment of discharge fees, was frequently employed because many EPBs desperately needed fee-based revenues to supplement budget allocations they received from local government leaders.

The importance of discharge fees as a revenue source is highlighted by the practice of some EPBs to charge more than legally stipulated fees when dealing with particularly prosperous enterprises. At the same time, EPBs often did little to collect fees from money-losing enterprises because they felt it was not worth the effort. In addition, late fees were typically not imposed on enterprises behind in their payments lest those enterprises be discouraged from making any payments at all.

Informal Rules in NPDES Implementation

To what extent do respect for authority, political or professional relationships (counterparts to *guanxi*), and face affect administration of the NPDES permit program? While we could find no clear parallel to "respect for authority" as an influence in the United States, powerful individuals sometimes attempt to influence NPDES permits. We discuss this first and then consider whether U.S. equivalents of *guanxi* and face affect NPDES implementation.

Influence of Political Officials on Particular NPDES Cases

High political officials appear to have only marginal effects on particular NPDES permits in states where US EPA implements NPDES on a daily basis. According to US EPA staff we interviewed in the agency's Region 9 office in San Francisco, mayors, legislators, corporate officers, and so forth, frequently call or write attempting to reduce the stringency of the agency's NPDES enforcement. However, US EPA personnel administering the permit program are effectively buffered from those attempts. At most, NPDES personnel (in Region 9 at least) would be asked to brief top regional office staff on how a particular permit case was being handled.

The Region 9 staff we interviewed felt that outside attempts to alter its decisions have failed because supervisors at US EPA have consistently respected their professionalism in handling NPDES enforcement. Moreover, citizens, NGOs, and the media have been watchful of US EPA decisions, particularly on high profile NPDES cases. These entities can bring countervailing pressures, for example, by exposing attempts of politicians to influence agency staff. No equivalent opportunities exist for citizens, NGOs, or the media in China.

In sharp contrast to the situation at US EPA's Region 9 office, some state agency staff implementing NPDES have been pressured to cut back on enforcing NPDES requirements. Based on interviews with state environmental personnel, Hunter and Waterman found "considerable support" for the claim that state implementation of NPDES occurs in a "highly political arena." As examples, they cite observations from two of their interviewees, both top-level enforcement officials from state environmental agencies:

> [A New Mexico official] delineated how, during the tenure of a past Republican governor, considerable pressure was exerted on agency personnel to ease enforcement practices. In one case he even asserted that "a sweetheart deal" was worked out between the governor's office and the number three violator on the state's enforcement priority list. Likewise, an official from Alaska complained that after his office assessed penalties against a particularly egregious violator, a past "governor . . . simply gave the money back." (Hunter and Waterman, 1996: 158)

State environmental agency personnel interviewed by Hunter and Waterman also emphasized the pressure exerted by industry in NPDES enforcement. For example, an environmental official in Arizona complained that business interests there have an "undue influence." The official went on to say that Arizona "is a 'very conservative state.' Development is 'the most important issue' " (Hunter and Waterman, 1996: 158).

If a state running the NPDES program does a poor job of enforcement, US EPA can intervene and conduct its own enforcement. The situation in Virginia when George Allen was governor during the 1990s provides an example. During the Allen administration, the number of penalties imposed by Virginia's Department of Environmental Quality for NPDES violations dropped precipitously, and the administration signaled to industry that the state would back off on environmental enforcement.

During this same period, US EPA worked with the U.S. Department of Justice to sue Smithfield Foods, Inc., a meat-packing company located in Smithfield, Virginia. The government's lawsuit charged Smithfield Foods with presenting false information in its discharge-monitoring reports and having numerous permit violations. Smithfield Foods had been operating for several years under an interim consent order in which the Virginia Department of Environmental Quality had allowed the company to satisfy interim discharge limits for ammonia and phosphorous. The federal suit undermined the validity of the state's interim agreement allowing Smithfield Foods to operate while violating permit conditions. In

August 1997, the federal district court in Norfolk, Virginia found in favor of the
U.S. government and assessed a $12.6 million fine against Smithfield Foods.[10]

The Smithfields Foods' case was only one of many instances in which Virginia
had eased its enforcement of permit requirements. A 1997 report by a State of
Virginia legislative audit commission described numerous cases in which egre-
gious violations of permit conditions met with little or no enforcement response
during the Allen administration (JLARC, 1997). The report also cited interventions by high-level state officials that resulted in reduced enforcement of permit
requirements. When a new governor took office, Virginia's NPDES enforcement
record improved notably.

Relationships Between Agencies and Regulated Facilities

As noted, professional and personal relationships (*guanxi*) between EPB staff and
personnel at regulated factories in China often affect how permits are written and
enforced. Do connections between environmental agency staff and personnel at
regulated facilities play any role in administering NPDES?

Procedures for writing permits limit the extent to which relationships between
U.S. permit writers and staff representing regulated parties can affect permit requirements. In response to an application for a permit, environmental agency staff
applies well-established procedures based on BAT and BCT rules and best professional judgment. Dischargers and agency staff may negotiate while a permit
is being written, but negotiations are limited to technical issues, such as the equipment needed to satisfy permit conditions. Indeed, analysts have characterized the
permit issuance process as "highly technical and non-political" (Hunter and
Waterman, 1996: 38). Permit writers are largely concerned with ensuring that their
professional judgments are defensible from a technical and scientific perspective.
In many cases, regulators work from files and application materials and have limited contact with applicants.

Interestingly, in many states and US EPA regional offices, the individuals who
prepare NPDES permits are different from those who enforce permit conditions.
In those settings, relationships that may have developed while a permit was being written have little opportunity for ongoing development.

In contrast to permit writers, environmental agency staff who make monitoring and enforcement decisions can be influenced by relationships with dischargers. Agency staff who have positive professional ties with regulated parties often place great trust in the information provided by those parties. This trust can
affect discretionary choices, such as decisions on the frequency and type of inspection an agency conducts and how an agency responds to noncompliance incidents. While there is a typical hierarchy of enforcement responses—telephone
calls, letters, official notices of violation, administrative proceedings, and court
actions—agencies exercise discretion in determining when and how to step up
the pressure on permit violators. These choices are affected by the trust (or mis-
trust) created as a result of long-term interactions between agency staff and per-

sonnel at regulated facilities. However, whether permit conditions must eventually be met is not a discretionary decision.

We used our interviews with US EPA staff to explore whether loss of face was an issue in NPDES implementation. Although "face" was not a term used by interviewees, the equivalent of loss of face was raised in one context: the loss of credibility that occurs when inexperienced environmental agency staff makes errors in writing or enforcing permit conditions. In some states, the rate of turnover of staff implementing NPDES has been high, and the possibility that inexperienced staff might make embarrassing mistakes in implementing NPDES has been an ongoing concern.[11] This problem also arises occasionally in US EPA regional offices.

ENFORCEMENT OF PERMIT REQUIREMENTS

China's Reliance on Non-adversarial Enforcement

As in the United States and other countries, environmental enforcement in China involves monitoring an enterprise's compliance status and taking action in response to noncompliance. Assessment of compliance with permit conditions is based on self-monitoring and self-reporting by enterprises and scheduled factory inspections by EPB staff. In contrast to the situation in the United States, China's environmental agency personnel make many *informal* visits to factories they regulate, and they use these visits to exchange information and enhance *guanxi* with factory personnel.

Of the three Chinese environmental programs we analyzed, the record of enterprise compliance with discharge permits was the strongest. This is not surprising because permit requirements were frequently based on status quo discharge conditions and concentration limits in permits were often less rigorous than effluent standards.

Interestingly, enforcement policies issued by SEPA are different from the enforcement approaches taken by environmental protection bureaus. SEPA views development of a rigorous, coercive enforcement strategy as a key task for EPBs. However, EPBs included in our research tailored the strictness of their enforcement to the particular circumstances faced by regulated parties. If an enterprise was having financial difficulties, an EPB would typically adopt a sympathetic, non-confrontational posture. Similarly, if an enterprise was trying to meet environmental requirements but failed because of its financial problems or limited technical know-how, an EPB would avoid coercion. Indeed, the only instances in which EPBs adopted severe enforcement methods were when a profitable enterprise was willfully causing significant harm or when an environmental enforcement campaign was being waged.

The one environmental program that was enforced strictly by EPBs was the discharge fee system. Pollutants were monitored regularly and concerted efforts were made to collect fees. This attention to fee payment is not surprising because many EPBs depended on revenues from fees to support core activities. Arguably, all other EPB programs to control water pollution were enhanced by the EPBs' fee-collection efforts. For example, the fee-collection process provided data characterizing discharges, and revenues from the fee program supported growth of EPB staffs.

EPBs have flexibility in responding to noncompliance, and many have developed cooperative enforcement strategies without policy guidance from SEPA. These locally-designed, cooperative approaches reflect a perspective held by many Chinese environmental regulators we interviewed: the law is not to be followed literally just because it is the law. EPBs often find they can make considerable progress in abating pollution by helping enterprises find solutions and by bargaining with enterprises over requirements, deadlines, and penalties. Many EPB personnel we interviewed felt that relatively few enterprises willfully disobey environmental rules and deserve serious sanctions. In their view, most enterprises that violate requirements do so because they face financial difficulties or have limited technical capabilities.

NPDES Enforcement in Theory and Practice

In contrast to the flexible enforcement approaches adopted in China, agencies that implement NPDES in the United States are expected to follow well-defined procedures in responding to permit violations. Although schedules for bringing violators into compliance are negotiable, permit conditions are not. Results from assessing compliance in each state are summarized in Quarterly Noncompliance Reports (QNCRs). US EPA maintains a Permit Compliance System, a database for tracking the compliance status of all permitted facilities.[12]

As in China, compliance monitoring in the United States occurs in two ways: self-monitoring (and self-reporting) by regulated parties and inspections by environmental agency staff. The U.S. system for self-monitoring differs from the one in China in that U.S. permit holders that falsify data are subject to severe penalties under both civil and criminal law.

Notwithstanding possible penalties, fraudulent monitoring has occurred frequently in the United States. Laboratory tests for measuring trace quantities of many toxics regulated under NPDES are expensive to perform, and some laboratories have used improper shortcuts to save money while billing clients for the expensive, properly run tests.[13] In other instances, such as the previously-mentioned case involving Smithfield Foods, contractors hired by permit holders have submitted falsified monitoring data.

Enforcement of NPDES permits is supposed to follow US EPA's Enforcement Management System, a scheme designed to yield consistent implementation of federal permit requirements across all states. For example, the Environmental Management System calls on US EPA or a state agency responsible for NPDES to provide a "formal enforcement response" to significant noncompliance within sixty days of the time the noncompliance appears in a Quarterly Noncompliance Report. The "significant noncompliance" designation signals that the violation should receive high priority. A formal enforcement response includes use of administrative pollution abatement orders or imposition of fines.

High Variability in Enforcement Activity

US EPA guidance calls for a rigorous strategy of coercive enforcement, but that guidance is not followed strictly. Evidence for spotty enforcement is contained in audit reports prepared by US EPA's Office of Inspector General. Citing senior officials at US EPA headquarters, the *New York Times* noted that the audit "reports point to problems not isolated in the relatively few states where audits were done" (Cushman, 1998: 1).

Consider, for example, the audit covering NPDES implementation in Alaska, Idaho, and Washington by US EPA Region 10 in Seattle, Washington. Auditors reviewed all twenty-five instances of significant noncompliance reported for one or more quarters between October 1994 and December 1996. Region 10 failed to take formal enforcement action against nineteen of the twenty-five dischargers, and thus it departed from guidance in the Enforcement Management Strategy (US EPA, 1998a: iii). For ten of these dischargers, violations were for two or more consecutive quarters. Here also rules of the Environmental Management System were broken, in this case, because Region 10 failed to provide justification for not initiating a formal enforcement response.

Auditors turned up other deficiencies when they examined how permit applications were being processed in Region 10. During the two and one-half years preceding the audit, the regional office had issued thirty-three NPDES permits in Alaska and Idaho, but it had a backlog of one thousand applications waiting to be processed, and seventy percent of those applications were at least four years old (US EPA, 1998a: ii). The audit also found that the QNCRs were sometimes developed using data that was either obsolete or incomplete.

The Office of Inspector General also audited the NPDES program administered by the State of Kansas. In this case, auditors highlighted the state's failure to act on expired permits. As of August 1997, auditors found that Kansas had allowed 182 (of a total of 832) permits to expire for periods up to six years (US EPA, 1998b: 4). After a permit had expired and a new application was filed, discharge restrictions in the expired permit continued to be enforceable.

In contrast to the negative results found in some states, North Carolina's NPDES program received glowing reports. One analyst concluded that North Carolina had one of the nation's best NPDES programs with an overall compliance rate of 94 percent in 1985, and only one percent of major non-municipal dischargers classified as significant noncompliance violators in 1986 (Lowry, 1992: 75).[14]

Role of Citizens and Media in Triggering Enforcement Responses

US EPA's Enforcement Management System includes guidance on how to translate compliance information in Quarterly Noncompliance Reports into "timely and appropriate enforcement actions" (US EPA, 1998a: 30). QNCRs are based mainly on information in discharge monitoring reports submitted by regulators.

Although the Enforcement Management System highlights use of QNCRs to trigger enforcement actions, other approaches are commonly used. For example, in US EPA's Region 9, complaints by citizens and NGOs and anonymous tips about NPDES permit violations play key roles in causing the regional office to take enforcement actions in Arizona, the only state in Region 9 where US EPA runs the NPDES program.

For states other than Arizona, Region 9 is prompted to take enforcement action when cases are referred to it by state environmental agencies implementing NPDES. States typically make such referrals on difficult cases where US EPA can be used as leverage to force cleanups. Media pressure also triggers enforcement within the region. For example, a series of articles in the *San Francisco Chronicle* during the summer of 1997 prompted Region 9 to work with the State of California to subject organic waste from animal feedlots to NPDES requirements.

Factors that bring about follow-up action in Region 9 also apply in other regional offices. A number of US EPA personnel interviewed by Hunter and Waterman indicated that citizen reports of NPDES violations played a major role in compliance monitoring and enforcement. US EPA often initiates enforcement in response to referrals from state environmental agencies. Based on an analysis of over 27,000 NPDES enforcement actions conducted by US EPA between 1975 and 1988, Hunter and Waterman (1996: 69) found that states implementing NPDES "pass off their most serious cases to EPA personnel."

Infrequent Use of Courts to Enforce NPDES

Environmental agency staff often highlight the importance of criminal and civil sanctions in implementing NPDES. However, it appears that *threats* of sanctions as opposed to the sanctions themselves are what really counts. Hunter and Waterman found that only about 7 percent of the 27,000 NPDES cases they analyzed involved even the filing of court documents, not to mention the imposition of court imposed penalties.

One explanation for why US EPA and state environmental staffs *infrequently* try to collect fines from polluters centers on the absence of economic incentives:

> The fines ultimately collected from violators are invested into the general fund rather than back into the agency's budget (Hunter and Waterman, 1996: 58).

This point was made by environmental officials in many states where Hunter and Waterman conducted interviews.[15]

Other factors contribute to US EPA's infrequent use of court actions to collect penalties for NPDES permit violations. For example, agency staffs must devote much time and budget to make a case for penalties. In addition, judicial rules of evidence impose a heavy burden on those attempting to prove that permit conditions were violated willfully. Moreover, legal proceedings often involve years of delay, and penalties sought by US EPA are frequently reduced significantly on appeal (Hunter and Waterman, 1996: 55). Finally, US EPA and state environmental agencies cannot bring court actions on their own. US EPA must be represented in court by the U.S. Department of Justice, and state environmental agencies must rely on state attorneys-general. This inability to initiate lawsuits on their own is still another factor discouraging environmental agencies from using the courts.[16]

In comparing discharge permit enforcement activities in the United States and China, the following differences stand out:

- Bargaining and negotiation over permit compliance is far more common in China than in the United States, and China's environmental agencies have more flexibility in interpreting environmental rules than their counterparts in the United States.
- Citizens, NGOs, and the media play a more dominant role in fostering compliance in the United States than in China.
- Court actions and the threat of court actions are much more important as enforcement tools in the United States than in China.

Despite these differences, enforcement of discharge permit conditions in the United States and China are similar in some important respects. Environmental agency personnel in both countries are able to decide when to force companies to comply strictly with permit system regulations and when to use discretion within the framework of the law.[17] In addition both countries rely heavily on monitoring data gathered by polluters. Moreover, environmental agencies in both countries frequently lack the staff and budgetary resources to enforce regulations strictly. Thus it is not surprising that complaints about inadequate enforcement of environmental requirements are heard commonly in both countries.

NOTES

1. Some states have adopted discharge fee systems. For example, the State of California imposes discharge fees. In contrast to the Chinese fee program, fees in the California system are intended to cover the costs of issuing permits. The fees are not based on the mass flowrate of pollutants released.

2. NPDES was established by the Federal Water Pollution Control Act Amendments of 1972. The law was later renamed the U.S. Clean Water Act.

3. In some states, discharge fee systems contribute to the budgets of state environmental agencies.

4. Environmental agencies in the United States can use administrative procedures to impose fines on polluters without going to court. However, court actions may be required if dischargers refuse to comply with administratively imposed penalties.

5. The emphasis of the discharge permit system on enterprises is demonstrated by experience in cities initially selected for the trial implementation of the system (see Appendix A). In most of those cities, permits were issued only to enterprises.

6. For examples of the judiciary's influence on NPDES, see Rodgers (1994: 342–363).

7. Effluent guidelines and other regulations governing implementation of NPDES are in the *Code of Federal Regulations*, Title 40, Parts 122 to 133 and Parts 401 to 503.

8. Issues negotiated in NPDES *pretreatment* permits also cover a narrow range. US EPA regulations (and sometimes local ordinances) greatly restrict the discretion of those who write pretreatment permits. Personal and professional relationships typically have little influence on permit conditions.

9. Our colleague, Katherine Kao Cushing, identified a similar informal rule based on her analysis of compliance by Chinese pharmaceutical companies with water pollution control laws:

> As long as the factory has some kind of wastewater treatment system on site and is making a good faith effort to comply with standards and pay discharge fees (if it is financially able to do so), violations of local discharge standards are tolerated by the EPB (Cushing, 1998: 145).

Cushing developed this informal rule based on case studies of nine pharmaceutical factories in Shanghai, Shenyang, and Dalian, and interviews with EPB staff in Shanghai and Shenyang.

10. This paragraph is based on interviews granted on condition of anonymity with staff at US EPA headquarters, US EPA Region 3, and Virginia's Department of Environmental Quality. It is also based on a fact sheet issued by the US EPA Region 3 office ("Response to Request for Information to RA Concerning VA Enforcement").

11. This assertion is based on the views of US EPA staff who granted us interviews on the condition of anonymity.

12. The Permit Compliance System also includes other information, such as compliance schedule requirements.

13. For example, US EPA's Office of Inspector General reported that a former director of Hess Environmental Laboratories in Pennsylvania "admitted falsifying test results and billing customers more than $223,000 for testing that, in most cases, was never done" (US EPA, 1997: 38). In addition, a former manager at the laboratory reported that some regulatory limits on toxic contaminants in wastewater were met, when, in fact, those limits had been violated.

14. For other evidence of the high variability of the quality of enforcement across states, see Hunter and Waterman (1996: 50–75).

15. CALPIRG (1999) compiled data on enforcement of NPDES in California between January 1997 and March 1999, and the results were similar to those presented by Hunter and Waterman. The CALPIRG study found that only 44 of 2,590 violations of discharge permit conditions in three regions of California resulted in fines. The 2,590 cases included 404 that were classified as "major violations."

16. Attorneys-general obtain referrals for court actions from many agencies, and they must exercise discretion in deciding which cases to prosecute. Often, cases pushed by

state environmental agencies are given low priority by attorneys-general because they believe cases from other agencies are stronger or more urgent.

17. This sentence paraphrases an argument made by Hunter and Waterman based on their empirical study of how environmental agency staffs in the United States enforced NPDES permit conditions:

> [Environmental agency] enforcement personnel may choose to comply strictly with regulations, to use their own discretion within the framework of the law, to rely on a supervisor's judgment, or to employ completely unauthorized discretion. (Hunter and Waterman, 1996: 8)

Our empirical study of DPS enforcement suggests that a similar argument could be made to describe how EPBs enforce China's discharge permit system.

Appendix A

Study Design: Objectives, Methods, and Definitions of Compliance

This appendix describes choices we made about which regulatory programs to study and what research methods to use. It also includes our definitions of compliance.

SELECTION OF ENVIRONMENTAL REGULATIONS

In deciding on which regulations to analyze, we gave priority to programs that encouraged industrial facilities to be in continuing, not just initial, compliance with environmental requirements. *Initial compliance* is a successful demonstration that a facility is capable of satisfying a particular regulation. In contrast, *continuing compliance* involves meeting a requirement over years of routine facility operations.[1] Because of our interest in continuing compliance, we eliminated from consideration China's programs for environmental impact assessment and the three synchronizations. These programs are important, but they only ensure that enterprises satisfy discharge standards when they begin operating a new (or renovated) facility.

Based on an analysis conducted before starting our fieldwork, we decided to concentrate on compliance with the discharge permit system. We singled out this program because it was promising and new, and because it aimed at ensuring continual compliance with effluent standards. As discussed in Chapter 2, the National Environmental Protection Agency created the permit system in response to limitations of China's discharge standards. NEPA staff responsible for creating the permit program believed environmental quality was continuing to deteriorate because discharge standards restricted concentrations of pollutants rather than their mass flowrates. The staff reasoned that even though many enterprises were meeting the concentration-based national effluent standards, ambient water quality was getting worse because the total quantity of emitted waste was

173

unregulated.[2] By issuing permits, EPBs could restrict both the mass and concentration of pollutants in wastewater discharges.

During our initial fieldwork, we observed a controversy concerning linkages between the new permit program and the well-established discharge fee system.[3] Enterprises were complaining to EPBs about inconsistencies between the two systems: was an enterprise to meet the concentration-based effluent standards linked to the fee system, or the mass flowrate and concentration constraints spelled out in permits? Often the concentration restrictions in permits were less stringent than those in effluent standards. Because of enterprises' concerns with these inconsistencies, we felt we could not analyze compliance with the permit system without making compliance with the fee system a part of our study.

The fee program was created to motivate enterprises to meet national discharge standards. Under this program, enterprises are charged a fee if they release wastewater that violates standards.[4] In most cities, the fee is based on both the extent of violation of the concentration-based effluent standards and the total volume of wastewater discharged.

In principle, if an enterprise that violates effluent standards pays required fees, it is still obligated to meet the standards. In practice, however, an informal rule of behavior has evolved: if an enterprise's discharge is not causing major damage, an EPB will often consider the enterprise's actions acceptable if the enterprise pays applicable fees even though it violates effluent standards. Thus, when we analyze compliance with the discharge fee system, we distinguish between compliance with formal rules and the informal interpretation of compliance: payment of applicable discharge fees while violating effluent standards.

In summary, results from our preliminary studies led us to revise our initial plan to investigate compliance with discharge permits. Inconsistencies between concentrations in permits and effluent standards were causing problems with permit system implementation. Because of the linkages between permits, fees, and effluent standards, we decided to study all three programs.

OVERALL RESEARCH APPROACH

Our research strategy involved complementary use of case studies and a survey. We use "case study" to mean an investigation of compliance with environmental regulations by a particular enterprise. We included only a small number of enterprises in our case study work, and each was selected intentionally (not at random). Each case focused on a single enterprise and key organizations involved in compliance events, such as the mayor's office, the local EPB, and the relevant industrial bureau. The term "survey" is used here to refer to an investigation based on questionnaires completed by a sample of enterprises representative of the population; the latter consists of companies at which permits, fees, and effluent standards were applied in the cities included in our survey.

We employed case studies to obtain details on the decision processes that enterprises, EPBs, and others used in making choices affecting compliance. The case study work provided details concerning how and why compliance with environmental requirements took place. In contrast, we used our survey to provide more general results.

By conducting both case studies and survey research we obtained insights that we could not have gained by either method alone. We did not want to rely exclusively on a survey because little information on compliance by Chinese enterprises was available from prior research. Without doing the case study work first, we would have had trouble designing appropriate survey questions, and our survey might have missed important explanations of compliance outcomes. Moreover, the case studies allowed us to understand how EPBs and enterprises responded to requests for data from higher-level government agencies. Without this understanding, we might have misinterpreted the meaning of environmental compliance statistics tabulated by national agencies. Although case studies have advantages, they also have a key weakness: generalization is impossible using the small sample sizes typically associated with case study research. The survey portion of our investigation attempted to compensate for this weakness. By conducting surveys of compliance by a large number of enterprises, we hoped to extend our ability to generalize.

SELECTION OF CITIES

At the time we began our research in the early 1990s, programs involving discharge standards and fees had been used in all Chinese cities for more than fifteen years, but the permit system had only recently been adopted on a trial basis in selected cities. As of 1995, experience with the permit system was limited to less than ten years, even in cities that had participated in the program since it was initiated. Those first participants—seventeen cities and one river basin—began issuing permits between 1987 and 1989.

In selecting cities to include in our study, we limited our attention to those that had been involved in the trial implementation of the DPS for at least five years. In a city with less than a five-year record, the implementation would have been too short to be evaluated fully. To meet this time-related constraint, only cities from the first group of seventeen cities and one river basin assigned to participate in the trial implementation of the DPS between 1987 and 1989 were considered (see Table A.1).

Before starting our field research, we decided, based on available resources, to examine only four cities. Our rationale for selecting the four cities was based on a preliminary statistical study of factors affecting industrial pollution abatement in China (Rozelle, Ma, and Ortolano, 1993). That analysis, which employed 1990 data for eighty-two cities, showed that per capita gross domestic product

Appendix A

Table A.1   Cities Participating in Initial Permit System Implementation

City	Region	Per Capita GDP[a]	Size[b]	Fraction of State-Owned Enterprises[c]
Shenyang	Northeast	Medium	Large	Average
Dandong	Northeast	Low	Middle	Low
Beijing	North	High	Large	Average
Tianjin	North	Medium	Large	High
Jinan[d]	North	Medium	Large	Average
Zibo[d]	North	Medium	Middle	Low
Anyang	North	Low	Middle	High
Shanghai	Central	High	Large	High
Jinhua	Central	Medium	Middle	Average
Changzhou	Central	Medium	Middle	Low
Xuzhou	Central	Low	Large	High
Hefei	Central	Low	Middle	High
Xiangtan	Central	Low	Middle	High
Shunde	South	High	Small	Low
Xiamen	South	High	Small	Low
Lanzhou	West	Medium	Middle	High
Neijiang	West	Low	Large	Average
Chongqing	West	Low	Large	High
Shihezi	West	Low	Small	High

[a]The scale for per capita GDP is as follows: high level, GDP per capita > 10,000 *yuan*; medium level, 10,000 *yuan* > GDP per capita > 5,000 *yuan*; and low level, GDP per capita < 5,000 *yuan*.

[b]The classification of city size is based on standards used by the Chinese National Statistics Bureau: large municipality, population > 5,000,000; middle-sized municipality, 5,000,000 > population > 1,000,000; and small city, population < 1,000,000.

[c]The classification for the fraction of enterprises within a city that are state-owned is based on an analysis of data for 82 cities (Rozelle, Ma, and Ortolano, 1993): high, > 80 percent; average, 60–80 percent; and low, < 60 percent.

[d]Jinan and Zibo are cities located in the Xiaoqing River Basin, the one river basin selected to participate in the trial implementation of the permit program.

(GDP), the fraction of state-owned enterprises, and the number of environmental staff per enterprise was correlated with levels of industrial wastewater pollution reduction. Those results also suggested that relationships between these three variables and industrial pollution control levels are different for big, medium, and small cities.

We initially considered using four variables—city size, per capita GDP, percentage of state-owned enterprises, and number of environmental staff per enterprise—as criteria for selecting the four cities to include in our research. However, we decided to drop the number of environmental staff per enterprise because it did not vary much across the initial cities participating in the permit system's trial implementation. Thus only three variables from the statistical analysis—city

Table A.2   Cities Included in Our Research

City	Region	Per Capita GDP	Size	Fraction of State-Owned Enterprises
Beijing	North	High	Large	Average
Jinan[a]	North	Medium	Large	Average
Anyang	North	Low	Medium	High
Changzhou	Central	Medium	Medium	Low
Shunde	South	High	Small	Low
Chongqing[a]	West	Low	Large	High

[a]Included in our research after the initial selection of cities.

size, per capita GDP, and percentage of state-owned enterprises—were used to guide our selection of cities. Although we tried to pick cities representative of various locations and socioeconomic contexts, our attempt to do so was limited because, based on our original design, only four cities were to be visited.

After considering the above-noted factors, we selected Anyang, Beijing, Changzhou, and Shunde for inclusion in our study. We made this choice before starting our field studies in 1993. During that field work, one of us (Xiaoying Ma) became involved in World Bank research projects on the control of industrial pollution in Chongqing and Jinan. By coincidence, both cities were among the first assigned to participate in the trial implementation of the permit system. This work with the World Bank provided us with an unforeseen opportunity to gather additional information for our study. However, because of time and resource constraints, only informal interviews with EPB staff and factory managers were conducted in Chongqing and Jinan. We were unable to conduct either case studies or survey research in those cities.

Table A.2 lists characteristics of the four cities included in our original research design plus the two cities—Chongqing and Jinan—that were added later. As shown in the table, the cities are from four geographical regions, and they vary in terms of size, level of economic development, and fraction of state-owned enterprises.

SELECTION OF ENTERPRISES

We conducted *case studies* in Anyang, Beijing, Changzhou, and Shunde. In each city, we selected enterprises based on discussions with the local EPB and industrial bureaus. Four criteria were used in choosing enterprises. First, for reasons similar to those offered in the discussion of the choice of cities, we limited our research to enterprises that had been involved in the permit system's trial implementation for at least five years. Second, we wanted enterprises with different compliance records because this would allow us to identify variables explaining why some enterprises met environmental requirements and others did not. Third, we sought enterprises that varied in terms of ownership type and level of profitability because we wanted to examine how these enterprise characteristics affected compliance. Fourth, we considered only industrial categories that were major sources of organic pollution in China (for example, the chemical sector and the pulp and paper sector).[5] Table A.3 summarizes attributes of the twelve enterprises we selected as case studies.

We conducted *surveys* in Anyang, Changzhou, and Shunde with the support of the local EPBs. Although we also tried to survey enterprises in Beijing, we abandoned our efforts because it was not convenient for the Beijing EPB to assist us with the survey.

We used a stratified sampling approach to select enterprises. In a given city, we first identified the population to be sampled: all enterprises at which effluent standards, wastewater discharge fees, and the discharge permit system were be-

Table A.3   Characteristics of Case Study Enterprises

Enterprise[a]	Form of Ownership[b]	Economic Status	Compliance Status[c]
Anyang:			
A1 Power Plant	SOE	Profitable	Full compliance
A2 Chemical Fiber Plant	SOE	Profitable	Partial compliance
A3 Paper Mill	SOE	Unprofitable	Noncompliance
Beijing:			
B1 Brewery	SOE	Profitable	Partial compliance
B2 Chemical Works	SOE	Profitable	Partial compliance
Changzhou:			
C1 Chemical Plant	SOE	Unprofitable	Noncompliance
C2 Chemical Works	SOE	Unstable[d]	Partial compliance
C3 Printing and Dyeing Plant	SOE	Unprofitable	Noncompliance
C4 Printing and Dyeing Plant	TVE	Profitable	Full compliance
Shunde:			
S1 Sugar Plant	SOE	Profitable	Partial compliance
S2 Printing and Dyeing Company	TVE	Profitable	Full compliance
S3 Dyeing Company	TVE	Unprofitable	Partial compliance

[a]Names of all enterprises are pseudonyms.

[b]SOE = state-owned enterprise; TVE = township and village enterprise.

[c]Full compliance = met effluent standards; partial noncompliance = did not meet effluent standards, but paid pollution discharge fees; noncompliance = neither met effluent standards nor paid fees.

[d]"Unstable" indicates that the enterprise was profitable in some years and unprofitable in others.

Table A.4   Characteristics of Surveyed Enterprises

	Total	Anyang	Changzhou	Shunde
Ownership:				
SOEs	57	22	29	6
TVEs	15	0	6	9
Other[a]				
Profit Status:	4	2	1	1
Profitable[b]	56	15	27	14
Unprofitable	20	9	9	2
Industrial Sector:				
Textiles	27	5	8	14
Chemicals	17	9	8	0
Light Industry	15	7	7	1
Other Sectors[c]	17	3	13	1
TOTAL	76	24	36	16

[a]"Other" refers to collectively-owned enterprises in urban areas.

[b]Profitable enterprises included those for which the net revenue in 1992 was greater than or equal to zero.

[c]"Other Sectors" include slaughterhouses, and enterprises producing pharmaceuticals, machinery, and construction materials.

ing applied. This amounted to 228 enterprises (50 in Anyang, 124 in Changzhou, and 54 in Shunde). Next, we eliminated enterprises used as case studies. Then, for a given city, we grouped the remaining enterprises into three categories: state-owned enterprises, township and village enterprises, and collectively-owned enterprises in urban areas. Finally, we selected enterprises from each group at random.[6]

Our survey included seventy-six enterprises: twenty-four in Anyang, thirty-six in Changzhou, and sixteen in Shunde. Collectively, they constitute about one-third of the 228 enterprises in the population.[7] As indicated in Table A.4, the enterprises vary significantly across industrial sectors, profit status, and ownership type.

We pretested our survey questionnaire and data collection methods at three enterprises in Beijing, the first city in which we conducted case studies. We asked environmental managers working for these enterprises to fill out a preliminary version of our survey questionnaire. Based on discussions with those managers, we revised the questionnaire to improve both the wording of questions and the clarity of response items. The final version of the questionnaire was fourteen pages long, and it included both closed and open-ended questions.

After selecting enterprises to include in our survey, we obtained the help of the local EPBs in arranging meetings of environmental managers working at the sampled enterprises. (These managers were the survey respondents.) In each city, we distributed questionnaires at a meeting and asked managers to fill them out and return them to the EPB office within a week.

DATA SOURCES

Data for the *case studies* came from three main sources. One source was our interviews with staff at case study enterprises, as well as officials from the National Environmental Protection Agency[8] and EPBs in Anyang, Beijing, Changzhou, and Shunde. In each city except Anyang, we conducted additional interviews at related government agencies, including the mayor's office, the municipal people's congress, the local economic and planning commissions, and various industrial bureaus. A second source of data consisted of reports, newsletters, regulations, and other documents we obtained from EPBs and NEPA. Our third source included statistical yearbooks, such as the environmental statistical yearbooks issued by NEPA, files at EPB offices, and records maintained by enterprises.

We obtained data for the *survey* portion of our study from the following sources: (1) personal interviews at the city EPBs in Anyang, Changzhou, and Shunde; (2) the survey questionnaire completed by environmental managers; and (3) secondary statistical data, such as that contained in environmental annual reports issued by EPBs.

Although the twelve case studies and the surveys of seventy-six enterprises constitute the main sources of data for our research, those are not the only sources. Because of unforeseen opportunities created by the previously-mentioned affiliation with some World Bank projects, we were also able to conduct interviews with factory managers, EPBs, and other agencies in Chongqing and Jinan. Table A.5 contains a city-by-city breakdown of our sources of primary data. We also relied on the literature on politics and economic development in post-Mao China and environmental policy implementation in China and other countries.

Table A.5   Sources of Data for the Six Cities

	Interviews				
Cities	Enterprises	EPBs	Other Agencies	Case Studies	Surveys
Initial Selections:					
Anyang	X	X		X	X
Beijing	X	X	X	X	
Changzhou	X	X	X	X	X
Shunde	X	X	X	X	X
Later Additions:					
Chongqing	X	X	X		
Jinan	X	X	X		

WORKING DEFINITIONS OF COMPLIANCE

Any research on compliance with environmental rules must grapple with what it means to say a waste discharger complies with the rules. In general terms, compliance is the full implementation of environmental requirements (US EPA, 1992). When compliance occurs, all requirements are met and desired reductions in pollutant releases are achieved.

Although this general conception of compliance is widely embraced, definitions vary greatly when people actually try to measure compliance. For example, an agency may classify an enterprise as being out of compliance with concentration-based effluent standards if more than 5 percent of its wastewater (in terms of volume discharged per time period) does not meet the standards. In contrast, another agency may claim an enterprise is in violation if it fails to satisfy effluent standards more than five days out of every one-hundred successive days. Thus an enterprise may be in compliance according to one definition and out-of-compliance by another. Variations in working definitions of compliance also result because of differences in the goals of participants in a regulatory process. Regulatory agencies and enterprises often have different interpretations of what it means to satisfy environmental rules.

Relevant regulations and guidelines do *not* define compliance for the three environmental programs examined in our research: effluent standards, the discharge fee program, and the discharge permit system. Moreover, EPBs use disparate measurements to determine whether an enterprise satisfies requirements of each of the three programs. For example, some EPBs determine whether an enterprise meets effluent standards by using both data reported by enterprises and data gathered by EPBs. Some EPBs combine these two data sources by assigning weights to each of them. Other EPBs rely only on their own measurements to determine whether a particular discharge exceeds standards, and still others use only data reported by enterprises.

In order to put results for different cities on a comparable basis, we developed uniform working definitions to evaluate compliance for each of the three environmental programs. We developed working definitions that made sense to us and the EPBs and employed data that was readily available. For effluent standards, we defined compliance as follows: an enterprise is in compliance if 90 percent or more of the volume of its wastewater release for a given year satisfied applicable effluent standards. Five of the six cities in our research adopted the national effluent standards. The exception, Beijing, used more stringent standards. For each city, we used data reported by enterprises to EPBs to determine compliance with effluent standards.[9]

For the discharge fee program, an enterprise required to pay fees was classified as *not* being in compliance if it either delayed its fee payments or did not make required payments for more than three months in a year.[10] Otherwise, the enterprise was in compliance. By this definition, a company that met effluent standards and therefore owed no fees was in compliance.

For the discharge permit system, an enterprise was *not* in compliance for a given year if the mass flowrate of COD in its effluent (as measured by an EPB) exceeded the maximum allowable COD specified in the enterprise's permit at any time during the year.[11] If none of the monitoring data obtained by an EPB indicated a violation within a given year, the enterprise was in compliance. Most EPBs included in our study measured permit compliance this way.

OVERVIEW OF COMPLIANCE RESULTS

In determining compliance with effluent standards, we used data from annual reports submitted by enterprises to EPBs. We calculated compliance with requirements of the discharge fee system using both our survey questionnaire results and the EPBs' records, and we employed data in EPB files to assess compliance with permit requirements. Table A.6 summarizes our results. For the seventy-six enterprises in our survey, rates of compliance in 1992 with effluent standards, discharge permits, and the discharge fee program were 36 percent, 69 percent, and 68 percent, respectively.

A much lower percentage of enterprises satisfied effluent standards (36 percent) than permit requirements (69 percent). This outcome is explainable by differences in the strictness of targets. In all three cities where we conducted surveys, pollutant concentrations in effluent standards were often more stringent than concentration limits in discharge permits. Consequently, many enterprises could meet permit requirements without satisfying effluent standards.

Table A.6   Compliance with Environmental Requirements in Surveyed Cities (1992)

	Total	Anyang	Changzhou	Shunde
Effluent standards[a]				
Number of enterprises in compliance	26	8	14	4
Number of valid observations	73	23	35	15
Compliance rate (%)	36	35	40	27
Discharge permits				
Number of enterprises in compliance	47	12	25	10
Number of valid observations	68	21	31	16
Compliance rate (%)	69	57	81	62
Discharge fees				
Number of enterprises in compliance	22	NA[b]	12	10
Number of valid observations	32	NA	21	11
Compliance rate (%)	68	NA	57	91

[a]Each of the three cities adopted the national effluent standards.

[b]NA = Not available. The pollution discharge fee program in Anyang was being modified at the time of our survey.

About 68 percent of the enterprises we surveyed paid discharge fees on time. However, satisfaction of fee-payment requirements is *not* the ultimate goal of the system. Rather, the goal is to motivate polluters to meet effluent standards. The compliance rate of 68 percent implies that, of the enterprises violating effluent standards, 68 percent paid fees on time and 32 percent did not. Ignoring differences in the numbers of enterprises used to calculate compliance rates for different programs, the figures for standards and fees can be interpreted as follows: about 64 percent of the enterprises failed to meet effluent standards, and 32 percent of those enterprises (that is, the ones that failed to meet standards) did not pay their fees on time.[12]

What are the key factors leading only 36 percent of enterprises to satisfy effluent standards? Why is compliance with permit conditions relatively high (69 percent)? Which enterprises neither met effluent standards nor paid discharge fees? And why did those enterprises fail to pay fees? Chapters 3 through 8 investigate these questions by examining factors influencing how enterprises make decisions on whether to satisfy environmental regulations.

NOTES

1. These definitions of initial and continual compliance are based on Russel, Harrington, and Vaughan (1986).

2. Chapter 6 details the reasons NEPA introduced the DPS.

3. The initial fieldwork was conducted by Xiaoying Ma in 1991 at several enterprises participating in the DPS trial implementation in Beijing.

4. Discharge fees are not restricted to water pollution; for example, fees are paid for emissions of air pollutants that violate applicable discharge standards. In our study, we considered only fees for wastewater releases.

5. We singled out organics in wastewater because many Chinese environmental officials consider organic pollution—as measured by chemical oxygen demand—as the most significant of the "conventional pollutants." EPBs in virtually all Chinese cities regulate and monitor COD in wastewater releases.

6. EPBs in Anyang, Changzhou, and Shunde provided us with lists of all enterprises at which standards, fees, and the permit system were applied.

7. We issued eighty-six questionnaires, and seventy-six were returned with a quality high enough to be used in this study. Each of the seventy-six respondents provided usable answers to most (but not all) questions.

8. NEPA became the State Environmental Protection Administration in 1998, long after our field research was completed.

9. Local EPBs provided us with (self-monitoring) data on the fraction of the volume of wastewater meeting effluent standards for each enterprise for each day or week of a particular year. If the concentration of any pollutants monitored in a wastewater discharge exceeded effluent standards, 100 percent of the wastewater volume discharged that day or week was classified as not meeting standards. If no pollutants in an enterprise's effluent were found violating effluent standards, 100 percent of the wastewater volume discharged that day or week was classified as meeting standards. An annual percentage of

wastewater volume satisfying effluent standards was calculated by adding all the daily or weekly wastewater meeting standards in a given year. Although enterprises differ in terms of which pollutants are regulated, virtually all enterprises have COD concentration limits. Most enterprises use the COD concentration of their effluents to calculate the percentage of wastewater meeting standards.

10. We chose a three-month period because most cities included in our study made an assessment of an enterprise's discharge fees once every three months.

11. We focused on chemical oxygen demand because NEPA considered it as the most significant of the "conventional pollutants." Also, technologies that control COD discharges tend to reduce the levels of other pollutants.

12. The percentage of enterprises that failed to meet effluent standards equals 100 percent minus the 36 percent that met standards.

Appendix B

Classes of Water Use in China

Table B.1   Classes of Water Use in China

Class of Water Use	Description of Use
I	Water that flows through national nature reserves
II	Source of municipal drinking water supply (first grade conservation area); conservation areas for rare aquatic species; and areas for fish spawning
III	Source of municipal drinking water supply with treatment required (second grade conservation area); conservation areas for common aquatic species; and areas for swimming
IV	Source of industrial water supply and recreational use other than swimming (e.g., boating and fishing)
V	Source of industrial cooling water, irrigation water, and ordinary landscape

Appendix C

National Effluent Standards

The 1988 national wastewater discharge standards were applicable at the time of our field research and they are summarized in Tables C.1 and C.2. These standards were revised in 1996. Details on the revisions are given by NEPA (1996).

Table C.1   Comprehensive Wastewater Discharge Standards for Type I Pollutants (National Standards—GB8978–88)[a]

Pollutant	Maximum Allowable Concentration in Effluent (mg/l)
Total mercury	0.05
Alkyl (organic) mercury	Below detectable limit
Total cadmium	0.1
Total chromium	1.5
Hexavalent chromium	0.5
Total arsenic	0.5
Total lead	1.0
Total nicke	1.0
Benzo[a]pyrene	0.00003

[a]The complete version of the national wastewater discharge standards has been published by NEPA as *Guo Biao* 8978–88.

Table C.2   Comprehensive Wastewater Discharge Standards for Type II Pollutants (National Standards—GB8978–88)

	Maximum Allowable Concentration in Effluent (mg/L)				
	Level I		*Level II*		*Level III*
Pollutant[a]	*New Enterprise*	*Existing Enterprise*	*New Enterprise*	*Existing Enterprise*	
pH	6–9	6–9	6–9	6–9	6–9
Color (dilution multiple)	50	80	80	100	–
Total suspended solids	70	100	200	250	400
BOD$_5$	30	60	80	80	300
COD$_{Cr}$	100	150	150	200	500
Petroleum	10	15	10	20	30
Oil and grease	20	30	20	40	100
Volatile phenols	0.5	1.0	0.5	1.0	2.0
Cyanide	0.5	0.5	0.5	0.5	1.0
Sulphide	1.0	1.0	1.0	2.0	2.0
NH3–N	15	25	25	40	–
Fluoride (F^{-1})	10	15	10	15	20
Phosphate	0.5	1.0	1.0	2.0	–
Formaldehyde	1.0	2.0	2.0	3.0	–
Aniline	1.0	2.0	2.0	3.0	5.0
Nitrobenzene	2.0	3.0	3.0	5.0	5.0
Anionic surfactant detergent	5.0	10	10	15	20
Copper	0.5	0.5	1.0	1.0	2.0
Zinc	2.0	2.0	4.0	5.0	5.0
Manganese	2.0	5.0	2.0	5.0	5.0

[a]Except for pH and color, units for parameters are in mg/l.

Effluent Standards Applicable to Different Classes of Water Use

Table D.1   Effluent Standards Applicable to Different Classes of Water Use

		Class of Water Use				Municipal sewerage system with secondary treatment
	I	*II*	*III*	*IV*	*V*	
Effluent standards for Type I pollutants[a]	X	X	X	X	X	X
Effluent standards for Type II pollutants	NA[b]	NA				
Level I standards			X			
Level II standards				X	X	
Level III standards						X

[a]Limits for Type I and II pollutants are given in Appendix C.

[b]NA = Not applicable. For water bodies designated for Class I and II use, no new pollution sources are permitted. Existing sources that release contaminants into water bodies designated for Class I and II water use must ensure that the ambient water quality standards are met.

Bibliography

AMPG (Anyang Municipal People's Government), 1989, *Anyang Shi Renmin Zhengfu Pizhuan Shihuanbaoju "Anyangshi Paifangshui Wuranwu Xukezheng Guanli Yijian (Shixing) De Tongzhi."* [A Notice on Approving the "Methodology for DPS Management in Anyang (Trial)." Submitted by Anyang EPB] Anyang People's Government Document No. 43.

Andrews, Richard N. L., 1997, "United States," in Jänicke Martin, and Helmut Weidner (eds.), *National Environmental Policies: A Comparative Study of Capacity-Building*, Springer-Verlag, Berlin.

Anyang EPB, 1989, *Anyangshi Paifang Shuiwuranwu Xukezheng Guanli Yijian (Shixing)*. [Methodology for DPS Management in Anyang (Trial)]. Anyang EPB Document No. 119 (89).

Ash, Robert F. and Richard L. Edmonds, 1998, "China's Land Resources, Environment and Agricultural Production," *The China Quarterly*, 156: 836–879.

APM (Anyang Paper Mill), 1989, *Guanyu Yaoqiu Zhanhuan Zhixing Zongliang Shoufei De Qingshi Baoggao*. [A Report Asking A Postponement in Implementing the Mass-Based Pollution Charges], internal document, December.

Bahm, A. J., 1969, *The Heart of Confucius: Interpretations of Genuine Living and Great Wisdom*, Walker/Weatherhill, New York.

Banister, Judith, 1998, "Population, Public Health and the Environment in China," *The China Quarterly*, 156: 986–1015.

Bartel, Ann and Lacy Thomas, 1985, "Direct and Indirect Effects of Regulation: A New Look at OSHA's Impact," *Journal of Law and Economics*, XXVIII: 1–25.

Baum, Richard, 1998, "The Fifteenth National Party Congress: Jiang Takes Command?" *The China Quarterly*, 153: 141–156.

Bernstein, Janis, 1993, *Alternative Approaches to Pollution Control and Waste Management*, The World Bank, Washington, D.C.

Bo, Wen, 1998, "Greening the Chinese Media," *China Environment Series*, Issue 2, The Woodrow Wilson Center, Washington, D.C.

Bohm, Robert A., Chazhong Ge, Milton Russell, and Tintian Yang, 1998, "Environmental Taxes: China's Bold Initiative," *Environment*, 40(7):10–13 and 33–38.

191

Boxer, Baruch, 1992, "China's Environment: Issues and Economic Implications," in Joint Economic Committee, Congress of the United States, *China's Economic Dilemmas in the 1990s*, M. E. Sharpe, Armonk, NY.

CALPIRG (California Public Interest Research Group), 1999, "Three Strikes and You Profit: A CALPIRG Study of Clean Water Enforcement in California." Unpublished, Sacramento, CA: CALPIRG.

CASS (Chinese Academy of Social Science), 1995, *Jiushi Niandai Huanjing Yu Shengtai Wenti Zaocheng Jingji Sunshi Gusuan*. [An Estimate of Economic Losses Caused by Pollution and Ecological Problems in the 1990s], unpublished report, Beijing.

CCICED (China Council for International Cooperation on Environment and Development), 1994, *Chongqing Gongye Wuran Kongzhi Zhanlue Yu Zhengze Yanjiu Baogao*. [A Report on a Strategy for Industrial Pollution Control and Policy Study in Chongqing Municipality], discussion report.

CEYCC (China Environment Yearbook Compiling Committee), 1993, 1994, etc. *Zhongguo Huanjing Nianjian* [China Environment Yearbook], *Zhongguo Huanjing Kexue Chubanshe* [China Environmental Science Press], Beijing.

Chai, Joseph C. H., 1997, *China: Transition to a Market Economy*, Clarendon Press, Oxford, U.K.

Chan, Hon S., K. C. Cheung, and Jack M. K. Lo, 1993, "Environmental Control in the PRC," in Nagel, Stuart S., and Miriam K. Mills (eds.), *Public Policy in China*, Greenwood Press, Westport, CN, 63–81.

Chan, Hon S., Koon-Kwai Wong, K. C. Cheung, and Jack Man-Reung Lo, 1995, "The Implementation Gap in Environmental Management in China: The Case of Guanzhou, Zhengzhou and Nanjing," *Public Administration Review*, 55(4): 333–340.

Chang, Phyllis L., 1989, "Deciding Disputes: Factors that Guide Chinese Courts in the Adjudication of Rural Responsibility Contract Disputes," *Law and Contemporary Problems*, 52(3): 102–142.

Charlton, Ellen M., 1997, *Comparing Asian Politics: India, China, and Japan*, Westview Press, Boulder, CO.

Cheng, Lucie and Arthur Rosett, 1991, "Contract with a Chinese Face: Socially Embedded Factors in the Transformation from Hierarchy to Market, 1978–1989," *Journal of Chinese Law*, 5: 143–55, 207–44.

Ch'ü, T'ung-tsu, 1961, *Law and Society in Traditional China*, Mouton & Co., Paris.

Clarke, Donald D., 1991, "Dispute Resolution in China," *Journal of Chinese Law*, 5: 245–296.

Cohen, Jerome A., 1966, "Chinese Mediation on the Eve of Modernization," *California Law Review*, 54(2): 1201–1226.

Corne, Peter H., 1997, *Foreign Investment in China: The Administrative Legal System*, Hong Kong University Press, Hong Kong.

Cushing, Katherine Kao, 1998, *Wastewater Treatment and Cleaner Production in the Chinese Pharmaceutical Industry: How Institutions, Incentives and Capabilities Influence Organizational Behavior*, Ph.D. dissertation, Stanford University, Stanford, CA.

Cushman, John H., Jr., 1998, "E.P.A. and States Found to be Lax on Pollution Law," *New York Times,* national edition, June 7: 11 and 17.

Dasgupta, Susmita and David Wheeler, 1996, "Citizen Complaints as Environmental Indicators: Evidence from China," unpublished manuscript, Environment, Infrastructure and Agriculture Division, Policy Research Department, The World Bank, Washington, D.C.

DiMento, Joseph, 1986, *Environmental Law and American Business: Dilemmas of Compliance*, Plenum Press, New York.

Dong, Furen, 1991, "Behavior of Chinese State-Owned Enterprises under the Two-Tier System," unpublished paper, Chinese Academy of Social Sciences, Beijing.

Du, Lingfeng, 1992, *Guojia Yusuan Yu Shuishou* [State Budget and Taxation], *Zhongguo Caizheng Shubanshe* [China Finance Press], Beijing.

Dunn, Seth, 1997, "Taking a Green Leap Forward," *The Amicus Journal*, 18(4): 12–14.

EBCEY (Editorial Board of China Environmental Yearbook), 1997, *1996 China Environmental Yearbook,* China Environmental Yearbook, Inc., Beijing.

———, 1998, *1997 China Environmental Yearbook,* China Environmental Yearbook, Inc., Beijing.

Edmonds, Richard L., 1994a, *Patterns of China's Lost Harmony: A Survey of the Country's Environmental Degradation and Protection*, Routledge, London.

———, 1994b, "China's Environment: Problems and Prospects," in Denis Dwyer (ed.), *China: The Next Decades*, Longman Scientific & Technical, Essex, England.

Epstein, Edward J., 1994, "Law and Legitimation in Post-Mao China," in Potter, Pitman B. (ed.), *Domestic Law Reforms in Post-Mao China*, M. E. Sharpe, Armonk. NY.

Farson, Seth, 1997, "Major Shift for China: Big State Industries Will Be Sold," *New York Times*, national edition, September 12: A–1 and A–8.

Gao, Xi-Ching, 1989, "Today's Legal Thinking and Its Economic Impact in China," *Law and Contemporary Problems*, 52(2): 89–115.

GDSB (Guandong Statistics Bureau), 1994, *Guangdong Tongji Nianjian* [Guangdong Province Statistical Yearbook], *Zhongguo Tongji Chubanshe* [China Statistics Press], Beijing.

Guthrie, D., 1998, "The Declining Significance of Guanxi in China's Economic Transition," *China Quarterly*, 154: 254–282.

Harkness, James, 1998, "Recent Trends in Forestry and Conservation of Biodiversity in China," *The China Quarterly*, 156: 911–934.

Hartzell, Richard W., 1988, *Harmony in Conflict: Active Adaptation to Life in Present-Day Chinese Society*, Vol. 1, Caves Books, Ltd., Taipei.

Hu, Wengzhong and Cornelius L. Grove, 1991, *Encountering the Chinese: A Guide for Americans*, Intercultural Press, Inc., Yarmouth, Maine.

Huang, Yasheng, 1990, "Web of Interests and Patterns of Behavior of Chinese Local Economic Bureaucracies and Enterprises During Reform," *The China Quarterly*, 123: 431–458.

Hunter, Susan and Richard W. Waterman, 1996, *Enforcing the Law: The Case of the Clean Water Acts*, M. E. Sharpe, Armonk, NY.

Jahiel, Abigail R., 1994, "Policy Implementation Through Organizational Learning: The Case of Water Pollution Control in China's Reforming Socialist System," Ph.D. dissertation. University of Michigan, Ann Arbor.

———, 1997, "The Contradictory Impact of Reform on Environmental Potection in China," *The China Quarterly*, 149: 81–103.

———, 1998, "The Organization of Environmental Protection in China," *The China Quarterly*, 156: 757–787.

Jefferson, Gary H. and Inderjit Singh, 1997, "Ownership Reform as a Process of Creative Reduction in Chinese Industry," in Joint Economic Committee, Congress of the United States, *China's Economic Future: Challenges to U.S. Policy*, M. E. Sharp, Armonk, NY, 176–202.

Jefferson, Gary H. and Thomas G. Rawski, 1994, "Enterprise Reform in Chinese Industry," *Journal of Economic Perspectives*, 8(2): 47–70.

Ji, You, 1998, *China's Enterprise Reform: Changing State/Society Relations After Mao*, Routledge, London.

Jiang, Hong and Shan Guan, 1991, *Zhongguo Qiye Xingwei Lun* [On Chinese Enterprises' Behavior], *Haiyang Zhuban She* [Ocean Press], Beijing.

JLARC (Joint Legislative Audit and Review Commission), 1997, *Review of the Department of Environmental Quality,* House Document No. 67, Commonwealth of Virginia, Richmond.

JMPG (Jinan Municipal People's Government), 1990, *Methodology of the DPS Management in Jinan*, a document prepared by Jinan EPB and the Jinan Municipal People's Government.

JSSB (Jiangsu Statistics Bureau), 1994, *Jiangsu Tongji Nianjian* [Jiangsu Province Statistical Yearbook], *Zhongguo Tongji Chubanshe* [China Statistics Press], Beijing.

Ju, Yanan, 1996, *Understanding China: Center Stage of the Fourth Power*, State University of New York Press, Albany, NY.

Knup, Elizabeth, 1997, "Environmental NGOs in China: An Overview," in Frank, Aaron, ed., *China Environment Series* (1st edition), The Woodrow Wilson Center, Washington, D.C.

Koo, Anthony, Elizabeth Li, and Zhaoping Peng, 1993., "State-Owned Enterprises in Transition," in Walter Galenson, ed., *China's Economic Reform*, The 1990 Institute, South San Francisco, CA.

Kornai, Janos, 1980, *Economics of Shortage*, North-Holland, Amsterdam.

Krupnick, Alan, 1991, "Incentive Policies for Industrial Pollution Control." Prepared for presentation at the 1992 Meeting of the American Economic Association. New Orleans, LA, January 2–5.

Leys, Simon, 1997, *The Analects of Confucius/Translation and Notes*, W. W. Norton & Co., New York.

Lieberthal, Kenneth, 1995, *Governing China: From Revolution Through Reform*, W. W. Norton & Co., New York.

———, 1997, "China's Governing System and Its Impact on Environmental Policy Implementation," in Frank, Aaron (ed.), *China Environment Series* (1st edition), The Woodrow Wilson Center, Washington, D.C.

Lo, Carlos Wing-Hung, 1995, *China's Legal Awakening: Legal Theory and Criminal Justice in Deng's Era*, Hong Kong University Press, Hong Kong.

Lockett, Martin, 1988, "Culture and the Problems of Chinese Management," *Organization Studies*, 9(4): 475–496.

Lotspeich, Richard and Amien Chen, 1997, "Environmental Protection in the People's Republic of China," *Journal of Contemporary China*, 6(14): 33–59.

Lowry, William, H., 1992, *The Dimensions of Federalism: State Governments and Pollution Control Policies*, Duke University Press, Durham, NC.

Lubman, Stanley, B., 1999, *Bird in a Cage: Legal Reform in China After Mao*, Stanford University Press, Stanford, CA.

Ma, Xiaoying, 1997, *Controlling Industrial Water Pollution in China: Compliance in the Context of Economic Transition*, Ph.D. dissertation, Department of Civil and Environmental Engineering, Stanford University, Stanford, CA.

National Environmental Modeling Center, 1999, *1998 Environmental Quality Report*, Beijing.

Naughton, Barry, 1992, "Hierarchy and the Bargaining Economy: Government and Enterprise in the Reform Process," in Kenneth Lieberthal and David Lampton, eds., *Bureaucracy, Politics, and Decision Making in Post-Mao China*, University of California Press, Berkeley, CA.

———, 1995, *Growing Out of the Plan: Chinese Economic Reform, 1978–1993*, Cambridge University Press, Cambridge, U.K.

NEPA, (National Enviromental Protection Agency), 1987, *Huanjing Tongji Nianbao* [Environmental Statistical Yearbook], Beijing.

———, 1988a, *Zonghe Wushui Paifang Biaozhun* [Comprehensive Wastewater Discharge Standards, GB 3838–88], Beijing.

———, 1988b, *Guanyu Yinfa Shuiwuranwu Paifang Xukezheng Guanli Zhanxing Banfa He Kaizhan Paifang Xuhezheng Shidian Gongzuo De Tongzhi* [A Notice for Issuing the 'Provisional Methodology for DPS Management' and for Carrying Out the DPS], Document No. 111, Beijing.

———, 1988c, *Shui Wuranwu Paiwu Xukezheng Guanli Zhanxing Banfa* [Provisional Methodology for DPS Management], Beijing.

———, 1988d, *Guanyu Kaizhan Shui Wuranwu Paiwu Xukezheng Shidian Gongzuo De Jidian Yijian* [Several Suggestions for Trial Implementation of the Discharge Permit System], in NEPA, 1991, *Implementation of DPS in China, Vol. 4 (Regulations, Policies, and Systems)*, Beijing.

———, 1989, *Shuiwuran Fangzhifa Shishi Xize* [Detailed Rules for Implementing the Water Pollution Prevention and Control Law], Beijing.

———, 1993, *Paiwu Xukezheng Zhidu Guifanhua Yanju* [A Study on DPS Standardization], The Research Team of DPS Standardization, internal report, Beijing.

———, 1996, *Integrated Wastewater Discharge Standards* (revised from GB 8978–88). GB 8978–1996, Beijing, October 4.

———, 1997, *1996 China Environmental Statistical Bulletin*, NEPA, Beijing.

NEPA, MOA, SPC, and SETC, (National Environmental Protection Agency, Ministry of Agriculture, State Planning Commission, and State Economic and Trade Commission), 1997, *Guanyu Jiaqiang Xiangzhen Qiye Huanjing Baohu Gongzuo De Guiding* [Regulations Concerning Environmental Protection at Township and Village Enterprises], Beijing, March 5.

NEPA, SPB, and MOF, (National Environmental Protection Agency, State Price Bureau, and Ministry of Finance), 1991, *Guanyu Tiaozheng Chaobiao Wushiu He Tongyi Zaosheng Paiwufei Biaozhun De Tongzhi* [A Notice on Adjustment of the Pollution Discharge Fee Rate for Wastewater and the Pollution Levy Rate for Noise], Document 262–91, Beijing.

NEPA and SPC, (National Environmental Protection Agency and State Planning Commission), 1994, *Environmental Action Plan of China, 1991–2000*, China Environmental Science Press, Beijing.

North, Douglass C., 1990, *Institutions, Institutional Change, and Economic Performance*, Cambridge University Press, Cambridge, U.K.

Note, 1998, "Class Action Litigation in China," *Harvard Law Review*, 111(6): 1523–1541.

O'Brien, Kevin, 1992, "Bargaining Success of Chinese Factories," *The China Quarterly*, 132: 1087–1100.

———, 1994, "Chinese People's Congresses and Legislative Embeddedness: understanding early legislative development." *Comparative Political Studies*, 27: 80–109.

Oi, Jean C., 1992, "Fiscal Reform and the Economic Foundations of Local State Corporatism in China," *World Politics*, (October): 99–136.

———, 1995, "The Role of the Local State in China's Transitional Economy," *The China Quarterly*, 144: 1132–1149.

———, 1998, "The Collective Foundation for Rapid Rural Industrialization," in Vermeer Pieke and Woei Lien Chong (eds.), *Cooperative and Collective in China's Rural Development*, M. E. Sharpe, Armonk, NY.

———, 1999, *Rural China Takes Off*, University of California Press, Berkeley.

Ortolano, Leonard, Katherine Kao Cushing, and Kimberley A. Warren (eds.), 1999, "Special Issue on China's Use of Cleaner Production as an Environmental Management Strategy," *Environmental Impact Assessment Review*, 19(5).

Palmer, Michael, 1998, "Environmental Regulation in the People's Republic of China: The Fact of Public Law," *The China Quarterly*, 156: 788–808.

Pearson, Margaret M., 1997, *China's New Business Elite: The Political Consequences of Economic Reform*, University of California Press, Berkeley, CA.

Pye, Lucian, 1981, *The Dynamics of Chinese Politics*, Oelgeschlager, Gunn & Hain, Publishers, Inc., Cambridge, MA.

Qian, Yingyi and Chenggang Xu, 1993, "Why China's Economic Reforms Differ: The M-Form Hierarchy and Entry/Expansion of the Non-State Sector," working paper. Publication No. 319, Economics Department, Stanford University, Stanford, CA.

Rawski, Thomas G., 1995, "Implications of China's Reform Experience," *The China Quarterly*, 144: 1150–1173.

Redding, S. Gordon, 1996, "Societal Transformation and the Contribution of Authority Relations and Cooperation Norms in Overseas Chinese Business," in Tu, Wei-ming, (ed.), *Confucian Traditions in East Asian Modernity: Moral Education and Economic Culture in Japan and the Four Mini-Dragons*, Harvard University Press, Cambridge, MA, 310–327.

Rodgers, William H., Jr., 1994, *Environmental Law*, 2nd ed., West Publishing Co., Minneapolis, MN.

Ross, Lester, 1988, *Environmental Policy in China*, Indiana University Press, Bloomington.

———, 1989, "The Changing Profile of Dispute Resolution in Rural China: The Case of Zouping County, Shandong," *Stanford Journal of International Law*, 26(1): 15–66.

Ross, Lester and Mitchell Silk, 1987, *Environmental Law and Policy in the People's Republic of China*, Quarum Books, New York.

Rozelle, Scott, Xiaoying Ma, and Leonard Ortolano, 1993, "Industrial Wastewater Control in Chinese Cities: Determinants of Success in Environmental Policy," *Natural Resources Modeling*, 7(4): 353–378.

Russell, Clifford, Winston Harrington, and William Vaughan, 1986, *Enforcing Pollution Control Laws*, Resources for the Future, Washington, D.C.

Sabatier, Paul and Daniel Mazmanian, 1983, *Can Regulation Work?* Plenum Press, New York.

SCEPC (State Council's Environmental Protection Commission), 1986, *Decision on Quantitative Assessment of Comprehensive Urban Environmental Control*, Beijing.

Scott, Richard W., 1995, *Institutions and Organizations*, Sage, Thousand Oaks.

SEPA (State Environmental Protection Administration), 1998, *1997 China Environmental Statistical Bulletin*, SEPA, Beijing.

Shi, Tianjin, 1997, *Political Participation in Beijing*, Harvard University Press, Cambridge, MA.

Shirk, Susan L., 1993, *The Political Logic of Economic Reform in China*, University of California Press, Berkeley, CA.

Sinkule, Barbara J. and Leonard Ortolano, 1995, *Implementing Environmental Policy in China*, Praeger, Westport, CN.

Smil, Vaclav, 1993, *China's Environmental Crisis: An Inquiry into the Limits of National Development*, M.E. Sharpe, Armonk, NY.

SPC (State Planning Commission) et al., 1973, *Gongye Sanfei Paifang Biaozhun* [Industrial 'Three Wastes' Discharge Standards, GBJ4–73]. Issued jointly by the State Planning Commission, the State Construction Commission, and the Ministry of Public Health, Beijing.

SPC and MF (State Planning Commission and the Ministry of Finance), 1993, *Guanyu Zhengashou Wushui Paiwufei De Tongzhi* [*A Notice on Collection of Wastewater Discharge Fee*], Beijing.

Spofford, Walter O., Jr., Xiaoying Ma, Zon Ji, and Kathlin Smith, 1996a, *Assessment of the Regulatory Framework for Water Pollution Control in the Xiaoqing River Basin: A Case Study of Jinan Municipality*, a report prepared by Resources for the Future for the Shangdong Provincial Environmental Project of The World Bank, Washington, D.C.

———, 1996b, *Assessment of the Regulatory Framework for Industrial Pollution Control in Chongqing*. Unpublished report for The World Bank Chongqing Project, Resources for the Future, Washington, D.C.

SPPG (Shandong Provincial People's Government), 1996a, *Guanyu Liji Guanting Xiaozaozhi Qiye De Tonggao* [A Public Notice on Closing Down Small-Sized Paper Mills], April 25, 1996.

———, 1996b, *Shandongsheng Renmin Zhengfu Guanyu Jiaqiang Shuiwuran Fangzhi De Jueding* [A Decision On Strengthening Water Pollution Prevention and Control, Shandong Provincial People's Government Document, No. 31]. Issued by Shandong Provincial People's Government (SPPG) on April 2, 1996.

SSB (State Statistical Bureau of the PRC), 1996, 1997, etc., *China Statistical Yearbook*, China Statistical Publishing House, Beijing.

State Council, 1982, *Zhengshou Paiwufei Zhanxing Banfa* [Provisional Measures for Collecting Pollution Discharge Fees], Beijing.

———, 1992, *Regulations on Transformation of Management Mechanisms at State-Owned Industrial Enterprises,*. Beijing, July 23.

———, 1996, *Guowuyuan Guanyu Huanjing Baohu Rogan Wenti De Jueding* [State Council Decisions Concerning Certain Environmental Protection Issues], Beijing, August 3.

State Council, SPC, and SEC (State Council, State Planning Commission, and State Economic Commission), 1986, *Jianshe Xiangmu Huanjing Baohu Guanli Banfa* [Management Guidelines on Environmental Protection for Construction Projects], Beijing.

Tang, Shui-Yan, Carlos Wing-Hung Lo, Kai-Chee Cheung, and Jack Man-Keung Lo, 1997, "Institutional Constraints on Environmental Management in Guangzhou and Shanghai," *The China Quarterly*, 152: 863–874.

Tanner, Murray S., 1994, "Organizations and Politics in China's Post-Mao Law-Making System," in Potter, Pittman B. (ed.), *Domestic Law Reforms in Post-Mao China*, M. E. Sharpe, Armonk, NY.

————, 1995, "How a Bill Becomes a Law in China: Stages and Processes in Lawmaking." *China Quarterly*, 141 (March): 40–64.

U.S. Council on Environmental Quality (CEQ), 1993, 24th Annual Report, CEQ, Washington, D.C.

U.S. Embassy Beijing, 1998, "The Fading of Chinese Environmental Secrecy," an unpublished report dated March, 1998, U.S. Embassy, Beijing.

US EPA (U.S. Environmental Protection Agency), 1984, Technical Guidance Manual for Performing Waste Load Allocations, Book VII: Permit Average Periods, Washington, D.C.

————, 1992, *Principles of Environmental Enforcement*, Washington, D.C.

————, 1997, Office of Inspector General Semiannual Report to the Congress, April 1, 1997 through September 30, 1997, Report No. EPA-350-R-97-002 (November, 1997), Office of Inspector General, Washington, D.C.

————, 1998a, "Water: Region 10's National Pollutant Discharge Elimination System Permit Program" (March 13, 1998), Report No. E1HWF7-10-0012-8100076, Office of the Inspector General for Audits, Western Division, San Francisco, CA.

————, 1998b, Kansas National Polluters Discharge Elimination System Program, Audit Report E1HWF7-07-0022-8100089, March 31, 1998, Office of Inspector General, Central Audit Division, Kansas City, Kansas.

Vermeer, Eduard B., 1991, "Management of Pollution Abatement by Chinese Enterprises," *China Information*, VI (1): 34–45.

————, 1995, "An Inventory of Losses Due to Environmental Pollution," *China Information*, X(1): 19–50.

————, 1998, "Industrial Pollution in China and Remedial Policies," *The China Quarterly*, 156: 952–985.

Vogel, Ezra F., 1989, *One Step Ahead in China: Guangdong Under Reform*, Havard University Press, Cambridge, MA.

Walder, Andrew G., 1992, "Local Bargaining Relationships and Urban Infrastructure Finance," in Lieberthal, Kenneth G. and David M. Lampton (eds.), *Bureaucracy, Politics and Decision-Making in Post-Mao China*, University of California Press, Berkeley, 308–333.

Walder, Andrew G., (ed.), 1998, *Zouping in Transition: The Process of Reform in Rural North China*, Harvard University Press, Cambridge, MA.

Wandi, Jiang, 1996, "Friends of Nature: China's New Environmental Watchdog," *Beijing Review* (August 5–11): 17–19.

Wang, Hui, 1994, *The Gradual Revolution*, Transaction Publishers, New Brunswick.

Wang, Xin and Robert Bloomquist, 1992, "The Developing Environmental Law and Policy of the People's Republic of China: An Introduction and Appraisal," *The Georgetown International Environmental Law Review*, 5: 25–75.

Warren, Kimberley A., 1996, "Going Green in China: An Organization Theory Perspective on Pollution Prevention in Chinese Electroplating Factories," Ph.D. dissertation, Department of Civil and Environmental Engineering, Stanford University, CA.

Weidenbaum, Murray and Samuel Hughes, 1996, *The Bamboo Network: How Expatriate Chinese Entrepreneurs are Creating a New Economic Superpower in Asia*, The Free Press, New York.

Wong, Christine P. W., 1991, "Central-Local Relations in an Era of Fiscal Decline: the Paradox of Fiscal Decentralization in Post-Mao China," *The China Quarterly*, 128: 691–715.

————, 1993, "Public Finance and Economic Decentralization," in Galenson, Walter, *China's Economic Reform*, The 1990 Institute, South San Francisco, CA.

Wong, John and Mu Yang, 1995, "The Making of the TVE Miracle – An Overview of Case Studies," in Wong, John, Rong Ma, and Mu Yang, *China's Rural Entrepreneurs: Ten Case Studies*, Times Academic Press, Singapore.

World Bank, 1994, China Urban Environmental Service Management, Report No. 13073-CHA, Environment and Urban Development Division, East Asia and Pacific Regional Office, The World Bank, Washington, D.C.

————, 1996, *China's Reform of State-Owned Enterprises*, Report No. 14924-CHA, China and Mongolia Department, East Asia and Pacific Region, The World Bank, Washington, D.C.

————, 1997, *Clear Water, Blue Skies: China's Environment in the New Century* (unpublished draft), The World Bank, Washington, D.C.

Xie, Zhenhua, 1996, *Zai Disici Quanguo Huanjing Baohu Huiyi Shang De Baogao* [A Report at the Fourth National Environmental Protection Conference], Beijing, (July).

Yang, Mayfair, 1989, "Between State and Society: The Construction of Corporateness in a Chinese Socialist Factory," *The Australian Journal of Chinese Affairs*, 22: 31–60.

Yeh, Kung-Chia, 1993, "Economic Reform: An Overview," in Walter Galenson, ed., *China's Economic Reform*, The 1990 Institute, South San Francisco, CA.

Zhang, Hongjun and Richard J. Ferris, 1997, "The Environmental Regulatory Regime of the People's Republic of China: A Primer Addressing Practical Concerns of Foreign Investors," *Environmental Law Reporter News & Analysis*, XXVII(5): 10228–10242.

Zheng, Shiping, 1997, *Party vs. State in Post-1949 China: The Institutional Dilemma*, Cambridge University Press, Cambridge, U.K.

Zhou, Xuezhi and Wenkui Tang, 1996, *Rural Environmental Protection in China* (Zhongguo Nongcun Huanjing Baohu), China Environmental Science Press, Beijing.

Zhu, Xingxiang, et al., 1991, *Zhongguo De Paiwu Xukezheng Zhidu* [Discharge Permit System in China], *Zhongguo Huanjing Kexue Chubanshe* [China Environmental Science Press], Beijing.

Index

accidents, 59
acid rain, 4
administrative acts, 33n6
administrative system: and environmental protection, 55–58, 60–65, 78–81, 154; hierarchy, 33–36, 38, 78; line and area relationships, 36–40; ministries and bureaus, 35–36, 52n3, 68–70; municipalities, 60–63; provincial officials, 65. *See also* government
agriculture, 2–3, 7, 73
Air Force personnel, 81
air pollution, 3–6
ambient water, 18–19, 159, 160, 173–74
aniline, 188
annual plans, 64
Anyang: and administrative rank, 81; COD limits, 103; factory visits, 122; fee assessment, 119–20, 133–36; fee calculation, 111, 140; fee collection process, 149n4; and models, 105; research rationale, 177
area relationships, 36–40
Arizona, 163, 168
arsenic, 187
assimilative capacity, 100
authority, respect for, 77–78, 161
awards, 87

banks, 67–68
Beijing: administrative system, 35; enforcement, 117; industrial bureau EPDs, 66; permit system, 103, 107; research rationale, 177; survey questionnaire, 179; water supply, 6–7
Beijing Environment and Development Institute, 73
benzopyrene, 187
best available technology (BAT), 159–60
best conventional technology (BCT), 159–60
boating and fishing, 185, 189
BOD_5, 188
breweries, 101–3
bribery, 84–85
bureaus. *See* finance bureaus; industrial bureaus; urban construction bureaus

cadmium, 19, 187
California, 169n1, 170n15
campaigns, 121, 128
capacity, 100
case studies, 174–75, 177–78, 180
CCP. *See* Chinese Communist Party
centralization, 26–27, 28, 40
Changzhou: COD standards, 103; enforcement example, 120–21; face-saving solution, 88–89; factory visits, 122; fee calculation method, 108–10; fee overpayment, 142–43; lawsuit attempt, 92–93; ownership form study, 144–49; research rationale, 177; unprofitable enterprises, 137–39

Chao Lake, 30
chemical fiber plant, 139–42
chemical industry: DPS impact, 103; and EPBs, 38, 66, 120; profitable SOE example, 139–42; unprofitable SOE example, 136–38
chemicals: standards, 187–88; for water treatment, 88–89, 137
China Environmental News, 74
China Environmental Protection Foundation, 76n23
Chinese Communist Party (CCP): and dispute resolution, 90; and NPC, 13–14; ownership reforms, 47–48; and personnel, 31n3; pre-1979 role, 42; and status, 81
chlorofluorocarbons, 18
Chongqing: and discharge fees, 67; and EPBs, 58, 69, 82; and legislatures, 58, 59; permits, 101; research rationale, 177; unprofitable enterprises, 145–46
chromium, 187
cities: environmental quality assessment, 27; prefectural level, 52n2; and Water Pollution Prevention and Control Act, 28. *See also* municipalities; urban construction bureaus
citizen complaints: in China, 70–72, 74, 154; in U.S., 156–57, 168
city selection, 175–77
class-action suits, 71
COD (chemical oxygen demand). *See* oxidizable organic matter
college campuses, 73
commercial bureaus, 68–69
Communist Party. *See* Chinese Communist Party
compliance: Chinese view, 162; cost factor, 137–38, 138–39, 139–42; deadlines, 26; definitions, 181–82; with effluent standards, 181, 182–83; v. fee payment, 119–20, 126, 174; initial v. continuing, 173; morale factor, 138; and ownership form, 144–49. *See also* monitoring
concentration-based standards, 20, 28, 98, 99, 101

conciliation, 90
conferences, 121
Confucianism, 77–78, 90, 93n2, 94n19
consensus, 36, 89
Constitution, Chinese, 15–16, 31n7
construction projects: approval requirement, 154; citizen complaints, 71–72; and enterprise development, 52; environmental impact, 24–25, 32n36; and planning commissions, 65. *See also* Ministry of Construction; urban construction bureaus
contaminants, 9, 11n7, 160, 187–88
contract responsibility system, 44–45
cooling, industrial, 185, 189
cooperative approach, 121–22
copper, 188
corruption, 84–85, 90
costs: of compliance, 137–38, 138–39, 139–42; of enforcement, 10; of pollution, 1, 3; of public projects, 46
counties, 33–34, 51
courts. *See* judicial system; lawsuits
criticism, 88
Cushing, Katherine Kao, 91, 170n9
cyanide, 30, 188

Dalian City, 71
data sources, 180
deadlines, 26
decentralization, fiscal, 43–44
Denqin County, 74
detergents, 188
DFS. *See* discharge fee system
dilution, 113n6
Dinanchi Lake, 30
discharge fee system (DFS): assessment criteria, 117–20, 129n1; Changzhou example, 108–10; compliance, 181, 183; distribution, 67–68, 75nn8–9; diversion, 67–68; fee overpayment, 142–43; fee types, 21, 117; implementation, 22–23; as incentive, 103; non payment, 115, 116, 117, 127, 130n6, 149n4; penalties, 21–22, 123; v. permit system, 99–100, 106–11, 129n2, 174; revenue from, 21–22,

23, 62, 123–26, 129, 162; SOEs v. TVEs, 144–49; v. treatment costs, 137–38, 138–39, 139–42; U.S. counterparts, 169n1, 169n3; and urban construction bureaus, 69–70
discharge permit system (DPS): affected facilities, 159–61; cities participating in, 176; compliance definition, 182; effectiveness, 97–98, 101–3, 111–12, 113n2; and EPBs, 159; v. fee system, 99–100, 106–11, 129n2, 174; implementation process, 98–99; information flow, 88; negotiability, 160, 164; rationale, 24, 98, 158–59; requirements, 100–101, 104–6, 111–12, 159, 165; revocations, 126–27, 161; U.S. counterpart, 153, 155–58, 159–61; violations, 115, 116, 117, 127
disputes, 63, 82, 89–93, 94n21
documentaries, 72, 73
DPS. *See* discharge permit system
drinking water, 185–89
drought, 6–7
dump sites, 4–6
dyeing industry, 86, 103, 138–39, 148

Earth Day, 73
economic commissions, 65
economic development, 16, 63, 82
effluent guidelines, 159–160
effluent standards: compliance, 181, 182–83; for specific substances, 187–88; testing method, 183n9; in the U.S., 153; by usage class, 19, 185, 189; violations, 115, 116. *See also* standards
enforcement: actual measures, 117–21; authorized measures, 115–16; campaigns, 121, 128; cost of, 10; DPS v. DFS, 107; fee collection, 149n4; and *guanxi*, 126–27, 161–62; mayoral role, 63; permit revocation, 126–27; SEPA v. EPB views, 165–166; in the U.S., 164–65, 166–69, 170n15, 171n17; at unprofitable SOEs, 133–138; at unprofitable TVEs, 138–39. *See also* disputes; penalties; violations

engineering skills, 49–50
enterprise selection, 177–80
environmental impact statements, 25–26, 32n26
Environmental Protection Agency, U.S. (US EPA), 155–56, 157–58, 162–65, 168; Seattle office, 167
Environmental Protection and National Resources Conservation (EPNRC), 14
environmental protection bureaus (EPBs): administrative rank, 80–81, 154; background, 8; banking in, 142–43; Beijing example, 107, 113n9; Changzhou example, 108–10; and citizen complaints, 70, 71–72; conferences, 121; and construction projects, 25; dispute resolution, 90–91; enforcement, 88–89, 117–21, 126–29; and fees, 21–23, 67–68, 75nn8–9, 123–26; and fiscal decentralization, 43; *guanxi* effect, 83–85, 161–162; and industrial bureaus, 65–67; and local people's congresses, 58; mayoral interference, 63–64, 82; monitoring activity, 20, 22, 60–62; and municipal governments, 59–60, 62–63; and other agencies, 10; and permits, 104–6; and planning commissions, 65; and SOEs, 46–47; staffing, 62–63, 75n7, 95n27, 105; and TVEs, 50; and urban construction bureaus, 69–70
environmental protection division (EPD), 65–67
Environmental Publicity and Education Center, 72
environmental responsibility system, 26–27
EPB. *See* environmental protection bureaus
EPD. *See* environmental protection division

face, 85–89, 162, 165
fees. *See* discharge fee system
fertilizer, 2–3
finance bureaus, 67
fish, 29, 86, 185, 189

five-year plans, 64
flowrates, 98, 101–4, 108
fluoride, 188
forests, 4, 7, 73, 74
formaldehyde, 188
four small pieces, 21–22, 123
Friends of Nature, 72–73, 74
fuel, 4
funding, 46, 69–70, 76n23. *See also*
    discharge fee system
future trends, 29–30, 60, 67

Global Village Institute, 73
Gorsuch, Anne, 158
government, 34, 36–40, 155, 157–58.
    See also administrative system; local
    governments
grants: and discharge fees, 21, 31n14,
    68; and fee overpayment, 142–43;
    and SOEs, 44; and TVEs, 53n12
grant-to-loan program, 44
grassland, 7
groundwater, 11n7
Guangdong Province. *See* Guangzhou;
    Shenzhen City
Guangzhou, 59–60, 81
guanxi, 82–85, 88–89, 91, 94n8. *See also*
    enforcement

habitat. *See* species loss
Hai River, 2, 30
halon, 18
Hartzell, Richard W., 86, 87
hazardous waste, 4
Hejin County, 51
households, 73
Huai River, 2, 6, 29–30
Hubei Province. *See* Wuhan
Hunan Province, 64
Hunter, Susan, 158, 163, 164, 168, 171n17

illness, 29
implementation: in China, 22–23, 81, 98–
    99; in U.S., 155–58
incentives, 87, 103
industrial bureaus, 65–67, 68–69, 121
industry: growth factor, 63; pollution
    prevention, 28–29; sectors, 38–40;
    solid waste, 6; wastewater, 3, 11n8

informal rules: dispute resolution, 89–
    93; face, 85–89, 162; and fee
    payment, 174; v. laws, 10; relation-
    ships (*guanxi*), 82–85, 88–89, 91,
    94n8; respect for authority, 77–78,
    161; and treatment plant, 170n9; in
    the U.S., 162–65
institutions, 9–10, 12n17
integrity, 86
intermediaries, 89–91
international agreements, 18
iron, 19
irrigation, 185, 189

Jahiel, Abigail: on EPBs, 62–63; on fee
    collection, 126; on future, 29–30, 60;
    guanxi example, 83–84; on Qu
    Geping, 79
Jiang Zemin, 47
Jinan: administrative system, 57, 58–59;
    discharge fees, 67–68, 108; EPBs, 60–
    62; industrial bureaus, 68–69; load al-
    location, 106; manager exchange pro-
    gram, 122; mayoral role, 64; permits,
    117; planning commissions, 65; re-
    search rationale, 177
joint ventures, 40
judicial system: for disputes, 90–91;
    and enforcement, 116, 117, 127–28,
    129; in U.S., 157, 158

Kansas, 167
Kornai, Janos, 45

lakes, 30
laws: Chinese view, 91–92, 94n19;
    circumventing, 84–85; formal v.
    informal, 10; national v. local, 93
lawsuits: in China, 71, 92–93, 136; in
    U.S., 156–57, 168–69, 170n16
lead, 187
"leading cadre's project," 93n7
legislation: authority for, 15–16; basic
    environmental law, 16; participating
    bodies, 13–15; special statutes, 17–
    18; Water Pollution Prevention and
    Control Act (1996), 28. *See also*
    local governments

Li, Elizabeth, 44
Liao River, 30
Liaoning Province. *See* Dalian City;
    Shenyang City
licenses, 68
Lieberthal, Kenneth, 31n3, 36, 40, 63
line relationships, 36–40
load allocation, 98–99, 104–6
loans, 21–22, 23, 31n14, 68. *See also* grant-
    to-loan program
local governments: components, 9, 33–34;
    mayoral offices, 63–64, 82, 121; munici-
    pal, 59–60; people's congresses, 58–59,
    71, 154; political factor, 156; SOEs and
    TVEs in, 50–52

Ma, Xiaoying, 177
management procedures, 16, 147
manganese, 188
mass-based standard, 28, 111, 112, 140–41
mayors, 63–64, 70–71, 82, 121
mayor's project, 93n7
media: in China, 71, 72–74, 154–55; in
    the U.S., 157, 168
mediation, 89, 94n21
meters, 108
Ministry of Construction, 78, 80–81
models, 104–6, 112, 159, 160
monitoring: data falsification, 166,
    170n13; and EPBs, 20, 22, 60–62,
    121; of flowrates, 108; frequency,
    32n17; municipal treatment works,
    69; purpose, 126; self-, 10, 99, 148–
    49, 166; in the U.S., 166, 167. *See
    also* citizen complaints; reporting
municipalities: administrative system,
    33–34; and EPBs, 59–63; and fees as
    revenue, 123; finance bureaus, 67–
    68; monitoring, 69; in U.S., 156,
    161; wastewater, 3, 11n8, 156

National Environmental Protection
    Agency (NEPA): and DPS, 98–100;
    edicts, 17; history, 8, 79–80; model
    guidelines, 104–6; plan for the
    1990s, 2; and responsibility system,
    26–27. *See also* discharge permit
    system; State Environmental
    Protection Agency

National People's Congress (NPC), 13–
    14, 74n1. *See also* PRC Environ-
    mental Protection Law
National Pollutant Discharge Elimina-
    tion System, U.S. (NPDES): and
    EPA, 168; formal rules, 159–61;
    informal rules, 162–65; role, 153,
    155–58
nature reserves, 8, 185, 189
negotiation, 44–45, 160, 164
NEPA. *See* National Environmental
    Protection Agency
newsletters, 73
newspapers, 74
NGO. *See* nongovernmental organiza-
    tions
NH3–N, 188
nickel, 187
Ninth Five Year Plan, 30
nitrobenzine, 188
nitrogen, 2–3
nomenklatura system, 33n3, 42
nongovernmental organizations
    (NGOs): in China, 72–73, 76n23,
    155; in U.S., 156–57, 168
North, Douglass, 12n17
North Carolina, 167
NPC. *See* National People's Congress
NPDES. *See* National Pollutant
    Discharge Elimination System, U.S.

Oi, Jean, 48
oil, 160, 188
overstandard fees, 21
ownership, 40–41, 47–48, 144–49
oxidizable organic matter: compliance
    cost, 141–42; definition, 10; in Ninth
    Five Year Plan, 30; paper mill
    example, 134; and permit system,
    101–4, 159; standards, 19–20,
    183n5, 184n11, 188; in U.S., 160
ozone layer, 18

paper mills: in Chongqing County, 59;
    DPS impact, 103; and fee assess-
    ment, 119, 133–36; in Guangzhou,
    81; and Huai River, 29; in Shandong
    province, 146; treatment plant, 134

Pearson, Margaret, 84–85
penalties: Anyang method, 111;
    Changzhou method, 109; v.
    discharge fees, 107; discharge fee
    system, 21–24; for effluent standard
    violations, 115, 116; late payment,
    127, 130n6; Shunde method, 110–
    11; and taxes, 63, 115. *See also*
    enforcement; violations
people's congresses. *See* local govern-
    ments; National People's Congress
permits. *See* discharge permit system
personnel: EPB, 62–63, 75n7, 95n27;
    fee collectors, 130n17; manager
    exchange, 122; morale, 138;
    relationships, 82–85, 86, 94n8, 122,
    161–62, 164; skills, 148; in SOE v.
    TVE, 137, 145, 148; in U.S., 165
petroleum, 188
pH, 160, 188
pharmaceutical industry, 91, 170n9
phenols, 188
phosphate, 188
planning commissions, 64–65
plant closures, 145–46
political pressure, 156, 157–58, 162–64
pollutants, 160
pollution levy fund, 21–22, 67–68, 142–
    43
population, 1
power plants, 81, 119–20
pragmatism, 128–29
PRC Environmental Protection Law,
    16–17, 21, 24, 99
prevention, 16, 28
prioritization, 2–6
private sector, 40–41
production methods, 28–29
profitability, 120–21, 130n8, 133–39
profit retention, 43, 44–45
projections, 1
protectionism, 53n11
public. *See* citizen complaints
public projects, 46

Qingdao City, 87
Quarterly Noncompliance Reports
    (QNCRs), 166, 167

Qu Geping, 78, 79, 154–155

radio, 71
rank, 34–36, 80–81
Reagan, Ronald, 158
reciprocity, 82–85, 93n2
recycling, 73
Red Star, 87
reforms. *See* ownership; state-owned
    enterprises
registration, 99
regulations, 10
*Regulations on Transformation of
    Management Mechanisms at State-
    Owned Industrial Enterprises*
    (1992), 65, 154
renovation projects, 44–45
reporting: as implementation step, 99;
    omissions, 88, 166; overstatement,
    109–10; self-, 10, 166; in the U.S., 166
research approach, 174–80
responsibility, 16, 26–27, 44–45
rice bowl, 137, 145
Ruckleshaus, William, 158
rules. *See* informal rules; laws

sanctions, 10
SDPC. *See* State Development and
    Planning Commission
SEC. *See* State Economic Commission
self-construction fees, 22
self-construction fund, 67–68
self-monitoring. *See* monitoring
self-reporting. *See* reporting
SEPA. *See* State Environmental
    Protection Agency
SETC. *See* State Economic and Trade
    Commission
Shandong province, 26, 59, 146. *See also*
    Qingdao City
Shanghai, 100
Shanxi Province. *See* Hejin County
Shenyang City, 91
Shenzhen City, 86
Shunde: COD limits, 103; factory visits,
    122; fines and fees, 110–11; model-
    ing, 105; ownership form study, 144–
    49; research rationale, 177

Sichuan Province. *See* Wan County
Smil, Vaclav, 1, 7
Smithfield Foods, 163–164
social services, 42
SOE. *See* state-owned enterprises
soil erosion, 7
solids, 160, 188
SPC. *See* State Planning Commission
species loss, 8
standards: ambient water, 18–21, 98, 159, 160; capacity-based, 98, 100 goal-based, 100–101. *See also* effluent standards
State Council: and construction projects, 25; 1996 decision, 74; edicts, 17; and fees, 21; and responsibility system, 26–27, 78–80; role, 14; and SOEs, 46; and TVEs, 30
State Development and Planning Commission (SDPC), 34
State Economic and Trade Commission (SETC), 34
State Economic Commission (SEC), 25
State Environmental Protection Agency (SEPA): and construction projects, 25; enforcement policy, 165; history, 8, 69, 78–80; information access, 88; rank, 36, 80–81; role, 9, 153–54; and urban assessment, 27–28; and violations, 10. *See also* National Environmental Protection Agency
state-owned enterprises (SOEs): fee compliance, 144–49; incentives, 87; and local governments, 50–52; management procedure, 147; number of, 50; post-1991, 46–48; pre-1979 reform, 40, 41–42; profitable, 130n8, 139–42 ranks, 36, 38; reforms, 40, 41–42, 44–45, 46–48; 1984-1991 reforms, 44–45; sizes, 52n5; v. TVEs, 49–50; unprofitable, 130n8, 133–38, 145–46, 150n19
State Planning Commission (SPC), 2, 25
students, 73
sulfide, 188
sulfur dioxide, 4
surveys, 174–75, 178–79, 180

swimming, 185, 189

Tai Lake, 30
tanneries, 30
tax system: and fee overpayment, 142–43; and fines v. fees, 63, 115; revenue sharing, 50; and SOEs, 46–47, 52n5
tax-for-profit system, 43
technology, 49, 159–60
television, 73, 74
"Ten, One Hundred, One Thousand, Ten Thousand" plan, 28–29
third parties, 89–91
Three Norths Program, 17
Three River's Plain, 73
three synchronizations, 25–26, 103, 147
township and village enterprises (TVEs): environmental protection, 29–30; fee compliance, 144–49; and local governments, 50–52; management, 147–48; number of, 50; post-1978 reform, 40, 48–49; v. SOEs, 49–50; unprofitable, 138–39, 150n19
townships, 34, 51. *See also* local governments; municipalities
training, 122, 146, 147–48
Trans-Century Green Project, 30
treatment plants: funding, 69–70; and good faith, 170n9; in Jinan, 64; monitoring, 69; operating costs, 137–38, 138–39; for paper mill, 134; in TVEs v. SOEs, 147
trial programs, 32n22, 44, 120, 158–59
TVE. *See* township and village enterprises

unemployment, 137, 145
United States: enforcement, 164–65, 166–69, 170n15; EPA (*see* Environmental Protection Agency, U.S.); NPDES (*see* National Pollutant Discharge Elimination System, U.S.); state level, 155–56, 163, 168
urban construction bureaus, 69–70
US EPA. *See* Environmental Protection Agency, U.S.
usage classification, 19, 185, 189

Vermeer, Eduard, 130n8
villages, 34, 51
violations: contextual conditions, 91; corrections, 113n2; discharge permit, 116; of effluent standards, 115, 116; face-saving solutions, 88–89, 162; fees, 116. *See also* enforcement; penalties
Virginia, 163–64
visits, informal, 122

Wan County, 4
Wang Hanbin, 92
warnings, 117, 122
Warren, Kimberley, 148
wastewater: annual industrial release, 3; industrial v. municipal, 11n8; load allocation, 98; oxidizable organic matter, 10; regulations, 10; standards, 19–21; treatment plants, 64
wastewater discharge fee, 22

water: ambient, 18–19, 159, 160, 173–74; contaminants, 9, 11n7, 160, 187–88; drinking, 185–89; pollution sources, 2–3; shortages, 6
Waterman, Richard, 158, 163, 164, 168, 171n17
wetlands, 73
workshops, 122
World Wide Fund for Nature (WWF), 73
Wuhan, 83, 125–126
WWF. *See* World Wide Fund for Nature

Xiaoqing River, 59, 106
Xie Zhenhua, 8, 28

Yunnan Province. *See* Denqin County

Zhu Rongji, Premier, 23
Zibo, 106
zinc, 188

About the Authors

XIAOYING MA completed her Ph.D. in the Civil and Environmental Engineering Department at Stanford University. An environmental economist at the Asian Development Bank, Dr. Ma has been working on environment-related projects in the People's Republic of China, Indonesia, and Tajikistan since her graduation from Stanford University in 1997.

LEONARD ORTOLANO is UPS Foundation Professor of Civil Engineering and Director of the Program on Urban Studies at Stanford University. A specialist in water resources and environmental planning, Dr. Ortolano has been doing research on industrial pollution control in China since 1987. He has served as a consultant to numerous environmental management firms and regulatory agencies in the United States and abroad.

on the road with
Lisa Harper

TOUGH LOVE,
TENDER MERCIES

3 short stops in the Minor Prophets

Tyndale House Publishers, Inc.
Wheaton, Illinois

Visit Tyndale's exciting Web site at www.tyndale.com

TYNDALE is a registered trademark of Tyndale House Publishers, Inc.

Tyndale's quill logo is a trademark of Tyndale House Publishers, Inc.

Tough Love, Tender Mercies

ISBN-13: 978-1-4143-0277-5

ISBN-10: 1-4143-0277-0

Printed in the United States of America

11   10   09   08   07   06   05
7   6   5   4   3   2   1

God has graciously woven incredible men and women in my life (apart from my family) to teach me about His character. Some have tutored me through Biblical exposition, some through honest confrontation, and all by modeling Christ-likeness. The following is a short list of not-so-minor, modern day *prophets* for whom I am deeply grateful: Pastor Roy Carter, Helen Cummings, Julie Dilworth, Margaret Dye, Kim Hill, Sue Johnson, Jack and Pammy Markle, Wendy Martin, Dr. Charles McGowan, Teresa Moshell, Eva Self, and Pastor Scotty Smith.

I'd also like to thank several people who've labored long hours on my behalf:

Karen Watson, Carol Traver, and Kathy Simpson at Tyndale House Publishers; Naomi Duncan at the Ambassador Agency; my editor, Lisa Jackson; and my "road warrior," Libby Willems.

CONTENTS

How to Use the DVD   *ix*

Introduction   *xi*

First Stop: Hosea

1. An Unlikely Love Story   *3*

2. Surnames and Slur-names   *15*

3. Crème Brûlée and Castor Oil   *29*

4. Crime, Punishment, and Promise   *45*

Second Stop: Zephaniah

1. God Doesn't "Do" Recess   *59*

2. Just Desserts   *75*

3. The Biggest Kahuna of All   *87*

4. Unmistakable Hope   *99*

Last Stop: Malachi

1. When Your Tara's Trashed   *115*

2. The Consequences of Cheap Charity   *127*

3. Another Face of Grace   *139*

4. The Truth about Transcendent Joy   *155*

Final Thoughts   *167*

Notes   *171*

How to Use the DVD

As you work your way through the book, you'll notice that certain questions have a DVD symbol next to them. Whenever you see this symbol, pop in the enclosed DVD, cue up the right chapter, hit play, and see what the book club has to say about this portion of Scripture.

You can watch as you go—one chapter at a time—or make some microwave popcorn and watch the whole thing while relaxing on the couch!

We really hope you enjoy "eavesdropping" on our conversations about God—and we hope they prompt some heartfelt and lively discussions with your friends, too!

Lisa

Introduction

If you mention the Bible in a crowded elevator, you'll find that most people shuffle uncomfortably and stare at the illuminated buttons hoping for a quick getaway (unless you're at a Christian convention, of course). The Bible just isn't a very popular subject these days. It's characterized as legalistic, archaic, hate crime-inciting literature by its worst detractors and a collection of mostly benign morality tales by many others. Some Christians even dismiss it as old-fashioned, boring, and irrelevant. But none of those adjectives are remotely accurate—the Bible isn't malicious, dull, or immaterial. It is, however, quite possibly the most misinterpreted book in history.

And for that very reason, the On the Road series was developed. This is the second book in a series written and formatted specifically to help people better engage with and understand the Bible. All kinds of people—people who flock to Bible studies and people who'd rather wrestle an alligator than read the Bible. We hope that even if you don't consider yourself a Christian, you'll be able to use the following pages as a sort of *scriptural tour guide* to help you interact with the captivating plots, dramatic imagery, and relevant promises.

In this particular book, we're going to visit a section of Scripture called the Minor Prophets, a place rarely traveled but very

rewarding. And to show just how relevant these ancient tales are to your life today, we'll compare each prophet's story with a contemporary movie theme. Our first stop will be at a place called Hosea, where we'll ponder Julia Roberts' famous *Pretty Woman* role and how it relates to God's mercy. The second stop will find us comparing one of actor Morgan Freeman's characters to the characteristic of God's holiness in a place called Zephaniah. And the third stop will take us to a hardscrabble town full of Scarlett O'Hara-wannabes in a place called Malachi.

Please keep in mind this is an intentionally informal trip. It's not one of those tours where you have to wear matching T-shirts or hats in order to look like everyone else on the bus. Nor do you need to have appropriately religious answers to every question. We want you to wrestle honestly with the difficult concepts and allow yourself to linger over the persistent promise of God's grace. We also hope you'll invite others to take the trip with you. Especially your friends and family who fit in the category of "elevator shufflers" and those who avoid the Bible like some dinnertime telemarketer.

Our sincere prayer is that after choosing to take this brief biblical tour, you'll have a clearer picture of "who" God is and how very much He adores you.

First Stop:

Hosea

1

An Unlikely Love Story

LISTEN TO YOUR LIFE. SEE IT FOR THE FATHOMLESS
MYSTERY THAT IT IS. IN THE BOREDOM AND PAIN OF IT NO
LESS THAN IN THE EXCITEMENT AND GLADNESS: TOUCH,
TASTE, SMELL YOUR WAY TO THE HOLY AND HIDDEN HEART
OF IT BECAUSE IN THE LAST ANALYSIS ALL MOMENTS ARE
KEY MOMENTS, AND LIFE ITSELF IS GRACE. *Frederick Buechner*

I wouldn't mind looking like Julia Roberts. It's not
that I'm really unhappy with my own looks—
though I wouldn't mind having my pre-forty-year-
old metabolism back—and I don't have any aspira-
tions to be a contestant on *Extreme Makeover*. But
with her close-to-perfect figure and megawatt
smile, Julia always seems to get the good guy. At
least in the movies. And the film that probably best

showcases her appeal is *Pretty Woman.* That movie launched her career as a superstar and was also one of the highest-grossing romantic comedies in recent history.

Read Hosea 1–3 in the New Living Translation or *The Message* and synopsize these chapters in your own words.

If Hollywood optioned the rights to your life story, what actress would you choose to play yourself? Why?

You probably remember the story line: Julia Roberts portrays a likable prostitute (she doesn't really *want* to be a lady-of-the-evening—she just doesn't have any other viable choices—but we're led to believe that she still has a good heart and certain values she wouldn't compromise!) opposite handsome Richard Gere's extremely successful businessman character. Theirs is a very unlikely romance, which began when his curiosity and sheer pragmatism intersected—he had never learned how to drive a car with a manual transmission and needed someone to drive his borrowed stick-shift sports car. After a few hours in Julia's charming presence, which did not include a stereotypical fishnet-hose-and-bad-teeth prostitute persona, Richard asks her to be his no-strings-attached date for several weekend business functions.

Of course, within a short time they become smitten with each other and go on to overcome her profession, his fear of commitment, and the dismay

of his clued-in business associates. By the end of the movie, they have fallen madly in love. It sounds pretty far-fetched, doesn't it? Only Hollywood could write a story where a gum-smacking prostitute ends up with a good-looking, Ivy League–educated millionaire, right? Well, not exactly. I think Tinseltown borrowed the "very bad girl gets very good guy" plot from an Old Testament book called Hosea.

It's been said that all great stories include the four main themes of Scripture: Creation, the Depravity of mankind, Redemptive love, and Death (or Heaven). Which one of your favorite books or movies is a good example that incorporates those themes?

Polygamy, Politics, and Pagans

Hosea kicks off a twelve-book section located at the very end of the Old Testament, commonly called the Minor Prophets. I used to think they were called *minor* because the men who wrote them were diminutive! But they're actually designated this way because they're relatively short books, unlike the longer prophetic books like Isaiah and Jeremiah. Yet, in spite of their brevity—most are no more than a few chapters in length—the Minor Prophets are full of passion, intrigue, and unforgettable images of God. And my favorite image of all is found in Hosea, the first stop on our tour.

However, before we begin our trip, we need to learn a few things about this divine district we'll be visiting. Now, for those of you who tend to take

NOTES

mental field trips during history lessons, I suggest you grab some coffee and dark chocolate to help you focus because the following information is the key to enjoying the rest of the tour!

The twelve Minor Prophets were written over a span of about four hundred years (from 835 BC to 400 BC), after the reigns of David and Solomon. And those four hundred years represent an extremely tumultuous time in Israel's history. They were in turmoil partly because of bad leadership. After forty years of strong leadership, King David died, leaving the keys to the throne to his smart son, Solomon. But although Solomon's SAT scores were at the top of the class, he flunked the final exam of leadership.

Solomon was a brilliant, literary man (he wrote most of Proverbs, and possibly some of the other Wisdom books) with a bevy of beautiful wives from other countries. In the beginning of his reign, he

did you know?

The notation **BC** stands for "before Christ" and represents the time period **preceding** His birth. **AD** is an abbreviation for the Latin words **anno Domini** which translated means "the year of the Lord" and represents the time period **after** Jesus was born. Those two terms—BC and AD—have been used worldwide for well over a thousand years to designate the time periods before and after Jesus Christ's birth. However, in modern literature the politically correct terms **BCE** and **CE** are fast replacing BC and AD. BCE stands for "before the common era" and CE stands for "common era." These terms have the same time "value" as BC and AD, but have effectively removed the reference to Christ. For obvious reasons, I still prefer the dating notations BC and AD.

followed in his father's wise footsteps. But then he made the dumb decision to let his foreign wives continue practicing the idolatry they grew up with instead of converting to faith in the one true God, Jehovah. Furthermore, Solomon foolishly allowed those same pagan wives to control the kids. So when he died and the need for a successor arose, chaos broke lose in the harem. His Jerry Springer version of a family couldn't begin to agree on which of his sons should become the next king of Israel.

Read 1 Timothy 3:1-5 and 8-12. Why do you think God included being a good father in the list of qualifications for church leadership? What parenting characteristics do you think best correlate with effective leadership?

The infighting that followed Solomon's death resulted in a vicious split in the kingdom of Israel. The northern kingdom retained the name *Israel,* and is sometimes also called *Ephraim,* which was the name of Israel's largest tribe. The southern kingdom—now called *Judah*—retained Jerusalem, the beautiful "City of God," as its capital. The gist of this split in God's family is that His people now warred amongst themselves as often as they fought with foreign nations.

Finally, the theocracy of Israel was in turmoil because rather than trusting God to protect them, they made alliances with former enemies like Assyria in a dangerous game of political roulette. When they aligned themselves with people they used to cross swords with, they also swung the door to their

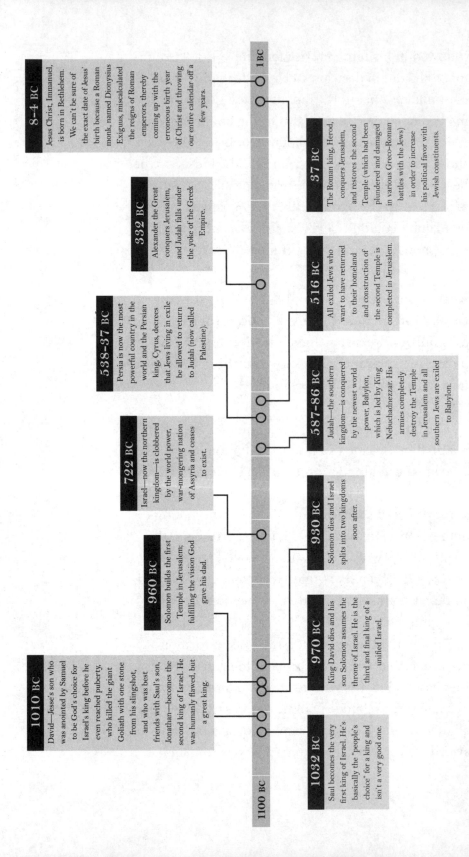

1100 BC

1BC

1032 BC
Saul becomes the very first king of Israel. He's basically the "people's choice" for a king and isn't a very good one.

1010 BC
David—Jesse's son who was anointed by Samuel to be God's choice for Israel's king before he even reached puberty, who killed the giant Goliath with one stone from his slingshot, and who was best friends with Saul's son, Jonathan—becomes the second king of Israel. He was humanly flawed, but a great king.

970 BC
King David dies and his son Solomon assumes the throne of Israel. He is the third and final king of a unified Israel.

960 BC
Solomon builds the first Temple in Jerusalem, fulfilling the vision God gave his dad.

930 BC
Solomon dies and Israel splits into two kingdoms soon after.

722 BC
Israel—now the northern kingdom—is clobbered by the world power, war-mongering nation of Assyria and ceases to exist.

587–86 BC
Judah—the southern kingdom—is conquered by the newest world power, Babylon, which is led by King Nebuchadnezzar. His armies completely destroy the Temple in Jerusalem and all southern Jews are exiled to Babylon.

538–37 BC
Persia is now the most powerful country in the world and the Persian king, Cyrus, decrees that Jews living in exile be allowed to return to Judah (now called Palestine).

516 BC
All exiled Jews who want to have returned to their homeland and construction of the second Temple is completed in Jerusalem.

332 BC
Alexander the Great conquers Jerusalem, and Judah falls under the yoke of the Greek Empire.

37 BC
The Roman king, Herod, conquers Jerusalem, and restores the second Temple (which had been plundered and damaged in various Greco-Roman battles with the Jews) in order to increase his political favor with Jewish constituents.

8–4 BC
Jesus Christ, Immanuel, is born in Bethlehem. We can't be sure of the exact date of Jesus' birth because a Roman monk, named Dionysius Exiguus, miscalculated the reigns of Roman emperors, thereby coming up with the erroneous birth year of Christ and throwing our entire calendar off a few years.

sanctuary wide open, allowing other religions to waltz into their once monotheistic way of life. Instead of being "one nation under God," Israel was becoming a compromised spiritual smorgasbord. Needless to say, they were in a heap of trouble.

How would you compare Israel's inner turmoil with the segregation and jealousy among Christian denominations today? If you attend a church that is affiliated with a specific denomination, was there a unique issue or tradition that attracted you to it in the first place?

Several notable Bible scholars assert that God's prophets only spoke when Israel was in trouble, that God normally communicated to His people through kings and priests and He didn't use prophets until things really got out of control. And things were certainly out of control in Hosea's hometown, spiritually speaking anyway.

did you know?

Israel is the only nation ever given the status of **theocracy**—that is, a nation specially chosen by God to represent a covenant relationship with Him. The Old Testament Historical Books reveal how God created Israel to be His nation and chose the Israelites to be His representatives to the other nations, His ambassadors to the world. These "chosen people" were ordained to be kings and priests unto God, and all other nations were to be blessed by their contacts with Israel (see 2 Corinthians 4:6). But like Christians today, Israel was prone to wander and their spiritual apathy and idolatry led to their downfall.[1]

Like Charles Dickens's opening line in *A Tale of Two Cities*, it was "the best of times and the worst of times" in Jerusalem. It was the best of times because the national economy was thriving and Judah was experiencing unprecedented favor with surrounding nations. But it was the worst of times because God's chosen people were turning their backs on Him.[2] They were spending more time at the mall than the synagogue. They were frolicking in their newfound freedom and material excess and flinging loyalty to God out the window. Hedonism replaced holiness. So God chose Hosea—and Hosea's marriage—to express His disapproval and to forecast the consequences of Israel's actions.

FAST FACT
The first nine books of the Minor Prophets are classified as being **pre-exilic**, which means they were written **prior** to that very dark period in Israel's history when southern Jews were exiled from their homeland and forced to live in Babylon. The last three books of the Minor Prophets are classified as **post-exilic**, which means they were written **after** the Jewish exiles had returned to Jerusalem.

Read Exodus 34:14-16; Deuteronomy 32:16; and Isaiah 62:5. How does our "marriage" to God differ from a human marital relationship? In what ways are they similar?

Dating Diblaim's Daughter

While we know much about ancient world powers and monks who made dating mistakes (no pun intended), we know very little about this man named Hosea. Based on the content of his prophecy, we do know that it was written in the eighth century BC, and that he preached during the reigns of four successive kings of Judah (somewhere between 770 to 710 BC).[3] We also know that Hosea's name literally means *salvation* in Hebrew. But other than that, all we know about him comes from the poignant story God asked him to live and record.

Thus, in the absence of knowable details, I'm going to use considerable creative license to describe what Hosea *might* have been like. Since he was a prophet, and therefore an all-around good guy, I picture him wearing high-water pants, a short-sleeved white shirt with a tie his grandmother gave him for his bar mitzvah, old-fashioned black leather oxfords, and Coke-bottle glasses. He was the vice president of his high school math club and a loyal member of the FPGCP—the Future Prophets of God's Chosen People—club. Definitely not the type of guy who cruised questionable watering holes looking for chicks. Frankly, Hosea wasn't the type of guy who had a girlfriend. He probably didn't even go to his senior prom . . . he just stayed home and played Nintendo.

So what God asked this nice guy to do next was all the more surprising:

> *When the* LORD *first spoke through Hosea, the* LORD *said to Hosea, "Go, take to yourself a wife of whoredom and have children of whoredom, for the land commits great whoredom by forsaking the* LORD*."*   Hosea 1:2

The girl God told Hosea to marry had a social life very different from his. While he'd never taken a date to a Friday night football game, her phone number was plastered all over the boys' locker room. She was a quintessential party animal who'd been through more boyfriends than Jennifer Lopez. And it was her bad behavior that made her the perfect metaphor for God's chosen people, because they had a pretty racy reputation too. They'd betrayed the Creator of the universe by indulging in meaningless flings with idols and numerous affairs with false prophets. Faithfulness wasn't their forte.

It's amazing that Hosea doesn't question God in light of His request. He doesn't protest, "Hey, wait a minute, God. I don't like this idea! I don't want my marriage to be some prophetic metaphor! I want to marry a nice girl, not some tramp who's been with every guy in the neighborhood." Hosea doesn't say anything. He simply obeys God:

> *So he went and took Gomer, the daughter of Diblaim, and she conceived and bore him a son.*
>
> Hosea 1:3

 Many people—including theologian and church father John Calvin—have questioned why God would ask one of His children to marry a woman He knew would commit adultery. If you had to write a paper or engage in debate on this subject, how would you *justify* God asking Hosea to marry a "whore"?

When God asks me to do something difficult and I do what He says, I typically expect a good return on my investment. Especially if it cost me personal inconvenience or emotional pain. For instance, recently I was given too much change at a fast-food drive-through window. When I realized I'd been mistakenly given change based on twenty dollars instead of ten, I turned my car

around, parked, and went into the restaurant to give the extra money back. I was in a big hurry and didn't really have the time to go inside—that's why I was picking up *fast* food from a drive-through in the first place. But I didn't want anyone to get in trouble when they came up ten bucks short in the register at the end of the day, plus God's pretty clear that honesty is important, even when it comes to little things.

However, when I went inside that trashy taco joint and briefly explained the situation to the cashier, you would've thought I passed her a note that said, "This is a stickup and I'm wearing men's underwear," because she seemed alarmed and kind of disgusted at the same time. Then she sighed in exaggerated exasperation and told me to wait because she was going to have to get the assistant manager in order to straighten things out. Things didn't go much better with him, though. He told me that my actions weren't covered in their training manual and he wasn't sure how to put money *back* into the register without some type of transaction. I explained that I "just wanted to do the right thing" and he gave me the now familiar "thief wearing boxers" look.

I ended up leaving the money on the counter and walking out of the restaurant with several pairs of eyes watching me warily. I didn't expect a parade or a story in the local paper lauding my integrity, but I didn't expect to be treated like a wacko either.

Sometimes doing the right thing doesn't get the response you hope for. God doesn't promise an

NOTES

immediate or *public* blessing as a result of our obedience.

Hosea found that out the hard way.

What's the most difficult thing you've sensed God asking you to do recently?

2

Surnames and Slur-names

For we Christians there is no greater solace than
to know we are known by God and still loved.

R. C. Sproul

Several years ago, my friend Kim Hill (who you
will see on the DVD included with this book) and I
got to go to a luxurious spa near Santa Fe, New
Mexico. We'd read about this particular spa in a
travel magazine—it's consistently ranked as one of
the best in the country—so we were excited when
they confirmed our appointments. We decided to
get there early so we'd have plenty of time to
wander around the gardens we'd read about. And
when we arrived, we weren't disappointed; the
grounds were as breathtakingly beautiful as
described.

After changing into fluffy white robes and special sandals, a kung fu–clad waiter appeared out of nowhere with cups of steaming herbal tea. I was thinking, *I could get used to this kind of pampering* when Kim's attendant came to whisk her away for a facial. Since my appointment wasn't for another hour and a half, the hostess recommended a visit to their world-famous outdoor hot springs. She explained that there was a coed pool or a "women's only" pool if I preferred. She also said that clothing was optional.

I had read about their renowned hot springs, and I did want to experience everything the spa had to offer—especially the free services—since I might never have the opportunity for a return visit. But I didn't savor the idea of splashing around outside in my birthday suit. So I leaned in discreetly and told her that I hadn't brought a bathing suit with me and wasn't comfortable being naked in public. "Oh, no problem!" she replied in spa-appropriate perkiness. "We have rental suits." Then she cheerfully pulled a bin of used bathing suits out from behind the desk.

Saying no has never been one of my gifts; plus, I reasoned, *This is a very reputable spa, so I'm sure they wash these in hot water after each use.* I gingerly sorted through the pile and found one rather large—but clean-looking—black one-piece. I grimaced, mostly because it was wet and cold, when I stretched it on in the tiny locker room outside the "women's only" pool. But since everyone else seemed to be cavorting at the coed springs, I thought I might have lucked out and would get to enjoy my soak in silence.

I did spend about four glorious minutes alone before a trio of bronzed, Swedish blondes invaded the oasis. They, of course, opted to leave their clothes *off.* They frolicked about like dolphins desperately needing Ritalin and babbled incessantly in their foreign tongue. All the while, I tried to make myself invisible so they wouldn't make fun of my winter pallor and conventional modesty or notice that big dimples were forming in the plastic bra of my rented bathing suit. As I huddled there in the world-famous hot springs, dodging bouncing bottoms and trying to hide dented cups, I thought, *This isn't working out quite the way I'd hoped.*

Crazy Christenings and a Wanton Wife

I wonder if Hosea ever felt the same way. If he ever thought the union God asked him to commit to wasn't anything close to the marriage he'd hoped for.

It probably started out nice enough. Although Gomer's romantic résumé included more than a few flings with bad boys, she was most likely appreciative of Hosea's good-guy ways at first because monogamy brought with it an unfamiliar, yet wonderful, feeling of security. And surely Hosea was a sweet, attentive husband. Maybe he even surprised her on their first anniversary with the keys to a cute little brick bungalow so they could have a place of their own. He got a preaching job with a pension and she joined a book club. They had two children and bought a minivan. But just when everyone assumed Gomer's promiscuity was history and Hosea didn't get such a bad deal after all, she got pregnant again, and this time she lived up to her former reputation:

> *So he went and took Gomer, the daughter of Diblaim, and she conceived and bore him a son. And the LORD said to him, "Call his name Jezreel, for in just a little while I will punish the house of Jehu for the blood of Jezreel, and I will put an end to the kingdom of the house of Israel. And on that day I will break the bow of Israel in the Valley of Jezreel." She conceived again and bore a daughter. And the LORD said to him, "Call her name No Mercy, for I will no more have mercy on the house of Israel, to forgive them at all. But I will have mercy on the house of Judah, and I will save them by the LORD their God. I will not save them by bow or by sword or by war or by horses or by horsemen." When she had weaned No Mercy, she conceived and bore a son. And the LORD said, "Call his name Not My People, for you are not my people, and I am not your God."*
>
> Hosea 1:3-9

The book of Hosea—along with several other places in Biblical narrative—records the significance of *naming* a child. What's the genesis of your name—how did your parents choose it?

Like other Jewish fathers, Hosea knew that a child's name was extremely important. And in the case of his kids, it was even more so because God Himself named them. He christened Hosea's first son "Scattered" (*Jezreel* means "scattered" in

Hebrew), which described what would soon happen to God's chosen people when the northern kingdom fell to Assyria, and is an apt description of the people of Israel today. God then named their daughter "No Mercy" (*Lo-ruhama* means "she has not received mercy" in Hebrew), which was a chilling reminder of God's waning patience with Israel's wandering heart. And I think the final moniker is also the saddest, because the second son's name—*Lo-ammi*—means "not my people" in Hebrew,⁺ which basically meant God was absolutely fed up with His people's disobedience. It probably also meant that the last little boy bore no resemblance to Hosea.

Read Psalm 136. Over and over in this psalm it says that God's love endures forever. How can that be true if God is implying here in Hosea that He *won't* show mercy anymore and His people will cease being His people? Do you think God ever truly abandons His people?

After saddling her three offspring with prophetic forenames, God paints a vivid picture of Gomer's— and metaphorically, God's people's—indiscretions:

> *For their mother has played the whore; she who conceived them has acted shamefully. For she said, "I will go after my lovers, who give me my bread and my water, my wool and my flax, my oil and my drink."* Hosea 2:5

In modern context, Gomer went barhopping while Hosea stayed home and played single parent

FAST FACT
Numerous Bible scholars think both the little girl (**Lo-ruhama**) and the second son (**Lo-ammi**) weren't Hosea's biological children because the Hebrew text doesn't include the term **bore him**—meaning "born to Hosea"— as it did with the first son, Jezreel.

to three young children. He drove in the carpool, he packed their sack lunches, he helped them with their homework, he put Band-Aids on their scraped knees, he read them stories, he listened to the sweet semantics of their bedtime prayers, and then he tucked them in. All while their momma was making out with traveling salesmen who plied her with cheap jewelry and mixed drinks.

Desperate Housewives and Divine Hedges

Do you know someone like Gomer? A woman in your neighborhood or an acquaintance from work who wears low-cut shirts, lots of makeup, and jeans that would cut off a normal person's circulation? Do you know someone who flirts shamelessly with all members of the male species between junior high and hip-replacement age, and makes a habit of chucking her marriage vows out the window? Do her illicit romances resemble Roman candles, taking off like a rocket but fizzling out fast? Think Edie Britt on the trashy sitcom *Desperate Housewives*. Sadly, femmes fatales like this are notoriously slow learners. They typically labor under the myth that they'll find perfect love and contentment in the *next* relationship. Thus, straying becomes a dangerous addiction capable of destroying them and those who love them. Gomer's marriage certainly looked like it was headed for destruction.

And don't forget the symbolism of this Minor Prophet merger. God told Hosea to propose to Gomer because her unfaithfulness would be the perfect metaphor for His people's spiritual unfaithfulness. But somehow adultery seems more

FAST FACT
Recent statistics reveal that 24 percent of men and 14 percent of women have had sex outside of marriage. But findings of infidelity are hotly debated, and earlier studies said up to 68 percent of men and 66 percent of women confessed to extramarital bed-hopping. "People routinely lie to investigators about infidelity," warns Peggy Vaughan, author of **The Monogamy Myth**. Statistics are a bit more stable—and sobering—regarding the effect adultery has on marriage; approximately 65 percent of couples divorce in the aftermath of an adulterous affair.[56]

appalling in a human relationship, doesn't it? For a woman to abandon her three babies and husband appears unpardonable, yet letting dust bunnies pile up on your Bible seems pretty harmless. I mean, does dabbling in other religions *really* deserve His divine wrath? Is spiritual distraction really that big a deal?

Yes, to both questions. God elucidates His desire for uncompromising loyalty in Hosea. Through this story He bellows that straying from His affection is every bit as serious as marital infidelity—which was punishable by death, according to Jewish law!

Compare spiritual adultery to physical adultery. In what ways do you think the emotional consequences are similar?

When you're betrothed to the Creator of the universe, putting your wedding ring in your purse in order to experience a wild night out on the town isn't a harmless option. But just like Gomer, we, as God's people today, tend to breach the boundaries of our divine union with Him anyway. And so the ultimate Bridegroom goes to great lengths to ensure the longevity of His relationship with us.

More Info

"If a man commits adultery with the wife of his neighbor, both the adulterer and the adulteress shall surely be put to death" (Leviticus 20:10).

"If a man is found lying with the wife of another man, both of them shall die, the man who lay with the woman, and the woman" (Deuteronomy 22:22).

Therefore I will hedge up her way with thorns, and I will build a wall against her, so that she cannot find her paths. She shall pursue her lovers but not overtake them, and she shall seek them but shall not find them. Then she shall say, "I will go and return to my first husband, for it was better for me then than now." And she did not know that it was I who gave her the grain, the wine, and the oil, and who lavished on her silver and gold, which they used for Baal.   Hosea 2:6-8

I was a rocker as a baby. Not the leather-pants-with-electric-guitar kind of rocker, but a full-body-pitching-to-and-fro-on-my-forearms-and-knees kind of rocker. I rocked so enthusias-tically that Mom said they were often jolted awake by the loud *wham* when I'd finally rolled the crib from one side of the room to the oppo-site wall. They tried putting locks on the crib wheels, but she said my constant back-and-forth movement would ultimately work the wheels free and I'd scoot across the room for another drywall-denting encounter. They weren't too alarmed by my nocturnal gymnastics—at least I wasn't eating glue or poking hairpins in the elec-trical outlets—until our pediatrician noticed that I was becoming very pigeon-toed as a result. When X-rays revealed that my legs were begin-ning to curve abnormally, my parents consulted an orthopedic specialist.

I really liked going to his office at first. The receptionist always gave me one of those lollipops with a loop handle, which I thought was much more grand than the plain suckers I was used to from the bank. (This introduction to sweets proba-bly started me down the path toward expensive gourmet dark chocolate, but that's another story!) Although they looked like a medieval torture device, the Forrest-Gumpish leg braces the doctor

first prescribed to correct my gait weren't really that bad. Besides, I got brand-new, red Mary Janes to go with them!

But my pigeon-toed walk only got worse, because I was still rocking myself to sleep since I didn't have to wear the braces to bed! And despite my mother's pleas, I rocked and rolled to my heart's content—until the next doctor's visit. I can't remember his name, but I can still remember what he told Mom in front of me. He said that unless I stopped rocking, she would have to tie me spread-eagled to the bedposts at night so I couldn't move; otherwise I'd never walk correctly. He may have winked at Mom while suggesting that sadistic therapy. He was probably just kidding, and half-hoping he could frighten me into rock-less slumber.

However, I was only four or five years old at the time and I thought he was serious. And though I didn't know the word for it yet, mild claustrophobia was already part of my little-girl psyche. I'd rather sit on a porcupine or swim with sharks than be tied up motionless for eight hours! So his teasing warning worked. I don't know how many nights I stared at the ceiling, barely moving a muscle, before I was able to fall asleep without lurching back and forth. But eventually I stopped rocking. And I can walk a straight line today because of his creative prescription for my own protection.

Therefore I will hedge up her way with thorns, and I will build a wall against her, so that she cannot find her paths. Hosea 2:6

God prescribed a thorny bush to barricade Gomer from harm, to keep her from hurting herself again. He *will protect* His beloved . . . even when it means protecting us from our own destructive behavior. And He'd rather teach us the lesson of loyalty by drawing a little blood with a thorn than have to bind up the painful, self-inflicted wounds of betrayal.

Can you think of an example when God built a "hedge" to keep you from making a bad decision and ultimately hurting yourself? Did you recognize that it was His merciful protection at the time? Why or why not?

Supernatural Mercy and Shiny New Names

When we were in high school, my friend Cindy and I were both prone to making up silly nicknames—and sometimes inserting those names in songs and poetry—for our friends. These little ditties usually involved rhyming their names with an object, like Lisa-Pizza or Windy-Cindy. And what we lacked in creativity, we made up for with animated zeal!

One day, we walked into a class together, laughing and talking about who-knows-what, and ran right into one of our good friends named Shelly. She'd been absent from school for a while and seemed a little downcast, so I quickly hugged her and announced perkily for the whole classroom to hear, "Hey there, Shelly-BELLY!"

Never one to be impassive, Cindy responded by

gasping and giving me a horrified look because Shelly wasn't exactly petite. But I hadn't meant *anything* by using the word *belly*—it certainly wasn't in reference to her size; it was simply the first rhyming word that popped in my goofy, teenage mind. I felt terrible, and the more I apologized, the more embarrassed she became. In the years that have passed, I've thought about that awkward moment with sweet Shelly many times, and I hope God erased that stupid, probably hurtful, nickname from her mind and heart.

Along with your given surname, most of us have also been saddled with a slur-name. Maybe that hurtful nickname was unintentional, as in Shelly's case, or maybe it was hurled over and over to shame and belittle you. Is there a slur-name from your past that still stings?

The last ten verses of Hosea chapter 2 describe God's mercy for His people, in spite of how they've prostituted their affections. It's a beautifully redemptive passage, that begins with God's promise to allure Israel on a trip into the wilderness. Then He refers to the tender things He's going to say to His beloved. But as much as I relish the idea of a special date night in the country with our Creator, I can't help but be drawn to the end of the chapter. Because that's when our gracious heavenly Father turns His attention back to those precious kids.

> *I'll have mercy on No-Mercy. I'll say to Nobody, "You're my dear Somebody," and he'll say "You're my God!"* Hosea 2:23 (*The Message*)

We don't know how Hosea's children felt about their birth names. Perhaps they were too little to understand the prophetic connotation. But I'll bet they held their heads higher and sat straighter and probably even hid shy smiles behind their hands when the schoolteacher called out their *new names* at roll call!

My first real boyfriend was a catch named Keith. We started "going together" in the eighth grade, and the first gift he gave me to celebrate our serious case of puppy love was a gold ID bracelet with his name inscribed on it in big block letters. I was so proud of that bracelet. I didn't care that it turned my arm green. All I cared about was having Keith's name dangling from my wrist for all the other Farrah-haired girls to see. Because wearing his name meant we were a pair. We were *committed* to each other. Well, as much as you can be committed to another thirteen-year-old, anyway.

When God chooses to circle back to these three wounded kids and redeem their slur-names, He recognizes them as belonging to Him. He gives them His ID bracelet, in effect saying, "These little ones are mine and I'm committed to them." Never forget that the omnipotent Creator of the Universe is also a tender, merciful Father who is fiercely possessive and protective of His children. And His jewelry won't turn your skin green either.

> *Don't be afraid, I've redeemed you. I've called your name. You're mine.*
>
> Isaiah 43:1 (*The Message*)

Read Isaiah 43:1; John 15:12-15; Galatians 4:4-7; and Revelation 2:17. What are some of the *new names* God has given you? Which one is the most meaningful and/or healing for you personally? Why?

3

Crème Brûlée and Castor Oil

EVERYONE WHO RETURNS FROM A LONG AND DIFFICULT
TRIP IS LOOKING FOR SOMEONE WAITING FOR HIM AT THE
STATION OR THE AIRPORT. EVERYONE WANTS TO TELL HIS
STORY AND SHARE HIS MOMENTS OF PAIN AND EXHILARA-
TION WITH SOMEONE WHO STAYED HOME, WAITING FOR
HIM TO COME BACK.   *Henri Nouwen*

If you've seen *Pretty Woman*, then you no doubt
remember the romantic ending when Richard Gere
bounds up the fire escape ladder with an armful of
roses to declare his love for Julia Roberts—who, by
the way, has already wisely decided to give up her
dubious profession. (If you haven't seen the film,
I'm certainly not advising you to rent it because I
don't want to deal with the backlash of irate calls

and e-mails from the CMP—the self-appointed Christian Movie Police!) Anyway, it's a sappy, but effective scene where true love conquers impressive odds. I cried a few happy tears the first time I watched it, even though I knew I *shouldn't* be cheering for an immoral union! I just couldn't help myself because it was such a sweet way to end the story.

What with chapter 2's restorative romp in the wilderness and the children's second divine christening, one would assume this Minor Prophet's story couldn't get much sweeter. But we haven't gotten to the best part yet! Much-loved pastor, author, and professor Dr. James Montgomery Boice called Hosea, "the second greatest story in the Bible," saying it was second only to the gospel itself, and referred to the passage we're about to peruse as, "the *greatest* chapter in the Bible." Richard and Julia's rendezvous in the stairwell pales next to Gomer and Hosea's reconciliation:

> *And the LORD said to me, "Go again, love a woman who is loved by another man and is an adulteress, even as the LORD loves the children of*

did you know?

A **shekel** was about 11 grams, a **homer** was about 6 bushels, and a **lethech** was about 3 bushels. The value of these added up to about 30 shekels, the "going rate" for a slave (see Exodus 21:32), and the price Judas was paid to betray Jesus. It's also interesting that Hosea added barley to the bid, because that was the offering God insisted on when jealousy followed the suspicion of adultery in a marriage (see Numbers 5:11-15).

Israel, though they turn to other gods and love cakes of raisins." So I bought her for fifteen shekels of silver and a homer and a lethech of barley. And I said to her, "You must dwell as mine for many days. You shall not play the whore, or belong to another man; so will I also be to you."

Hosea 3:1-3

One of the reasons Dr. Boice called this chapter *great* is because of the literal circumstances surrounding Gomer and Hosea's reunion. They were reunited in a slave market. You see, Gomer's adultery had likely spiraled her downward into prostitution, and when other men stopped paying for her dinner, drinks, and living expenses—her bread and water, wool and flax, oil and drink (see Hosea 2:5)— she started selling her body to pay the bills. And when men stopped paying her for sex, she had to find some other way to support herself. One wrong choice led to another until Gomer felt she had no option but to sell herself into slavery to survive. She bottomed out on the auction block.

Historical documents reveal much about what the slave market Gomer found herself in was like.[8] And it sure wasn't pretty. Slaves were always sold naked—so buyers could examine the "merchandise"—and typically the bidding audience was male. I can only imagine the lewd comments those men made as they circled and salivated over her on the auction block. Things like, "Why should I pay for something I've already had for free?" or "Can I sample this slave before deciding whether or not I want to buy her?" All the while Gomer stood there

FAST FACT
Some Bible scholars think the **cakes of raisins** are in reference to what people ate during the ceremonial worship of Baal—a popular idol at this time in history. [7]

silently, staring at her feet, wishing she could go back in time and change the choices that led to this living hell. Probably wishing she could just die and get it over with.

But then she hears a familiar voice. A kind voice calling out from the raucous crowd, "I want to buy her." And she looks up to see Hosea, her estranged husband. He's standing there in his best outfit—the pants are too short and his shirt is buttoned up too high—wearing an expression of grace and compassion. She can scarcely believe it's him. It's been such a long time since she's seen him. She hasn't dropped by the house or bothered to call in months. Not even on the kids' birthdays. Yet there he is, grinning at the auctioneer like he's just won a date with the homecoming queen.

Has someone ever paid off a significant debt on your behalf (i.e., your parents' paying off your student loan or an out-of-control credit card balance)? If so, how did it make you feel?

FAST FACT

There were three things that led to slavery in ancient cultures like Hosea's: one was to become a slave as a result of conquest (i.e., the Israelites in Egypt prior to the Moses-led Exodus), another was to be born into slavery, and the final reason for slavery was debt.

Remember, Hosea had the legal right to have Gomer put to death for her indiscretions. According to Jewish tradition, he should've been standing there with a couple of burly policemen, prepared to give his adulterous wife what she *really deserved*. But he's not there for vengeance. He emptied out his 401(k) and took the Greyhound to the slave sale. He's pushed through a rough crowd of beer-chugging, dirty-joke-telling hooligans not to punish his wife, but to redeem her.

Then GOD ordered me, "Start all over: Love your
wife again, your wife who's in bed with her latest
boyfriend, your cheating wife. Love her the way I,
GOD, love the Israelite people, even as they flirt and
party with every god that takes their fancy."

Hosea 3:1 (*The Message*)

I was at the airport recently and I bumped into
an acquaintance who works for a "big dog" in the
Christian recording industry. We chatted about the
cities we were flying to and the different conferences we'd be attending. She started talking about
how her employer could usually make women cry
at events, then she went on to boast about how
much money they made at the merchandise table
when women did get emotional. She walked off
when her flight began to board, then turned back
toward me and said breezily, "Weep and buy, baby!
Weep and buy!"

I was stunned by her candor, but sadly it's not
the first time I've seen crass commercialism all
dressed up in a religious costume. I was at a conference a few months ago where one of the speakers
hawked her books and tapes by announcing, "God
told me that you *need* the words He's spoken to me.
These books and tapes are messages He gave me
specifically for you." Yuck. That kind of manipulation makes me sick.

It also makes me think. When do I compromise
holiness for personal gain? When have I let my
greed outwrestle grace? When have I leased my
soul for a few lousy silver coins? Spiritual solicita-
tion doesn't have to involve naked bodies or seedy

motels. You can *prostitute your heart* for God without taking your clothes off. But you'll still feel dirty afterward.

And His mercy is the only thing that will take the stain out.

Drinking Medicine after Dessert

A few months ago I received a tongue-lashing from one of Nashville's finest. Some people from Tyndale House Publishers were in town to film promotional material. They wanted to shoot some photographs outside, and I told them there was a picturesque setting near my house called the Natchez Trace Parkway. The "Trace" is a beautiful 444-mile long winding road that commemorates an ancient American Indian trail. Deer, wild turkey, and other wildlife often graze alongside the roadside, and there's hardly any traffic. It's my favorite place to ride my Harley, and I thought it'd be the perfect place to take pictures.

And it was, until a Tennessee state trooper pulled up. I grinned and introduced myself, thinking he was going to give my friends from the Windy City a proper Southern welcome. Instead he swaggered up and demanded to speak with whoever was in charge. After Carol, our production manager, explained that we were just taking a few pictures for an upcoming book, he gruffly asked for each of our driver's licenses. Then he walked back to his patrol car (probably to check and see if any of us had criminal records so he could fire his gun or at least frisk us!) and took so long that we started preparing for the worst. We whispered anxiously,

"Surely he can't actually arrest us for taking a picture, can he? Do you think we should call a lawyer? Does anybody have an overdue speeding ticket?"

He finally returned and began to sternly list the potential consequences of our actions, as well as the violations he *could* have charged us with. He *could* have impounded every single one of our vehicles. He *could* have destroyed the film and taken all of the camera equipment into federal custody. And he *could* have arrested each one of us for the unapproved use of government property in a commercial venture. He said we might as well have been taking photographs at a top-secret military base. We listened to his tirade intently, realizing that with one wrong move we might be wearing orange jumpsuits. And after hearing the list of charges, I was very thankful to avoid jail time, and surprised to get off *scot-free!*

Read Hosea 4 in the New Living Translation or *The Message*. Synopsize this chapter in your own words.

Chapter 4 in Hosea begins with some very serious charges God makes against His people:

> *Hear the word of the LORD, O children of Israel,*
> *for the LORD has a controversy with the inhabit-*
> *ants of the land. There is no faithfulness or stead-*
> *fast love, and no knowledge of God in the land;*
> *there is swearing, lying, murder, stealing, and*
> *committing adultery; they break all bounds, and*
> *bloodshed follows bloodshed.* Hosea 4:1-2

This divine lecture is like chasing crème brûlée with castor oil. It's the bitter after the sweet. Because after beautifully illustrating His love for His people through Hosea's mercy toward his wayward wife, God uses the same pen to rebuke Israel. He rebukes them for having no faithfulness or devotion. But I think the third charge is the most serious of all—when God says they have *no knowledge of Him.*

Several years ago I had a very interesting experience at a women's retreat. Since I was teaching at this particular event, the sponsor asked me to meet with the worship team before everything got started in order to make sure the songs they'd chosen complemented the theme. So we got together in their dressing room and discussed the direction of the program and the Bible passages I was going to be teaching.

We chatted amiably, and they said the songs they were going to "perform" fit *perfectly* with the message. I didn't have any reason to doubt them— aside from the fact that their outfits were skintight and sparkly. However, when they pranced onstage and began to belt out Broadway show tunes, I realized that perhaps I should have asked more specific questions about their song list! They were entertaining and enthusiastic—if not talented— performers; but after spending the whole day with them I'm pretty sure they didn't know what Christ-centered worship was.

One edition of *Webster's* defines *devotion* as "profound dedication; consecration" or "earnest

attachment to a cause, person, etc." Who/what would you list as your most earnest attachments?

Forgetful Followers

Speaking of music, several years ago I attended a Dove Awards ceremony in Nashville, which is the Gospel Music Association's version of the Grammy Awards. Only instead of Evian and Dom Perignon flowing backstage, the Dove Awards serve Aquafina and Diet Coke. There are no twenty thousand-dollar gift baskets for the presenters—more likely a coupon for Chick-fil-A and a T-shirt. And the winners don't make the covers of *People* or *Rolling Stone*. But it's still like prom night for many in the Christian music industry. Artists, musicians, and managers come decked out in their finest. Which in "Music City, USA" means lots of boots, big hair, and long black coats!

There are also quite a few people like me in the audience: People who aren't personally connected to Christian music, but are somehow connected to someone who is. We're the smallest fish in the proverbial pond. So there I was, a metaphorical minnow—holding in my stomach because my pants were too tight and hoping my hair looked okay— when I spotted a friend from church. Not one of my close friends, but definitely a friend. We'd had lunch together and I'd been to her house a few times. So I swam through the tide of people to say hello. She was standing in the midst of a group of people that included a big fish. A big, famous fish with lots of money, connections, and clout. But this

FAST FACT

The English word **knowledge** that we read in Hosea chapter 4 has been translated from the Hebrew word, **da'at**, which can also mean "understanding" or "learning." This word occurs ninety times in the Old Testament, the first of which can be found in Genesis 2:9.[9]

big fish wasn't talking directly to my friend, so I greeted her without interrupting "Jaws." She completely ignored me.

I thought, *Oh, she must not be able to hear me because it's so loud in here,* so I said my friend's name a little louder and waved at her. At which she glanced my way with an insincere smile and thinly disguised irritation, then turned her back toward me, effectively shutting me out of the circle of people she was desperately trying to impress.

Remember the scene in *Pretty Woman* when Julia Roberts is rudely dismissed by a haughty salesgirl in an elegant boutique? That's kind of what my so- called friend's snub felt like. I couldn't believe she was acting like she didn't even know me. And Hosea says that's how we treat our heavenly Father.

God's not a small fish, either. In fact, He's the One who created *all* the fish in the sea, along with the entire universe surrounding the sea! He's the King of kings and Lord of lords . . . *the* God of history. And He lovingly charted the course for our personal history. He knew we would abandon Him and prostitute our hearts with other lovers. He knew those same lovers—mere idols that could only imitate affection—would eventually leave us disappointed and desperate for real love. He knew we'd basically sell our souls in search of unconditional acceptance. So He wrote a miraculous plan by which to redeem us once and for all. To teach us that His love is perfect, that it will never fail or fade, even on our worst days. It's an amazing story about being loved beyond our wildest dreams. But somehow we

still manage to forget it, and we have the audacity to act like we don't even know our Redeemer.

Hosea's words describe what people look like who *don't know God*. Read Psalm 1 for a description of someone who *knows God*. What are some of his distinctive features? Can you find another Psalm that portrays someone who's familiar with God?

Perhaps the most infamous case of spiritual amnesia belongs to the apostle Peter. He walked and talked with God incarnate. They hung out together for three years. He watched Him walk on water and heal leprosy and bring corpses back to life. Peter experienced the redeeming love of God firsthand, through a Savior with skin on. And he still pretended that God was a total stranger.

> *The gang that had seized Jesus led him before Caiaphas the Chief Priest, where the religion scholars and leaders had assembled. Peter followed at a safe distance until they got to the Chief Priest's courtyard. Then he slipped in and mingled with the servants, watching to see how things would turn out.*
>
> *The high priests, conspiring with the Jewish Council, tried to cook up charges against Jesus in order to sentence him to death. But even though many stepped up, making up one false accusation after another, nothing was believable.*
>
> *Finally two men came forward with this: "He said, 'I can tear down this Temple of God and after three days rebuild it.'"*

The Chief Priest stood up and said, "What do you have to say to the accusation?"

Jesus kept silent.

Then the Chief Priest said, "I command you by the authority of the living God to say if you are the Messiah, the Son of God."

Jesus was curt: "You yourself said it. And that's not all. Soon you'll see it for yourself: The Son of Man seated at the right hand of the Mighty One, arriving on the clouds of heaven."

At that, the Chief Priest lost his temper, ripping his robes, yelling, "He blasphemed! Why do we need witnesses to accuse him? You all heard him blaspheme! Are you going to stand for such blasphemy?"

They all said, "Death! That seals his death sentence."

Then they were spitting in his face and banging him around. They jeered as they slapped him: "Prophesy, Messiah: Who hit you that time?"

All this time, Peter was sitting out in the courtyard. One servant girl came up to him and said, "You were with Jesus the Galilean."

In front of everybody there, he denied it. "I don't know what you're talking about."

As he moved toward the gate, someone else said to the people there, "This man was with Jesus the Nazarene."

Again he denied it, salting his denial with an oath: "I swear, I never laid eyes on the man."

Shortly after that, some bystanders approached Peter. "You've got to be one of them. Your accent gives you away."

Then he got really nervous and swore. "I don't know the man!"

Just then a rooster crowed. Peter remembered what Jesus had said: "Before the rooster crows, you will deny me three times." He went out and cried and cried and cried.

Matthew 26:57-75 (*The Message*)

In his provocative book, *Blue Like Jazz*, Donald Miller talks about being maligned because of his faith in God:

> *Later I had a conversation with a very arrogant Reed professor in the parking lot in which he asked me what brought me to Reed. I told him I was auditing a class but was really there to interact with the few Christians who studied at Reed. The professor asked me if I was a Christian evangelist. I told him I didn't think I was, that I wouldn't consider myself an evangelist. He went on to compare my work to that of Captain Cook, who had attempted to bring Western values to indigenous people of Hawaii. He looked me in the eye and said that the tribes had killed Cook.*
>
> *He did not wish me a greater fate at Reed.*[10]

Although I haven't been verbally accosted in a parking lot because of my faith in God, I *have* been accused of being judgmental, homophobic, narrow-minded, and intellectually inferior. And those insults came from unbelieving *friends*. Others haven't been quite so gracious. Every now and then I get tired of being demonized and marginalized for being a Christian. Sometimes I'd like to sleep in on

Sundays, read trashy novels, laugh at Bill Maher's late-night remarks, yell at drivers who don't yield, and just generally bond with popular culture. It's on those days—when I'm lounging in the shallow end of a self-pity sin pool—that I can identify with Peter. I can understand why he pretended not to know Jesus.

Have you ever been in a social situation where you were embarrassed to be a Christian? Have you ever pretended *not to know* God, like Peter did? If so, how did you feel after the fact?

Read Hosea 5–7 in the New Living Translation or *The Message* and describe, in your own words, what God is saying in this section.

Hosea's congregation was just as "forgetful" as Peter. Chapters 4 through 7 enumerate the sins caused by their charade, culminating when God unmasks the insincerity of their religious "revival":

> *What shall I do with you, O Ephraim? What shall I do with you, O Judah? Your love is like a morning cloud, like the dew that goes early away.*
> Hosea 6:4

> *Ephraim mixes himself with the peoples; Ephraim is a cake not turned.*
> Hosea 7:8

> *Strangers devour his strength, and he knows it not; gray hairs are sprinkled upon him, and he knows it not.*
> Hosea 7:9

> *Ephraim is like a dove, silly and without sense, calling to Egypt, going to Assyria.*
> Hosea 7:11

They return, but not upward; they are like a treacherous bow; their princes shall fall by the sword because of the insolence of their tongue. This shall be their derision in the land of Egypt.

Hosea 7:16

Morning dew that quickly evaporates. A half-cooked pancake. Someone clueless who needs a good colorist. A goony bird. And a faulty weapon that can't shoot straight. These are images of something short-lived, unappealing, foolish, or broken. They are images of fraudulent religion and bogus repentance.

And they represent us.

They do not cry to me from the heart.

Hosea 7:14

Read Hosea 6:6 and Micah 6:6-8. What kind of offering *is* pleasing to God? And what are some tangible ways to "live out" that kind of offering?

4

Crime, Punishment, and Promise

THE REASON WE NEVER ENTER INTO THE DEEPEST REALITY
OF OUR RELATIONSHIP WITH GOD IS THAT WE SO SELDOM
ACKNOWLEDGE OUR UTTER NOTHINGNESS BEFORE HIM.

Thomas Merton

My brother, John—whom I absolutely adore—was
born with a silver tongue and an endless supply of
crocodile tears. He used both to his greatest advantage when we were growing up! I'll never forget
the time Mom caught him with a brimful of stolen
merchandise. He was about five or six, and he was
enamored with the hat pins on display at the
B&W—our modest neighborhood grocery store.
There were animal pins, car pins, and sports team
pins. They came enameled, hand-painted, or gold-
plated. Every time we went to the store, which was

several times a week, John begged Mom for one. She bought him several, but they were a foolish purchase for a little boy who'd likely lose them within a day or two, so she didn't buy nearly as many as he wanted.

However, one day she noticed that John had a gleaming multitude on his ball cap. And she knew he couldn't possibly have turned in enough Coke bottles for that many pins. So she asked him where he got them. His panicked expression revealed the answer. But then his countenance quickly changed to one of grieved remorse. He dramatically explained that he just "*had* to confess his sin." He wailed that he knew better. He cried a river of anguish over his thievery!

Mom was already wise to John's theatrics and didn't swallow his Oscar-worthy confession one bit. Instead of winking at his new shoplifting habit, she took him back to the B&W to confess. And she made him pay for every single pin that he swiped. Good parents will punish bad behavior. That's how children learn not to make the same mistake again.

Read Hosea 8–10 in the New Living Translation or *The Message* and summarize these chapters in your own words.

The middle of this Minor Prophet's journal (chapters 8 through 10) reveals how God will punish His kids for their bad spiritual behavior:

> *For they sow the wind, and they shall reap the whirlwind. The standing grain has no heads; it*

shall yield no flour; if it were to yield, strangers
would devour it. Hosea 8:7

My God will reject them because they have not
listened to him; they shall be wanderers among the
nations. Hosea 9:17

Their heart is false; now they must bear their guilt.
The LORD *will break down their altars and*
destroy their pillars. Hosea 10:2

Ephraim shall be put to shame, and Israel shall be
ashamed of his idol. Samaria's king shall perish like
a twig on the face of the waters. Hosea 10:6-7

You have plowed iniquity; you have reaped injus-
tice; you have eaten the fruit of lies. Because you
have trusted in your own way and in the multitude
of your warriors, therefore the tumult of war shall
arise among your people, and all your fortresses
shall be destroyed, as Shalman destroyed Beth-
arbel on the day of battle; mothers were dashed in
pieces with their children. Thus it shall be done to
you, O Bethel, because of your great evil. At dawn
the king of Israel shall be utterly cut off.
Hosea 10:13-15

NOTES

Hosea begins a prayer for the Israelites in 9:14,
but then abruptly stops. Why do you think he
stopped praying? When have you been tempted
to stop?

Some scholars suggest that Hosea gave this
speech as a warning to God's people of the upcoming judgment during Sukkoth,[11] which was a big
celebration the Jews observed every fall. Sukkoth

marked the end of harvest; it was a time when they rejoiced that the backbreaking work was over for another year. Think Oktoberfest . . . everyone was in the mood to party! The men traded in their overalls for Wranglers and starched shirts. The women showed off new hairstyles and fresh manicures. Kids squealed happily on the Tilt-a-Whirl, while young couples held hands and ate funnel cakes. A good time was had by all during the festival of Sukkoth—everyone except for Hosea.

Hosea didn't ride any rides or chow down on a corn dog. Instead he walked around wearing a sandwich board that said, "Watch Out! Wrath Is Right around the Corner!" His Israelite neighbors thought he had stayed out in the sun too long. They probably chuckled behind his back and said, "Poor old Hosea, he's always been a bit gloomy. Gomer really should get him started on Prozac!" But they weren't laughing a few years later when his divinely inspired prediction came true. When the Assyrian soldiers marched into town and destroyed their homes, killed their young men, and forced them out of their homeland for good.

More Info

For the unabridged version of the fall of Israel to Assyria, read 2 Kings 17:6-23.

 Read Psalm 119:71 and Proverbs 3:11-12. Have you ever experienced God's grace, disguised as discipline? If so, explain.

Diapers and Devotion

Hosea uses quite a few colorful images to make his point in this oracle. He talked about gooey pancakes and goony birds and whirling tornadoes and wimpy

twigs. But my favorite image of all is found in chapter 11:

> *When Israel was a child, I loved him, and out of Egypt I called My son. . . .*
>
> *I taught Ephraim to walk, taking them by their arms; but they did not know that I healed them. I drew them with gentle cords, with bands of love, and I was to them as those who take the yoke from their neck. I stooped and fed them. . . .*
>
> *"How can I give you up, Ephraim? How can I hand you over, Israel? How can I make you like Admah? How can I set you like Zeboiim? My heart churns within Me; My sympathy is stirred."*
>
> Hosea 11:1, 3-4, 8 (NKJV)

Read Hosea 11–14. What does this portion of the book tell you about God?

I'd rather dig ditches than change a dirty diaper. My eyes water and my stomach threatens to do very embarrassing things. My "mommy" friends tell me this will change if I have children. But I'm not so sure. It'd be nothing short of a miracle. Except in the case of Benjamin.

Benjamin is my best friend Kim's little boy. As I'm writing this, he's about to turn eight years old, but it seems like yesterday that he was a toddler. (Since I don't have children of my own, the only "cute kid" stories I have are about my friends' children. I could tell stories about my two dogs, but those just don't have quite the same emotional

More Info

Admah and Zeboiim were the two cities God destroyed along with Sodom and Gomorrah—see Genesis 10:19; 19:23-25; and Deuteronomy 29:23 for the rest of that story.

impact!) One Sunday, when Benji was about eighteen months old, I was working in the church nursery and he was in my class. It was soon apparent that he needed a diaper change. Now there were several other adults volunteering in the classroom that day, all of whom had children of their own and wouldn't have blinked twice about changing him. But none of them really knew Benji. They didn't love him like I did. So I scooped him up and carried him to the changing table and took a deep breath. I won't go into detail—let's just say it was beyond bad.

But it didn't matter. Overwhelming tenderness took over and allowed me to change the world's most disgusting diaper without flinching—because I adored that little guy. I loved his wispy blond hair, his chubby little legs, and the way he reached his arms up when he wanted me to carry him. I loved the way he said, "Weesa," when he was first learning to talk and the way he always asked for a "Coookeee," when he woke up from his nap. Benjamin pretty much had my heart wrapped around his little finger back then (and still does).

Hosea paints a beautiful picture of our heavenly Father's tenderness when he uses the image of a toddler to represent God's people. When he says God taught us how to walk. That He reached down from His throne in heaven to gently grasp our sticky little hands. That He lovingly guided us away from sharp corners and slippery surfaces. That He broke our falls so we wouldn't be seriously hurt. He *stooped down* to us. To feed us. To

clean up our messes. The God of all glory bent
down to love us as His very own.

Read Exodus 4:22-23 and Isaiah 54:5. Hosea
uses both "God as our Father" and "God as our
Husband" to illustrate our relationship with
Him. Which one makes you feel more secure?
Do you know why?

Real Repentance

Kim (Benji's mom) showed me a letter she received
the other day from a woman who felt convicted
about making bootleg copies of one of Kim's record-
ings. Most people in our culture don't think burning
copies of CDs is a big deal. It seems only musicians
and record labels consider it illegal. But this woman
must've heard an effective sermon from someone,
because her letter detailed exactly what she did
wrong (she made five copies of Kim's record for
other people) and humbly asked for Kim's forgiveness. They weren't just flowery words either; she
had enclosed a check for the five CDs she said she
had "stolen" from Kim.

The difference between my little brother's
hat-pin histrionics and that woman's remorse is
very much like the distinction between Israel's
insincere repentance in chapter 6 and the prayer of
genuine repentance in the last chapter:

> *Take away all iniquity; accept what is good, and we*
> *will pay with bulls the vows of our lips. Assyria shall*
> *not save us; we will not ride on horses; and we will*
> *say no more, "Our God," to the work of our hands.*
> *In you the orphan finds mercy.* Hosea 14:2-3

In his commentary on Hosea, Dr. Boice points to three characteristics that make this confession the real deal. The first is an *awareness of sin.* Notice they actually use the word *iniquity* in their plea for God's forgiveness. The Hebrew word for iniquity is *'awon,* which can also be translated *sin, guilt,* and *wickedness.*[12] They didn't just say, "We're sorry you got mad at us, God," as if He was being overly strict and their behavior wasn't really that far out of line. They owned up to their stuff. They called it wicked. They acknowledged the seriousness of their transgressions.

Read Jonah 3:6-10 (it's just a few pages to the right from Hosea). What strikes you as sincere about the repentance portrayed here?

Second, this prayer includes the *recognition of specific sins.* Confessing corporate sin is easy: "God, please forgive America for being such a greedy nation." "God, please forgive our church for being too concerned with the color of the carpet in the sanctuary." Naming our intimate, individual sin is harder. "Please forgive me for stealing five CDs from you." "God, please forgive me for being such a jerk to my mother-in-law." "Please forgive me for being jealous of my girlfriend's engagement." When God's people talked about Assyria and horses, they were admitting specific sins, the fact that they put their trust in foreign alliances, military prowess, and false idols instead of Jehovah.

And finally, their request includes an *appeal for God's mercy.* They understand that they don't deserve God's forgiveness. That they can't just

raise their hands in church, or cry during a moving worship service, or put a fat check in the offering plate, and earn a divine pardon. There are no "Get out of Jail Free" cards for sale at the synagogue. God's heart is stirred by humility. A broken and contrite spirit is what unleashes God's amazing grace.

Read Hosea 6:1-3 and 14:2-3. What differences did you notice immediately?

Dancing toward Divine Restoration

Many years ago I met a couple who appeared to be the Christian version of Barbie and Ken. They were both very attractive and successful and had several cute, smart kids. They were well respected at church and in the community. But then it was discovered that she was having an affair with another man. And it wasn't just any man either. It was the husband of a young woman she had befriended and mentored.

People were horrified when they found out. "Barbie" lost her shine and most of her friends. But she didn't lose Ken. Week after week, they came to church together. I think everyone was surprised when they didn't leave town, or at least change churches. But they didn't; it was as if part of her repentance included facing the shame knowing that some people would continue to whisper about how she had betrayed her husband *and* her friend. They both looked tired, but he exuded a sort of determined grace. It was evident in the way he opened doors for her and held her hand and looked in her eyes. He was probably the only person at church who still considered his wife beautiful.

In spite of our prostituted affections, our spiritual forgetfulness, our arrogance, and our idolatry, God still thinks His people are beautiful. He still thinks we're worth pursuing:

> *I will make a fresh start with Israel. He'll burst into bloom like a crocus in the spring. He'll put down deep oak tree roots, he'll become a forest of oaks! He'll become splendid—like a giant sequoia, his fragrance like a grove of cedars! Those who live near him will be blessed by him, be blessed and prosper like golden grain. Everyone will be talking about them, spreading their fame as the vintage children of God. Ephraim is finished with gods that are no-gods. From now on I'm the one who answers and satisfies him. I am like a luxuriant fruit tree. Everything you need is to be found in me.*
> Hosea 14:4–8 (*The Message*)

Read Zechariah 12:10–13:1 and Romans 11:25-27. Do you think God was talking about something that would happen in Israel's immediate future, or an "ultimate fulfillment" of restoration in the above passage (Hosea 14:4–8)?

When I was growing up, I spent a few weeks every summer at a Christian camp called Lake Swan, near Gainesville, Florida. We waterskied and played soccer and had great chapels and late night gabfests. One of the most common topics of conversation was the Sadie Hawkins dance on the last night of camp. It wasn't actually a *dance* though, because this was a pretty conservative Christian camp where the powers-that-be decided God's beloved couldn't boogie. So we actually just stood around in our dress clothes in the cafeteria. But it was still the highlight—or the lowlight, depending on your perspective, personality, and appearance—of the summer.

The real drama took place during the Sadie Hawkins Day race on the afternoon of the undance dance. The counselors would line all the boys up on one side of a field and line all the girls up on the other side—facing the boys. When the head counselor blew the whistle, each girl was supposed to chase whatever boy she wanted to go to the undance with that night. They'd probably get sued for having a Sadie Hawkins race today because I'm sure some of these kids suffered emotional damage. Especially the slow and the shy.

But the rest of us didn't know any better. So we spent countless hours before the race plotting who was going to chase whom. For several years, the most wanted young man was Jeff McGarvey. Jeff was a preacher's kid from my hometown with curly brown hair and a killer jump shot. The guys admired his basketball skills and most of the girls admired his legs in basketball shorts. He was the Brad Pitt of Lake Swan.

One race day when I was fourteen or fifteen, Jeff asked if he could talk to me outside the girls' cabins. This wasn't that unusual because we'd known each other since we were little—his mom was my piano teacher—and we were pretty good friends. I thought maybe he needed a ride home from camp. But that's not what he came to ask. He hemmed and hawed and then told me that he really wanted to go to the dance with me and asked if I would chase him. When I said yes, he told me where he'd run to when the whistle blew so that I could be the one to catch him.

The girls' line was buzzing when we lined up that day. And much of the excitement revolved around Jeff, because lots of girls were planning to pursue him. But I didn't whisper with the rest of my friends—I just stood there grinning. I wasn't sure why he chose me; I wasn't the prettiest girl in camp or the sweetest. But I sure felt like the luckiest, because when the whistle sounded, I didn't have to take off running like everybody else. I just waited a little while and then casually jogged over to the place where Jeff and I agreed to rendezvous.

I wore a peach polyester dress that night and smiled so much my mouth hurt. Because I was standing around in the cafeteria with Jeff McGarvey. The catch of the camp had picked *me*. It was sort of like an adolescent adaptation of *Pretty Woman*!

The thread that runs through all fourteen chapters of Hosea is God's affection for His undeserving people. Despite our dirty and divided hearts, He has invited us to the dance of all dances.

Read Hosea 14:9; Psalm 107:43; and Ecclesiastes 12:13-14. How would you synopsize the message of these passages in your own words?

Second Stop:

Zephaniah

1

God Doesn't "Do" Recess

IF WE GLOSS OVER OUR SELFISHNESS AND RATIONALIZE THE
EVIL WITHIN US, WE CAN ONLY PRETEND WE ARE SINNERS
AND THEREFORE ONLY PRETEND WE HAVE BEEN FORGIVEN.

Brennan Manning

Morgan Freeman is one of my favorite actors; I
loved him in *Driving Miss Daisy, Glory,* and *The
Shawshank Redemption.* Even in a dark, sad film like
Shawshank, Freeman has an air of dignity about
him. My good friend Susie is close to him and his
wife, and she thinks the world of them both. So
even though I've never met Morgan Freeman, I
trust Susie's opinion and root for his movies to be
box-office hits! And when thinking about a movie

that would illustrate our next Minor Prophet pit stop, I couldn't help but notice how Mr. Freeman's flick, *Lean on Me*, fit.

Lean on Me was a popular movie that came out in 1989. It's based on the true story of a principal named Joe Clark (portrayed by Morgan Freeman) and the school he captains in New Jersey named Eastside High. The film is set in the early eighties, when Eastside resembles an out-of-control juvenile detention center more than a school. Drug dealers and gang members rule the halls, chaos rules the classrooms, truancy is at an all-time high, and standardized test scores are at an all-time low. After the school is labeled a "cauldron of violence" in the media and the majority of students fail the state's minimum basic skills test (which basically means they can't read and write), the mayor reluctantly agrees to hire Joe—a former military drill instructor and maverick—to try to get things under control.

The first thing Joe Clark does when he gets to Eastside is to expel three hundred troublemakers in a school assembly. Calling them, "Drug-dealers, drug-takers, and hoodlums," he declares they aren't going to disrupt or intimidate the other students one more day. Pandemonium breaks out when the ruffians realize they are being permanently suspended, and armed security guards have to carry some of them out, kicking and screaming. And that's just the beginning of what Mr. Clark calls a "war" to reinstate a safe learning environment at Eastside. He also orders that all school doors leading to the outside be chained so that the drug dealers and gangbangers can't get back in.

This violates the state fire code and gives his political adversaries ammunition—but he doesn't care about that. What he cares about is keeping his students safe from thugs!

Pretty soon his efforts start paying off: Teachers are able to focus on teaching instead of policing, students engage in class discussions like never before, kids of all races are socializing and studying together in response to his emphasis on unity, and some who'd all but given up hope for a better life start dreaming again. But in spite of those dramatic improvements, Principal Clark still has his vocal critics. They call him an egomaniac and a dictator. They protest his authoritative leadership style and refer to him as "Crazy Joe" in the papers. And they completely miss the point that for the first time in a very long time, the students at Eastside High School are actually being educated.

Zephaniah's portrayal of God is somewhat like Joe Clark. And the world Zephaniah lived in was a whole lot like Eastside High.

Who's the most demanding teacher you had in **school? Did you come to appreciate his/her lessons later in life? If so, have you ever expressed your gratitude to that teacher?**

God's Kids Gone Wild

The book of Zephaniah is short, even among the Minor Prophets; the whole thing is only fifty-three verses long. Thus, one would assume it'd be a hot topic for preachers and Bible teachers because brevity usually means fewer naps in the listening audience. But Zephaniah isn't a teacher's pet; in fact, apart from one verse (Zephaniah 3:17), this book is more like the Rodney Dangerfield of the Bible—it just "don't get no respect!" Perhaps because from the very beginning it reads like the *Wrath and Destruction Diaries*:

> *"I will utterly sweep away everything from the face of the earth," declares the* LORD. *"I will sweep away man and beast; I will sweep away the birds of the heavens and the fish of the sea, and the rubble with the wicked. I will cut off mankind from the face of the earth," declares the* LORD.
>
> Zephaniah 1:2-3

Read Genesis 6:7 and 7:23. Do you notice any difference between the waves Noah rode and the devastation Zephaniah describes?

Yikes. It's sure not a pleasant way to start. Kind of makes you want to turn the page to something a little less punitive, doesn't it? Why is God *so* mad? Well, for starters, besides being adulterers and idolaters, His people were big, fat liars.

Read Zephaniah 1–3 in the New Living Translation or *The Message* and synopsize these chapters in your own words.

I'm sure you remember the sniper attacks that occurred in the fall of 2002. Our nation was still reeling from September 11 when some nut with a high-powered rifle started picking people off at random in and around the Washington, D.C., area.

Ten people were killed and several others were injured, including a thirteen-year-old boy being dropped off at school, during the three-week reign of terror.

John Allen Muhammad was soon identified, arrested, and convicted as the notorious sniper. He was eventually sentenced to death for the Beltway murders and after the verdict was announced, several jurors commented about his lack of remorse. One juror said, "The total lack of remorse seemed to cap it off for us." Another said he studied Muhammad's demeanor throughout the trial and never saw anything close to remorse.[13] The man killed ten innocent people and wasn't even sorry.

Just like those thugs who complained when Joe Clark booted their behinds out of Eastside and the unconscionable John Allen Muhammad, the Israelites didn't think they had done anything wrong. They had Asherah poles in their backyard and bordellos near the Temple, yet they still had the nerve to show zero remorse.

They certainly couldn't blame their insolence on ignorance, because there'd been a long line of prophets who warned them about their sinful behavior. They'd been taught by the best. They'd listened to Jonah's tape series, The Top Ten Reasons for Quick Repentance, they were on the mailing list of the ministry Isaiah founded, and they'd watched Hosea's life story on cable. They'd been to Promise Keepers and Women of Faith and completed *fifty* days of purpose. God's people *knew* how they were supposed to live; they just weren't living like it.

FAST FACT
Asherah was the name of the Canaanite fertility goddess whose devotees frolicked around a "sacred" wooden pole in worship ceremonies. Thus, an Asherah pole was a blatant form of idolatry and probably sexual deviance. That's why God told Gideon to tear it down and burn it (Judges 6:25-27)!

So God handpicks another prophet named Zephaniah to express His righteous anger, as well as His relentless love.

Read Hebrews 1:1. Since God could've used "many ways"—like a cataclysmic event or a pillar of fire—to communicate His anger, why do you think He chose a human prophet in this instance?

Hey Dude, Where's My Torah?

As in the case of Hosea, we don't know many personal details about this concise preacher, except for what he reveals about himself in the first verse:

> *The word of the LORD that came to Zephaniah the son of Cushi, son of Gedaliah, son of Amariah, son of Hezekiah, in the days of Josiah the son of Amon, king of Judah.* Zephaniah 1:1

Some people teach that Zephaniah descended from a king because he includes Hezekiah in this genealogy (Hezekiah was the fourteenth king of Judah from 715–686 BC), and he goes back four generations to include him. He's the only minor prophet to trace his ancestry back that far, which makes sense if he was trying to say, "Hey y'all, my great-great-grandfather was King Hezekiah!" However, Hezekiah was a common name in their culture—kind of like Tom or Mike in ours. And since Zephaniah doesn't specifically refer to his forefather as *King* Hezekiah—the way he does with King Amon—we don't know for sure that he was born with a silver spoon in his mouth. But we do

FAST FACT
Zephaniah is the ninth and last of the **pre-exilic** Minor Prophets, which you may remember refers to those that were written prior to the fall of Jerusalem and Judah's exile to Babylon in 586 BC.

know a lot about his environment because of the
reference to the "days of Josiah" he was living in.

Josiah was only eight years old when his daddy,
King Amon, died. He was the first king to be sworn
in wearing a Sponge-Bob T-shirt. But he had wisdom well beyond his age in light of this epilogue:

> *Josiah was eight years old when he began to reign,
> and he reigned thirty-one years in Jerusalem. His
> mother's name was Jedidah the daughter of
> Adaiah of Bozkath. And he did what was right in
> the eyes of the LORD and walked in all the way of
> David his father, and he did not turn aside to the
> right or to the left.*   2 Kings 22:1-2

Josiah's wise leadership and unwavering faithfulness are even more impressive when you consider
what happened eighteen years after he became king:

> *One day in the eighteenth year of his kingship,
> King Josiah sent the royal secretary Shaphan son
> of Azaliah, the son of Meshullam, to The Temple
> of GOD with instructions: "Go to Hilkiah the high
> priest and have him count the money that has been
> brought to The Temple of GOD that the doormen
> have collected from the people. Have them turn it
> over to the foremen who are managing the work on
> The Temple of GOD so they can pay the workers
> who are repairing GOD's Temple, all the carpen-
> ters, construction workers, and masons. Also,
> authorize them to buy the lumber and dressed stone
> for The Temple repairs. You don't need to get a
> receipt for the money you give them—they're all
> honest men."*

NOTES

The high priest Hilkiah reported to Shaphan the royal secretary, "I've just found the Book of GOD's Revelation, instructing us in GOD's ways. I found it in The Temple!" He gave it to Shaphan and Shaphan read it.

Then Shaphan the royal secretary came back to the king and gave him an account of what had gone on: "Your servants have bagged up the money that has been collected for The Temple; they have given it to the foremen to pay The Temple workers."

Then Shaphan the royal secretary told the king, "Hilkiah the priest gave me a book." Shaphan proceeded to read it to the king.

When the king heard what was written in the book, God's Revelation, he ripped his robes in dismay. And then he called for Hilkiah the priest, Ahikam son of Shaphan, Acbor son of Micaiah, Shaphan the royal secretary, and Asaiah the king's personal aide. He ordered them all: "Go and pray to GOD for me and for this people—for all Judah! Find out what we must do in response to what is written in this book that has just been found! GOD's anger must be burning furiously against us—our ancestors haven't obeyed a thing written in this book, followed none of the instructions directed to us."

2 Kings 22:3-13 *(The Message)*

In March 2004, an anonymous tipster in California told authorities that Maria Genoveva Torres was impersonating a medical doctor and seeing patients in her home. When police investigators drove past her house, they indeed saw a crowd of adults and children lined up on the front porch. So two undercover officers went to Torres's house. The one officer complained of stomach pain, so Torres told him to remove his shirt and lie down on the floor. Then she informed him that he had colitis. She "treated" him by placing a penny on his stomach, putting a lighted candle on the penny, covering both with a glass, and rubbing the glass in a circular motion before offering him a substance she claimed would release the blockage in his stomach. She was arrested a few days later.[14]

Only the grace of God could enable Josiah to run Judah so well without instructions—operating without a license, if you will. God's people had wandered so far away from Him that they'd literally *lost the Bible!* Can you imagine if you went to church and the pastor strode up to the pulpit and said, "Hey, you guys aren't going to believe what happened! Remember that book called *the Bible* we're always talking about? Well I was cleaning out a storage room the other day and *I found one!*"?

Why should modern Christians be thankful for Johannes Gutenberg and William Tyndale? If you aren't sure, go to a library and check out their biographies or at least Google their stories!

It's not unusual for me to walk up to the podium at a Christian women's event and ask the audience to open their Bibles to a particular passage, only to realize that hardly anyone *brought* their Bibles! I

typically smile and say something like, "I see most
of you have the Bible memorized and didn't feel the
need to bring it" to gently make a point. To remind
them to carry the Word of God in their heart *and*
their hands.

Many American households own more than one
Bible. I did a quick inventory of mine and found
eleven. I have several different translations; some
are written in modern language, some have key
Hebrew and Greek words emphasized, and one is an
antique that was published in 1856. They're all
different styles: hardbound, softbound, bonded
leather, calfskin, cloth, and a cute, handy-dandy
purse-sized edition. My sentimental favorite is a
Christmas present from my mom when I was in
high school that's now held together with duct tape.

Of course, all those Bibles don't do me any good
if they just sit on shelves collecting dust. Like vita-
mins and chocolate, I have to actually open the
container and ingest the contents to be positively
affected.

> *You shall therefore lay up these words of mine in*
> *your heart and in your soul, and you shall bind*
> *them as a sign on your hand, and they shall be as*
> *frontlets between your eyes. You shall teach them to*
> *your children, talking of them when you are sitting*
> *in your house, and when you are walking by the*
> *way, and when you lie down, and when you rise.*
>
> Deuteronomy 11:18-19

> *This Book of the Law shall not depart from your*
> *mouth, but you shall meditate on it day and night,*
> *so that you may be careful to do according to all*

that is written in it. For then you will make your
way prosperous, and then you will have good
success.   Joshua 1:8

All Scripture is breathed out by God and profitable
for teaching, for reproof, for correction, and for
training in righteousness, that the man of God may
be competent, equipped for every good work.
                                  2 Timothy 3:16-17

How many Bibles do you have in your home or
apartment? If there is more than one, which
one is your favorite? Why?

Double-Minded Devotees

Oh sure, some of Zephaniah's peers still went to
church even in the absence of the Torah. That's
made clear in his opening remarks about who was
headed for a serious whipping:

> *I will stretch out my hand against Judah and*
> *against all the inhabitants of Jerusalem; and I will*
> *cut off from this place the remnant of Baal and the*
> *name of the idolatrous priests along with the*
> *priests, those who bow down on the roofs to the host*
> *of the heavens, those who bow down and swear to*
> *the LORD and yet swear by Milcom, those who*
> *have turned back from following the LORD, who*
> *do not seek the LORD or inquire of him.*
>   Zephaniah 1:4-6

Zephaniah describes three kinds of sinners here:
First, there were those among the Israelites who
worshiped stone idols like Baal and practiced the

idolatry of astrology. They'd never gone to Temple or professed to worship Jehovah, but they didn't seem all that bad. They drove minivans, coached Little League, and barbequed on the weekends.

Read Deuteronomy 4:19 and Jeremiah 8:2. Some people—including Christians—think reading their horoscope in a newspaper or magazine is completely harmless. What do you think?

FAST FACT

Astrology was a major player in the game of idolatry. Sometimes people even erected altars on their roof so as to have a clear view of the stars while they worshiped (see Jeremiah 19:13; Amos 5:25-26; and Acts 7:37-43).

Second, there were those Jews who *used* to go to Temple, but now they didn't want anything to do with it. They probably had a run-in with some jerk at church and decided to just chuck the whole thing. They were sick of God and His stupid people.

And last, there were those who still went to church. They professed to worship God *and* idols. They were the ones who would "bow down and swear to the Lord and yet swear by Milcom."

Shortly after September 11, 2001, I was driving on the interstate next to downtown Nashville when I noticed a huge sign that said, "Pray for Our Nation." The words themselves didn't surprise me. Proverbs like that had popped up on billboards and front lawns and McDonald's signs across the country. But this particular one grabbed my attention and I couldn't help but grin and shake my head, because it was plastered across the sign that also advertised the world's largest triple-x-rated bookstore. How ironic that the people peddling smut were also encouraging motorists to seek God's help.

It was incongruous for the Israelites to bow to

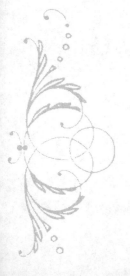

both God and Milcom. And believe it or not, it was even more disgusting than a pornographer recommending prayer. *Milcom* was another name for *Molech*, the national god of the Ammonites.[15] Furthermore, the ceremonial worship of Molech included the ritual sacrifice of children:

> *The LORD spoke to Moses, saying, "Say to the people of Israel, Any one of the people of Israel or of the strangers who sojourn in Israel who gives any of his children to Molech shall surely be put to death. The people of the land shall stone him with stones. I myself will set my face against that man and will cut him off from among his people, because he has given one of his children to Molech, to make my sanctuary unclean and to profane my holy name. And if the people of the land do at all close their eyes to that man when he gives one of his children to Molech, and do not put him to death, then I will set my face against that man and against his clan and will cut them off from among their people, him and all who follow him in whoring after Molech."* Leviticus 20:1-5

> *They built the high places of Baal in the Valley of the Son of Hinnom, to offer up their sons and daughters to Molech, though I did not command them, nor did it enter into my mind, that they should do this abomination, to cause Judah to sin.* Jeremiah 32:35

God's people showed no remorse for their sin. They'd lost their Bibles. And some said they loved Him, then went out and threw their precious babies

NOTES

into the roaring fire of a pagan god. No wonder He was mad.

One of my favorite scenes in *Lean on Me* takes place right after Morgan Freeman (Principal Joe Clark) orders the security guards to expurgate the drug dealers and hoodlums from Eastside. The rest of the student body watches in disbelief and cheers as the riffraff is forced off the stage and out of school forever. Principal Clark then says ominously, "The next time it may be you. And if you do no better than them, it *will* be you!" After a brief, inspirational charge, he strides past the stunned audience and out of the auditorium. Then one darling young woman turns to the friend beside her and says, "Mr. Clark don't *play!*"

That phrase sums up much of Zephaniah's message: God doesn't wink at sin; God doesn't compromise His holiness; God doesn't sit idly by while His people cavort with idols . . . *God don't play.*

Some of you might be thinking, *Well, I know some real stinkers who've never paid a divine penalty for rotten behavior. God sure seems to be twiddling His thumbs while they have a moral meltdown. Why doesn't He wallop them for their whopper sins instead of spanking me for minor infractions?* If you've pondered along those lines, you're not alone. There have been many times when I've questioned the way God doles out punishment. When I've wondered why He doesn't obliterate certain people into grease spots— or at least singe them a little.

More Info

God also warns His people about worshiping Molech/Milcom in Leviticus 18:21. The entire chapter deals almost exclusively with laws for sexual behavior. This leads some scholars to believe there was some type of sexual perversion associated with the already horrific ritual of child sacrifice.[16]

But we need to remember that the lack of overt, tangible punishment doesn't mean anyone *ever* gets away with rebellion against God. There will always be a price to pay for sin. The highest price of all is to be separated from Him. Some people may be laughing it up now, but there will be hell to pay. And while Christians will not face eternal separation from God, we can certainly suffer the consequence of waning intimacy with Him.

A friend of mine's husband stored pool chemicals in their linen closet, on the shelf underneath her makeup and feminine hygiene products. Pretty soon, she began to suffer with a low-grade fever, nausea, and overall fatigue. At first she thought she just had a stubborn case of the flu, but she couldn't get over it. After a battery of tests and lots of questions, they finally figured out that she was being poisoned by those pool chemicals in their bathroom. They were making her sick from the inside out.

Sin is kind of like that. It may not result in dramatic, immediate consequences, like being zapped into a pillar of salt. But unconfessed sin *will* make us sick. It will leach into our hearts and poison our souls. It will distance us from our merciful Creator.

What's the most serious form of discipline you received as a child? If you're a parent, what's the most serious form of discipline you use with your kid(s)?

2

Just Desserts

GRACE MEANS YOU'RE IN A DIFFERENT UNIVERSE
FROM WHERE YOU HAD BEEN STUCK, WHEN YOU HAD
ABSOLUTELY NO WAY TO GET THERE ON YOUR OWN.

Anne Lamott

As much as I learned to like Sadie Hawkins Day at
Lake Swan Camp, I still liked waterskiing more. I
loved to skim across the water, and jump wakes,
and spray whoever got too close with a wall of
water! So when I got to work on the camp staff
when I was in high school, I was thrilled that they
picked me to be one of the first female ski instruc-
tors. While the rest of the girls were changing
linens in the cabins or cutting up vegetables in the
kitchen, I got to hang out with a bunch of cute

guys and teach kids to ski! And sometimes, when we weren't instructing, we got to work on new stunts to show off in the unofficial ski show that took place most afternoons during free time.

Most of the stunts involved barefoot skiing, which, if you don't know, means waterskiing without the help of skis! Back then we didn't have a boom for the boat or wakeboards or any other sissy equipment like they have nowadays to assist people who hope to skim across a lake at forty-five miles an hour on bare feet. All we had was a fast boat, a rope, and teenage tenacity. When I finally learned how—after many eyelid-peeling, bone-jarring attempts—I was pretty full of myself. There weren't any other girls at camp that year who could ski barefoot, and I was proud of my newfound elite status. So when the guys asked me if I wanted to try a "beach start," I didn't hesitate before saying yes!

I'd seen most of them try beach starts and only a few had pulled one off. They'd walk up the beach about twenty or thirty feet from the water, sit in the sand with their feet crossed over the tow rope, grip the foam handle as hard as they could, and then yell, "Hit it!" to the boat driver. It was a daring feat (actually, *stupid* would be a more apt adjective!) that rarely worked. Usually the guy who attempted the beach-start just ended up with a fanny full of sand, blisters on his hands, and huge, purple bruises on his inner thighs from the rope handle. But I threw caution to the wind and pranced up the beach with the tow rope, anyway.

I don't remember much about my beach-start,

other than the green and black bruises that lasted for weeks and the grit that found its way into every single orifice in my body. And aside from hormones, I'm not sure why I tried something so dumb! Especially after witnessing the consequences of my friends' sandy battles.

Before going any further in Zephaniah, we need to look at one more reason for his peers' spiritual downfall. They foolishly ignored the ugly consequences of those who'd forsaken God before them.

> *In the fourth year of Hezekiah and the seventh year of Hoshea son of Elah king of Israel, Shalmaneser king of Assyria attacked Samaria. He threw a siege around it and after three years captured it. It was in the sixth year of Hezekiah and the ninth year of Hoshea that Samaria fell to Assyria. The king of Assyria took Israel into exile and relocated them in Halah, in Gozan on the Habor River, and in towns of the Medes.*
>
> *All this happened because they wouldn't listen to the voice of their GOD and treated his covenant with careless contempt. They refused either to listen or do a word of what Moses, the servant of God, commanded.*   2 Kings 18:9-12 (*The Message*)

The people of Judah had watched their relatives and rivals in the northern kingdom get clobbered by Assyria. They'd read news reports about the cruelty of the soldiers during the siege. They'd heard about the grisly deaths. About families being torn apart after soldiers killed the father and abused the mother. But they disregarded all of it and kept right on doing whatever they felt like.

Read Micah 6:8. Which of these spiritual disciplines are you most tempted to ignore?

The Lord's Day

Judah's pride caused the other proverbial shoe of God's punishment to drop:

> *Be silent before the Lord GOD! For the day of the LORD is near; the LORD has prepared a sacrifice and consecrated his guests. And on the day of the LORD's sacrifice—"I will punish the officials and the king's sons and all who array themselves in foreign attire. On that day I will punish everyone who leaps over the threshold, and those who fill their master's house with violence and fraud.*
>
> *"On that day," declares the LORD, "a cry will be heard from the Fish Gate, a wail from the Second Quarter, a loud crash from the hills. Wail, O inhabitants of the Mortar! For all the traders are no more; all who weigh out silver are cut off. At that time I will search Jerusalem with lamps, and I will punish the men who are complacent, those who say in their hearts, 'The LORD will not do good, nor will he do ill.' Their goods shall be plundered, and their houses laid waste. Though they build houses, they shall not inhabit them; though they plant vineyards, they shall not drink wine from them."*
>
> *The great day of the LORD is near, near and hastening fast; the sound of the day of the LORD is bitter; the mighty man cries aloud there. A day of wrath is that day, a day of distress and anguish, a day of ruin and devastation, a day of darkness and gloom, a day of clouds and thick darkness, a day of*

*trumpet blast and battle cry against the fortified
cities and against the lofty battlements.*

*I will bring distress on mankind, so that they
shall walk like the blind, because they have sinned
against the LORD; their blood shall be poured out
like dust, and their flesh like dung. Neither their
silver nor their gold shall be able to deliver them
on the day of the wrath of the LORD. In the fire of
his jealousy, all the earth shall be consumed; for a
full and sudden end he will make of all the inhabitants of the earth.*   Zephaniah 1:7-18

What "Christian" business practices do you think God despises today?

Double yikes! My friend's little boy used to run
upstairs and put on a second pair of pants when he
knew he was getting a spanking; if I were Judah,
I'd have done the same thing! Because the Day of
the Lord sounds like a very, very bad day for unbe-
lievers.

Several years ago I was invited to be a guest on a
Christian television show. It wasn't a "big" TV

did you know?

ecause the Jewish merchants had become wealthy through dishonest
ractices, they were singled out to depict the severity of God's judg-
ent. The Fish Gate (now called the Damascus Gate) was located on
e north side of town and was a high-traffic sales area; the Second
uarter was a district inside the city walls; and "inhabitants of
ortar" refers to the valley of Siloam, which was also a hopping
siness district.

show—most people have never even heard of it—but it was syndicated in front of a live audience, so I was kind of excited. My old boss used to say, "A blind squirrel only finds a nut every now and then," and that's sort of how I felt. At my level of obscurity, any coverage is good coverage. So I wore an outfit that makes me look thinner and prepared a couple of devotions that I thought might work on television.

My first disappointment came when the makeup artist told me proudly that she used to work on the women from the comedic variety show, *Hee Haw.* I smiled bravely, but winced inwardly while she teased my hair to new heights. Then I found out that the program order they e-mailed earlier in the week had been revised. Instead of being the second guest in the interview portion of the show, I was going to be the very first person on camera. They wanted me to "warm up" the audience *before* the host came on and then sit in for a short interview. Finally, after reminding me to talk with a lot of enthusiasm and look at the cameras, not the people in the audience—all seventy-five of them—the producer told me he'd prefer it if I left my Bible backstage. He said, "I know you're a Bible teacher and all, but we really just want you to tell funny stories tonight." He said most people tuned in to be entertained, not taught.

I think a lot of Christians fit that description. I'd certainly rather laugh at funny stories from the pulpit or be wowed by powerful illustrations than consider things like distress, anguish, ruin, devastation, darkness, and gloom. And I sure don't want to be pegged as some dreary, turn-or-burn Bible

thumper. Frankly, I'm still a bit worried about including Zephaniah in this book because I'm afraid readers will stomp out of Starbucks vowing never to buy anything with my name on it again!

But God's holiness is every bit as real as His grace. And I'd rather be branded as boring than face what God says awaits those who don't think He'll punish sin and write Him off as harmless:

> *On Judgment Day, I'll search through every closet and alley in Jerusalem. I'll find and punish those who are sitting it out, fat and lazy, amusing them-selves and taking it easy, who think, "God doesn't do anything, good or bad. He isn't involved, so neither are we." But just wait. They'll lose every-thing they have, money and house and land. They'll build a house and never move in. They'll plant vineyards and never taste the wine.*
> Zephaniah 1:12-13 (*The Message*)

Read Deuteronomy 28:29 and Zephaniah 1:17. DVD In what ways can disobedience lead to spiritual blindness? Have you ever felt like you were "groping" during a season of rebellion?

Dual-Purpose Phrase

My pastor, Scotty Smith, talks about God with such interesting and memorable phraseology that I find myself parroting points of his sermon throughout the week. Zephaniah must've felt the same way about Joel, because he borrows his classic phrase, "the Day of the Lord," and uses it through-out this sermon.

In Zephaniah, the *Day of the Lord* has two applications. The first involves the immediate consequences that Judah will face as a result of her sin. And as with the spiritual lesson God taught His kids in the northern kingdom through war with Assyria, God will also use a foreign army to discipline Judah. Just twenty-three years after Josiah's death (remember, Zephaniah prophesied during Josiah's reign), the army of Babylon rolls into Jerusalem and wreaks havoc. The Temple is destroyed, houses are burned, dead Jewish bodies are strewn everywhere, and God's children are carted off to live in exile. Thus, the first application of the Day of the Lord is historical. Bad stuff really happened to unrepentant sinners.

However, at the end of the Day of the Lord lecture God says, "The *whole land* shall be devoured" (emphasis mine). All the Hebrew scholars I studied say that points to a final judgment. This is what the apostle John wrote about in the last book of the Bible:

Then I saw a great white throne and him who was seated on it. From his presence earth and sky fled away, and no place was found for them. And I saw the dead, great and small, standing before the throne, and books were opened. Then another book was opened, which is the book of life. And the dead were judged by what was written in the books, according to what they had done. And the sea gave up the dead who were in it, Death and Hades gave up the dead who were in them, and they were judged, each one of them,

More Info

The phrase "the Day of the Lord" is used nineteen times in the Old Testament and four times in the New Testament. It usually refers to the wrath God will pour out on sin, both historically and on the final day of judgment (see Isaiah 13:6 and Joel 1:15), but it can also represent God's ultimate blessing for those who trust in Him (see 2 Peter 3:10-13).

according to what they had done. Then Death and
Hades were thrown into the lake of fire. . . . And if
anyone's name was not found written in the book
of life, he was thrown into the lake of fire.

Revelation 20:11-15

**Read Psalm 103:11-12, Daniel 7:9-10, 12:1, and
1 John 1:9. Do you think the books Daniel (the
"book" is not mentioned in John) refers to
include *every* thing we've done against God,
or just those sins we haven't truly repented
for?**

Thus, we better pay attention, because the
second application of the Day of the Lord is
prophetic. In other words, it involves us! Thankfully, we'll be spared God's wrath if our name is in
the Book of Life. If we have a personal relationship
with Jesus Christ. But what about our friends and
family? What about our next-door neighbors? How
will the Day of the Lord affect them?

**How does your concern for your unbelieving
friends and family affect you in practical ways
(i.e., Do you pray for them? Do you invite them
to events with your Christian friends? Have you
told them your story?).**

Sams's Last Chance

After issuing one of the harshest sentences in Scripture, Zephaniah reveals the bottomless compassion
of God with another invitation to repent:

Gather together, yes, gather, O shameless nation,
before the decree takes effect—before the day passes

away like chaff—before there comes upon you the
burning anger of the LORD, before there comes
upon you the day of the anger of the LORD. Seek
the LORD, all you humble of the land, who do his
just commands; seek righteousness; seek humility;
perhaps you may be hidden on the day of the anger
of the LORD.   Zephaniah 2:1-3

Compare the offer of repentance in Amos 5:6 to
the one Zephaniah just wrote. What's the
significant difference?

In the pivotal scene of *Lean on Me*, there's a
chubby little freshman named Thomas Sams, (nick-
named "Sams") who was kicked out of school along
with all the other ruffians. He has a cherubic face
and an impish grin; it's obvious that Sams isn't a
hopeless case like the criminals he hangs around
with. But he was caught skipping school and smoking crack and was punished accordingly.

Early the next morning, when the principal pulls
up to school in his car, Sams is sitting there waiting for him with a hangdog expression. At first
Mr. Clark gruffly refuses Sams's plea to return to
school because Sams won't admit his offenses. But
when he continues to beg for another chance, Mr.
Clark says abruptly, "Come with me, Sams," and
drags him up to the school roof. There he roughly
encourages Sams to jump. Sams cries pitifully and
says he doesn't want to die. To which Mr. Clark
replies that he might as well jump, because smoking crack will kill him just as sure as jumping off a
roof! Through his tears, Sams finally confesses that

he did do what he was accused of, but he promises to change. Sighing, Mr. Clark tells him that he'll let him come back to school, but that he's going to be "on his case" every single minute.

And he is. Poor Sams gets in trouble with Mr. Clark constantly. He gets reprimanded for even the most minor infractions. He gets lectured for dressing sloppy, for eating off someone else's plate in the cafeteria, and for singing in the hallway. But he responds to the discipline beautifully. He stops skipping school and smoking crack and smarting off. He starts passing his classes. And by the end of the movie he has become one of Eastside High's shining stars . . . and Mr. Clark's biggest fan.

Sams reminds me of a girl I went to high school with named Peggy. Not that she was a sloppy dresser, smoked crack, or pilfered snacks, but she had an infectious, rebellious spirit. Other students were drawn to her living-on-the-edge personality; wherever she went, a party soon followed. And so did trouble. As a matter of fact, the only time I was ever chased on foot by the police was when I spent the night at Peggy's and she talked me into an unforgettable escapade . . . but that's a whole other story!

Needless to say, I assumed she would eventually end up wearing an orange jumpsuit and making license plates.

Boy was I surprised when I ran into her at a conference a few years after college. No longer the consummate party girl, Peggy had become a radiant Christian whose grin had absolutely nothing to do with evading law enforcement officers! She was working with a campus ministry, helping students find their identity in the love of God instead of guzzling beer. And she loved to tell her story—the story of how God entered her out-of-control life and gave her the love, stability, and sense of belonging that she was so desperate for.

Prostitutes can become faithful wives. Party girls can become missionaries. God is truly the God of second chances.

If only Judah had responded like Peggy and Sams.

 What's the most merciful second chance you've ever been given in a human relationship?

3

The Biggest Kahuna of All

THE WORLD DWARFS US ALL, BUT GOD DWARFS THE WORLD.
THE WORLD IS HIS FOOTSTOOL, ABOVE WHICH HE SITS
SECURE. HE IS GREATER THAN THE WORLD AND ALL THAT IS
IN IT, SO THAT ALL THE FEVERISH ACTIVITY OF ITS BUSTLING
MILLIONS DOES NO MORE TO AFFECT HIM THAN THE CHIRP-
ING AND JUMPING OF GRASSHOPPERS IN THE SUMMER SUN
DOES TO AFFECT US.   *J. I. Packer*

When Benji—my diaper-changing show-and-tell—
was a toddler, he had a very strong personality and
couldn't seem to understand that he wasn't the
boss of his household. He knew his big brother
Graham was under his parents' authority, but he
thought he was somehow exempt. After several
head-butting confrontations with her baby, my

friend Kim finally found a novel way to help him understand his position. She made him stand in front of the mirror once or twice a week and repeat over and over again, "I am not in charge. I am not in charge."

Who had the most strong-willed personality in your family when you were growing up? If it wasn't you, how has this person's personality changed over time? If it was you, how has your personality changed over time?

The following passage is Zephaniah's effort to teach a bunch of stubborn, strong-willed people that *they are not in charge* . . . God is.

> *For Gaza shall be deserted, and Ashkelon shall become a desolation; Ashdod's people shall be driven out at noon, and Ekron shall be uprooted.*
>
> *Woe to you inhabitants of the seacoast, you nation of the Cherethites! The word of the LORD is against you, O Canaan, land of the Philistines; and I will destroy you until no inhabitant is left. And you, O seacoast, shall be pastures, with meadows for shepherds and folds for flocks. The seacoast shall become the possession of the remnant of the house of Judah, on which they shall graze, and in the houses of Ashkelon they shall lie down at evening. For the LORD their God will be mindful of them and restore their fortunes.*
>
> *"I have heard the taunts of Moab and the revilings of the Ammonites, how they have taunted my people and made boasts against their territory. Therefore, as I live," declares the LORD of hosts,*

the God of Israel, "Moab shall become like Sodom,
and the Ammonites like Gomorrah, a land
possessed by nettles and salt pits, and a waste
forever. The remnant of my people shall plunder
them, and the survivors of my nation shall possess
them."

This shall be their lot in return for their pride,
because they taunted and boasted against the people
of the LORD of hosts. The LORD will be awesome
against them; for he will famish all the gods of the
earth, and to him shall bow down, each in its place,
all the lands of the nations.

You also, O Cushites, shall be slain by my sword.

And he will stretch out his hand against the
north and destroy Assyria, and he will make
Nineveh a desolation, a dry waste like the desert.
Herds shall lie down in her midst, all kinds of
beasts; even the owl and the hedgehog shall lodge
in her capitals; a voice shall hoot in the window;
devastation will be on the threshold; for her cedar
work will be laid bare. This is the exultant city
that lived securely, that said in her heart, "I am,
and there is no one else." What a desolation she has
become, a lair for wild beasts! Everyone who passes
by her hisses and shakes his fist.

Zephaniah 2:4-15

Much has been written and proposed about the
four nations—Philistia, Moab/Ammon, Cush
(Ethiopia), and Assyria—that Zephaniah included
in this diatribe. They were all players in ancient
world politics. And they all did despicable things in
the eyes of the Lord.

Philistia was a wicked nation that constantly opposed Israel and "Israel's God." They were known as crass opportunists who captured entire populations and then sold them off as slaves (Amos 1:6).

Moab and Ammon (taken together because of their proximity and similar history—kind of like Alabama and Mississippi) had the most eyebrow-raising origins. When God destroyed Sodom and Gomorrah, His lone disciple, Lot, settled in the hill country with his two daughters (remember, their mom became a salty statue for disobeying God's get-out-of-town orders). These girls must've taken after their sinful mama, because they got Lot drunk on two separate occasions, had sex with him, and then each bore a son from those incestuous romps. Gross, huh? Lot's older daughter was brazen enough to name her little boy, *Moab*, which literally means "from father." The younger daughter named her son *Ben-ammi*, which means "son of my people." Ben-ammi became the father of the Ammonites (Genesis 19:30-38). Both countries were condemned for explicit brutality (Amos 1:13; 2:1).

More Info

For more on the stories of how God fulfilled His promise to punish these foreign nations, read Amos 1:6-8; Ezekiel 30:24-25; and 2 Kings 19:32-37.

There aren't as many colorful details about Cush, otherwise known as Ethiopia. But Isaiah makes it clear that they were stinkers too, "feared near and far" (Isaiah 18:1-2).

Assyria is the last and largest nation mentioned. She's also Judah's most immediate threat. Nineveh, Assyria's capital city, was big and glittery (think Las Vegas) and known for widespread idolatry and violence (Nahum 1:14; 3:1-3).

Some people reading these passages today attempt to make modern associations by singling out foreign countries with similar reputations. Then they utter menacing and small-minded predictions like, "Russia better watch out because God's not going to put up with those commies much longer!" Poor things are missing the point. Zephaniah could have used any combination of existing nations he wanted, because *everyone* was in spiritual rebellion. But he specifically chose Philistia, which was *west* of Judah; Moab and Ammon, which were *east* of Judah; Cush, which was *south* of Judah; and Assyria, which was due *north*. God inspired Zephaniah to use the countries surrounding Judah to demonstrate the fact that He governs *the whole world!*

Not just countries that stamp "In God We Trust" on their currency. Not just people who vote Republican. And not just southerners who dress up on Sunday. The synopsis of Zephaniah's last discourse is that God rules over every single nation, tribe, tongue, and people group. This concept is so contrary to our contemporary way of thinking that it's like carrying a six-pack of beer into an AA meeting!

But when the apostle Paul said, "Therefore God has highly exalted him and bestowed on him the name that is above every name, so that at the name of Jesus every knee should bow, in heaven and on earth and under the earth, and every tongue confess that Jesus Christ is Lord, to the glory of God the Father" (Philippians 2:9-11), he wasn't just whistling Dixie. He was pointing to the absolute omniscience and authority of God the Father, through Jesus the Son.

Just like Zephaniah before him, Paul was explaining that God is in control of everyone, everywhere. We are *so* not in charge.

It's often said that America is "God's favorite nation." How would you respond to that statement?

Do you have any friends who practice another faith, like Buddhism or Islam? If so, have you ever told them how you came to believe in the claims of Christ?

There Are Three Pointing Back at You

And in case Judah was feeling a little cocky, thinking, *Hey, we're not like those foreign pagans, we're God's chosen people,* Zephaniah turns his attention back home and recites a poem God wrote just for them:

> *Woe to her who is rebellious and defiled, the oppressing city! She listens to no voice; she accepts no correction. She does not trust in the LORD; she does not draw near to her God.*
>
> *Her officials within her are roaring lions; her judges are evening wolves that leave nothing till the morning. Her prophets are fickle, treacherous men; her priests profane what is holy; they do violence to the law. The LORD within her is righteous; he does no injustice; every morning he shows forth his justice; each dawn he does not fail; but the unjust knows no shame.* Zephaniah 3:1-5

It's certainly not Yeats. It sounds more like something Donald Trump would compose for a firing episode on *The Apprentice*. I can just imagine those Jews turning red-faced and slinking lower in their pews when Zephaniah began to read this Scriptural sonnet. They probably squirmed in their seats and tried to figure out how they could slip out of church without making a scene. But then he got to the last stanza. And, as is often the case in Hebrew poetry, the latter part pointed to God's remarkable faithfulness.[17]

JERUSALEM / GOD'S PEOPLE	GOD
Doesn't listen	Is never absent
Doesn't accept discipline	Makes His justice clear
Doesn't trust God	Is totally trustworthy
Doesn't draw near to God	Is always accessible

Which of the four spiritual indictments listed here—*not listening, not accepting discipline, not trusting God, not drawing close to God*—do you struggle with the most?

They probably breathed a sigh of relief when God's steadfast character was proclaimed, but only for a second. Because Zephaniah concluded the poem with this:

> *But evil men and women, without conscience and without shame, persist in evil.*
>
> Zephaniah 3:5 *(The Message)*

God was charging Judah with being no different than the nations around her. Nations that didn't have a church on every corner, a Bible in every home, preachers on television, and prayer in schools.

Do you think that ancient poetic shoe fits America today?

The Sad Reality of Self-Reliance

I like to read biographies, especially ones that involve some element of risk or adventure. And most of the tales I read are uplifting; they typically include some element of overcoming adversity or making the best of a difficult situation. But I read one a couple of years ago that still haunts me; it's the story of a young man named Chris. His story begins in April 1992, five miles outside of Fairbanks, Alaska, where—now hitchhiking and going by the alias "Alex"—Chris is picked up by a sympathetic driver named James Gallien. When Gallien asked Alex where he was headed, the young man said Denali National Park where he planned to "live off the land for a few months."

Gallien became suspicious. The young stranger didn't seem to be carrying enough gear and wasn't dressed appropriately for a months-long stay in the wilderness. Spring comes late to the back country; most of the terrain was still under a layer of deep snow. But Gallien also knew that Alaska attracts countless soul searchers who hope to reground their lives in the solitude and expanse of the pristine surroundings. As author Jon Krakauer writes, "The bush is an unforgiving place, however, that cares nothing for hope or longing."

During the drive to Denali, the two had a pleasant conversation. Alex was personable and chatty.

Realizing that Gallien was an experienced hunter and outdoorsman, the passenger took advantage of their time together, asking about "the kind of small game that live in the country, the kinds of berries he could eat."

When Gallien offered to drive out of his way to buy Alex some basic essentials, he was politely rebuffed. "No, thanks," Alex replied. "I'll be fine with what I've got." At the drop-off point—ten miles from the highway—Gallien learned that he was the only person who knew about Alex's venture. After thanking his trucker acquaintance, Alex's last words exuded self-confidence: "I'm absolutely positive I won't run into anything I can't deal with on my own."[18]

Gallien later told authorities that he just couldn't talk Chris McCandless out of roughing it in the wild on his own. At the trailhead Gallien gave the young man a sandwich and a pair of rubber boots, took a photo of a grinning "Alex" at his behest, and then drove away. Gallien didn't know his real name until several months later.

He didn't know that Chris was from the Washington, D.C., area. He didn't know that Chris graduated from Emory University with honors. He didn't know that Chris was the only son of a loving family who missed him terribly. James Gallien didn't know that Chris would die alone in the Alaskan bush sixteen weeks later.

Chris McCandless spent those four, long months living in an abandoned blue and white bus. Several years before, hunters had hauled it into the wilderness to shelter them from the elements and serve as a crude base camp. Little did they know it would become an independent young man's coffin.

Chris left behind a journal on that bus. A journal that recorded a few, seemingly small mistakes, which led to his untimely death. He wrote about getting sick after eating some plants and how his body was weakened as a result. He wrote about how he tried to hike back to civilization—only ten miles away—but how he was forced to turn back by a swollen river.

The last words he wrote were written on a note that two hikers found tacked by his door. The note said: "S.O.S. I need your help. I am injured, near death, and too weak to hike out of here. I am all alone, this is no joke. In the name of God, please remain to save me. I am out collecting berries close by and shall return this evening. Thank you, Chris McCandless. August?"[19]

Chris McCandless had been dead for several weeks when they found his body huddled in a blue sleeping bag inside that old bus.

My first reaction when I finished reading his story was, *That didn't have to happen.* In fact, in Jon Krakauer's book, *Into the Wild,* which this story was excerpted from, he describes two routes to civilization Chris could have taken when he tried to hike out. One, a hand-operated tram, was only a quarter-mile downstream from where he turned back. The other, a National Park Service cabin, was just six miles away and was plainly marked on most maps. But, of course, Chris didn't think he needed a map. Plus, his friends said even if he had a map, "his mule-headed obsession with self-reliance

would have kept him from staying anywhere near the bus; rather he would've headed even further into the bush."[20]

I can't help wondering how his family must've grieved his senseless death. How his parents probably wished their beloved son hadn't tried to be quite so self-reliant. How they probably wished he'd taken a shortwave radio, or at least a map, with him on that ill-fated Alaskan adventure.

Though not nearly as horrific as Chris's experience, my self-reliance has gotten me into trouble too. Once, when I was stubbornly snowboarding during a blizzard (while everyone else was wisely inside, drinking hot chocolate by the fireplace), my snowboard got wedged under a log buried several feet beneath the surface of the snow. My newfangled boots were attached to the metal bindings on the board, so I was effectively trapped. As I stood there, waist deep in powder in a remote, wooded area, I realized no one could hear me or see me. It was bitterly cold, I was all alone, and I was scared.

It took over an hour to work myself free, and by the time I limped into the lodge, I was hypothermic. A while later, someone commented that I had been fortunate not to lose my toes. I was so grateful to be alive and fully-toed that I started making jokes to lighten the tense atmosphere. But my friends weren't remotely amused—my foolhardy antics had increased their blood pressure and ruined their weekend. They made me promise to try to temper my independent streak. I'm learning that living by the mantra "I won't run into anything I can't deal with on my own" is actually just a shortcut to disaster.

Like my friends, our heavenly Father clearly has a dim view of independence. He demands to be in charge. Philistia, Moab, Ammon, Ethiopia, Assyria, and some people who thought they were safe because they were religious learned that lesson the hard way.

> *But I will sing of your strength; I will sing aloud of your steadfast love in the morning. For you have been to me a fortress and a refuge in the day of my distress.*   Psalm 59:16

How would you describe the difference between having total dependence on God and an unhealthy dependence on other people?

Read Matthew 21:33-46. What are the similarities between Jesus' parable and Zephaniah's poetry?

4

Unmistakable Hope

GRACE IS NOT SIMPLY LENIENCY WHEN WE HAVE SINNED.
GRACE IS THE ENABLING GIFT OF GOD NOT TO SIN. GRACE
IS POWER, NOT JUST PARDON.   *John Piper*

My dad and mom, along with all three of her sisters
and their husbands, and two of my cousins and their
families, live on Stone Island, which is about thirty
minutes north of Orlando in central Florida. Let me
clarify that: They all live in *separate houses* on Stone
Island. I like to tease that we're kind of like the
Kennedy family—only without the political aspira-
tions and impressive pedigree! It's not really an
"island" either, more of a peninsula with a drainage
ditch on one side. I think the developers just thought
they'd sell more lots by calling it an island.

But it is a beautiful place to live. It's off the beaten path, there's not a strip mall for miles. Plus, it's right on the St. Johns River, so there's abundant wildlife—including manatees, turkeys, and alligators. Because of the water and the hot weather, it's basically a natural greenhouse, too. Even people with black thumbs grow bougainvillea to die for. The only major downsides to life on Stone Island are the mosquitoes and the danger of flooding during hurricane season.

You might remember that in 2004, three hurricanes hit Florida with a vengeance. This caused record-breaking winds and flooding on Stone Island. Just about everyone's home sustained some damage—from flyaway roofs to toppled trees. But no one was hit worse than my Aunt Darlene. In the first hurricane, Aunt Darlene's pool screen was ripped off like a loose Band-Aid, and then a week after having it replaced, it was torn off again, this time taking the whole gutter system with it. And because of their close proximity to the water, they ended up with a foot and a half of water in the lower level of their home. You couldn't even tell they had a pool because their entire backyard "became one with the river."

Aunt Darlene and Uncle Dale took it in stride. They didn't cry or moan about their losses, even when they were forced to evacuate their home with no time to gather anything but basic necessities. They simply moved in with Dale's dad, bringing little more than the clothes on their backs. They assumed their insurance company would assess the damages within a week or two, write them a check,

and then they'd be able to start repairing the damages. So they called contractors and roamed the aisles of Home Depot.

When two months passed without an adjuster's visit, they grew more than a little weary of commuting to work, wearing the same few outfits, and eating out. They just wanted to go home. So when the call finally came to schedule the assessment, they were overjoyed. Darlene prepared a neat list detailing their damages, and Dale brought an extra set of waders so the adjuster wouldn't get his feet wet. They waited expectantly for him like little kids on Christmas Eve.

Their adjuster had been transferred to Florida from Pennsylvania to help out with the deluge of claims, and it was obvious that he wasn't too happy about it. He complained that he'd been working nonstop for weeks and he wasn't too thrilled about having to wear waders, either. But Darlene and Dale were so excited he was actually there, they weren't bothered by his grouchiness. And when he got distracted by the alligator in their backyard and started to videotape that instead of the damage, they weren't concerned. At least it seemed to put him in a better mood. However, they didn't know just how engrossed he'd become on his video safari. That for fifteen minutes his focus would fixate on that one bumpy-backed reptile. That he'd track the gator right into their camouflaged pool. And that before they'd have time to react and scream for him to stop, he'd disappear beneath the waves with a big swoosh, camera and all!

NOTES

What has been the primary focus of your life lately? Does it move you toward God or distract you from Him?

We're all in danger of becoming too engrossed in our own pursuits, our personal needs, passions, and desires—our own little stories. Brent Curtis and John Eldredge elaborate about this in the book, *The Sacred Romance*:

> *For hundreds of years, our culture has been losing its story. The Enlightenment dismissed the idea that there is an Author but tried to hang on to the idea that we could still have a larger story, life could still make sense. . . .*
>
> *But once we had rid ourselves of the Author, it didn't take long to lose the larger story.*[21]

The reason God spoke through prophets like Hosea and Zephaniah is that His people were forgetting the larger story. They weren't living in the wondrous reality that they'd been chosen to live in covenant relationship with the Lord of the universe! And in keeping with the theme of forgetfulness and meta-narratives, I want to take a minute to talk about how we also tend to miss the larger, more important story.

For instance, some of you have probably gotten so distracted by a question, historical fact, or by the cool shoes of someone sitting next to you, that you've forgotten to ask the all-important question: How does Zephaniah point to Jesus? Because while Zephaniah is a divinely inspired book that chronicles Jewish history and God's pending judgment on

Judah, ultimately, it's supposed to point us toward the gospel!

Read Luke 24:13-26. How would you explain verse 26 in your own words? And what does it have to do with Zephaniah?

If I've just confused you, don't turn the page yet, because Peter explains this far better than I can.

> *Concerning this salvation, the prophets who prophesied about the grace that was to be yours searched and inquired carefully, inquiring what person or time the Spirit of Christ in them was indicating when he predicted the sufferings of Christ and the subsequent glories. It was revealed to them that they were serving not themselves but you, in the things that have now been announced to you through those who preached the good news to you by the Holy Spirit sent from heaven, things into which angels long to look.* 1 Peter 1:10-12

In other words, we live in the day of fulfillment. We can "get" Zephaniah's message even better than the people it was written to, because we're able to look at their history through the lens of the Cross. We can see how some of the Jews responded to Josiah's reforms and the revival that followed. We can also examine the way God disciplined Judah via Babylon and the exile. And how He shepherded them back home after they learned their lesson. We can appreciate the *big* picture—the prevail-

More Info

For more on Josiah's reforms and the mini-revival that took place after Zephaniah's prophecy, read 2 Kings 22:8–23:25 and 2 Chronicles 35.

ing story line of His faithfulness. Because hindsight reveals that God *never* abandons His beloved.

Read 2 Kings 23:26-27. Why do you think God's anger still burned even after the revival?

So does all the *wrath* Zephaniah talks about have nothing to do with us? Well, not exactly.

From where I'm sitting, I can see the folder holding my tax return. It makes me feel like getting up and going to the refrigerator. I don't like doing my taxes or paying my taxes. I'm always thankful when April 15 is behind me for another twelve months. And I'm assuming most of you feel the same way. I haven't met a person yet who jumps up and down with enthusiasm about paying taxes.

What if you got a personal letter from the IRS that said, "Dear whatever-your-name-is, someone else has paid your taxes in full and left an open tab so you'll never have to sweat April 15 again"? Wouldn't that be incredible? *That's a small picture of what Jesus did on the cross.* His blood paid the price for our transgressions, forever. The theme of judgment is very real in Scripture—it required the death of God's Son. Then, and only then, was God fully satisfied as our Judge. He put down His gavel, took off the black robe, and came out from behind the podium to embrace us. Our Judge became our Father. Therefore, if you put your faith in Christ, you will *never* face the punishment your sins deserve. You won't face the wrath of abandonment or damnation. But our heavenly Daddy will still discipline us when we need it.

Sometimes He'll just hold up a mirror and make us say, "I am not in charge," but sometimes we'll have to face His paddle.

My mother insists she only spanked me a few times when I was growing up, but there's one incident when I tried to be in charge that we both remember well. I was nine or ten years old and had done something rotten—which probably involved pummeling my little brother—when she told me to come inside because I was going to "get a spanking."

Being told to lie still, facedown on a bed and then having to wait for your mom's belt to whistle through the air before connecting with your behind is an awful place to be. Especially if your brother deserved the pummeling that got you in the fix. So when my mom said, "This is going to hurt me more than it hurts you," I replied, "Then maybe we should switch places."

My siblings and I weren't normally sassy kids. My parents simply wouldn't put up with disrespectful comments or attitudes. Therefore, when I uncharacteristically piped up prior to my spanking, Mom was shocked. But her shock quickly morphed into determination because she was not about to have a mouthy, juvenile delinquent for a daughter!

However, when she finished resurfacing my bottom, she didn't leave the room. She waited for me to stop crying. To stop quivering and convulsing my shoulders while dramatically gulping for air. Then she held me. She told me that it really did hurt her heart to punish me, but that it was part of her job as a mom. She told me that she disciplined

NOTES

me *because* she loved me. And I believed her. I never talked back during spankings again either!

That's the way it works with God, too. For those who put their hope in Him, even divine punishment will prove to be restorative.

> *I know, O LORD, that your rules are righteous, and that in faithfulness you have afflicted me.*
>
> Psalm 119:75

 What spiritual "spanking" has taught you the biggest lesson?

From Time-Out to "Let's Celebrate!"

Now let's really try to read the last few passages in Zephaniah through the lens of the gospel:

> *Sing aloud, O daughter of Zion; shout, O Israel! Rejoice and exult with all your heart, O daughter of Jerusalem! The LORD has taken away the judgments against you; he has cleared away your enemies. The King of Israel, the LORD, is in your midst; you shall never again fear evil.*
>
> Zephaniah 3:14–15

The single Greek word **teleō** is translated into the three English words "It is finished," which Jesus said just before giving up His spirit on the cross. **Teleō** has also been found written across ancient tax receipts, where the meaning was "paid in full" (see John 19:30 and Colossians 2:13-14).[22]

Stop and think for a minute or so about the last three chapters.

Has Zephaniah been out partying with Lot's daughters? Because this would make more sense if he was drunk! How can he possibly segue from, "God is so mad at you, you're going to be squished like a pancake" to "Sing and rejoice"? The *only* way this scriptural whiplash makes sense is for us to remember the larger story. To realize that God is using Zephaniah as a megaphone to declare a promise to satisfy sin Himself! *He's pointing to Jesus!* It's a preview of definitive mercy.

Read Zephaniah 3:9-11. Some people think these verses are only talking about the Israelites who've been living as exiles "beyond the rivers of Cush." If so, why does God say He'll change the speech of the "peoples"—denoting more than one people group—in verse 9? Do you think He could be referring to a multicultural *remnant*?

I think the very best picture of divine mercy is found in chapter 3, verse 17. When most people say they "love" the book of Zephaniah, this is usually the only verse they're thinking about!

> *The LORD your God is in your midst, a mighty one who will save; he will rejoice over you with gladness; he will quiet you by his love; he will exult over you with loud singing.*   Zephaniah 3:17

Have you ever pondered the concept of God singing over you? Since He's *rejoicing* over us, the song would have to be sweet. Full of words telling us how much He loves us. Restorative words. Lyrics most of us are absolutely desperate for.

One of the most wonderful things I've experienced in ministry started out awkwardly. I was at a Christian women's conference that was being held in a convention center. There were several thousand women at the event, and when they closed out the day with an opportunity for them to come forward and pray, over a thousand women responded.

I know that sounds like a good thing, but on this particular day it didn't feel like it. I was standing on the stage while Kathy Troccoli was singing, and I kept thinking, *This just feels way too emotional.* They were crying so loudly, I could barely hear Kathy's song. And while tears can be a wonderful, tangible expression of God working in a person's heart—the Bible even speaks of God storing the tears we shed (Psalm 56:8)—sometimes when you have a big group of emotive women bawling in unison, it can become more about hormones than the Holy Spirit! I couldn't help but sense that was the case here. I thought, *Boy, somehow we need to turn the attention back to God's faithfulness instead of who has the hardest life.*

Kathy must have sensed the same thing, because the next time she passed by, she shoved the microphone toward me and said, "Pray Lisa!" I thought, *Oh good night! I don't know what to say!* But I did know that in a crowd like that, a lot of women were struggling in their marriages, some were dealing with prodigal children or husbands, some were suffering with cancer and infertility, and some were probably grieving the death of someone they loved. So I started praying about those things. And as I was praying, God whispered for me to pray something else. Now, I'm not saying I heard an audible voice from God, like Moses or Abraham did. But, you know how sometimes He speaks to you *so clearly?* I mean, you just *know* it's His voice; it's not your mama's, it's not your counselor's, it's not your imagination. Scripture's pretty clear about us being able to recognize His voice, too (see John 10:1-5).

My first response was, *Lord, I don't think that's going to go over very well.* Because what He asked me to pray just didn't seem very appropriate at a *Christian* women's conference, where at least half the women had matching purses and shoes. I thought the crowd was too conservative to use the words He said. And I'd much rather be liked than be seen as some kind of liberal nut job. But I didn't want another holy spanking, either, so I went ahead and prayed what He impressed me to say: I prayed for women who were struggling with homosexuality and living in lesbian relationships. Yeah, I know. They were probably surprised, too.

But nothing dramatic happened. Within a few hours I was on a plane back to Nashville and that was the end of it. Or so I thought.

A few weeks later, I got a letter that was postmarked from the state the conference had been in. It was from a girl named Lori (not her real name), who wrote that she'd been to the conference and wanted to tell me something that happened. She explained that she'd been to that particular conference six or seven years in a row, and that she didn't go because she wanted to; she just went to appease her mom. She said she'd been raised in a Christian home, but rebelled in college. She'd been involved in the lesbian lifestyle for years, but was able to keep her mother in the dark because she didn't live in the same town.

Lori wrote, "I don't know if you remember, but the altar call at the conference was really emotional." I grinned when I read it and thought, *Yeah, I remember!* She said that she was sitting on the bleachers in the very back of the convention center with her arms crossed, thinking, *I hate this! These are all a bunch of hypocrites and nothing here applies to my life.* Then she said she "dared" God—though she wasn't even sure He existed anymore. "God, if you're real, I dare you to make that lady (talking about me) say the word *lesbian*, because I've been here year after year and I've never heard anyone say it."

The minute she "dared God," I said the word *lesbian* in my prayer. She said she was so shocked that she jumped up and ran to the bathroom, locking herself in until she couldn't hear any more noise outside. Then she walked out to the parking lot alone and drove away. A week or so later, she was driving down the highway and found herself at the very end of her rope. She had lost her job and the relationship with her latest girlfriend had ended. She said she basically asked God the same thing she had asked at the conference, but with a lot less anger and bravado: *God, if you're real, show yourself to me in a way that I can't miss it.*

As soon as she finished her candid request, she recognized a familiar song on the radio and reached over to turn up the volume. She was surprised to hear Kathy's voice, singing the very song she had sung during the altar call. Lori said she never listened to Christian radio, and wasn't sure why it was even tuned to that station. Then she said, to make it even more of an eye-opener, Kathy's song must have been recorded at the conference, because when it ended, rather than a DJ or an advertisement coming on, my prayer was

tagged on and she heard "the word" she'd asked for all over again.

Lori said the experience was *so unmistakably God,* that she pulled her car over to the shoulder of the road and asked Him to take control of her life.

Everywhere I go, I meet people like Lori. People whose self-reliance, self-centeredness, or lack of self-control once distanced them from God. I meet them in Los Angeles and Louisiana, Arizona and Africa. In the mall and in the mirror. And I never tire of hearing the stories about how God changed their lives. How He transformed prolific prodigals into precious saints. How He breathed living hope into the hopeless. How He changed lyrics of despair into songs of deliverance. How even the darkest, hidden sin can be forgiven by the God who sees everything . . . and still chooses to redeem His ragamuffins. Every good movie—like every good novel— gives us a glimpse of the larger story of the gospel. A scene that *should* have been in *Lean on Me* would be Morgan Freeman making some amazing sacrifice, that makes no rational sense, so that hoodlums like me, you, and Lori could come back inside the fold.

That's the underlying hope in Zephaniah, and that's the truth of the gospel.

> *What wondrous love is this, O my soul, O my soul!*
> *What wondrous love is this, O my soul!*
> *What wondrous love is this that caused the*
> * Lord of bliss*
> *To bear the dreadful curse for my soul, for my soul,*
> *To bear the dreadful curse for my soul.*

When I was sinking down, sinking down,
  sinking down,
When I was sinking down, sinking down,
When I was sinking down beneath God's
  righteous frown,
Christ laid aside His crown for my soul,
  for my soul,
Christ laid aside His crown for my soul.

To God and to the Lamb, I will sing, I will sing;
To God and to the Lamb, I will sing.
To God and to the Lamb Who is the great
  "I Am";
While millions join the theme, I will sing,
  I will sing;
While millions join the theme, I will sing.

And when from death I'm free, I'll sing on,
  I'll sing on;
And when from death I'm free, I'll sing on.
And when from death I'm free, I'll sing and
  joyful be;
And through eternity, I'll sing on, I'll sing on;
And through eternity, I'll sing on.[23]

Do you have a "Lori"—a seemingly "prolific" sinner (of course, they're no worse than the rest of us!)—in your circle of friends or family? Have you ever talked with that person about God's radical mercy?

Last Stop:
Malachi

1

When Your Tara's Trashed

IT IS GOOD THAT WE HAVE SOMETIMES SOME TROUBLES AND
CROSSES; FOR THEY OFTEN MAKE A MAN ENTER INTO
HIMSELF, AND CONSIDER THAT HE IS HERE IN BANISHMENT,
AND OUGHT NOT TO PLACE HIS TRUST IN ANY WORLDLY
THING.   *Thomas à Kempis*

Because I'm forty and single, some well-inten-
tioned but misguided women decided it was okay
to gloss over the truth about a gentleman they
wanted to set me up with. Their rationale was that
a woman my age should be happy if my blind date
was breathing without a machine. Which is why,
not too long ago, I found myself sitting across from
a man old enough to be my father, feigning interest
in pictures of his grandchildren. He thought our

date was a smashing success; I thought it was a disaster. We just didn't have anything in common, aside from the fact that he was in World War II and I studied about it in high school.

Read Malachi 1 in the New Living Translation or *The Message*. Synopsize the theme of this chapter in two or three sentences.

Scarlett O'Hara and Malachi don't seem to have much in common either, do they? Self-centered southern belles and Old Testament prophets aren't your typical compare-and-contrast illustration. But while movies aren't divine narrative, the Scarlett-Malachi matchup actually makes more sense than me and my date.

Unless you were raised by wolves, you probably remember who Scarlett O'Hara was. She was author Margaret Mitchell's creation who came to life—via actress Vivien Leigh—on the big screen in the classic film *Gone with the Wind*. Miss Leigh's Scarlett was an unforgettable character; an all-too-human heroine who survived the horrors of the Civil War and single-handedly made wearing velvet curtains trendy.

I can remember clearly the day my dad took my sister Theresa and me to see the movie. I was seven or eight, and the first hour seemed impossibly long once my Milk Duds were gone. The Civil War battles scared me, and I hated the portrayal of slavery. But like everyone else in the theater, I was mesmerized by Scarlett. It wasn't her sweet personality that held us captive—even I could see

she was stuck-up and Melanie was the nice one—
it was the no-holds-barred, passionate way she
dealt with unrequited love and devastating
circumstances. She was compellingly feisty;
you just couldn't wait to see what she'd do
next!

Scarlett's most riveting scene took place right
before intermission, after she'd narrowly escaped
the clutches of death in the flames of Atlanta and
finally made her way back to Tara, her beloved
childhood plantation home. She's hungry and
exhausted, her hoop skirt is bent, and the romantic notion she had of war and dances with dashing
soldiers has been replaced by the reality of death
and destruction. All she wants to do is go home.
To clean cotton sheets, comfort food, mint juleps
on the veranda, and servants who spoil her.

But we all gasped when Scarlett finally made it
back to Tara, because the fog cleared to unveil a
very different picture than the one she carried in
her mind and heart. The paint was peeling, the
columns were crumbling, the garden was overrun
with weeds, and her adoring daddy had become a
deranged stranger. Scarlett's dream of home had
become a disappointment of nightmarish propor-
tions.

I sat on the edge of my seat in the theater
wondering what Scarlett was going to do now.
And I cried when she raised her fist with the last
scrawny carrot from their garden and vowed,
"With God as my witness, I'll never be hungry
again!" Then the curtain came down and dad took
us back out to the lobby for more Milk Duds.

If you asked your close friends and/or family (the cerebral, literate ones who've actually read or watched Scarlett's saga) whether you're more like spunky Scarlett or merciful Melanie, which one do you think they'd choose? Explain why.

Mirror-Image Messes

The cast of characters is different, but Malachi's story is strikingly similar. The first wave of Israelites is returning to Jerusalem after many years of captivity in Babylon. They've been dreaming about going home for as long as most could remember. Grandparents had enthralled Jewish children with stories about the Promised Land where they'd once lived and where they hoped to be buried. They talked about hiking up the hill to the Temple for feast days. They reminisced about tables heavy with incredible food. Tender lamb, hot falafel, pomegranates as big as a man's fist, and olive oil as clear as water. The bards of Babylon never defaced the picture of home they had.

But just like Scarlett, when they finally make it back to Jerusalem, they find it isn't anything like the vision of Canaan they'd carried throughout their confinement. The walls surrounding the city are in ruins. Squatters and wild animals now live where kings had slept. The once-fertile fields are full of rocks and choked with weeds. Wells have dried up. The land of milk and honey is a mess. And God's people are sick with disappointment.

They raise their fists—minus the carrots—toward the heavens and ask God, "If You're so good, then why are our lives so bad?" Then when

He speaks mercy through the prophet Malachi, reminding them that He loves them, they poke out their bottom lips like petulant teenagers and ask, "Oh yeah, how?"

Although Malachi would have probably been much more comfortable wearing a sandwich board advertising, "The End Is Near . . . Turn or Burn" than fussy window treatments turned into a velvet dress, their dramas are close cousins. And the common denominator in their stories is selfish discontent.

Cleaning Out Closets

Malachi's associates were unbelievably arrogant. How dare they question God? He created them. He made a covenant with them and called them into a loving relationship with the God of the universe. He rescued them from darkness, brought them out of slavery, gave them food and directions in the desert, and made them victorious over their enemies.

Yet their response to His protection and provision had been anything but grateful. They continuously wandered away from His affections into the arms of idols. God disciplined them with things like Babylon so they'd behave and return to the safety and security of His perfect love. But their default setting was stuck on "rebellious." God's offspring were selfish, spoiled-rotten brats . . . just like Scarlett O'Hara. And on bad days, just like you and me.

Most of us don't have to dig too far back in our behavioral closet to find our inner Scarlett. I could spend all day confessing the times I've asked God questions like those postexilic whiners did. And when God graciously reminds me of His mercy, I've often pouted just like them: *Oh yeah, if You really love me, then why does my life look like this? How many Mother's Days do I have to spend alone? If You won't give me a husband and children, can't You at least give me a high metabolism and good skin?*

Sometimes when I consider my circumstances, I doubt God's goodness. What about you . . . what questions have you been hurling at the heavens lately?

Read Deuteronomy 6:13, 16 (see also Luke 4:12 and 1 Corinthians 10:9). Jesus quoted from these two verses when Satan tempted Him (read Matthew 4:1-11 for the Paul Harvey part). What's a modern example of "putting God to the test"?

Divine Drumroll

Malachi is a book of distinctive placement because it's the very last book in the Old Testament. It marks the end of what Hebrews calls the *Old Revelation* (Hebrews 1:1-4) and the beginning of more than four hundred aptly named *Silent Years*. Almost half a millenium will pass—the *Intertestamental Period*—before God speaks again through a hirsute prophet with bug breath named John the Baptist. When you consider God's sovereignty in the development of the Holy Writ, Malachi is kind of like His last Old Testament monologue. God doesn't make another sound until the Gospels. Malachi is the "da-ta-ta-dah"—the divine drumroll that precedes the introduction of Jesus!

Biblical historians can't give an exact date for when Malachi was written. However, because of the

assumption of the second Temple in both the second and third chapters and the fact that Malachi addresses many of the same issues that Ezra and Nehemiah did (marriages to pagans, children who can't speak Hebrew, social injustice, corruption of the priesthood, anemic tithing, etc.), most scholars agree this book was penned between 460–450 BC. This gives even more credence to our movie metaphor, because that really is the time period when the first wave of captives returned to Judah to find utopia ransacked.

My friend, Victor Farragali, pronounces Malachi, *Ma-La-Chee*, and playfully insists that he's the only Italian writer in the Bible! But actually *Malachi* is a Hebrew word that's translated into two words, *my messenger*, in English. And much like the other messengers before him—devoted Hosea, tearful Jeremiah, and lyrical Zephaniah—Malachi is the oral liaison between the Lord and His people. I think what makes Malachi unique is the tangible hope in his words. In the middle of an extremely difficult season, he clears his throat and eloquently points to the coming Messiah.

> **More Info**
>
> Malachi is the last of the three *post-exilic* books in the Minor Prophets, which means this prophecy was given *after* the Jewish exiles had returned home to Jerusalem from those fifty-some years of captivity in Babylon.

Boxing with God

Malachi is also unique in its literary composition; no other book in the Bible is written quite like it. It's comprised of a thesis, followed by six prophetic disputation speeches, followed by a summation and challenge. I know that probably sounds like a high-school English review and is about as riveting as watching an infomercial on ponytail holders! But what all that verbose seminary language really means is that Malachi's friends have adopted some bad theology in regards to the predicament they find themselves in, so they question God. And boy, does He answer them!

Biblical scholars say Malachi is the most repetitive book in the Old Testament and the simplest in form. However, the speech form used—*rhetorical disputation*—is rare in prophetic writings and takes some getting used to.

Below is an example of *rhetorical disputation* in the first few verses of Malachi.

Malachi 1:2-5

Assertion (by God): "I have loved you." (1:2a)

Questioning (by Israel): "How have you loved us?" (1:2b)

Response (by God): "Is not Esau Jacob's brother?" declares the LORD. "Yet I have loved Jacob but Esau I have hated. I have laid waste his hill country and left his heritage to jackals of the desert." (1:2b-3)

Implication (by Israel): "Your own eyes shall see this." (1:5a)

The term **rhetorical** means that it's used for style and effect, not necessarily to elicit a response, and **disputation** draws attention to the debate that's taking place.

It sounds like a parent-teen disagreement, doesn't it? That's actually a pretty accurate template! Basically, the *assertion* is the undisputed truth, because it's spoken from God's mouth through His messenger, Malachi. The *questioning* is audacious, because it represents the clay questioning the Potter, the created questioning the Creator. The *response* is what I call "the big uh-oh," because

this is when God starts responding to their inso-lence. (It reminds me of those times when I pushed my mom too far and she used my entire given name. When my mom uses my middle name, I know I'm in big trouble!) And finally, the *implica-tion* is the application of "uh-oh"—the conse-quence—the spanking after Mom said, "Because I'm your mother and I said so, that's why!"

Do you think *asking God questions* and *doubting God's faithfulness* are synonymous? Do you think it's ever permissible to question God? Explain why or why not.

All seven questions in Malachi follow this basic disputation/debate outline, which makes it user-friendly and easy to study once you understand the format. But tread softly, because it's as convicting as it is well-written. Malachi is like wasabi (the green stuff some hapless sushi diners mistake for avocado paste)—just a little bit goes a long way!

Impudent Inquiry
"How have you loved us?" Malachi 1:2
"How have we despised your name?" Malachi 1:6
"How have we polluted you?" Malachi 1:7
"Where is the God of justice?" Malachi 2:17
"How shall we return?" Malachi 3:7
"How have we robbed you?" Malachi 3:8
"How have we spoken against you?" Malachi 3:13

Talk about impudence! We've already confessed our inner Scarletts, so we've admitted we aren't perfect, but I really can't imagine asking *all seven* questions! I'm pretty sure I would've quit pestering God after two . . . at the most three. What's wrong with these people? Are they slow learners? I know we're sinners saved by grace and all, but we aren't nearly as bad as Malachi's peers were, are we?

Read James 1:2-8. Synopsize what this passage says about someone who doubts God.

Read Judges 6:36-40. When Gideon asked to make just one more request (verse 39, NIV), the literal Hebrew translation meant to *say*, *speak*, *promise*, *tell*, or *command*. Why do you think God allowed Gideon the audaciousness of *telling* Him to perform a miracle before he (Gideon) would trust Him? Describe a situation when you *told* (or were tempted to tell) God to do something before you would trust Him.

Do you remember the book *The Scarlet Letter*? It was almost certainly on your "must-read" list in high school, so most of us have at least looked at the CliffsNotes. The protagonist of the book is a Puritan woman named Hester Prynne. Hester has a brief, tumultuous love affair with the town pastor and winds up having a child out of wedlock. The religious zealots and pious leaders in Ms. Prynne's town demand that she discloses the identity of the baby's father or else face severe punishment. But Hester won't budge. And the cute, cowardly pastor stays silent, too. So the town condemns her and, in one of the most dramatic scenes, forces Hester Prynne to wear a red letter *A* around her neck. The *A* stands for adultery. That crimson letter forever

brands her as a sinner; it was the ultimate mark of disgrace in her community.

Read Luke 24:36-51. What did Jesus do to **tangibly ease the disciples' doubts? How has He recently eased your doubts about a difficult circumstance or relationship you find yourself in?**

When I taught the book of Malachi in church recently, I wanted to do something to help us relate with the ancient people who listened to God speak through Malachi. So I showed a video clip of the movie *The Scarlet Letter,* the scene where Hester (played with just a touch of Scarlett's defiance by actress Demi Moore) is forced to wear the red letter. When the clip was over, I pulled out a big box filled with lots of large red letters. I told the class what each letter stood for: *S* represented sexual sin; *P* represented pride; *C* represented a critical spirit; *L* represented lying and deceit; and *I* represented idolatry. Then, one at a time I hung all five letters around my neck. (I could've used the whole alphabet, but I just wanted to make a point, not hang out all my dirty laundry.) There was an uncomfortable silence in the room for a moment because most of the women assumed they were also going to have to take letters representing their sin out of the box and wear them to small groups.

We didn't do that—true conviction is a work of the Holy Spirit, not human manipulation or theatrics—but we did talk soberly about how we'd be

> **More Info**
>
> In Malachi 1:6, God refers to Himself as the "Lord of hosts," which is one of sixteen Old Testament names for God. The Hebrew word for "Lord" in this text is *Adonai,* which denotes lordship—and brings to mind a great classic Michael Card song!

much more humble if we did have to wear our transgressions visibly, like Hester Prynne. With necklaces highlighting our sinful notoriety, we'd probably never again argue our affinity with the worst of Biblical sinners. We'd probably never forget our tendency to wander like the Israelites or whine like Scarlett. And we wouldn't have to be reminded quite so often of how desperate we are for God's mercy.

We have been called into a dynamic love affair, one that gives more than we could have ever hoped and demands more than we would freely give. To receive God's grace in Christ is to be brought into a revolutionary reign, not ushered into a quiet rest home! God's love is as disruptive as it is delightful, as demanding as it is delicious. God loves us exactly as we are today, but He loves us too much to leave us as we are and where we are.[24]

We aren't any better than Malachi's buddies. We are just as arrogant, just as faithless, just as stubborn, and just as blind to our own sin. But thankfully, God loves us way too much to leave us brokenhearted and disillusioned with our fists defiantly raised toward Him.

More Info

The phrase "from the rising of the sun to its setting" (Malachi 1:11 and Psalm 50:1) is a way of referring to the whole earth. Some theologians assert that this is Malachi's way of pointing toward a millennial era when the Lord will be praised throughout the earth and His name honored by all people (Philippians 2:10).[25]

Watch *Gone with the Wind* with some friends and keep track of Scarlett's most colorful displays of selfishness. After the movie, discuss how you identify with her, and if you're in a safe group, share how you've emulated her bad behavior recently.

2

The Consequences
of Cheap Charity

ALL OUR OFFERINGS, WHETHER OF MUSIC OR MARTYRDOM,
ARE LIKE THE INTRINSICALLY WORTHLESS PRESENT OF A
CHILD, WHICH A FATHER VALUES INDEED, BUT VALUES ONLY
FOR THE INTENTION.   *C. S. Lewis*

One of my good friends, Kari (her name's been
changed to protect her less-than-innocent relatives),
has an unpleasant mother-in-law. She's long-winded
and narrow-minded and is one of the worst gift-
givers of all time. Soon after Kari married her son,
this mother-in-law gave Kari a dated Christmas
ornament that was three years old! She's also given
Kari used clothing, macramé tissue holders, and a
vast assortment of junk that appealed to her stingy
whims.

Read Malachi 2 in the New Living Translation or *The Message*. Synopsize the theme of this chapter in two or three sentences.

I had a boyfriend in high school who rivaled Kari's mother-in-law when it came to tacky presents. One Christmas when we were at an all-time romantic high and I was expecting gold-plated jewelry, he gave me a big mirror framed in shells. Nice for a beach house, not so hot for a teenager in love. For Valentine's Day one year he gave me a stuffed elephant. Although I was young and trim, I still didn't think a pachyderm was an appropriate romantic gesture. To his credit, he said he thought the elephant was a fox when he bought it (this was the era of using *foxy* as an adjective for feminine attractiveness). And, from certain angles, Dumbo did appear rather fox-like! I never got mad at my old beau's gift-giving faux pas because I knew his heart was in the right place.

The problem with Kari's mother-in-law wasn't her taste, her frugality, or even her bank account; she seemed to have plenty of money to spend on herself. The problem was that her heart was in the wrong place. She was a mean-spirited miser. Her seemingly thoughtless gifts were actually conscious attempts to slight the recipient. Kari wasn't a picky prima donna daughter-in-law, either. She didn't mind the bargain basement ornaments or used sweaters with strange hairs embedded in them. What bothered her was the flagrant disregard for her feelings. The cheap gifts were

indicative of how little her mother-in-law valued their relationship.

What's the best tangible gift you've ever received (for any occasion), and why was it so special?

Judging by the gifts being hauled to the Temple in Malachi's neighborhood, these Israelites didn't value their relationship with God much either. Instead of offering Him their best—big bulls, ripe olives, and unblemished lambs—they were offering skinny cows, bruised fruit, and crippled sheep. The metaphorical religious mafia had infiltrated the priesthood, and God's own employees were trying to pull the wool over His eyes. They were advertising "perfect" sacrifices—the kind God requires—at top dollar, then substituting damaged goods and squirreling away the profit for themselves. However, these petty thief priests weren't the sharpest tools in the shed, because they thought their little money-laundering scheme was under God's radar.

> **More Info**
> Based on the book of Haggai, Nehemiah 5, and Malachi 3:8-12, it's obvious that the agricultural industry was in a slump and farms around Jerusalem were in desperate need of a good pest control company.[26]

What's the best gift you've ever given someone? Why was it special or significant to the recipient?

But God is omnipresent, He's everywhere; He's omniscient, He knows everything; He's omnificent, He created everything; and He's omnipotent, He has unlimited power. Nothing is ever under His radar; nothing escapes His perception! He sees the posture of every heart, from the cheap to the charitable.

Does the thought of God's all-seeing, all-knowing presence give you security or anxiety?

Cheaters Never Prosper

> *A son honors his father, and a servant his master. If then I am a father, where is my honor? And if I am a master, where is my fear? says the* Lord *of hosts to you, O priests, who despise my name. But you say, "How have we despised your name?" By offering polluted food upon my altar. . . . For from the rising of the sun to its setting my name will be great among the nations, and in every place incense will be offered to my name, and a pure offering. For my name will be great among the nations, says the* Lord *of hosts. But you profane it when you say that the Lord's table is polluted, and its fruit, that is, its food may be despised. But you say, "What a weariness this is," and you snort at it, says the* Lord *of hosts. You bring what has been taken by violence or is lame or sick, and this you bring as your offering! Shall I accept that from your hand? says the* Lord. *Cursed be the cheat who has a male in his flock, and vows it, and yet sacrifices to the Lord what is blemished. For I am a great King, says the* Lord *of hosts, and my name will be feared among the nations.* Malachi 1:6-7, 11-14

Whew! They got caught with their proverbial con-man pants around their ankles! When God talks about pure offerings, He's dead serious. And when He says to give Him the firstfruits of our produce, He's referring to the very best, not inexpensive substitutes.

> *Honor the LORD with your wealth and with the firstfruits of all your produce; then your barns will be filled with plenty, and your vats will be bursting with wine.*   Proverbs 3:9-10

Of course, not as many people make a living in agriculture anymore. We don't all pay our bills by farming or put jars of olives in the collection plate on Sunday. And the closest most of us come to sheep is wearing wool in the winter. So I've written "heart and mind" next to Proverbs 3:9-10 in my Bible. Because I think the context of *firstfruits* can be expanded to include our time and attention. In other words, we should be thinking about God more than anyone else. He should be more important to us than anything. Instead of slinking toward Him with scratch-and-dent sacrifices, we should run to Him with offerings we've spent our whole allowance on. And we should be able to stand before Him with big silly grins—like kindergarteners with a plaster-of-paris handprint we made all by ourselves—knowing that He's just going to love what we've brought Him!

Reread Proverbs 3:9-10. Make a list of literal **_firstfruits_ you've given—or have been convicted to give—God. Do you find it harder to part with money or time? Explain.**

We should be like the generous widow Luke describes in his Gospel account (Luke 21:1-4). The story goes like this: Jesus observes wealthy people putting lavish sums into the offering box, then watches a poor widow put in two copper coins, not even enough for a Starbucks latte. But He commends her pittance as the best gift, saying it was greater than the sum of the other gifts because those people gave from their abundance but she gave all she had. She gave her first and only fruit.

When it comes to giving to God, I want to be more like the widow and less like Malachi's peers and Kari's mother-in-law. I want to spend less of my attention and affection at the altar of me, and give God my very best.

Take out your checkbook ledger and calendar and peruse the activity of the last six months. Can you honestly describe the time and money you've given God as *firstfruits*? Do you think you need to make some new entries?

Rabbits and Rattlers

The next passage we're going to consider is a whopper, but before we go there I'm going to take the risk of chasing a rabbit. The bunny trail begins with the word *prolegomenon,* which means "a treatise or introduction to a book." It's a fancy word for a prologue. And because I lean toward being a verbose windbag, I love words like *prolegomenon.* But, I'm also aware most people take mental field trips when rambling writers use multisyllabic terminology. So I'll get right to the point: The following will serve as

a prolegomenon to the next nugget in Malachi, a prologue to explain the context of marriage and divorce in this ancient culture.

D. A. Carson (a wonderful writer and professor at Trinity Seminary) says, "Any text without a context becomes a pretext for a proof text." In other words, reaching into the Scripture and grabbing one or two verses, then writing a book or wrapping a theology around them, is very dangerous. For example, in Luke 10:19 Jesus says, "Behold, I have given you authority to tread on serpents and scorpions, and over all the power of the enemy, and nothing shall hurt you." And this single, solitary verse has spawned an entire back-woods denomination that revolves around snake handling. People who subscribe to this particular doctrine believe if you have enough faith, you can swing dance with snakes and come out unscathed.

But that's not the point of this passage. Jesus is referring to the transforming power of redemption; snakes and scorpions are just figurative terms for demonic entities. I'll bet the ill-advised people who agonized after being bitten (some even died) wish they'd read Luke's entire Gospel before getting up close and personal with a rattlesnake! The only responsible way to read and understand Scripture is to consider the context—how the passage relates to the whole book God breathed.

Fickle Men and Fractured Covenants

> *Did he not make them one, with a portion of the Spirit in their union? And what was the one God seeking? Godly offspring. So guard yourselves in*

NOTES

*your spirit, and let none of you be faithless
to the wife of your youth. "For the man who hates
and divorces, says the LORD, the God of Israel,
covers his garment with violence, says the LORD
of hosts. So guard yourselves in your spirit,
and do not be faithless."*

Malachi 2:15-16

In much the same way as the viper verse, these words can be taken out of context if considered in part rather than in the whole of God's message. And the result ends up being a critical spirit as dangerous as a poisonous serpent. For instance, verse 16 is commonly quoted, "God hates divorce," which is an inaccurate translation of the Hebrew text. But it sure is popular in Christian settings.

I wince when I hear that phrase used as ammunition in church or Bible studies, because the latest statistic shows that over 50 percent of confessing Christians have been through a divorce. It's like their greatest failure being broadcast over a loudspeaker in a place where people don't need another excuse to throw rocks. If another believer vehemently announced in public, "God hates chunky, chatty women who buy shoes when they're depressed," I'd sure feel exposed and humiliated!

Let's back up and review the questions these verses are responding to (Malachi 1:6-7): "How have we despised your name?" "How have we polluted you?" God's reply does seem to say that anyone who's gone through a divorce has despised His name, right? Well, not exactly.

Read Isaiah 43:1-4 and 54:4-5. What adjectives would you use to describe God's relationship with us in light of these verses? What is your favorite aspect of that relationship? Would you describe God as "possessive" when it comes to us?

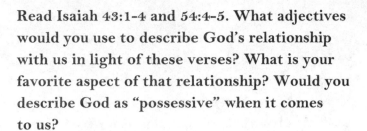

Remember, the Jews whom Malachi was addressing had just returned from captivity in Babylon to find the crown jewel of Judah in ruins. Instead of something beautiful like the Taj Mahal, they found Tara after the Civil War. Although they rebuilt the Temple, it wasn't nearly as impressive as Solomon's first Temple. Kind of like a Motel 6 compared to the Marriott Marquis. God's people got sick and tired of their second-class surroundings and difficult circumstances, and their dissatisfaction spread to their marriages.

With the priests leading the parade, Israelite men began to divorce their wives and marry pagans. Now, in all fairness, the wives of their youth had changed a bit since that first dreamy-eyed kiss. They were probably a little wider through the hips because the only groceries they could afford now were loaded with carbs. Plus, their children were begging for PlayStations and Game Boys, but the men weren't bringing home enough money to pay the bills, much less go to Target. And those financial problems made them a little grouchier than usual. You could say it was the Israelite women's season of "Nagging and Sagging."

And their fair-weather husbands didn't want to put up with their complaints. So when they met some foreign hotties at the bowling alley, they decided to trade in their first wives for these newer, younger models. They even used an obscure Mosaic law as an excuse to make their betrayal sound spiritual. Verse 15 refers to their disloyal deeds, to the way these religious men were dumping their spouses, getting hair transplants, buying convertibles, and marrying teenagers. In keeping with the Margaret Mitchell motif, these fickle men were walking out on their families and effectively saying, "Frankly, my dears, I don't give a darn!"

Reread Malachi 2:11; Jeremiah 2:26-28; and Judges 3:5-6. Why was it such a big deal for the Israelites to marry non-Israelites? Share examples of some biblical romances between God's people and pagans that were nothing but trouble. (Hint: one guy had really long hair until his girlfriend got her way!)

Love Instead of Legalism

Sadly, this type of faithless behavior is often still swept under the rug in our culture and *God hates divorce* is spewed with such venom that wounded victims assume it means God hates *people* who are divorced. The church has done such a good job of perpetuating this myth that many who've been bloodied in battle leave Christian environments to search for first aid elsewhere. We've done a deplorable job of communicating and reflecting the love God has for adults and children who've been damaged in the combat of divorce, as well as the forgiveness He extends to the repentant.

Let me be clear, lest I sound like a softie when it comes to the permanence of marriage. I don't think God is ambivalent about divorce. Nor do I believe He condones no-fault divorces. In fact, there are multiple biblical passages that clearly explain God's desire for marriage to be a lifelong commitment. But that desire isn't rooted in petty legalism; it's cemented in compassion.

My parents divorced when I was little. Their split didn't look anything like the divorces depicted on television. They didn't remain friends or have nostalgic conversations about the past. It was an ugly, violent shredding of the covenant they'd made to each other and to God.

Largely due to the emotional and financial instability following the divorce, Mom made another mistake in her second marriage. My stepfather was handsome and charming and promised the security she was desperate for, so she married him two years later. They've been married for thirty-five years now, but it's been a long, difficult road because my stepfather is a stubborn, agnostic man (whom I love dearly and pray will come to faith in Christ). Dad's story is even more colorful, but similar. His second marriage ended in divorce less than ten years after it began. In short, the painful consequences of their divorce have had ripple effects throughout the rest of my parents' lives.

My older sister and I bear different emotional scars. We were nine and five at the time, and we were both devastated. I won't reveal her private journey, but I will tell you how I responded when Dad left. I became the best little girl I could

NOTES

possibly be, basically a pathological people-pleaser. I thought if I could just be good enough, no one would ever leave me again. And while God continues to redeem the days the locusts ate from our cabinets, we're still experiencing the effects of our parents' fallout even today, as forty-something women.

Do you think it's possible for a Christian to be emotionally intimate and unequally yoked (married to a non-Christian)? Explain.

God isn't a cosmic killjoy who gets His jollies by making people feel guilty or forcing them to endure abuse. He's a merciful, loving Father who grieves over the emotional trauma caused by people being unfaithful to one another and to Him. Divorce breaks His holy heart because of the way it hurts people, not because someone broke the rules.

And praise God that divorce isn't part of His perfect plan because if it was, if His attitude was "Hey, if the going gets tough, you can always bail out," then surely He would have left us for good a long time ago. These words in Malachi aren't just about human husbands and wives; they're about God's commitment to love us no matter what. We've certainly been a less-than-loyal bride. We've wandered after other lovers and still had the audacity to question His love for us. He has every reason to abandon us, yet He remains true to His Word.

3

Another Face of Grace

AND ALL THINGS AS THEY CHANGE PROCLAIM THE LORD
ETERNALLY THE SAME.   *Charles Wesley*

July 4, 2004, was a terrible day. I was in the middle
of a breakup with the man I had started falling in
love with, so I went over to Kim's to help her do
some stuff around the house and take my mind off
the newly invisible man. But while I was in her
garage installing shelves, the ladder I was perched
on slipped and crashed to the cement floor, twelve
feet below. I was only knocked out for a few
seconds and was pretty sure I wasn't hurt badly,
but the goose egg over my eye prompted Kim to
ask me a series of worried questions: "What's your
full name? What's your address? What's today's
date? Who's the president?" She wanted to make

sure I didn't have a serious head injury. She insisted that we had to go to the hospital, but I didn't want to be in the ER all night with a bunch of drunks who'd barbequed their fingers with fireworks. And while I was playing the belligerent patient to Kim's "Marcus Welby," something much worse than my fall happened.

Read Malachi 3 in the New Living Translation or *The Message*. Synopsize the theme of this chapter in two or three sentences.

My little dog, Reba (don't ask, I didn't name her!), who was left outside next to the fence during the mishap, got tangled up in her leash and died. I still get teary thinking about it and I'm not even one of those people who wear T-shirts with my pet's picture. It was awful; Kim had gone outside to get her and came back inside with a dazed look on her face. She told me she was dead. I was still woozy, so I thought I'd misunderstood her. I asked Kim to repeat herself, and then—because the news was so unbelievably awful—I asked if she was teasing. She said, "No, Reba's really dead" and then started laughing hysterically. It wasn't "happy" laughing either, more "quiet-room-with-padded- walls" laughing. Kim's a steady, kind person, but finding me sprawled out on the floor of her garage covered in blood and then finding Reba in the first stages of rigor mortis had wreaked havoc on her typically calm demeanor.

And to top it all off, after taking Reba to the vet to be "disposed of," Kim had a hair appointment

with the guy who gave me the dog. He loved that terrier much more than I did. The only reason he asked me to keep her was because his kids were allergic to dog hair and his wife had put her foot down. When Kim got to the salon, she gently told him about Reba's accident. He responded by telling her he'd just had sinus surgery and couldn't blow his nose; then he tilted his head back and excused himself from the room. He had several more griev-ing, tilting moments during Kim's haircut, and she came back looking like she'd lost an argument with a Weed Eater.

It was a really bad day.

The Israelites certainly knew what it was like to have bad days. They'd had a very long season of very bad days. And it showed.

> *You have wearied the LORD with your words. But you say, "How have we wearied him?" By saying, "Everyone who does evil is good in the sight of the LORD, and he delights in them." Or by asking, "Where is the God of justice?"*   Malachi 2:17

The attitude behind these ostensibly innocuous words is: "Why are the pagans driving around in BMWs, when we're driving these trashy Yugos? How come the Babylonians have such big houses while we—Your chosen people—are living in cramped apartments with no air-conditioning? This isn't fair; we deserve better than this!"

When's the last time your man left or your dog died . . . or something even worse happened and you told God you deserved better?

Rabbit Trail Recurrence

There's a huge difference between *understanding* God's love for us, and the sense of entitlement displayed by Malachi's peers at the end of chapter 2. When our security rests in God's love for us, it is manifest in humility, gratitude, and love for others. We become God- and others-centered. But entitlement will always manifest itself in an arrogant demand to have our needs and wants met. Entitlement is *self-centered.*

It's critical for us to learn that the opposite of arrogance is *not* insecurity; frankly insecurity and arrogance are fruit from the same tree. Christians who wear their feelings on their sleeve, are quick to take offense, and reek of anxiety are *not* humble; they're big, fat babies! The opposite of arrogance is *security.* It's the deep-seated confidence that God holds us in the palm of His hand and nothing can separate us from His love. That kind of security is what gives us the ability to focus on God instead of ourselves.

However, God's children usually lean toward whiney insecurity instead of confidence in His compassion. Malachi 2:17 is certainly not the only self-centered verse in the Bible. The ugly refrain of "I deserve better than this!" reverberates throughout Scripture.

> *And he arose and came to his father. But while he was still a long way off, his father saw him and felt compassion, and ran and embraced him and kissed him. And the son said to him, "Father, I have sinned against heaven and before you. I am no longer worthy to be called your son." But the*

*father said to his servants, "Bring quickly the best
robe, and put it on him, and put a ring on his
hand, and shoes on his feet. And bring the fattened
calf and kill it, and let us eat and celebrate. For
this my son was dead, and is alive again; he was
lost, and is found." And they began to celebrate.*

*Now his older son was in the field, and as he
came and drew near to the house, he heard music
and dancing. And he called one of the servants and
asked what these things meant. And he said to him,
"Your brother has come, and your father has killed
the fattened calf, because he has received him back
safe and sound." But he was angry and refused to
go in. His father came out and entreated him, but
he answered his father, "Look, these many years I
have served you, and I never disobeyed your
command, yet you never gave me a young goat, that
I might celebrate with my friends. But when this
son of yours came, who has devoured your property
with prostitutes, you killed the fattened calf for
him!"* Luke 15:20-30

*Then Job answered and said: "Today also my
complaint is bitter; my hand is heavy on account of
my groaning. Oh, that I knew where I might find
him, that I might come even to his seat! I would lay
my case before him and fill my mouth with argu-
ments. I would know what he would answer me
and understand what he would say to me. Would
he contend with me in the greatness of his power?
No; he would pay attention to me."* Job 23:1-6

*Ahab told Jezebel all that Elijah had done, and
how he had killed all the prophets with the sword.*

NOTES

Then Jezebel sent a messenger to Elijah, saying, "So may the gods do to me and more also, if I do not make your life as the life of one of them by this time tomorrow." Then he was afraid, and he arose and ran for his life and came to Beersheba, which belongs to Judah, and left his servant there.

But he himself went a day's journey into the wilderness and came and sat down under a broom tree. And he asked that he might die, saying, "It is enough; now, O LORD, take away my life, for I am no better than my fathers."   1 Kings 19:1-4

When God saw what they did, how they turned from their evil way, God relented of the disaster that he had said he would do to them, and he did not do it.

But it displeased Jonah exceedingly, and he was angry. And he prayed to the LORD and said, "O LORD, is not this what I said when I was yet in my country? That is why I made haste to flee to Tarshish; for I knew that you are a gracious God and merciful, slow to anger and abounding in steadfast love, and relenting from disaster. Therefore now, O LORD, please take my life from me, for it is better for me to die than to live. And the LORD said, "Do you do well to be angry?"

Jonah 3:10—4:4

The older brother had a bad case of egocentric Ebola; he thought he deserved a party much more than his prodigal little brother. Job thought he deserved better than boils, bad advice, and being broke; he demanded an audience with God to tell Him how hacked off he was. Elijah pouted royally after the miracle on Mount Carmel; he didn't think he deserved to be bullied by Queen Jezebel. And another minor prophet, the water-phobic Jonah, thought he deserved a better assignment than preaching to a bunch of hellions in Nineveh. He sure didn't think those reprobates deserved God's reprieve.

Read Psalm 139:23-24. Do you think God uses the same "degree of heat" to purify us as individuals—in other words, do you think the conviction of the Holy Spirit is homogenous? Or do you think some people respond to God's prompting before things get really toasty?

Heavenly Hopes

Throughout the course of biblical history, right up to our post-postmodern selves, God's people have a habit of *doin' the Scarlett*. With one hand on our hip and the other in an angry fist, we shout for God to give us what we deserve. It's a wonder He doesn't say, "Here" and hand us a lightning bolt.

Yet instead of handing down the wrath we deserve for having the cheek to question His judgment, God almost always responds like a patient, compassionate dad.

> *Behold, I send my messenger and he will prepare the way before me. And the Lord whom you seek will suddenly come to his temple; and the messenger of the covenant in whom you delight, behold, he is coming, says the LORD of hosts.*
>
> Malachi 3:1

His response to the demands of these former captives is to remind them that Jesus is coming: "Behold, I send my messenger and he will prepare the way before me." Remember the guy with a goat coat and a fondness for locust lasagna? The first verse of chapter 3 points to him, to God's next messenger, John the Baptist. Then the other prophetic shoe drops, and I'm guessing Malachi's grin was a mile wide when he said this: that Jesus—their long-anticipated Messiah, the Lord they were seeking, *the* messenger of the covenant—was coming!

I got to fulfill a lifelong dream and go to Africa last year. I loved watching and listening to the women in Kenya sing about heaven. They swayed to the music and sang in Swahili and acted as if they really wanted to be raptured! Many of them have such hard lives that heaven is something they actually look forward to. I think most of us are so preoccupied with feathering our nests on earth that heaven fades into a forgettable caricature, like something from *Lord of the Rings* or *Anne of Green Gables*. If we have any thoughts of heaven at all, it's usually about postponing all the cloud-sitting and crown-throwing so we can have more time here to reach our goals, or get married, or enjoy our children and grandchildren and all the cool stuff we've accumulated.

More Info

Deuteronomy and Malachi are the only books in the Old Testament that begin with a sort of "megaphone" address to all of Israel. Among other similarities, both books emphasize tithing and the blessing that accompanies it (Malachi 3:6-12; Deuteronomy 26:1-19).

Read 1 Samuel 12:1-25 and Psalm 51. Share how God used a relationship or situation to refine you, to strip away your pretense, purify

your idolatrous heart, and draw you closer to Himself.

But when we forget that this world *isn't* our home and lose sight of eternity, very bad days have much bigger consequences. Trivial annoyances become life-sucking tragedies. Bad traffic becomes a catalyst for cussing. Failed romances become yearlong depressions. And a bad haircut ruins a perfectly good day. Just like my new friends in Nairobi, we need to keep things in perspective and remember that our Messiah, the Lord in whom we delight, is coming again!

Ode to Obedience

After God reminds this defiant bunch about the advent of the Messiah, He gives them a little dissertation on discipline. He explains that instead of the justice they're demanding—which would actually mean the annihilation of humanity—He's going to refine them.

> *But who can endure the day of his coming, and who can stand when he appears? For he is like a refiner's fire and like fullers' soap. He will sit as a refiner and purifier of silver, and he will purify the sons of Levi and refine them like gold and silver, and they will bring offerings in righteousness to the* LORD. *Then the offering of Judah and Jerusalem will be pleasing to the* LORD *as in the days of old and as in former years.* Malachi 3:2-4

All too often these verses are read with furrowed brows and a scary, James Earl Jones voice; but if you look long enough, you'll find God's affection. God compares His kids to expensive gold and precious silver. Elements so valuable, international economies are still based on them. He goes on to explain that refining is restorative, that discipline burns off the dross in our lives and makes us more beautiful. The treasure between the lines in this passage is that grace masquerades as discipline.

Sheila Walsh says that some of God's best gifts are wrapped in boxes that make our hands bleed when we open them. Which is the essence of what David said in the Psalms:

> *I know, O LORD, that your rules are righteous, and that in faithfulness you have afflicted me.*
>
> Psalm 119:75

David knew a lot about discipline—he lost his baby boy because of his adulterous dalliance with Bathsheba—but he also experienced the love of God in the midst of the negative consequences of his sin.

Reread Malachi 2:17–3:5; Jeremiah 9:7-11, 23-24; and Zechariah 13:8-9. What are the common themes regarding God's refining process in these passages? What adjectives would you use to describe the biblical refining process?

One of my closest friends, Eva Whittington Self, was paralyzed in a car accident when she was a senior in high school. When she finally

came home from the rehab hospital, she had learned most of the basic life skills she needed to function from a wheelchair, but there were still a few things she couldn't do by herself. Like putting her pants on.

One morning, a few days after Eva had gotten home, her mother, May Bell, told her she thought it'd be a good day to learn how to put her pants on by herself. Eva said she would eventually be able to do that, but it was still too hard to manage alone. But her mom—usually a timid, tender-hearted woman—insisted that Eva put on her jeans by herself. After arguing about it, Eva got mad and ordered her mom out of her room. Before she left, May Bell stretched the jeans out on the bed so they'd be within Eva's reach.

Eva said she was furious when her mom left, but after fuming awhile, she leaned down and grabbed her jeans by the waistband. It took about ten minutes to work them up to her knees. Then she threw herself back on the bed, angry and exhausted, and sobbed. After a few minutes she leaned forward again, and started pulling the pants up. Another ten or fifteen minutes passed, and she was able to work the pants up to her hips. Breathing hard, she fell back on the bed and started crying again. Then she took a deep breath, and started inching the waistband over the bulky plastic back brace. It took Eva more than half an hour, but she finally got her pants all the way up and buttoned. Then, wet with perspiration, she fell back on the bed a third time. And that was when she heard her mother crying.

NOTES

Do you think the process of being refined/ purified by God always includes pain? Explain why or why not.

May Bell had been in the next room the whole time. It must have broken her heart to hear Eva struggle, but she loved her too much to let her take the easy way out. May Bell knew that her daughter's path to independence would involve pain. In much the same way, our heavenly Father loves us way too much to withhold discipline. The Refiner's fire is fueled by mercy.

Reread Malachi 3:1. Who's been the most effective human messenger of the gospel in your life—someone who consistently points you to the living hope we have in Christ? Why is their "message" so effective?

Reread Malachi 3:2-4. How would you describe "offerings in righteousness"? Is there an offering that God's impressed you to give that you're having a hard time giving (it doesn't have to be a financial offering; it could be rejoicing about your child leaving the nest to attend college, etc.)?

did you know?

The Old Testament makes a distinction between blessings that accompany Israel's sojourn into the Promised Land and those that come only after the unleashing of whatever punishments were needed. Virtually all the blessings in the prophetic books have to do with God's merciful restoration, that would follow Israel's conquest and exile.[27]

Never Left Behind

And in light of God's infinite mercy, He doesn't conclude this passage with that helpful homily on correction. Instead, the exclamation point at the end of the lesson is all about His immutable—unchanging—affection for us.

> For I the LORD do not change; therefore you,
> O children of Jacob, are not consumed.
>
> Malachi 3:6

Even though we fuss and pout, rant and rave, and demand better circumstances; even though we're full of imperfections that need to be burned away; even though we are tiresomely repetitious in our rebellion, *God won't leave*. His presence doesn't wane, even in His chastisement.

Do you ever wonder if your rebellious heart will **weary God to the point that He will walk away from you? Explain, and be honest. Don't worry about the theological correctness of your answer!**

In yet another movie—*Hope Floats* with Sandra Bullock and the rakishly cute, Harry Connick Jr.—there's a riveting scene involving Birdee (Sandra's character) and her estranged husband, Bill. He comes to see her at her mother's house (where she's been living with their young daughter, Bernice, ever since Birdee found out about Bill's affair with her best friend) to ask for a divorce. He explains that he's in love with Connie (the proverbial *other woman*), and wants to start a new life. Bernice (played by a talented young actor named Mae Whitman) overhears the conversation and bursts into the room declaring, "I want to go with you, Daddy!" She races upstairs, jams a few things into a miniature suitcase, and bolts out the door following him to his car.

But when Bernice tries to put her bag in the trunk, her daddy grabs it and places it decisively on the ground. He then squats down beside her and explains that she can't come with him because he "needs some time alone with Connie." Of course, like most eight-year-olds who haven't seen their daddy in months, Bernice begs him not to leave her behind. And when Bill gets in the car and starts the engine, she pleads with everything she has. "You want me, Daddy! You told me you did in your letter! Please! You want me!" But instead of relenting, he rolls up the window and drives away, leaving his little girl standing in the road literally screaming in anguish.

Bernice's sorrow over her father's desertion is heartwrenching. The first time I saw it, I cried harder than I had when watching *Old Yeller*. It hit way too close to my emotional home. Because I can still remember the sinking feeling I had when my own dad's car drove away after one of our "visitation weekends" following my parent's divorce. Perhaps because of human moments like those, I think some of us are secretly afraid that our heavenly Father might leave us. That if we behave really badly or if He finds a cuter kid, He'll walk out on us.

But God isn't like any flesh-and-blood parent

you know. Even great, godly dads who are
committed and compassionate pale next to our
heavenly Father. He will not abandon His children
for any reason. We don't have to worry about
watching His taillights fade as He drives away
from us.

**Read Romans 8:31-39 and John 10:27-30. How
would you synopsize these two passages in your
own words?**

The book of Malachi is riddled with God's love.
He points disobedient people to the coming Messiah.
He disciplines us instead of destroying us, and then
He says He'll never walk away. God's compassions
will never fail; they are new every morning . . . even
in the dawn of very, very bad days.

**Write a letter to someone who's recently expe-
rienced a divorce or marital separation. Without taking sides or trying to "counsel," simply
communicate your prayer for them to experience God's comfort and peace in the midst of
their pain.**

*What peace it brings to the Christian's heart to
realize that our heavenly Father never differs from
Himself. In coming to Him at any time, we need
not wonder whether we shall find Him in a receptive mood. He is always receptive to misery and
need, as well as to love and faith. He does not keep
office hours nor set aside periods when He will see
no one. Neither does He change His mind about
anything. Today, this moment, He feels toward*

His creatures, toward babies, toward the sick, the
fallen, the sinful, exactly as He did when He sent
His only-begotten Son into the world to die for
mankind.[28]

The Truth about Transcendent Joy

WHAT I NEEDED MORE THAN PARDON WAS A SENSE THAT
GOD ACCEPTED ME, OWNED ME, HELD ME, AFFIRMED ME,
AND WOULD NEVER LET GO OF ME EVEN IF HE WAS NOT
TOO MUCH IMPRESSED WITH WHAT HE HAD ON HIS HANDS.

Lewis Smedes

When I was in college, I joined a sorority. I know
there are some negative stereotypes of fraternities
and sororities: of spoiled coeds skipping classes,
clandestine meetings with cultish themes, and
drunken toga parties. But that wasn't my experience. The Greek system in small-town Alabama
was much more *Little House on the Prairie* than
Animal House.

There was one aspect of sorority life that I
disliked, however, and that was the element of

exclusivity. I didn't like the way some girls were invited to join the "club," while others were rejected. I remember one meeting in particular when we were all sitting around in a big circle and one of the "sisters" was vehemently blackballing several other young women who'd expressed interest in joining our sorority. She was so condescending; she belittled the other girls' brains, looks, and backgrounds. Then she started making fun of one girl's size and said she was *too fat* to be one of us.

Her words were so ugly and insensitive that we all just sat there stunned. But then Susan, a chubby senior sister, stood up, looked across the room at "Miss Haughty," and let her have it. Susan said that she of all people had no room to talk because the only reason she was pledged the year before was because so many girls had graduated and they just needed a few warm bodies. Susan said they had to call an emergency meeting to settle a split vote over Miss Haughty's inclusion because so many members felt she didn't meet the sorority's standards. Susan finished her stern rebuke with words something like this: "We decided to take a chance on you and have regretted it ever since. You need to remember just how lucky you are to be wearing that green jersey before you open your big mouth again!" It took all the restraint I had not to stand up and cheer. Comeuppance can be a beautiful thing.

Read Malachi 4 in the New Living Translation or *The Message*. Synopsize the theme of this chapter in two or three sentences.

Skipping Thanksgiving

> *Your words have been hard against me, says the*
> *LORD. But you say, "How have we spoken against*
> *you?" You have said, "It is vain to serve God.*
> *What is the profit of our keeping his charge or of*
> *walking as in mourning before the LORD of hosts?*
> *And now we call the arrogant blessed. Evildoers*
> *not only prosper but they put God to the test and*
> *they escape."* Malachi 3:13-15

Much like that spiteful sorority girl, the gang
hanging around Malachi had forgotten how blessed
they were to be God's beloved. They were so
engrossed in the depressing stories of their individual lives that they missed the divine drama—the
meta-narrative—God had graciously written them
into.

**Rercad Malachi 3:13-15. Malachi's peers and
the religious leaders had done much more than
just question God. Reread Malachi 1:6-7, 12
and 2:9, 11, 17 and list some of their other
grievances against God.**

"How have we spoken against you?" is the last of
the seven questions that make up the book of
Malachi. The first was when God declared His love
for them and they replied, "How have you loved
us?" (Malachi 1:2). They went on to raise their
eyebrows in feigned innocence every time God
pointed out their sinful behavior. But despite their
pretense, they were guilty of doubting His love for
them, declaring Him unworthy of their best sacri-

fices, and accusing Him of being unjust. Now, as if their prior offenses weren't bad enough, they have the nerve to ignore their need for repentance.

I wish I could say I can't identify with them; that my perspective is more holy than theirs; that I tend to focus on God's purpose and plan more than my own personal hopes and expectations. But I don't. All too often, I'm just like them, like some selfish sorority girl or modern-day Scarlett O'Hara. My sense of entitlement usually outweighs my sense of gratitude for being chosen as His beloved.

What's the most repetitious *doubting* question you find yourself asking God? Share two or three examples of *good/beneficial* questions you've asked God. What do you think is the main difference between a doubting spiritual question and a beneficial spiritual question?

Peculiar Joy

If the canon wasn't closed and God still used human writers as His megaphone, I firmly believe Philip Yancey would be among that select literary group. The words he puts in print consistently give me a clearer picture of God, and his recent book, *Rumors of Another World*, is no exception. In it, he retells the story of John Merrick, the man whose life was memorialized in the movie *The Elephant Man*.

You probably remember that John Merrick was cruelly called the Elephant Man because he was born with a rare disorder called neurofibromatosis, which is a horribly disfiguring disease. As a result, his mother gave him to a factory owner; John had to work for his upkeep from the time he was four

years old. When he was fourteen, a carnival show-
man discovered him and decided he could make
money by exploiting John's deformities.

When the carnival came to London, it was set up
across the street from a hospital. Philip Yancey
explains that a surgeon, Dr. Frederick Treves,
noticed the crude drawing advertising "The
Elephant Man" and, overcome with curiosity, paid
a shilling to look at John Merrick.

This is Dr. Treves's description of what he saw
from Mr. Yancey's book *Rumors*:

> . . . *a bony mass protruding from his brow; spongy
> skin, with a fissured surface resembling brown
> cauliflower hanging in folds from his back; a huge,
> misshapen head the circumference of a man's waist;
> the mouth a distorted slobbering aperture; the nose
> a dangling lump of skin; a bag of flesh like the
> dewlap of a lizard suspended from the chest. His
> right arm was overgrown to twice its normal size,
> its fingers stubby and useless. Flaps of skin in the
> shape of a paddle descended from one armpit;
> deformed legs supported him only if he held onto
> a chair. A sickening stench emanated from the
> fungous skin growths.*[29]

Upon viewing John Merrick, Dr. Treves was
curious about his medical condition and arranged
to have him examined at the hospital. They
performed tests and took photographs and tried to
communicate with him. However, because of his
misshapen mouth, Mr. Merrick couldn't speak
clearly. No one at the hospital could understand

him. Nor could they imagine the inhumane conditions he was forced to endure. Therefore, at the end of the examination, Dr. Treves put his card in John's pocket and took him back across the street to the carnival, which—unbeknownst to him— would leave town the following day.

Two years later, the carnival was closed down for good. The manager kept all of John Merrick's earnings and put him on a train back to London. Although he wore a cloak and veil, he was abused by other passengers because of his appearance and had to be rescued by policemen when the train arrived. While trying to discern his identity, the police found the soiled card of Dr. Treves in John's pocket and called him. Dr. Treves, who'd thought of John Merrick many times since their brief encounter but didn't know how to find him again, hurried to the station and took this pitiable man back to the hospital.

 Read Malachi 3:16. What do you think they actually said when they "spoke with one another"? Why do you think God heard it? Who are the people in your life, whom, when you speak with them, you remember the Lord?

It was Dr. Treves who discovered that rather than being an ignorant imbecile, John was a very bright man with a beautiful spirit. Treves wrote:

> *His troubles had ennobled him. He showed himself to be a gentle, affectionate and loveable creature . . . without a grievance and without an unkind word*

*for anyone. I have never heard him complain. I
have never heard him deplore his ruined life or
resent the treatment he had received at the hands of
callous keepers. His journey through life had been
indeed along a* via dolorosa, *the road had been
uphill all the way, and now, when the night was
blackest and the way most steep, he had found
himself, as it were, in a friendly inn, bright with
light and warm with welcome.*[30]

John Merrick's disposition defied the laws of
behavioral science. In light of the treatment he'd
received since childhood, he should have grown into
a man with the temperament of a beaten dog.
Instead, the words he uttered most often during the
last years of his too-short life (he died in his sleep of
asphyxiation when he was twenty-eight years old)
were, "I am happy every hour of the day."

His happiness is shocking in context. His
circumstances would have led lesser men down a
path of bitterness, anger, and hatred. But John
chose joy. His heart leaped beyond the depressing
boundaries of his condition. And that is the
message of Malachi: The hope we have in God and
His Son is transcendent. His mercy is irrespective
of the human milieu.

> *'Tis true my form is something odd,*
> *but blaming me is blaming God.*
> *Could I create myself anew,*
> *I would not fail in pleasing you.*
>
> *Was I so tall, could reach the pole,*
> *or grasp the ocean with a span;*

I would be measured by the soul.
The mind's the standard of the man.[31]

Watch *The Elephant Man* with some friends and then discuss how the grand themes of creation, human sin, and redemption are revealed in John Merrick's story.

The Dance of the Delighted-In

After Reba died, I went out the very next day and bought two Jack Russell terrier puppies. I've since admitted my acquisition was probably due to a concussion because Jack Russell terriers are the canine version of the Energizer Bunny. They're strong-willed, hyperactive, and obsessed with creating tunnels from Tennessee to China. And like most terriers, they're very smart; which I thought was an admirable trait until a friend told me when dogs rival their owners in intelligence, there's bound to be trouble!

She's got a point; it would certainly be easier to have a compliant dog that would be happy with a chew toy, live to obey my every command, and never dig under the fence or develop a crush on my geraniums. But now I can't imagine life without Harley and Dot (they, too, were named by their breeders; I think "Harley and Dot" sounds like a sweet old couple from Kansas in a Winnebago) because it's so much fun to watch them romp with enthusiastic abandon! I've learned to be quick to correct their destructive behavior—things like biting people and power cords. But the responsibility of training them pales next to the delight of

watching them play. Their behavior epitomizes unbridled joy. It's the kind of behavior God refers to at the end of Malachi's oracle when He talks about His children leaping about like calves set free from a claustrophobic barn.

> *For behold, the day is coming, burning like an oven, when all the arrogant and all evildoers will be stubble. The day that is coming shall set them ablaze, says the LORD of hosts, so that it will leave them neither root nor branch. But for you who fear my name, the sun of righteousness shall rise with healing in its wings. You shall go out leaping like calves from the stall. And you shall tread down the wicked, for they will be ashes under the soles of your feet, on the day when I act, says the LORD of hosts.*
>
> Malachi 4:1-3

Reread Malachi 3:17; Exodus 19:4-6; Deuteronomy 7:6; and Psalm 135:4. List your most treasured relationships. Describe some ways you've communicated your love to those people. Apart from His Word, how has God communicated that you're someone He treasures?

Doom and gloom can certainly be found in the words of the Minor Prophets, but the Good News of the gospel (Its message of hope is in the Old Testament, too!) is that all the flaming wrath isn't meant for us. It's directed at the wicked, at those who don't trust and obey God. That glorious reprieve alone should make us jump around like cows on caffeine!

Look up the word *possession(s)* in a concordance (preferably an exhaustive concordance like *Strong's*). Then list a few directives God gives about the things we own. How is God's ownership of us different from the way we typically express ownership?

Reread Malachi 4:2. How do you metaphorically "leap" before the Lord in light of His love for you? When was your most recent jumping incident?

Peculiar People

God's Word is crammed full of stories about rescue and redemption, provision and protection. He employs metaphors like "strong tower," "mighty fortress," and a "mother hen" when explaining His care and concern for us. The reason we can laugh at the days to come—like the poster girl of Proverbs—is because we know *Who* holds our future in His hands. Our lives should reflect hope, joy, and contentment that defy our circumstances. The world should find the posture of our heart quite peculiar, much like it did John Merrick's.

The apostle John helps clarify the reason for our

did you know?

When "Elijah the prophet" is mentioned in Malachi 4:5, it's actually a euphemism for the Messiah's arrival (Some would call it an interpretive challenge!). Remember, John the Baptist was a type of Elijah at Christ's first advent (Luke 1:17).[32]

atypical disposition with his recollection of Christ's words:

> *The thief comes only to steal and kill and destroy.*
> *I came that they may have life and have it*
> *abundantly.*   John 10:10

The hard-to-pronounce prophet Habakkuk is more dramatic when he talks about trusting God joyfully regardless of what we're walking through:

> *Though the fig tree should not blossom, nor fruit be*
> *on the vines, the produce of the olive fail and the*
> *fields yield no food, the flock be cut off from the fold*
> *and there be no herd in the stalls, yet I will rejoice*
> *in the* LORD; *I will take joy in the God of my*
> *salvation. God, the* LORD, *is my strength; he makes*
> *my feet like the deer's; he makes me tread on my*
> *high places.*   Habakkuk 3:17-19

And David, the shepherd boy who became king, says it well in one of his songs:

> *You have kept count of my tossings; put my tears in*
> *your bottle. Are they not in your book? Then my*
> *enemies will turn back in the day when I call. This*
> *I know, that God is for me. In God, whose word*
> *I praise, in the* LORD, *whose word I praise, in*
> *God I trust; I shall not be afraid. What can man*
> *do to me?*   Psalm 56:8-11

John the Elephant Man, John the Beloved Disciple, Habakkuk, and David all understood that their individual lives were just brief chapters in the divine love story about a faithful God and His flawed people. We, too, need to remember the big picture when our perspective narrows to ruined romances, tight budgets, and sullied dreams. When all we can see is our own version of Tara trashed, we must look for God's mercy. Malachi reminds us to remember the glorious end of the story when we're struggling in the in-between time.

Final Thoughts

I visited my good friend Susie (Morgan Freeman's
buddy) and her husband, Dan, in Colorado
recently. Since my move to Tennessee, we don't
get to see each other very often, so when we do it's
an occasion to celebrate—to giggle and reminisce
and drink too much caffeine. I thoroughly enjoy
every minute I get to spend with Susie because I
love the way she's wired.

For starters, she's from England so she has one
of those enchanting British accents. She could read
the phone book and people would crowd around to
listen! She has a quick wit and a hearty laugh. And
she's very straightforward—she doesn't wear
pretense well, which makes for a refreshingly
honest friendship. But, as wonderful as she was,
Susie has actually changed for the better in the past
few years. She's a bit softer in spirit and kinder.
There's a luminance to her face; she sort of glows,
even when she's not smiling.

Others have noticed Susie's sheen as well. We've

commented to each other and to her how her "good qualities" have increased and her shortcomings are diminishing. To which she grins and gives credit to Dan. She talks often about how God's mercy has been made visible in her husband. She says she just can't get over the way he loves her. During my visit, we were wandering around their property together when she looked me in the eyes with what can only be described as delight and said, "It's even better than I'd dreamed."

Dan obviously feels the same way because when he looks at Susie, he lights up like a Christmas tree. I didn't have the privilege of knowing him pre-Susie, but I'm sure his friends would have similar observations about him that we have about her. Susie's love has undoubtedly made Dan a better man.

I'm guessing that some of you are thinking, *Okay, this is about to make me sick. This is way too lovey-dovey to be realistic.* And a few of you just felt the green monster of jealousy roll over; you're wondering why someone like Dan hasn't appeared on your horizon. Other battle-weary marriage veterans are musing, *Typical honeymooners—just give them a few years.* But hang on to your sarcasm and doubt for a minute. Susie and Dan aren't newlyweds. They've been married for more than three years. Nor is their marriage postcard perfect. They've struggled through issues such as Susie adjusting to being a stepmother, job changes, and the death of parents.

I think the real reason the glow hasn't dissipated is because they both remember what life was like without the other. Susie was past forty when she met

Dan. While she loved her job, her friends, and her
family, she wasn't sure she'd ever get married, much
less marry a man even better than she'd dreamed of.
And sweet Dan had been through a difficult divorce.
He knew firsthand the bruises that breakup can
bring. Susie and Dan both recognize how blessed
they are because they remember where they've been.
They cherish the love they have because they know
what it's like to live without such love.

Their evident gratitude for each other reminded
me of how we should respond to the relationship
God initiated with us. Although we have repeated
the rebellious, deplorable behavior of our forefa-
thers—we've been as promiscuous as Gomer, as
pretentious as Zephaniah's peers, and just as
whiney and spiritually apathetic as a postexilic
Israel—God has chosen to redeem us. Even though
we are rebellious and demanding and easily
distracted, God doesn't give up on us.

He won't leave us alone in some dingy apartment with nothing but a few cats and an online
dating service to keep us company. He paid the
price for our plentiful sin so that we could be
reconciled into a glorious, eternal marriage with
Him. God stands at the end of earth's aisle in a
custom tuxedo woven by angels, and smiles
tenderly as we stumble our way toward Him in a
soiled dress. He willingly takes a whore to be His
bride. And we should spend the rest of our lives
radiating our gratitude. We must never forget
what our lives were like without Him.

Amazing grace, how sweet the sound that saved
a wretch like me.

NOTES

[1] John Phillips, *Exploring the Minor Prophets* (Grand Rapids, Mich.: Kregel Publications, 2002), 9.

[2] James Montgomery Boice, *The Minor Prophets* (Grand Rapids, Mich.: Kregel Publications, 1996), 14.

[3] Bruce M. Metzger, David A. Hubbard, Glenn W. Barker, general eds., *The Word Biblical Commentary*, vol. 31, *Hosea–Jonah.* (Waco, Tex.: Word Books, 1987), 9; *The MacArthur Study Bible* (Nashville: Word Publishing, 1997), 1251; Thomas Edward McComiskey, *An Exegetical and Expository Commentary of the Minor Prophets* (Grand Rapids, Mich.: Baker Book House, 1992), 3; *Hebrew-Greek Key Word Study Bible* (Chattanooga, Tenn.: AMG Publishers, 1996), 1043.

[4] *English Standard Version, Classic Reference Bible* (Wheaton, Ill.: Good News Publishers, 2001), 908.

[5] Karen S. Peterson, "Affair Statistics," *USA Today* (December 21, 1998).

[6] Kerby Anderson, *Adultery and Society*, Probe Ministries International, 2001, http://www.probe.org.

[7] McComiskey, *An Exegetical & Expository Commentary of The Minor Prophets*, 51.

[8] Boice, *The Minor Prophets*, 30–31.

[9] *Vine's Complete Expository Dictionary of Old and New Testament Words* (Nashville, Tenn.: Thomas Nelson, Inc., 1996), 131.

[10] Donald Miller, *Blue Like Jazz* (Nashville, Tenn.: Thomas Nelson, Inc., 2003), 119.

[11] E. B. Pusey, *The Minor Prophets*, vol. 1 (New York: Funk and Wagnalls, 1885), 87; Boice, *The Minor Prophets*, 61.

[12] *Hebrew-Greek Key Word Study Bible*, 1988.

[13] *CNN.com.* Article posted November 25, 2003.

[14] Damon Adams, "Catching Phony Physicians," August 23/30, 2004, http://www.amednews.com.

[15] *The MacArthur Study Bible*, 491.

[16] *Ibid.*, 180.

[17] McComiskey, *An Exegetical and Expository Commentary of the Minor Prophets*, 941.

[18] Jon Krakauer, *Into the Wild* (New York: Villard, 1996), 4-6.

[19] Ibid., 197-198.

[20] "Into the Wild," excerpt in *Outside* (January 1993): 10.

[21] Brent Curtis and John Eldredge, *The Sacred Romance* (Nashville, Tenn.: Thomas Nelson, Inc., 1997), 39, 40.

[22] *Vine's Complete Expository Dictionary of Old and New Testament Words*, 239; *Hebrew-Greek Key Word Study Bible*, 1268; *The MacArthur Study Bible*, 1625.

[23] "What Wondrous Love Is This?" (1835). Words attributed to Alexander Means. Music from *The Southern Harmony and Musical Companion* by William Walker. Public domain.

[24] Scotty Smith, *The Reign of Grace* (West Monroe, La.: Howard Publishing, 2003), 15.

[25] *The MacArthur Study Bible*, 1362.

[26] McComiskey, *An Exegetical & Expository Commentary of The Minor Prophets*, 1253.

[27] *Ibid.*, 1258.

[28] A. W. Tozer, *The Knowledge of the Holy* (New York: HarperCollins Publishers, Inc., 1961), 53.

[29] Philip Yancey, *Rumors of Another World* (Grand Rapids, Mich.: Zondervan, 2003), 192.

[30] Ashley Montagu, *The Elephant Man* (New York: Dutton, 1971), 24, 27.

[31] According to several Web sites, this poem was often quoted by John Merrick. See "The Elephant Man, John Merrick: An Extraordinary Man, An Extraordinary Life!" at http://www.geocities.com/hagios@bcglobal.net.

[32] *The MacArthur Study Bible*, 1367.

Get ready for the next great adventure!

*Enjoy these other great titles
from Tyndale House Publishers!*

Real Life.
Honest Women.
True Stories.

"Bask in the gentle wisdom of a trusted friend."
Ruth McGinnis, musician, speaker, and author

Fairy Tale Faith by Brenda Waggoner

Drawing on such beloved fairy tales as *The Princess Bride*, *The Lion King*, and *Sleeping Beauty*, Christian counselor Brenda Waggoner explores the miracle that is God's grace. Tackling issues such as self-esteem, body image, perfectionism, and loss, Waggoner helps women live gracefully in The Meantime while waiting for Happily Ever After. (ISBN 0-8423-7113-3, hardcover)

"This is the kind of woman I want to learn from!"
Kay Arthur

The Hungry Heart by Lynda Hunter Bjorklund

Everyone longs for intimacy. As Christians we know that intimacy, significance, and acceptance can be found in the arms of a loving and gracious God. Dr. Lynda Hunter Bjorklund teaches women how to get at that place with God and find the deep relationship that comes from really knowing the One who created you. (ISBN 0-8423-7938-X, softcover)